CANCER-GATE
How to Win the Losing Cancer War

Samuel S. Epstein, M.D.

POLICY, POLITICS, HEALTH AND MEDICINE SERIES
Vicente Navarro, Series Editor

Baywood Publishing Company, Inc.
Amityville, New York

Baywood Publishing Company, Inc.
26 Austin Avenue, PO Box 337
Amityville, NY 11701
(800) 638-7819
E-mail: baywood@baywood.com
Web site: baywood.com

Library of Congress Catalog Number:
ISBN: 0-89503-310-0 (cloth)
ISBN: 0-89503-354-2 (paper)

Library of Congress Cataloging-in-Publication Data

Epstein, Samuel S.
    Cancer-gate : how to win the losing cancer war / Samuel S. Epstein.
        p. cm. -- (Policy, politics, health, and medicine series)
    Includes bibliographical references and index.
    ISBN 0-89503-310-0 (cloth) -- ISBN 0-89503-354-2 (pbk.)
        1. Cancer--Government policy--United States. 2. National Cancer Institute (U.S.) 3.
    American Cancer Society. 4. Cancer--Prevention. I. Title. II. Series.

RA645.C3E67 2005
614.5'999'0973--dc22

                                                                                2004065964

About the Author

Samuel S. Epstein, M.D., Professor Emeritus of Environmental and Occupational Medicine at the School of Public Health, University of Illinois at Chicago, and Chairman of the Cancer Prevention Coalition, is an internationally recognized authority on the causes and prevention of cancer and on the toxic and carcinogenic effects of environmental pollutants in the air, water, soil, and workplace and of ingredients and contaminants in consumer products—foods, cosmetics and toiletries, and household products. He has published some 270 articles in leading scientific journals and has authored 11 books: *Mutagenicity of Pesticides* (1971), *Drugs of Abuse: Genetic and Other Chronic Non-Psychiatric Hazards* (1971), *The Legislation of Consumer Product Safety* (1974), the prize-winning *The Politics of Cancer* (1978), *Hazardous Wastes in America* (1982), *Cancer in Britain: The Politics of Prevention* (1983), *Safe Shopper's Bible* (1995), *The Breast Cancer Prevention Program* (1998), *The Politics of Cancer Revisited* (1998), e-book *Got (Genetically Engineered) Milk! The Monsanto rBGH/BST Milk Wars Handbook* (2001), and *Unreasonable Risk: How to Avoid Cancer from Cosmetics and Personal Care Products* (2001). He has also contributed numerous editorials and letters to leading national newspapers.

Dr. Epstein's past committee and society involvements include: Chairman of the Air Pollution Control Association Committee on Biological Effects of Air Pollutants; President of the Society of Occupational and Environmental Health; Co-Founder of the Environmental Mutagen Society; Director of Consumers Union; advisor to a wide range of public interest, environmental, citizen activist, and organized labor groups; Co-Chairman of the Commission for the Advancement of Public Interest Organizations; and President of the Rachel Carson Council, Inc.

Dr. Epstein's activities in the interface between science and public policy include: consultant to the U.S. Senate Committee on Public Works; drafting of Congressional legislation; frequently invited Congressional testimony; and membership of key federal agency advisory committees, including the Environmental Protection Agency's Health Effects Advisory Committee, and the 1973 Department of Labor Advisory Committee on the Regulation of

Occupational Carcinogens. He was the key expert involved in the banning of hazardous products and pesticides, including DDT, Aldrin, Chlordane, and the military use of Agent Orange in Vietnam. He is the leading international expert on the undisclosed hazards of: biosynthetic (recombinant) bovine growth hormone (rBGH) used for increasing milk production; sex hormones, used for fattening cattle in feedlots; food irradiation; and numerous dangerous ingredients in cosmetics and toiletries. He presented "Legislative Proposals for Reversing the Cancer Epidemic" to the Swedish Parliament in 1998 and to the U.K. All Parliamentary Cancer Group in 1999.

Dr. Epstein's honors include: British Empire Cancer Campaign Fellowship at The Hospital for Sick Children Great Ormond Street, and the Chester Beatty Cancer Research Institute (1957); Society of Toxicology Achievement Award (1969); National Conservancy Award of the National Wildlife Federation (1977); Yale University Henry Kaiser Award (1981); Environmental Justice Award (1989); Rachel Carson Legacy Award (1990); University of Tasmania Richard Jones Memorial Award (1993); Right Livelihood Award (the Alternative Nobel Prize; 1998); Bioneers Award (1999); Humanitarian Award from the National Silver Haired Congress (2000); and Project Censored Award (the Alternative Pulitzer Prize; 2000).

Dr. Epstein has extensive experience on major national television networks, including Sixty Minutes, Face the Nation, Meet the Press, MacNeil/Lehrer, Donahue, Good Morning America, and the Today Show. He has also made frequent appearances on Canadian, European, Australian, and Japanese television. He is a member of the National Writers Union, AFL-CIO, and National Association of Science Writers.

To my wondrous and loving wife, Cathy,
who has made all things possible.

Contents

Foreword

Cancer remains one of the deadliest diseases known to mankind. Beyond the millions of people living with cancer, millions more live in fear of one day being diagnosed with this disease, which now strikes nearly one in two men and more than one in three women in their lifetimes. Although physicians and scientists continually try to improve diagnosis and treatment, over half a million Americans will die of cancer in this year alone.

The Federal government enjoined the medical crusade against cancer in 1927 with a funding allocation for cancer research. Then in 1937, Congress established the National Cancer Institute (NCI) which operated with modest funding for several decades. However, it wasn't until 1971 that President Nixon declared a national "War Against Cancer," and the National Cancer Act was passed. At that time, Congress was assured that a major infusion of funding for cancer research could produce a cure before the American Bicentennial in 1976.

When Dr. Epstein published *The Politics of Cancer* in 1978, Congress had increased NCI's budget to $872 million, from $233 million in 1971. However, a cure was still nowhere in sight, and there was considerable debate as to how the war against cancer should be fought. Dr. Epstein and many of his colleagues in the public health community argued for a more aggressive assault on the preventable causes of cancer that people are unknowingly exposed to on a daily basis—at home, on the job, and in the environment—and often at low levels over their lifetimes.

Today, the annual budget for the National Cancer Institute is over $4.8 billion, approximately 20-fold greater than when the "War Against Cancer" was declared. One thing we have learned from this massive investment is that the hope for a simple cure was naïve. The uncontrolled and destructive cell growth that can attack any part of the body is far more complex than once thought. Although scientific knowledge about cancer has continued to expand, and significant progress has been made in new areas such as cancer genetics and improved techniques for diagnosis and treatment, the goal for a cure remains elusive.

Despite NCI's growth, Dr. Epstein contends that cancer prevention is still greatly overlooked. In 1992, Dr. Epstein and a group of some 50 national experts and former federal officials in public health and cancer prevention held a press conference to engage the public on this imbalance. The group argued that the national cancer program should break from its focus on cancer treatment and do more to reduce the number of people getting cancer in the first place. Pointing to the continued onslaught of new cases of cancer, they urged that the NCI devote as much resources in research and outreach for cancer cause and prevention as for diagnosis and treatment. The NCI could then provide workers, consumers, Congress, and regulatory agencies with vital information to reduce our exposure to carcinogens in air, water, food, and the workplace. The underlying goal of this change in policy was to reduce the rate of people getting cancer in each age group down to the low level seen in the first half of the century.

The direction the federal government takes in investing public resources in cancer research should be guided in the context of an open and vibrant debate among NCI, independent experts, and the public. Dr. Epstein's timely *Cancer-Gate: How to Win the Losing Cancer War* provides an analysis of our nation's struggle to reduce the incidence and mortality of cancer, and proposes a complex of strategies on the "War Against Cancer." I hope that this book will reinvigorate the Congressional and public debate on the direction of our cancer research and prevention efforts, with the aim to optimize the nation's resources to prevent as many deaths as possible and reduce the nation's burden of this deadly disease.

Congressman David Obey
January 2005

Preface

The *International Journal of Health Services (IJHS)* is unarguably the world's leading peer-reviewed public health journal. Apart from its rigorous scientific standards, the *IJHS*'s predominant emphasis is on the obligate relation between public health science and public health policy, and human rights.

It is my privilege and pleasure to have published extensively in the *IJHS* over the past 15 years. This book, *Cancer-Gate: How to Win the Losing Cancer War*, is, primarily, a compilation of these articles, three with named coauthors. The book's chapters have been organized thematically, rather than chronologically, in four parts: Cancer Policy and Politics; Hidden Carcinogens in Food; Pro-Industry Bias, Corporate Crime, and Poorly Recognized Industrial Risks of Cancer; and an Epilogue that summarizes the reasons for the losing cancer war.

Part I: Cancer Policy and Politics

These chapters detail evidence for the losing war on cancer since President Nixon declared the 1971 War Against Cancer. This action was in response to well-orchestrated public pressure by the scientific leadership and by lay spokespersons of major cancer institutions funded by the "cancer establishment"—the federal National Cancer Institute (NCI) and the nonprofit American Cancer Society (ACS).

Since 1971, and in spite of the cancer establishment's massive budgetary increases, the incidence of cancer, particularly non-smoking-related cancers, has escalated to epidemic proportions. Cancer now strikes more than one in two men and more than one in three women in their lifetimes. Not only has the cancer establishment trivialized this increase, but it has issued a series of highly misleading claims of major progress in the cancer war. Equally disturbing, the cancer establishment remains fixated on damage control—screening, diagnosis, treatment, and related research—with indifference to prevention research, an indifference that for the ACS extends to hostility. Furthermore, the NCI and ACS deny the public its undeniable right to know about well-documented scientific evidence on avoidable causes of a wide range of cancers. This mindset is compounded by pervasive institutional and personal conflicts of interest with the cancer drug industry and, in the case of the ACS, even with a wide range of petrochemical and other polluting industries.

Part I also proposes scientific recommendations and legislative strategies for reversing the cancer epidemic, including a complex of unique, recent regulatory initiatives by the European Commission.

Part II: Hidden Carcinogens in Food

These chapters deal with risks of cancer, still poorly recognized by the public, that are posed by industrialized food. Since the 1950s, cattle have been routinely implanted with synthetic or natural sex hormones in feedlots for some 100 days prior to slaughter, in order to increase muscle mass and reduce the costs of meat. However, hormonal meat poses poorly recognized risks of reproductive cancers, besides hormonal disturbances, in consumers.

From 1994, cows have been injected with genetically engineered bovine growth hormone (rBGH) to increase milk production. Apart from a wide range of toxic veterinary effects, rBGH milk is contaminated with high levels of a natural growth factor, posing major increased risks of human breast, colon, and prostate cancers. It may be noted that attempts by *Science* to discredit evidence on the risks of rBGH milk are consistent with its past pro-industry track record.

More recently, meat is being treated with high doses of radiation in order to reduce bacterial infection from grossly unsanitary conditions in slaughterhouses. Irradiation of meat produces profound chemical changes, including unique new chemicals, which pose risks of cancer and genetic damage, apart from nutritional deficiencies.

The NCI and ACS have remained silent or dismissive of the cancer and other risks of industrialized food, while the U.S. Food and Drug Administration and U.S. Department of Agriculture have approved the sale and consumption of these foods without any warnings.

Part III: Pro-Industry Bias, Corporate Crime, and Poorly Recognized Industrial Risks of Cancer

Science is one of the most prestigious international journals. Nevertheless, under previous editors, the journal had a strong pro-industry bias. Chapter 18 documents evidence for this charge, particularly *Science*'s dismissal of concerns about environmental pollution and occupational cancer as "chemophobia." This is all the more surprising in view of the longstanding and substantial evidence for suppression and manipulation of health and safety data—extending to the frankly criminal—by the petrochemical industry. This is well illustrated in Chapter 16.

Environmental and occupational exposures to industrial carcinogens are now well recognized as major avoidable causes of a wide range of cancers. Chapters 17 and 18 summarize such evidence for colorectal and breast cancers.

Part IV: Epilogue

A recently published article on why we are still losing the winnable cancer war summarizes the major themes of the book.

A pervading theme in the book is its specific proposals for reforming cancer policy to reflect such concerns, and specific strategies for cancer prevention. These proposals have been endorsed by the nation's leading independent cancer prevention and public health scientists, besides activist groups and nongovernmental organizations (see Appendix, p. 299). Further information on these proposals, as well as other material related to cancer policy, cancer prevention, and public health, is available at my website, www.preventcancer.com.

Acknowledgments

I would like to pay tribute to the late Drs. Wilhelm Hueper, Irving Selikoff, Thomas Mancuso, and William Lijinsky, pioneers in occupational and environmental cancer, and to Dr. Quentin D. Young, Past President of the American Public Health Association and now Chairman of the Health and Medicine Policy Research Group, for their emphasis on the critical, but infrequently exercised, role of physicians in public health policy on the causes and prevention of cancer.

I thank the following scientists for their advice and guidance on specific chapters: Chapter 9, Olav Axelson, Denis Bard, Chris Busby, Laurence Chérié-Chaline, Richard Clapp, Jacqueline Clavel, Marcel Goldberg, Lennart Hardell, Brigitte Lacour, Laurent Remontet, Annie Sasco, Joel Tickner, Jean-François Viel, and Theofanis Christoforou, Legal Advisor to the E.C.; and Chapter 14, Michael O. Blackstone, Stephen B. Hanauer, Joseph B. Kirsner, Philip J. Landrigan, and Marvin Schneiderman. I would also like to express appreciation to the 64 scientists, including past directors of federal agencies, for endorsing Chapter 2, Part A, the 103 scientists and NGOs for endorsing Chapter 6, and their 30 representatives involved in reviewing the strategies outlined in Chapter 8.

Warm recognition is due to Cong. David Obey (D-WI), for his insights and scrutiny of the NCI's failed policies and priorities; Cong. Henry Waxman (D-CA), for long-standing concerns on consumer product safety and escalating cancer rates, as exemplified by his 1987 request to me for a Congressional Record report on the status of the cancer war; Cong. John Conyers, for his 1979 invitation to draft legislation on "white-collar crime" in relation to industry malpractice—its knowingly exposing millions of citizens and workers to avoidable risks of cancer from industrial chemicals—and for his long-standing interest in legislative reform of cancer policies.

I also thank Edward Goldsmith, leading international ecologist, environmental scholar, and editor and publisher of *The Ecologist,* for decades-long encouragement. I am also grateful to Jakob von Uexkull, President of the Right Livelihood Award Foundation, for having supported my research with the 1998 Award (also known as the Alternative Nobel Prize). I would also like to thank the Horst

M. Rechelbacher, Fred Schneider, and Ann Oestreicher Foundations, and Marjorie Roswell, for their generous research support.

Thanks are also due to the University of Illinois, Chicago, for staunch support of my academic freedom, and to the School of Public Health and its scholarly and activist dean, Susan Scrimshaw, for providing me with a hospitable academic base for scientific research and public policy initiatives.

I would like to express appreciation and admiration to Dr. Vicente Navarro, founder and editor-in-chief of the *International Journal of Health Services (IJHS)*, for his long-standing leadership in international public health policy and for his insistence on the social responsibility of public health scientists. It is a pleasure to have worked with Linda Strange, copy editor of the *IJHS,* for her invaluable and skilled editing of the journal articles compiled in this book.

Finally, I would like to thank my secretary and administrative assistant, Julie Hlavaty, for her indefatigable help and support.

Introduction

Cancer-Gate: How to Win the Losing Cancer War is essential reading for all public policy makers and citizens alarmed by the health care crisis in America today. Its thesis is as simple as it is disturbing. Contrary to three decades of misleading promises and assurances from the federal National Cancer Institute (NCI) and the non-profit American Cancer Society (ACS), we are losing the winnable war against cancer largely because we have failed to adopt obvious fundamental prevention measures.

In the wake of this groundbreaking book, policy makers and the civil society must critically examine the reasons why the NCI and ACS have virtually ignored cancer prevention other than anti-smoking initiatives. These organizations have spent tens of billions of taxpayer and charity dollars seeking magic-bullet cures, while ignoring more fruitful avenues that could better protect us from industrial and other carcinogens in the first place. It's tautological that the more cancer we prevent, the less cancer there would be to treat.

Since 1971, the NCI's budget has increased 30-fold, while cancer incidence has skyrocketed. No elected official or CEO could survive such a track record of failure. And, as *Cancer-Gate* emphasizes, it is now clear that if we want to turn the tide and embark on a campaign to win the cancer war, there must be a new paradigm that strongly emphasizes the critical need for prioritizing practical cancer prevention programs which have been virtually ignored by the NCI and ACS. Such failure has surely been a contributing factor in the escalation of cancer rates to epidemic proportions, now striking nearly one in every two men and more than one in every three women in their lifetime. This translates into an approximately 50 percent increase in cancer in men and 20 percent increase in women over the course of just one generation. And, as study after study have shown, African American and other minority populations are even more severely affected by this crisis.

These startling facts are detailed in *Cancer-Gate*. The book's fundamental premise is that so much of the carnage is preventable. Preventable, that is if the NCI and ACS get off the dime and does their job.

Alarmingly, *Cancer-Gate* also documents how the NCI and ACS have become dangerously chummy with industrial polluters and special interests, particularly the pharmaceutical industry, which aggressively promotes new anti-cancer drugs, even when there is little evidence that they are effective. In this regard, the book notes a particularly disturbing comment from a recent NCI director who admitted that the NCI has become a "government pharmaceutical company." The *Chronicle of Philanthropy* similarly has charged that "the ACS is more interested in accumulating wealth than saving lives." And, for the first time, Epstein explains in this book how the NCI and ACS are sitting on mounds of information about avoidable industrial causes of cancer, while failing to make this information available to the public.

For years, I have argued that the disproportionate number of hazardous waste sites in African American communities is a cause of cancer and many other illnesses that can be traced to toxic substances in local communities. As such, I have also argued that the Department of Justice, in Republican and Democratic administrations alike, has failed to enforce Title VI of the Civil Rights Act and other laws, which prevent government actions, such as hazardous waste permitting, that result in disproportionate adverse effects on minority communities. The issues raised in this book chronicle what is yet another major health care failure, and makes the central point that so much of the disease and death—which hits minority communities hardest—is avoidable. As the ranking member of the House Judiciary Committee, Dean of the Congressional Black Caucus, former Chairman of the House Government Operations Committee, and representative of the people of Detroit, I have long felt that we are sinking too many precious dollars into federal institutions without sufficient accountability or reporting requirements that would provide measurable outcomes of these taxpayer-subsidized programs. *Cancer-Gate* emphatically makes the case for fixing this problem and for creating key reforms—right-to-know laws, budgetary shifts in favor of prevention inside the National Institute of Health, for a start—that will ensure that the public interest is protected and promoted through these hallowed institutions. Further, as the book implores, we need to take the special-interest influence out of our cancer institutions and to require that the tomes of data showing how cancer can be prevented are released to the public.

The book thus provides policy makers, grassroots organizers, and everyday citizens with a commonsense roadmap for change. If taken, these steps could save millions of lives who needlessly lost because there are not adequate federal laws to protect the public from cancer-causing pesticides, industrial air and water pollutants, medical x-ray technology, and exposure to carcinogens in the workplace. The reader, whether member of Congress or concerned citizen, will thus be empowered with critical information needed to start demanding change and protecting themselves and their families.

It's time to hold our government and these much vaunted institutions accountable, to make the cancer war part of our homeland security effort. For this is a war that we can win if the public merely demands that Congress require the NCI to disclose information on these chemical attacks on our communities.

This exposé of the NCI and ACS, and the proposed reforms of public policy, have been endorsed by over a hundred leading independent experts in cancer prevention and public health, as well as by activist citizen groups. *Cancer-Gate* is a must read for all who are alarmed by the modern cancer epidemic. The book should also serve as a roadmap for policy makers on how to reverse the 30-year failed war on this most deadly disease.

Congressman John Conyers, Jr.

PART I

Cancer Policy and Politics

Chapter 1

LOSING THE WAR AGAINST CANCER: WHO'S TO BLAME AND WHAT TO DO ABOUT IT

Cancer is now a major killing disease in the industrialized world, and its rates are sharply rising. In contrast, there have been major reductions in deaths from cardiovascular disease—still the number one killer in the United States—probably because of a recent decline in smoking and increased attention to diet and exercise.

With more than 900,000 new cases and 450,000 U.S. deaths in 1988, cancer has now reached epidemic proportions, with an incidence of one in three and a mortality of one in four. Analysis of overall cancer rates, standardized for age, sex, and ethnicity, has demonstrated a steady increase in cancer rates since the 1930s. In recent years, the incidence rate has risen more sharply, by some 2 percent a year, and mortality rates have risen by 1 percent a year.

Striking confirmation of these recent increases comes from estimates of the lifetime probability of getting cancer for people born at different times. For white males born in 1975–1985, for instance, the probability of developing cancer has risen from 30 to 36 percent, while the probability of dying from cancer has risen from 19 to 23 percent; probability rates for black males are even higher. Such increases in overall cancer rates are also reflected in the increasing incidence of cancers of the lung, breast, colon, prostate, testis, urinary bladder, kidney, and skin, and of malignant melanoma and lymphatic/hematopoietic malignancies, including non-Hodgkin's lymphoma. (It should, however, be noted that there have been substantial decreases in rates for cancers of the stomach and cervix, and less so, for rectal cancer.) Lung cancer is responsible for about one-third of the overall recent increase in incidence rates. It should be stressed that some 75 percent of all cancer deaths occur in people over 55 years of age, and that recent increases are largely restricted to these ages.

Published in *International Journal of Health Services*, Volume 20, Number 1, 1990.

STATIC CURE RATES

The overall cancer "cure rate," as measured by survival for more than five years following diagnosis, is currently (in 1990) 50 percent for whites, but only 38 percent for blacks. There is no evidence of substantial improvements in treatment during the last few decades, during which the five-year survival and age-adjusted mortality rates for the major cancer killers (lung, breast, and colon) and for cancers of most other organs have remained essentially unchanged. The only improvements have been for cancer of the cervix and for relatively rare cancers, such as testicular seminomas, Hodgkin's disease, and childhood leukemias treated with radiation and/or chemotherapy. Apart from immediate toxicity, such treatment, while usually effective, can increase the subsequent risk of developing a second cancer by more than tenfold.

INCREASING CARCINOGENIC EXPOSURES

Cancer is an age-old and ubiquitous group of diseases. Its recognized causes and influences are multifactorial and include natural environmental carcinogens (such as aflatoxins and sunlight), lifestyle factors, genetic susceptibility, and more recently, industrial chemicals. Apart from modern lifestyle factors, particularly smoking, increasing cancer rates reflect exposure to industrial chemicals and run-away modern technologies whose explosive growth has clearly outpaced the ability of society to control them. In addition to pervasive changes in patterns of living and diet, these poorly controlled technologies have induced profound and poorly reversible environmental degradation and have resulted in progressive contamination of air, water, soil, food, and workplaces with toxic and carcinogenic chemicals, with resulting involuntary exposures.

With the dawn of the petrochemical era in the early 1940s, by which time technologies including fractional distillation of petroleum, catalytic and thermal cracking, and molecular splicing had become commercially established, the annual U.S. production of synthetic organic chemicals was about 1 billion pounds. By the 1950s this had reached 30 billion pounds, and by the 1980s more than 400 billion pounds annually. The overwhelming majority of these industrial chemicals has never been adequately tested—if tested at all—for chronic toxic, carcinogenic, mutagenic, and teratogenic effects, let alone for ecological effects, and most of the limited available industrial data are at best suspect.

Occupational exposure to industrial carcinogens has clearly emerged as a major risk factor for cancer. In 1978, a blue-ribbon government commission (under the auspices of the then Health, Education and Welfare Secretary, Califano) estimated, on the basis of the only available exposure data, that up to 38 percent of all cancers in coming decades would reflect past and continuing exposures to just six high-volume occupational carcinogens (1). In spite of the recognized limitations of these estimates, both in overestimating exposure to certain of the named carcinogens, particularly asbestos, and in the failure to reflect a wide range of other possibly more significant exposures, their magnitude was surprisingly confirmed by industry consultants Stallones and Downs of the University of Texas School of Public Health, in a confidential report commissioned by the American Industrial Health Council. The National Institute for Occupational Safety and Health (NIOSH) estimates that some 10 million workers are now exposed to 11 high-volume carcinogens. Fivefold to tenfold increases in cancer rates for a wide range of organs have been demonstrated in some occupations. Also persuasive are British data on cancer mortality by socioeconomic class, largely defined by occupation, which show that the lowest class, particularly among males, has approximately twice the cancer mortality rate of the highest class (2).

Living near petrochemical and certain other industries in highly urbanized communities increases cancer risks, as demonstrated by the clustering of excess cancer rates. High levels of toxic and carcinogenic chemicals are deliberately and also accidentally discharged by a wide range of industries into the air of surrounding communities. Fallout from such toxic air pollutants is also an important source of contamination of surface waters, particularly the Great Lakes. While there are still no regulatory requirements in the United States for reporting and monitoring these emissions, unpublished government estimates indicate that they are in excess of 5 billion pounds annually.

Another example of the effects of run-away technology is the hazardous waste crisis. The volume of hazardous wastes disposed of every year in the United States has risen from under 1 million tons in 1940 to well over 400 million tons in the 1980s, more than 1 ton per U.S. citizen per year. The industries involved— fossil fuel, metal mining and processing, nuclear, and petrochemical—have littered the entire land mass of the United States with some 50,000 toxic waste landfills (20,000 of which are recognized as potentially hazardous), 170,000 industrial impoundments (ponds, pits, and lagoons), and 7,000 underground injection wells, not to mention some 2.5 million underground gasoline tanks, many of which are leaking. Not surprisingly, an increasing number of rural and urban communities have found themselves located on or near hazardous waste sites, or downstream, downgradient, or downwind from such sites. Particularly alarming is growing evidence of contamination of groundwater from hazardous waste sites, contamination that poses grave hazards for centuries to come. Once contaminated, groundwaters are difficult, and sometimes impossible, to clean up.

Environmental contamination with highly potent carcinogenic pesticides has reached alarming and pervasive proportions. Apart from high-level exposure of workers in manufacturing, formulating, and applicating industries, the contamination of ground and surface waters and the U.S. diet has become commonplace. Residues of ethylene dibromide in excess of 1,000 ppb in raw grains, cereals, and citrus fruits have been well known to industry and the Environmental Protection Agency (EPA) for as long as ten years after its very high carcinogenicity was first demonstrated; not until 1984, however, did EPA develop a

30 ppb tolerance, which was rejected by the Commonwealth of Massachusetts and the States of New York and Florida and replaced by much lower and less hazardous levels. While the exact numbers are uncertain, it is probable that tens of millions of homes nationwide are contaminated with varying and highly carcinogenic levels of chlordane/heptachlor, manufactured by Velsicol Chemical Co.; neither Velsicol nor EPA has made any attempt to monitor these homes for contamination with these highly persisting carcinogens. It should be noted that, on the basis of extensive hearings in 1975, the Agency concluded that exposure to chlordane/heptachlor posed an "imminent hazard" due to cancer (besides other chronic toxic effects), leading to a subsequent ban on their agricultural uses.

Much cancer today reflects events and exposures in the 1950s and 1960s. The production, use, and disposal of synthetic organic and other industrial carcinogens was then minuscule in terms of volume when compared with current levels, which will determine future cancer rates for younger populations now exposed. There is every reason to expect that even today's high cancer rates will be exceeded in the next few decades.

Concern has understandably focused on increasing cancer rates, but these substantially underestimate the extent and scope of the public health effects of environmental pollutants. Only a small proportion of the tens of thousands of petrochemicals in commerce, well under 500, are carcinogenic. However, many of these, together with many other noncarcinogenic petrochemicals, induce other chronic toxic effects, including neurological, respiratory, reproductive, hepatic, and probably immunological diseases, whose true causation is generally not suspected, much less investigated.

HOW INDUSTRY FIGHTS REGULATION

Twentieth-century industry has aggressively pursued short-term economic goals, recklessly uncaring or unmindful of harm to workers, local communities, and the environment. So far, industry has shifted responsibility for the damage it has caused and has externalized these costs onto society at large. Belated government efforts to control polluting industries have generally been neutralized by well-organized and well-financed opposition. With the exception of special purpose legislation for drugs, food additives, and pesticides, there were no regulatory requirements for pretesting industrial chemicals until the 1976 Toxic Substance Control Act, legislation that the industry had stalled for years and which is now honored more in the breach than in the observance.

Apart from the failure to pretest most chemicals, a key characteristic of industry's antiregulatory strategy has been the generation of self-serving and misleading data on toxicology and epidemiology and on regulatory costs and cost-benefit analyses. The record of such unreliable and often fraudulent data is so extensive and well documented as to justify the presumption that most industry data must be treated as suspect until proven otherwise.

Attempts by the Carter administration to develop comprehensive "generic" regulation of occupational carcinogens, later reversed by the Reagan administration, were attacked by the Manufacturing Chemists Association, which created the American Industrial Health Council to organize opposition. Such reactions generally reflect a short-sighted preoccupation with perceived self-interest rather than with efficiency and economy. The virtual uniformity of industry opposition to regulation is in marked contrast to the heterogeneity of the industries involved, in terms of both size and the diversity of their interests. Regulation has, in fact, generally resulted in substantial improvements in industrial efficiency and economy, particularly in large industries, by forcing development of technologies for recovery and recycling of valuable resources. A deplorable result of regulation, however, has been, and continues to be, the export of the restricted products or processes to the so-called lesser developed countries. Information on such exports is being systematized by Consumer Interpol, a program of the International Organization of Consumers Union based in Penang, Malaysia, which promotes consumer protection from dangerous products. The participants in this network are consumer, environmental, health, and other citizen groups concerned about unrestricted trade in hazardous substances. Besides the global dissemination of such hazards, the multinational corporations involved are also responsible for the loss of U.S. jobs and their replacement by cheap "expendable" foreign labor.

Apart from well-documented evidence on control and manipulation of health and environmental information, industry has used various strategies to con the public into complacency and divert attention from industry's own recklessness and responsibility for the cancer epidemic. Key among these is the "blame the victim" theory of cancer causation, developed by industry scientists and consultants and a group of pro-industry academics, and tacitly supported by the "cancer establishment." This theory emphasizes faulty lifestyle, smoking and fatty diet, sun bathing, or genetic susceptibility as the major causes of preventable cancer, while trivializing the role of involuntary exposures to occupational and environmental carcinogens. Another misleading diversion is the claim that there is no evidence of recently increasing cancer rates other than lung cancer, for which smoking is given the exclusive credit. While the role of lifestyle is obviously important, the scientific basis of this theory is as unsound as it is self-serving. Certainly, smoking is a major, but not sole, cause of lung cancer. But a wealth of evidence clearly incriminates the additional role of other causes of lung cancer, particularly exposure to occupational carcinogens and carcinogenic community-air pollutants. Illustratively, some 20 percent of lung cancers occur in nonsmokers; there have been major recent increases in lung cancer rates in non-smokers; an increasing percentage of lung cancer is of a histological type (adeno-carcinoma) not usually associated with smoking; high lung cancer rates are found with certain occupational exposures, independent of smoking; and excess lung cancer rates are found in communities where certain major industries are located. The chemical industry thus clearly uses tobacco as a smoke screen to divert attention from the role of carcinogenic chemicals in inducing lung cancer, besides other cancers.

When it comes to diet, the much touted role of high fat consumption, while clearly linked to heart disease, is based on tenuous and contradictory evidence with regard to breast and colon cancers. The evidence certainly does not justify the wild claims by lifestyle theorists (particularly in the National Cancer Institute and American Cancer Society) that some 30 to 40 percent of all cancers are due to faulty diet. For instance, a 1982 National Academy of Sciences report concluded that "in the only human studies in which the total fiber consumption was quantified, no association was found between total fiber consumption and colon cancer" (3). Similarly, a large-scale 1987 study, based on the eating habits of nearly 90,000 nurses, concluded that "there is no association between dietary fat and breast cancer" (4). However, U.S. diets are contaminated with a wide range of carcinogens that concentrate in fatty foods and whose presence is not disclosed to the consumer.

Another illustration of grossly misleading strategies relates to the identification of chemical carcinogens. When a particular chemical or product is threatened with regulation on the basis of animal carcinogenicity tests, the industry invariably challenges the significance of these tests, while routinely using negative test results as proof of safety. At the same time, industry insists on the need for long-term epidemiological investigations to obtain definitive human evidence of carcinogenicity. To test this apparent reliance on direct human evidence, researchers at Mt. Sinai Hospital in New York compiled a list of some 100 chemicals accepted as carcinogenic on the basis of valid animal tests, but for which no epidemiological information is available, and sent this list to some 80 major chemical industries (5). Respondents were asked whether any of the listed carcinogens had been or were in use and, if so, whether epidemiological studies had been conducted, were being conducted, or were planned to be conducted in the future, and if not, why not. The responses were revealing. The great majority of those industries using particular carcinogens replied that they had done no epidemiological studies, were not doing any, and did not intend to do any for various reasons, including alleged difficulty, impracticality, and expense, or because of their conviction that these chemicals could not possibly be carcinogenic to humans. A perfect catch-22: denigrate the animal tests and insist on human data, but make sure that the human studies are never done.

Industry positions are vigorously advocated by trade associations, such as the Chemical Manufacturers Association; public relations firms, such as Hill and Knowlton; front organizations, such as the American Council on Science and Health, supported by over 100 chemical and food industries (the contributions of whose director, Elizabeth Whelan, have been aptly characterized as "voodoo science"); and lay writers, such as Edith Efron (who charges that the American scientific community has been terrorized into submission by environmental "apocalyptics"). Disturbingly, another major source of support for antiregulatory strategies is an eager stable of academic consultants who advance the industry position in arenas including the scientific literature, federal advisory committees, and regulatory and Congressional hearings, generally without disclosing their indentured relationship to industry. (These consultants include: MacMahon, a Harvard epidemiologist who has cleared his contracted studies with industry before submitting them for publication; Demoupoulos, a pathologist at the New York University Medical Center who claims that asbestos and vinyl chloride are weak carcinogens and that the high cancer mortality rates in New Jersey are due to poor treatment by foreign-trained doctors in that state; Olson, a clinician at the Pittsburgh University School of Medicine who has testified that benzene cannot be carcinogenic in humans because it allegedly does not induce tumors in animals; Hayes, formerly of the Centers for Disease Control and Vanderbilt University School of Medicine, a toxicologist repeatedly on record as rejecting the human significance of animal carcinogenicity data on organochlorine pesticides; and Harbison, a toxicologist from the University of Arkansas Medical School who, in 1980, testified as a government witness that rodents are "good predictors of human cancer risk," and who, as an industry expert, blatantly testified just the opposite in 1985.)

GOVERNMENT AND THE CANCER EPIDEMIC

Presidents play a powerful role in setting national public health priorities, not unnaturally reflecting their own political agendas. Former President Reagan, however, was unique in having run for office on an ideological antiregulatory platform, and in having then systematically used his office to implement this ideology, often in contravention to the spirit and letter of the law. With the active support of Vice-President Bush as chairman of the 1981 "Regulatory Relief Task Force," Reagan systematically neutralized legislative mandates on controls of toxic and carcinogenic exposure by direct frontal assaults on regulatory agencies. (Such successes of the Reagan administration at the regulatory level are, however, in striking contrast to its failure to make any impression on the scientific underpinning of public health and environmental regulations. For instance, a 1985 report by the Office of Science and Technology Policy of the White House clearly affirmed such critical tenets as the value of animal carcinogenicity data in extrapolating to human risk, and the inability to set "safe levels or thresholds" for exposure to carcinogens.) Strategies employed included: staffing senior positions with unqualified, ideologically selected staff hostile to their agency mandates; budget cutting; insisting on formal cost-benefit analyses that focused on industry costs with little (or biased) consideration of the costs of failing to regulate, and which effectively stalled the regulatory process; illegal, behind-closed-doors meetings with industry; and making regulation dependent on the Office of Management and Budget, with its subservience to the White House.

An example is the White House decision to block the $1.3 million 1984 request by the National Institute of Occupational Safety and Health (NIOSH) to notify some 200,000 workers of risks from previously undisclosed exposure to workplace carcinogens, as identified in some 60 government studies, in order to allow medical follow-up and early diagnosis of cancer. The reason for this refusal of modest funding seems to have been a desire to shield corporations from possible claims. (On February 26, 1987, hearings were held before the Labor and Human Resources Committee on a bill sponsored by Senator Metzenbaum to require the Department of Health and Human Services to notify past or present workers known to be at risk of cancer and other occupational diseases. To the annoyance of Republican committee members, NIOSH officials supported the bill, which was opposed by administration spokespersons who claimed that it would duplicate existing efforts and generate "too much litigation." The senior dissenting officials received a subsequent "dressing down" from the administration. However, on March 27, 1987, unexpected support for the bill came from the 3000-member American Electronics Association, a trade group; from IBM; from the Digital Equipment Corporation; and from the General Electric Company.) Such a track record justifies the conclusions of a 1984 Congressional Study Group report that "efforts to protect public health and the environment from the dangers of toxic pollution have ground to a standstill under the Reagan Administration . . . [which was charged with being] a public health hazard" (6).

The U.S. Congress has gradually become sensitive to public health and environmental concerns, as exemplified in a plethora of legislation in recent decades. Such legislation has evolved fragmentarily, reflecting particular interests and priorities. New laws have focused on individual environmental media—air, water, food, or the workplace—or on individual classes of products or contaminants, such as pesticides or industrial chemicals, with tittle or no consideration of needs for more comprehensive and integrated approaches. Furthermore, the legislative language has traditionally been ambiguous, thus allowing maximal regulatory discretion to bureaucracies that, in some instances, have subsequently become closely associated with or even "captured" by the regulated industries. A noteworthy exception is the 1958 Delaney Amendment to the Federal Food, Drug, and Cosmetic Act, with its absolute prohibition against the deliberate introduction of any level of carcinogen into the food supply. Over the last three decades, this Amendment has been under repeated vigorous attacks by industry, usually with strong support of the Food and Drug Administration (FDA) and EPA. The latest such initiative is EPA's October 1988 proposal to scrap the Amendment for carcinogenic pesticides contaminating processed agricultural foods, and to substitute a "negligible [cancer] risk" regulation, based on manipulated numbers and unjustifiable assumptions. The FDA shares with EPA unwillingness to obey the Delaney law, and has been enthusiastic in developing a legal basis for exemptions for a wide range of carcinogenic coal-tar food dyes, and animal feed additives. Both FDA and EPA are planning to fling open the leaking floodgates to a wide range of carcinogens in the nation's food supplies.

Congress has also tended to abdicate decision making to scientific authority (or perceived authority), rather than questioning its basis in the open political arena. Of particular importance was passage of the 1971 Cancer Act in response to orchestrated pressures from the "cancer establishment," the National Cancer Institute (NCI), American Cancer Society (ACS), and clinicians aggressively pushing chemotherapy as a primary cancer treatment. The cancer establishment misled Congress into the unfounded and simplistic view that the cure for cancer was just around the corner, *provided* that Congress made available massive funding for cancer treatment research. The Cancer Act did just this, while failing to emphasize the need for cancer prevention, and also gave the NCI virtual autonomy from the parent National Institutes of Health, while establishing a direct chain of command between the NCI and the White House. Some 18 years and many billions of dollars later, by 1990 Congress still has not appreciated that the poorly informed special interests of the cancer establishment have minimized the importance of critically needed cancer prevention efforts and have singularly failed to support such efforts. Nor has Congress appreciated the need for a long-overdue investigation into the conduct and priorities of the NCI. Given the heterogeneity of Congressional interests, the complexity of the problem involved, the heavy lobbying by industry, the indifference or co-option of the general scientific community, and the well-orchestrated pressures of the cancer establishment, it is not surprising that Congress has yet to recognize that we are losing the war against cancer.

Until recently, state governments have largely deferred to federal authority, exercising relatively minor roles in cancer prevention. Reagan's federal deregulatory efforts began to reverse this relationship. Responsively, regulatory actions against carcinogens have emerged at the state level, such as the banning of chlordane/heptachlor and aldrin/dieldrin for termite treatment by Massachusetts and New York; the banning of daminozide (Alar) for apple ripening and tough restrictions on ethylene dibromide food tolerances by Massachusetts; and the introduction of informative occupational labeling laws by various states, such as the "right-to-know" workplace legislation in New Jersey.

In some cases, such state initiatives have evoked federal preemption by restrictive regulations—such as the 1983 Hazard Communication Standard of the Occupational Safety and Health Administration (OSHA)—despite Reagan's avowed commitment to getting big government off the backs of the people. In February 1987, a coalition of labor and citizen organizations asked the U.S. Court of Appeals to enforce its 18-month-old order directing the Occupational Safety and Health Administration to expand coverage of its communication standard from manufacturing to all workers. In an apparent about face, the Chemical Manufacturers Association supported this expansion in conformity with regulations developed for various states.

THE CANCER ESTABLISHMENT:
STANDING IN THE WAY OF PREVENTION

The cancer establishment still continues to mislead the public and Congress into believing that "we are winning the war against cancer," with "victory" possible only given more time and money. The NCI and ACS also insist that there have been major advances in treatment and cure of cancer, and that there has been no increase in cancer rates (with the exception of lung cancer, which is exclusively attributed to smoking). Yet, the facts show just the contrary.

The cancer establishment periodically beats the drum to announce the latest "cancer cure" and dramatic "breakthrough." These announcements reflect optimism and wishful thinking rather than reality. The extravagant and counterproductive claims for interferon as the magic cancer bullet of the late 1970s have been followed by the unpublicized recognition of its limited role in cancer treatment. Interferon is particularly effective, if not often curative, for two rare neoplasms: hairy cell leukemia and juvenile laryngeal papillomatosis. The latest NCI "breakthrough" claims for interleukin-2 as a cancer cure are grossly inflated and rest on questionable data. These claims fail to reflect the devastating toxicity and lethality of this drug, and gloss over the high treatment costs, which can run into six figures.

Equally questionable are claims by the NCI and ACS that overall cancer survival rates have improved dramatically in recent years. These claims, based on "rubber numbers" according to one prominent critic, ignore factors such as "lead-time bias"; earlier diagnosis of cancer, resulting in apparently prolonged survival even in the absence of any treatment; and the "overdiagnosis" of essentially benign tumors, particularly those of the prostate, breast, and thyroid, as malignant. Recently, the ex-director of the NCI, Vincent T. DeVita, resorted to blaming community doctors for using inadequate doses of chemotherapy drugs as the "real" reason why cancer cure rates are no better than they are.

The NCI misrepresentations are well reflected in budgetary priorities that are largely and disproportionately directed to cancer treatment research—to the serious neglect of cancer prevention. Even the very modest funding for cancer prevention is largely directed to endorsing industry's "blame the victim" concept of cancer causation. Thus, the NCI exaggerates the role of tobacco for a wide range of other cancers besides lung cancer and treats as fact the slim and contradictory evidence relating diet to colon, breast, and other cancers.

Apparently oblivious to mounting criticisms, the NCI continues vigorously to propagate these misrepresentations. A 1986 NCI document on cancer control objectives—the executive summary of which fails even to mention environmental and occupational exposures to carcinogens and focuses on diet and tobacco as the major causes of cancer—rashly promises that annual cancer mortality rates could be reduced by 50 percent by the year 2000 (7). More recently, Armand Hammer, chairman of the NCI National Cancer Advisory Panel (a three-member group that advises the President directly) and chairman of Occidental Petroleum Corporation (a major polluting industry and manufacturer of carcinogenic chemicals), announced a four-year fund-raising drive to add $1 billion to the NCI budget in order to "find a cure for cancer in the next ten years." None of this proposed funding is earmarked for cancer prevention, let alone the costs of Occidental's contributions to cancer causation.

More disturbing than indifference to cancer prevention is evidence uncovered in September 1982 by Congressman Dave Obey that the NCI has pressured the International Agency for Research on Cancer (IARC), funded in part by the NCI, to downplay the carcinogenicity of benzene and formaldehyde in IARC monographs that review and rank the carcinogenicity data on industrial and other chemicals (8). Such evidence is noteworthy since, contrary to the extensive scientific documentation and its own explicit guidelines, IARC has also downgraded the carcinogenicity of other highly profitable carcinogenic industrial chemicals, such as the pesticides aldrin/dieldrin and chlordane/heptachlor and the solvents trichloroethylene and perchloroethylene. (Apart from the noted exceptions, the IARC monographs are unique and well-systematized compendia of data on the chronic toxicity, carcinogenicity, and uses of a wide range of industrial and other chemicals.)

During the last two decades, consistent with its low priorities for cancer prevention, the NCI has played little or no role in providing the database in support of critical federal or state legislation and regulation on cancer prevention. Examples in which NCI scientific input could have been reasonably expected include attempts to prevent the exposure of much of the U.S. population to carcinogenic pesticides, such as ethylene dibromide residues in food or chlordane/heptachlor in the air of a high percentage of the many million homes treated for termites, and also exposure to industrial discharges of carcinogenic air pollutants or drinking water contaminants.

Following nearly a decade of fruitless discussions with the ACS, at a February 7, 1984, press conference a national coalition of major public interest and labor groups, headed by the Center for Science in the Public Interest (and myself), and supported by some 24 independent scientists, charged that: "[The ACS] is doing virtually nothing to help reduce the public exposure to cancer-causing chemicals. . . . Despite its promises to the public to do everything to "wipe out cancer in your lifetime," the ACS fails to make its voice heard in Congress and the regulatory arena, where it could be a powerful influence to help reduce public exposure to carcinogens." More specific criticisms included the following:

- ACS fails to support, and at times has been hostile to, critical legislation that seeks to reduce or eliminate exposure to environmental and occupational carcinogens. For example, ACS refused to join a coalition of major organizations, including the March of Dimes, the American Heart Association, and the American Lung Association, to support the Clean Air Act. ACS has rejected requests from congressional subcommittees, unions, and environmental organizations to support their efforts to ban or regulate a wide range of occupational and environmental carcinogens. Giant corporations, which profit handsomely while they pollute the air, water, and food with cancer-causing chemicals, must be greatly comforted by the ACS's silence.

- ACS's record on supporting efforts to ban carcinogens is dismal. Often, ACS's statements are expressly or implicitly hostile to regulation.
- ACS's approach to cancer prevention largely reflects a "blame the victim" philosophy, which emphasizes faulty lifestyles, rather than workplace or environmental carcinogens. For instance, ACS blames the higher incidence of cancer among blacks primarily on their diet and smoking habits, which diverts attention from the fact that blacks work in the dirtiest, most hazardous jobs, and live in the most polluted communities.

A few days after the press conference, ACS announced a "new set of policies," passing resolutions for the improved regulation of such chemicals as asbestos and benzene and the cleaning up of toxic waste sites. However, there has been little evidence of any real change of heart in the ACS since then.

THE LIFESTYLE ACADEMICS

The lifestyle academics are a group of highly conservative scientists, including Sir Richard Doll, the Warden and Director of the industry-financed Green College, Oxford (which according to a founding fellow, I. Herrman, was established in 1978 as a "special point of entry for industrial interests wishing to collaborate with university departments in research" (9); his protégé, R. Peto, a statistician also from Oxford; and more recently Bruce Ames, a California geneticist. The puristic pretensions of "the lifestylers" for critical objectivity are only exceeded by their apparent indifference to or rejection of a steadily accumulating body of information on the permeation of the environment and workplace with industrial carcinogens and the impact of such involuntary exposures on human cancer.

Consciously or subconsciously, these academics have become the well-touted and enthusiastic mouthpiece for industry interests, urging regulatory inaction and public complacency. Among the more noteworthy contributions of these academics is a series of publications claiming that smoking and fatty diet are each responsible for 30 to 40 percent of all cancers, and that sunlight, drugs, and personal susceptibility account for another 10 percent, leaving only a few percent unaccounted for, which, just for want of any better reason, was then ascribed to occupation. According to the lifestylers, this then proves that occupation is an unimportant cause of cancer, which really does not warrant much regulatory concern.

Apart from circularly referencing each other as authority for these wild guesses, the lifestylers have never attempted to develop any estimates of how many workers are exposed to defined levels of specific carcinogens. Without such estimates, there is no way of even attempting to determine just how much cancer is due to occupational exposure.

The lifestyle theory was further advocated in a 1981 report by Doll and Peto (10), dealing with causes of cancer in the United States, in which they denied evidence of increasing cancer rates other than for lung cancer, which was largely ascribed to tobacco without adequate consideration of the importance of community and occupational exposure to carcinogens. This study was sponsored by the Office of Technology Assessment, whose contract officer, Gough, was apparently unable to find any U.S. experts with knowledge of cancer in the United States and so selected British lifestyle advocates for the project. (Gough is also subsequently on record in a 1986 book on Agent Orange as dismissing epidemiological evidence on the hazards of dioxin, including rejecting evidence of its carcinogenicity based on extensive animal data.) To reach their misleading conclusions on static cancer rates, Doll and Peto excluded from analysis people over the age of 65 and blacks, just those groups with the highest and increasing cancer mortality rates. Not content with such manipulation, they claimed that occupation was only responsible for some 4 percent of all cancers, without apparent consideration of a wide range of recent studies dealing with the carcinogenic effects of such exposures. (Even if only 4 percent of cancers in the general population are occupational in origin, this implies that occupation is responsible for some 20 percent of all cancers in exposed workers.) This wild 4 percent guess was matched by "guesstimates" that diet was determinant in some 35 percent of all cancers. To trivialize the significance of animal carcinogenicity data on industrial chemicals, Doll and Peto minimized the predictive value of these tests, while emphasizing epidemiological data as the basis of regulation.

Doll is prompt to side with industry in downplaying evidence on carcinogenicity of industrial chemicals. For example, he recently lent enthusiastic support to the Australian Royal Commission on Agent Orange in its dismissal of the experimental and epidemiological carcinogenicity data on the herbicides 2,4-D and 2,4,5-T; Doll's position has since been effectively rebutted (11). (The 2,4,5-T component of Agent Orange was contaminated with high concentrations of 2,3,7,8-tetrachlorodibenzodioxin which, according to the Carcinogenic Assessment Group of EPA, is the most potent carcinogen it has ever evaluated, being some seven orders of magnitude more carcinogenic than the potent carcinogen, vinyl chloride.)

Bruce Ames is a geneticist who, in the 1970s, developed bacterial assays for mutagenicity which he advocated as highly reliable short-term tests for carcinogens; the predictability of his test is now recognized as similar to that of flipping a coin. He then published a series of articles stridently warning of increasing cancer rates and the essential need for tough regulation of industrial carcinogens, such as the fire retardant Tris and the fumigant ethylene dibromide. By the 1980s, when federal funding favored lifestyle theories rather than emphasis on industrial carcinogens, Ames made a 180-degree turn, and now, even more stridently, claims just the opposite, that overall cancer rates are not increasing, that industrial carcinogens are unimportant causes of cancer which do not need regulating, and that the real causes of cancer are natural dietary carcinogens, largely because mutagens can be found in a variety of foods. (Ames fails to extend his logic by claiming that feces are carcinogenic, although they are a rich source of bacterial mutagens! Moreover, assuming that Ames's exclusionary emphasis on dietary carcinogens has scientific validity, the critical issue is not which carcinogens are "natural" and which are industrial (asbestos is an example of a carcinogen belonging to both categories), but what exposures are preventable or at least reducible.) Ames has thus become a leading scientific spokesman for the chemical industry's ongoing struggle against regulation. However, the wide range of scientific flaws and misrepresentations in Ames's latest position has been effectively rebutted (12).

WHAT TO DO ABOUT CANCER

The cancer epidemic poses the nation with a grave and growing crisis of enormous cost to health, life, and the economy. In my 1979 book, *The Politics of Cancer,* I concluded with the following recommendations designed to reduce the toll of preventable cancer:

- Cancer must be regarded as an essentially preventable disease;
- The hidden political and economic factors which have blocked and continue to block attempts to prevent cancer must be recognized;
- The ineffective past track record of government in cancer prevention must be recognized;
- The critical roles in cancer prevention that public interest groups and informed labor leadership have exercised must be recognized and their further efforts fully encouraged and supported;
- Congress must resolve the major inconsistencies in a wide range of laws on environmental and occupational carcinogens;
- Substantially higher federal priorities for the prevention of cancer must be developed;
- Policies of the various federal agencies with responsibilities in cancer prevention must be effectively integrated and coordinated;
- Top business management must recognize the essential similarities between their long-term interests and goals and those of society. Prevention of occupational cancer and cancer in the community at large is of primary importance to both;

- The American Cancer Society must be influenced to balance its preoccupation with treatment with activist programs designed to prevent cancer;
- The medical and scientific community must accept a higher degree of responsibility and involvement in the prevention of cancer by actions on both the professional and political levels;
- Medical schools and schools of public health must be persuaded to reorient their educational and training programs from the diagnosis and treatment of disease and cancer to prevention;
- Chemicals in consumer products and in the workplace must be clearly and simply identified and labeled;
- New approaches must be developed for obtaining and for retaining honest and scientifically reliable data on the carcinogenicity and toxicity of new chemicals, in addition to those untested or poorly tested chemicals already in commerce; such data must be made accessible to public scrutiny. Maximum legal penalties should be directed against all those responsible, directly and indirectly, for distortion or manipulation of toxicological and epidemiological data on the basis of which decisions on human safety and risk are based;
- Apart from actions on a political level, we all have limited personal options. To some extent, it may be possible to reduce our own chances of developing cancer by making informed changes in lifestyle, in our use of consumer products, and in our work;
- The major determinants of preventable cancer are political and economic, rather than scientific, and as such must be addressed in the open political arena. Cancer prevention must become a major election issue, on a par with inflation.

A decade later, these goals still stand as valid, but none has been achieved, while cancer rates have steadily risen. To prevent similar conclusions a decade from now, the cancer prevention rhetoric must be translated into reality.

To compete with the well-financed propaganda of industry, tacitly supported by the cancer establishment and lifestyle academics, an educational offensive must be mounted to inform the public and develop grassroots pressures for a cancer prevention campaign. The cutting edge for such a campaign can be provided by the major public interest and citizen activist organizations, including the Natural Resources Defense Council, Sierra Club, Environmental Defense Fund, Health Research Group of Public Citizens, Environmental Action, Consumer Federation of America, National Campaign Against Misuse of Pesticides, Citizens Clearing House for Hazardous Wastes, the National Campaign Against Toxic Hazards, Greenpeace, the Rachel Carson Council, and the Center for Science in the Public Interest. Equally critical will be involvement of the Industrial Union Department of the AFL/CIO, and key unions such as the United Steel Workers of America; the United Rubber Workers; the Linoleum and Plastic Workers of America; the International Association of Machinists, Oil, Chemical, and Atomic Workers; the

Amalgamated Clothing and Textile Workers; and the United Auto Workers. (Liberal organizations and progressive labor groups, through effective research, writing, direct mail, and public advertising, are now challenging the ability of business to formulate the national agenda and shape the debate on basic social issues, such as worker rights, taxation, and environmental concerns, and on foreign policy. Such organizations include the Center for National Policy, Citizens for Tax Justice, the Democracy Project headed by Mark Green, the Economic Policy Institute headed by Jeff Faux, and the Council for Economic Priorities.) Many of these organizations have well-informed professional staffs, and some have played major roles in whatever limited legislative and regulatory successes have been achieved in the last two decades.

Active support at the local level is being provided by activist groups and labor organizations that have formed in response to community or regional concerns about such threats as hazardous waste dumps, contaminated drinking water, or lawn care chemicals; the motto of some such groups is, "Act locally, think globally." Further support can be provided by a small network of independent and government scientists, whose thinking ranks have recently been bolstered by the welcome involvement of professional organizations such as the American Public Health Association and the American Lung Association.

A potential source of cancer prevention funding is the multimillion dollar budget of the ACS raised by voluntary public contributions. An economic boycott of the ACS is now well overdue. Funding inappropriately used by the Society should be diverted to citizen activist groups, public interest organizations, and labor groups, which are more likely to achieve the goal of winning the war against cancer. Other potential funding sources include certification to participate by designation in United Way and Combined Federal Campaign.

Public interest, citizen activist, and labor organizations should develop coalitions with initially limited objectives, focused around specific areas of cancer prevention of local concern. These are now (as of 1990) being expanded into wider "rainbow" coalitions with more comprehensive goals. The 102nd Congress, revitalized by a Democratic renaissance, an increasing groundswell of consumer concerns and activism, and a supposedly sympathetic President George H. W. Bush, is now more likely to be receptive to such initiatives. This receptivity should be directed into increasing priorities for government concerns on cancer prevention, besides restoring the fragmented regulatory apparatus of government. It is also likely that key congresspersons could be galvanized into making cancer prevention one of their major political priorities, and that future presidential candidates could become interested in the potential grassroots appeal of a cancer prevention ticket.

Equally important are initiatives at the state level, the recent track record of state legislation offering encouraging precedents. These include the banning of chlordane and heptachlor for termite treatment by Massachusetts in 1985 and by New York in 1986, largely at the impetus of a citizen group, People Against

Chlordane; passage of a $1.5 billion hazardous waste clean-up bond by New York, the Environmental Quality Bond Act of 1986; and passage of Proposition 65, the Safe Drinking Water and Toxic Enforcement Act of 1986, by California.

Proposition 65, masterminded by the Sierra Club and the Environmental Defense Fund and supported by a coalition of California public interest citizen and labor groups, is a sophisticated referendum that imposes tough financial penalties on industries that knowingly discharge carcinogens into the drinking water supplies, and which makes mandatory the full public disclosure of such discharges by industry and state officials. A vocal opponent of Proposition 65 was Bruce Ames, who nonetheless failed to impress the California public with his lifestyle advocacy and his trivializing the significance of carcinogens in drinking water. Potential opposition by the petrochemical industry was anticipated and muted by the earmarking of some 50 percent of revenues from fines for the state superfund budget. However, Governor Deukmejian, responsive to special interest lobbying, attempted to neutralize the scope of the new legislation by restricting its application to epidemiologically confirmed carcinogens; however, this restriction has been reversed by the courts. Proposition 65 has excited national interest and is being used as a model for similar state initiatives.

Among early Congressional priorities should be enactment of comprehensive white-collar crime legislation. This would impose tough sanctions on individual executives, managers, and professionals of industries found guilty of willful "nondisclosure" of information on hazards to workers, local communities, and the nation. White-collar crime legislation should also be extended to U.S. and multinational corporations exporting to "lesser developed countries" carcinogenic products or processes that have been banned or regulated in the United States, especially in the absence of full disclosure of hazards directed to ultimate users and consumers. Attention should also be directed to developing comprehensive new "cradle to the grave" legislation as the basis for regulating toxic and carcinogenic chemicals. Such legislation should be designed to complement regulation by the judicious application of marketplace pressures, in the form of financial incentives and disincentives designed to wean industry away from unsafe practices, and to ensure that responsible industry is provided with a level playing field and not penalized or subjected to unfair competition by less responsible industry. At present, other than the prospect of toxic tort litigation, there are few incentives for industry to develop safer new products and processes. Legislation is needed to develop federal funding for research and development into such benign technologies and to ensure that they are closely coordinated with environmental, energy, and resource policies.

The growing receptivity of responsible industry to consumer concerns and pressures is illustrated by the Consumer Pesticide Project, spearheaded by the National Toxics Campaign and supported by a wide range of consumer and public interest groups, in conjunction with progressive agricultural interests. At a press conference in Washington, D.C., on September 11, 1989, this coalition announced the signing by major national supermarkets of an agreement to drastically reduce the residues of carcinogenic and hazardous pesticides on the produce they sell. The goals of this agreement are to identify progressive elements in the retail food industry that will support consumer and environmental groups to promote pesticide reform, to refute the dangerously lax federal standards, particularly for carcinogenic food residues, and to pressure EPA to develop more responsible policies. This initiative, which has met with serious opposition and even threats by intransigent industry interests, is likely to have far-reaching national repercussions, particularly as it represents the first serious attempt by responsible U.S. industry to police itself and to protect consumer health and welfare.

A critical legislative priority is an amendment to the National Cancer Act to give the highest possible priority to cancer prevention; to redress the historical imbalance existing in the NCI between cancer prevention and research on diagnosis and treatment; and to insulate the NCI from direct Presidential influence. Senior NCI staff should be restructured and boosted by professionals competent in environmental and occupational cancer and committed to cancer prevention. The National Cancer Advisory Board should be reconstituted with a balanced mix of independent prevention professionals, representatives of public interest and labor organizations, and concerned citizens, and should be subject to close Congressional scrutiny. Such scrutiny should ensure that the institutional resources are largely directed to cancer prevention, that grants and contracts fully reflect this priority, and that NCI staff play a key role in providing and supporting the scientific basis for legislative and regulatory cancer prevention efforts at the national and state levels.

Cancer is essentially a preventable disease. Given high national priority, this goal will be achieved.

POSTSCRIPT

With consumer concerns on carcinogenic contamination of food steadily mounting, as evidenced by Lou Harris polls and premium prices paid for organic foods, President George H. W. Bush on October 26, proposed weakening food safety regulation. His proposal authorizes EPA to allow dietary residues of carcinogenic pesticides at levels allegedly posing "negligible risk" of 1/100,000 excess lifetime cancers, equivalent to 35 annual cancers in the United States. These estimates not only are based on exposure and risk models reflecting questionable assumptions and "rubber numbers," but are restrictedly based on residues of a single carcinogenic pesticide on a single food commodity. Since most fruits and vegetables contain residues of a wide range of carcinogenic pesticides, residues of 50 pesticides on 50 foods would result in as many as 125,000 excess cancers, about 25 percent of current annual cancer deaths; EPA admits that it cannot estimate aggregate cancer risk in a total diet. Apart from these very high risks, the Bush proposals preempt stricter state initiatives, a major problem given that virtually all regulatory actions on food safety over the last two decades have been implemented by states and only reluctantly and belatedly followed by EPA.

Note — This chapter is based in part on keynote presentations at the National Safety and Health Conference of the International Association of Machinists, Washington, D.C., March 9, 1987; the Fifth National Pesticide Forum of the National Coalition Against the Misuse of Pesticides, Washington, D.C., March 21, 1987; the Conference on Global Development and Environmental Crisis, Friends of the Earth (Sahabat Alam), Penang, Malaysia, April 8, 1987; and on a position paper on the politics of cancer, published in the *Congressional Record,* E3449–E3454, September 9, 1987.

Chapter 2

DEBATE ON POLICIES OF THE NATIONAL CANCER INSTITUTE, AMERICAN CANCER SOCIETY, AND AMERICAN COLLEGE OF RADIOLOGY

On February 4, 1992, at a press conference sponsored by the public interest group Food and Water, Inc., on behalf of a group of 68 scientists, I presented a statement at the National Press Club in Washington, D.C., criticizing the cancer policies of the National Cancer Institute, the American Cancer Society, and some 20 cancer centers. A few days earlier, my commentary questioning the widespread use of mammography had been published in the *Los Angeles Times*. This chapter includes both of these statements (Parts A and B), the responses of the National Cancer Institute and American College of Radiology (Parts C and D), and my rebuttal to these responses (Part E).

On February 16, 1992, the *Washington Post* published an editorial criticizing my "denouncement" of the cancer establishment. I include here both this editorial and, again, my rebuttal (Parts F and G).

A. LOSING THE "WAR AGAINST CANCER": A NEED FOR PUBLIC POLICY REFORMS

Cancer now strikes one in three and kills one in four Americans, with over 500,000 deaths last year (1991). Over the last decade, some 5 million Americans died of cancer and there is growing evidence that a substantial proportion of these deaths was avoidable.

Part A published in *International Journal of Health Services,* Volume 22, Number 3, 1992.

We express grave concerns over the failure of the "war against cancer" since its inauguration by President Nixon and Congress on December 23, 1971. This failure is evidenced by the escalating incidence of cancer to epidemic proportions over recent decades. Paralleling and further compounding this failure is the absence of any significant improvement in the treatment and cure of the majority of all cancers. Notable exceptions are the successes with some relatively rare cancers, particularly those in children.

A recent report by the American Hospital Association predicts that cancer will become the leading cause of death by the year 2000 and the "dominant specialty" of American medicine. The costs in terms of suffering and death and the inflationary impact of cancer, now estimated at $110 billion annually (nearly 2 percent of the GNP), are massive. These costs are major factors in the current health care crisis, with per-case Medicare payments exceeding those of any other disease.

We express further concerns that the generously funded cancer establishment, the National Cancer Institute (NCI), the American Cancer Society (ACS), and some 20 comprehensive cancer centers, have misled and confused the public and Congress by repeated claims that we are winning the war against cancer. In fact, the cancer establishment has continually minimized the evidence for increasing cancer rates, which it has largely attributed to smoking and dietary fat, while discontinuing or ignoring the causal role of avoidable exposures to industrial carcinogens in the air, food, water, and the workplace.

Furthermore, the cancer establishment and major pharmaceutical companies have repeatedly made extravagant and unfounded claims for dramatic advances in the treatment and "cure" of cancer. Such claims are generally based on an initial reduction in tumor size ("tumor response") rather than on prolongation of survival, let alone on the quality of life, which is often devastated by highly toxic treatments.

We propose the following reforms, not as a specific blueprint, but as general guidelines for redefining the mission and priorities of the NCI:

1. The NCI must give cancer cause and prevention at least equal emphasis, in terms of budgetary and personnel resources, as its other programs, including diagnosis, treatment, and basic research; NCI's current annual budget is $1.8 billion. This major shift in direction should be initiated immediately and completed within the next few years. This shift will also require careful monitoring and oversight to prevent misleading retention of old unrelated programs under new guises of cancer cause and prevention.

2. A high priority for the cancer prevention program should be a large-scale and ongoing national campaign to inform and educate the media and the public, besides Congress, the Administration, and the industry, that much cancer is avoidable and due to past exposures to chemical and physical carcinogens in air, water, food, and the workplace, as well as to lifestyle factors, particularly smoking. It should, however, be noted that a wide range of occupational

exposures and urban air pollution have been incriminated as causes of lung cancer, besides smoking. Accordingly, the educational campaign should stress the critical importance of identifying and preventing the carcinogenic exposures and reducing them to the very lowest levels attainable within the earliest practically possible time.

3. The NCI should develop systematic programs for the qualitative and quantitative characterization of carcinogens in air, water, food, and the workplace, with particular emphasis on those that are avoidable. Such information should be made available to the general public, and particularly to subpopulations at high risk, by an explicit and ongoing "right to know" educational campaign, such as the specific labeling of food and consumer products with the identity and levels of all carcinogenic contaminants. While taking a lead in this program, the NCI should work cooperatively with federal and state regulatory health agencies and authorities, industry, public health and other professional societies, labor, and community-based citizen groups.

4. The NCI should cooperate with the National Institute of Environmental Health Sciences (NIEHS), and other NIH institutes, in investigating and publicizing other chronic toxic effects induced by carcinogens, including reproductive, neurological, hematological, and immunological diseases, besides cancer.

5. The NCI should cooperate with the National Institute for Occupational Safety and Health and other agencies to develop large-scale programs for monitoring, surveillance, and warning of occupational, ethnic, and other subpopulation groups at high risk of cancer due to known past exposures to chemical or physical carcinogens.

6. In close cooperation with key regulatory agencies and industry, the NCI should initiate large-scale research programs to develop noncarcinogenic products and processes as alternatives to those currently based on chemical and physical carcinogens. This program should also include research on the development of economic incentives for the reduction or phase-out of the use of industrial carcinogens, coupled with economic disincentives for their continued use, especially when appropriate noncarcinogenic alternatives are available.

7. The NCI should provide scientific expertise to Congress, federal and state regulatory and health agencies and authorities, and industry on the fundamental scientific principles of carcinogenesis including: the validity of extrapolation to humans of data from valid animal carcinogenicity tests; the invalidity of using insensitive or otherwise questionable epidemiological data to negate the significance of valid animal carcinogenicity tests; and the scientific invalidity of efforts to set safe levels or thresholds for exposure to chemical and physical carcinogens. The NCI should stress that the key to cancer prevention is reducing or avoiding exposure to carcinogens, rather than accepting and attempting to "manage" such risk. Current administration policies are, however, based on questionable mathematical procedures of quantitative risk

assessment applied to exposures to individual carcinogens, while concomitant exposures to other carcinogens in air, water, food, and the workplace are ignored or discounted.

8. The NCI should provide Congress and regulatory agencies with scientific expertise necessary to the development of legislation and regulation of carcinogens. Illustrative of such need is the Administration's revocation in 1988 of the 1958 Delaney amendment to the Federal Food, Drug and Cosmetic Act, banning the deliberate addition to foods of any level of carcinogen. This critical law was revoked in spite of the overwhelming endorsement of its scientific validity by a succession of expert committees over the past three decades. Neither the NCI, nor others in the cancer establishment, provided any scientific evidence challenging the validity of this revocation, including its likely impact on future cancer rates.

9. The limited programs on routine carcinogenicity testing, now under the authority of the National Toxicology Program (NTP), should be expanded and expedited with the more active and direct involvement of the NCI. (On a cautionary note, it should be emphasized that this program, which is clearly the direct responsibility of the NCI, was transferred to the NTP in 1978 because of mismanagement and lack of interest of the NCI.) Underutilized federal resources, particularly national laboratories, should be involved in carcinogenicity testing programs. The cost of carcinogenicity testing of profitable, and potentially profitable, chemicals should be borne by the industries concerned, and not by the NTP and the NCI and ultimately the taxpayer.

10. The NCI should undertake large-scale intramural and extramural research programs to characterize known carcinogenic exposures, both industrial and lifestyle, in terms of their estimated impact on cancer, and the practical feasibility of their avoidability or elimination within defined early periods.

11. The NCI should substantially expand its intramural and extramural programs on epidemiology research and develop large-scale programs on sensitive human monitoring techniques, including genetic and quantitative analysis of body burdens of carcinogens, and focus them specifically on cancer cause and prevention. The NCI should also take a key role in the design, conduct, and interpretation of epidemiological investigations of cancer by federal and state regulatory and health agencies and authorities.

12. The NCI should develop large-scale training programs for young scientists in all areas relating to cancer cause and prevention.

13. Continued funding by the NCI of its comprehensive cancer centers should be made contingent on their developing strong community out-reach programs in cancer cause and prevention, as opposed to their present and almost exclusive preoccupation with diagnosis and treatment. Centers should also establish tumor registries focused on identifying environmental and occupational carcinogens, and on the surveillance of occupational and other populations at high risk of cancer.

14. With the Congressional oversight and with advice from the NIH Office of Scientific Integrity, the NCI should take early action to disclose information on any interlocking financial interests between its Panel, Advisory Board, advisory committees and others in the cancer establishment, and major pharmaceutical companies involved in cancer drugs and therapy, and other industries. The NCI should also take the necessary precautions to prevent any such future conflicts.

15. The NCI should be enjoined from making or endorsing claims for new "cancer cures" unless these are clearly validated by data on reduced mortality rates and unless they conform to standard FDA regulations on claims for therapeutic efficacy.

16. The NCI should be removed from direct Presidential authority, and reintegrated within NIH, and thus made directly responsive to the scientific community at large and the advice and consent of Congress. Currently, the President appoints the Director of the NCI, who reports directly to the President, the twenty-three member executive National Cancer Advisory Board (NCAB), and three member National Cancer Advisory Panel (NCAP), which controls the policies and priorities of the NCI. The NCAP should be replaced by an executive committee recruited from advisory committees conforming to standard requirements of the Federal Advisory Committee Act for openness and balanced representation. Half of all appointees to NCI advisory committees should be recruited from scientists with credentials and record of active involvement in cancer cause and prevention. Appointments should also be granted to representatives of citizens', ethnic, and women's groups concerned with cancer prevention.

There is no conceivable likelihood that such reforms will be implemented without legislative action. The National Cancer Act should be amended explicitly to reorient the mission and priorities of the NCI to cancer cause and prevention. Compliance of the NCI should then be assured by detailed and ongoing Congressional oversight and, most critically, by House and Senate Appropriation committees. However, only strong support by the independent scientific and public health communities, together with concerned grassroots citizen groups, will convince Congress and Presidential candidates of the critical and immediate need for such drastic action.

Note — This statement was endorsed by 68 public health and other professionals (see Appendix, pp. 299–301).

B. MAMMOGRAPHY RADIATES DOUBTS

It has been widely (and with reason) charged that the makers and marketers of silicone breast implants, and self-interested plastic surgeons, made women their guinea pigs. But what of that other, and greater, scourge of women, breast cancer? There is reason to believe that women are equally ill-served by the cancer establishment, especially in its unrelenting promotion of mammography.

Breast cancer now strikes one in nine women, a dramatic increase from the one in 20 measured in 1950. This year (1992), 180,000 new cases and 46,000 deaths are expected. Hearings scheduled for February 5 in Washington by the Breast Cancer Coalition, an advocacy group loosely modeled on AIDS activists, could not seem more timely.

The coalition wants more federal funding for the National Cancer Institute (NCI) to increase its research into the causes and treatment of breast cancer, and to improve delivery of breast health care—including diagnostic screening. In pursuing these goals, the Coalition has been co-opted into supporting the policies of the cancer establishment—the NCI and the American Cancer Society—which is fixated on basic research, diagnosis, and treatment. Cancer prevention receives only an estimated 5 percent of the annual $1.8 billion NCI budget.

Breast cancer is not the only cancer on the rise. While its incidence has increased 57 percent since 1950, overall cancer has increased 44 percent, now striking one in three people and killing one in four. Male colon cancer is up 60 percent; testis, prostate, and kidney cancer up 100 percent; and other cancers, such as malignant melanoma and multiple myeloma, more than 100 percent. The cancer establishment trivializes evidence linking these increasing rates with avoidable exposure to cancer-causing industrial chemicals and radiation that permeate our environment—food, water, air, and workplace.

The cancer establishment maintains, on tenuous evidence, that a fatty diet itself is a major cause of breast cancer, while ignoring contaminants in fat. Carcinogenic pesticides, such as the highly persistent chlordane and dieldrin, which concentrate in animal fats, are known to cause breast cancer in rodents. Elevated levels of DDT and PCBs are found in human breast cancers. An Israeli study found that the breast cancer deaths in younger women recently dropped by 30 percent, despite a substantial increase in consumption of animal fat. This drop followed, and seems linked to, regulations that reduced previously high levels of DDT and related pesticides in dairy products. These pesticides act by

Part B was originally published in the *Los Angeles Times,* January 28, 1992, p. B7; republished in *International Journal of Health Services,* Volume 22, Number 3, 1992.

mimicking the action of estrogens or by increasing estrogen production in the body, which in turn increases the risk of breast cancer. A related concern is lifelong exposure of all women to estrogenic contaminants in animal fat, because of their unregulated use as growth-promoting additives in cattle feed.

In 1977, the NCI's director of endocrinology, Dr. Roy Hertz, warned, without effect, of breast cancer risks from these contaminants.

More ominous is the enthusiastic endorsement by the cancer establishment of massive nationwide expansion of X-ray mammography, including routine annual screening. While there is a general consensus that mammography improves early cancer detection and survival in postmenopausal women, no such benefit is demonstrable for younger women.

Furthermore, there is clear evidence that the breast, particularly in premenopausal women, is highly sensitive to radiation, with estimates of increased risk of breast cancer of up to 1 percent for every rad (radiation absorbed dose) unit of X-ray exposure. This projects up to a 20 percent increased cancer risk for a woman who, in the 1970s, received 10 annual mammograms of an average 2 rads each. In spite of this, up to 40 percent of women over 40 have had mammograms since the mid-1960s, some annually and some with exposures of 5 to 10 rads in a single screening from older, high-dose equipment.

Significant studies on radiation risks to the breast have been well known since the late 1960s, including evidence that mammography, especially in younger women, was likely to cause more cancers than could be detected. A confidential memo by Dr. Nathaniel Berlin, a senior NCI physician in charge of large-scale mammography screening in 1973, may explain why women were not warned of this risk: "Both the [American Cancer Society] and NCI will gain a great deal of favorable publicity [from screening, and] . . . this will assist in obtaining more research funds for basic and clinical research which is sorely needed."

Thus, once again, suspect technology was applied to women on a large scale, in spite of clear warning signals and with sufficient knowledge of the likely consequences. (On a smaller scale, but even more ethically appalling, was the use until last April of industrial polyurethane foam to coat silicone breast inserts, despite clear evidence that its manufacturing contaminants and breakdown products were carcinogenic. As with mammography, no serious studies have been launched to find out what happened to women in whom the foam was implanted, or indeed to women carrying any type of silicone implant.)

The risks of mammography, especially for premenopausal women, persist with the lower radiation doses (about one-half rad per screening) found in modern facilities with dedicated equipment and licensed operators. A large Canadian study conducted from 1980 to 1988 found a 52 percent increase in early breast cancer deaths in women aged 40 to 50 who had 10 annual mammograms, compared with women given just physical examinations. More recent concern comes from evidence that 1 percent of women carry a gene that increases their breast cancer risk from radiation fourfold.

The Coalition should insist that the NCI and American Cancer Society initiate an immediate, large-scale, well-publicized study to further investigate the role of past mammography in increasing breast cancer rates, and to investigate future cancer risk from mammography as currently conducted under widely varying conditions. Women should also be informed of their X-ray exposure and individual and cumulative risks each time they undergo mammography. The Coalition should demand an immediate ban on obsolete high-dose X-ray equipment, and the abandonment of routine mammograms on premenopausal women.

The Coalition should also encourage a crash program to develop and make available safe alternatives to mammography, apart from physical examination. Two that show the most promise are magnetic resonance imaging and transillumination with infrared light. The expansion of mammography should be put on hold, especially in view of the 1991 conclusion of the General Accounting Office that "there are more than enough machines to meet the screening needs of American women."

The Breast Cancer Coalition represents a welcome trend toward active grassroots involvement in public health. However, its current goals are too narrowly defined within the context of existing perspectives and institutional policies. The Coalition needs broader and more radical strategies if it is to reverse the modern epidemic of breast cancer.

C. NATIONAL CANCER INSTITUTE REAFFIRMS COMMITMENT TO PREVENTION

National Cancer Institute

Allegations that the nation is "losing the war on cancer" because of a lack of prevention research were characterized by spokesmen for the National Cancer Institute (NCI) today as old charges, lacking any basis in fact.

NCI officials also disputed the claim by Dr. Samuel Epstein, professor of Occupational and Environmental Medicine at the University of Illinois, and 60 other scientists, that little or no progress has been made in treating cancer, and backed the continuing use of mammography as the best available, early detection tool for breast cancer.

Part C was an NCI press release, dated February 4, 1992; published in *International Journal of Health Services*, Volume 22, Number 3, 1992.

"The NCI's efforts in research in cancer biology, cancer causation, cancer treatment, and cancer prevention and control are well balanced and peer reviewed," said Dr. Richard Adamson, director of the Division of Cancer Etiology, in a prepared statement. Moreover, he added, the Institute is "able to shift research into appropriate programs as science dictates" in order to reduce suffering and death from cancer. He further claimed that "In the coming year, the NCI will spend approximately one-third of its total budget on causation and prevention-related research, including the study of environmental agents in the workplace that may contribute to cancer risk. Over the past two years, NCI has also instituted new guidelines for intensified outreach and prevention programs at the nation's 57 NCI-designated cancer centers. These NCI-supported centers are engaged in all aspects of cancer research from basic research to clinical applications as well as prevention and control."

As part of its prevention efforts, NCI supports numerous studies of the total environment contributing to cancer causation, Adamson said, including studies on viruses, natural and synthetic chemicals, dietary and nutritional factors, fibers, ultraviolet radiation, ionizing radiation, and other factors.

"Unquestionably, however, lifestyle factors contribute to the toll of human cancer," Adamson stressed, "and the single most identifiable causes of cancer— and other diseases—in the United States is tobacco smoking." Numerous independent scientific studies now link tobacco use, particularly cigarette smoking, to lung cancer, as well as cancers of the larynx, oral cavity, pharynx, and esophagus. Tobacco use also has been implicated as a contributing factor in bladder, kidney, and pancreatic cancers.

In a separate statement, Dr. Edward Sondik, deputy director of NCI's Division of Cancer Prevention and Control, criticized Epstein's release of mortality data from the Canadian National Breast Cancer Screening Study, which has not yet been completely analyzed. The data purportedly show that women aged 40 to 49 who have annual mammograms have a 52 percent increase in breast cancer mortality over women who have physical exams only. "The dissemination of this [information] without any scientific basis is unethical," he said.

Although NCI does not view mammography as the ultimate technology for detecting early breast cancer, Sondik said, mammography, coupled with physical exam, has the potential to reduce mortality from breast cancer by at least 30 percent in women over 50. In addition, while studies in younger women have not been conclusive, he said, the evidence to date is that breast cancer screening is prudent for women between the ages of 40 and 49.

D. AMERICAN COLLEGE OF RADIOLOGY REFUTES EPSTEIN'S COMMENTS ON MAMMOGRAPHY

American College of Radiology

Dr. Samuel Epstein's comments on mammography which have been published in several major newspapers nationwide are a mixture of partial truths and outdated data, according to the American College of Radiology (ACR). The ACR, which is a national medical specialty association, added that Dr. Epstein's comments could unfortunately discourage women from having regular screening mammograms—the only tests proven to detect breast cancer at an early enough stage to reduce mortality.

The increase in the number of women who develop breast cancer is indeed alarming. Contrary to Dr. Epstein's suggestion that the increased incidence is a recent phenomenon, in fact the increase has been progressive over the past 50 years—long before the routine use of mammography. Extensive research is being done to determine the reasons for the increase. The most recent jump in incidence is primarily an artifact due to breast cancers being detected years earlier through the use of mammography. This produces an apparent increase in incidence. Another reason is that women are living longer and the older a woman, the greater the chance she has of developing the disease.

Dr. Epstein comments that there is no clear evidence that mammography benefits premenopausal women. There are, in fact, studies which show the benefit of screening women under 50. These include the Breast Cancer Detection Demonstration Project conducted by the National Cancer Institute and the American Cancer Society, and the Health Insurance Plan of New York study.

Dr. Epstein also raises the question of radiation risk. Studies of women exposed to high doses of radiation such as those women who survived the atomic bomb blasts in Japan show, along with other studies, that women 35 and older are at no demonstrable risk from radiation exposure to the breast, a fact which particularly applies to the very low doses which are used in modern mammography.

The Canadian study Dr. Epstein mentions is, unfortunately, seriously flawed because mammographic techniques and equipment varied throughout the trial. Quality control measures were not undertaken until late in the study. The

Part D was an ACR press release, dated February 4, 1992; published in *International Journal of Health Services,* Volume 22, Number 3, 1992.

researchers themselves noted that the quality of mammography was "poor" to "unacceptable" in the early years of the trial. Moreover, there is evidence that Canadian women with palpable cancers (usually later stage cancers) were encouraged to enroll in the screening trial. Many of these women died from their disease, leading Dr. Epstein to come to the erroneous conclusion that the increase in cancers and deaths was due to mammography screening.

The American College of Radiology has a peer review program which evaluates staff, equipment, and quality control procedures. Mammography facilities which meet the program's stringent requirements are accredited. This program also reviews exposure dose to ensure that mammography is performed at the lowest and safest dose possible while maintaining a high-quality test.

Researchers are constantly looking for other ways of detecting early breast cancer. Dr. Epstein mentions magnetic resonance imaging (MRI) and light-scanning. MRI is expensive and requires that contrast material be injected into the patient. It is one to two years away from the development of a prototype to exclusively evaluate the breast. Lightscanning has been shown to have absolutely no efficacy for detecting early breast cancers.

Investigations are underway to determine possible methods for preventing breast cancer. Numerous researchers are trying to determine its elusive causes. Until its causes are discovered or preventative measures devised, mammography screening provides the safest and best opportunity for detecting breast cancer at a stage at which curative treatment is possible.

Screening by mammography beginning at age 40 is widely accepted. It is recommended by the following organizations:

American Academy of Family Physicians
American Association of Women Radiologists
American Cancer Society
American College of Radiology
American Medical Association
American Osteopathic College of Radiology
American Society of Internal Medicine
American Society of Clinical Oncology
American Society for Therapeutic Radiology and Oncology
College of American Pathologists
National Cancer Institute
National Medical Association

E. CANCER ESTABLISHMENT CONTINUES TO MISLEAD PUBLIC: EPSTEIN REBUTS NATIONAL CANCER INSTITUTE AND AMERICAN COLLEGE OF RADIOLOGY RESPONSES

At a news conference on Tuesday, February 4, 1992, a group of 60-plus prominent scientists and physicians released a statement condemning the National
Cancer Institute (NCI) for ignoring or trivializing evidence of how carcinogens
in air, food, water, and workplaces are major factors in the cancer epidemic in
America. In addition, Dr. Samuel Epstein, professor at the University of Illinois
School of Public Health, presented data indicating significant cancer risks in
mammograms and their lack of effectiveness for premenopausal women.

The NCI and the American College of Radiology (ACR) responded to these
charges in separate statements. The following are Dr. Epstein's rebuttals, which
show both groups selectively use scientific data to mislead the public about
both the hazards of industrial carcinogens in our environment and of mammograms for younger women:

ACR STATEMENT REFLECTS IGNORANCE, SELF-INTEREST

Contrary to the ACR, the increase in breast cancer incidence since the 1970s has
been steeper than in previous decades. Furthermore, these increases exclude
effects of aging as they have been age-adjusted.

Also contrary to the ACR, a wide range of studies have failed to demonstrate
any benefit from routine mammography in premenopausal women (as opposed to
benefits in older women). These include the 1963 Health Insurance Plan of New
York, and the 1975 Dutch and 1977 Swedish studies (1, 2). The 1973–1981
Breast Cancer Detection Demonstration Project studies, on which the ACR
ineptly relies for alleged evidence of benefit, were "not designed for research
purposes, were not carried out in accordance with rigorous research standards,
and lack even an appropriate control group" (2, 3).

The high cancer risk from mammography was well known before the National
Cancer Institute and American Cancer Society, with active involvement of the
ACR, initiated their large-scale routine screening of premenopausal women in
the 1970s. The Biological Effects of Ionizing Radiation committee of the National

Part E was Epstein's press release, dated February 7, 1992; published in *International Journal of
Health Services,* Volume 22, Number 3, 1992.

Academy of Sciences, the world's leading authority on radiation, warned in 1972 of a "relative risk of about 0.8 percent increase in the spontaneous rate [of breast cancer] per rad" exposure. Thus, routine annual mammography over 10 years of premenopausal women with two rads per exposure (although much higher exposures were then commonplace) would lead to approximately a 20 percent increased cancer risk. Women were never warned of these risks while being falsely assured of benefits. Risks of routine mammography in premenopausal women still persist today, though at lower levels, at the best centers using designated equipment with lower exposures. However, women are still not warned of these risks or of the absence of any benefits.

The ACR has misrepresented the recent Canadian study which confirms mammography risks. This study reported a 52 percent increase in breast cancer mortality in young women given annual mammograms as opposed to unscreened controls. A 1991 editorial in *The Lancet* concluded that these findings could not be discounted by the criticisms on randomization and quality of mammography which ACR has resurrected. The editorial further pointed out that the Canadian findings are supported by similar results in several previous studies. *The Lancet* finally concluded that "there is no evidence to support introduction of service mammography for women under 50." It should be noted that this warning is endorsed by the American College of Physicians and the Canadian Breast Cancer Task Force.

Finally, ACR seems unaware of evidence that transillumination with infrared light scanning is a safe and highly promising alternative to mammography.

Considerations of malpractice aside, the recalcitrance of the ACR reinforces a growing grassroots conviction that cancer is too important to be left to self-interested professionals.

NCI RELEASE REAFFIRMS ITS DENIAL THAT WE'RE LOSING THE WAR ON CANCER

As detailed in a statement by 60 plus distinguished national scientists at a Washington, D.C., news conference on February 4, 1992, cancer rates are escalating; our ability to treat and cure cancer, apart from childhood and other rare cancers, has not improved for decades; and our environment, air, water, food, and workplace have become permeated with industrial carcinogens.

Meanwhile, the NCI and the American Cancer Society (ACS) have trivialized the evidence for increasing cancer rates and their relation to avoidable exposure to industrial carcinogens. Instead, together with the chemical industry, they focus on dietary fat itself (ignoring increasing contaminants, including pesticides), and smoking (ignoring increasing lung cancer rates in nonsmokers, and the important role of occupational exposures and urban air pollution) as the predominant causes of the cancer epidemic.

Furthermore, the NCI and ACS, with their fixations on diagnosis, treatment, and basic research, are indifferent to cancer cause and prevention, which accounts for only five percent of the NCI $2 billion budget (see budget line item of $90 million for Cancer Prevention and Control), and not 33 percent as the NCI alleges. The position of the NCI and ACS on prevention is further illustrated by their recent silence while the administration rolls back regulations designed to reduce avoidable exposure to industrial carcinogens, including the 1958 Delaney law banning the deliberate addition of any level of carcinogens to food; overwhelming evidence supports the scientific validity of this law.

The NCI and ACS position on prevention is compounded by their exaggerated claims on ability to treat and cure cancer. As detailed by authorities including the General Accounting Office (4), these claims reflect gross statistical manipulation, including the use of "relative survival" rather than mortality rates.

The statement by the 60 plus scientists calls for urgent reforms in federal cancer policies. These reforms must ensure that the NCI gives greater emphasis to cancer prevention, rather than to chasing the elusive but ever-promised cure for cancer, coupled with continuing oversight to ensure compliance. These reforms demand drastic legislative action and strong grassroots support.

F. THE CANCER WAR AND ITS CRITICS

The Washington Post

One of the continuing intramural conflicts in the government's "war on cancer" made an appearance last week when Samuel Epstein, a professor of environmental medicine from the University of Illinois, held a press conference to denounce the priorities of what he calls the "cancer establishment." Dr. Epstein, a longtime gadfly, accuses the major research groups and their funders of being "fixated on diagnosis and treatment" to the disadvantage of "preventive" research on environmental causes, like toxins. It's an argument based partly on a false distinction—obviously, "basic" research figuring out the mechanism by which cancer is triggered in an individual would mean great strides for both cure and prevention. The argument is fueled by the frustration of people watching the rates of many major cancers actually going up. Breast cancer, the main example

Part F was an editorial published in the *Washington Post,* dated February 16, 1992; republished in *International Journal of Health Services,* Volume 22, Number 4, 1992.

and the most mysterious, has risen 57 percent since 1950, and lung, pancreas, and some kidney cancers are also higher. Nobody knows just why.

Scientists from both the National Cancer Institute, which the federal government funds, and the private American Cancer Society sharply dispute Dr. Epstein's charges. Many call him a menace. They say that his demands for "preventive" research go at the matter backward—you can't work on "prevention" for a disease whose causes you don't know—and that he assumes a relationship with environmental toxins that they have in fact been unable to find. An added complicating factor is that tracing something like food contaminants in body fat is a lot more difficult than looking at airborne factors, and a fistful of studies can be waved for almost every conceivable link. These same cancer groups have been a major force in raising public awareness of the environmental factors that *have* been shown to be cancer-related—cigarettes, asbestos, and radon.

The "establishment" Dr. Epstein attacks is, of course, responsible for myriad advances over two decades, not only in cancer research but in spinoff discoveries in genetics, immunology, and the mechanisms of other diseases—including much current AIDS research. At least some of the apparent rise in incidence (how much is in dispute) is due to the improved detection methods they have developed. Dr. Epstein goes further than mere scientific criticism in some cases, alleging collusion with drug companies and hospital boards. On the level of purely scientific disagreement, it's not such a bad thing for scientific bureaucracies to field criticism, whether it likes the source or not. But given these organizations' proven record of advances, it seems ridiculous to accuse them of conspiracy or bad faith.

G. EPSTEIN REBUTS THE
WASHINGTON POST EDITORIAL

"The Cancer War and Its Critics" is a welcome expression of the overdue debate on federal cancer policies. However, the editorial misattributes criticisms of the cancer establishment, the National Cancer Institute (NCI), and American Cancer Society (ACS) exclusively to me—as well as seriously misrepresenting such criticisms.

These criticisms were based on a statement released on Feb. 4 by 65 prominent authorities in cancer research, public health, and preventive medicine, including former senior government scientists.

Part G, Epstein's response, was published in the *Washington Post*, March 10, 1992; republished in *International Journal of Health Services*, Volume 22, Number 4, 1992.

We expressed grave concerns about the failure of the war against cancer, evidenced over the past four decades by escalating cancer rates (now striking one in three and killing one in four), paralleled by absence of significant improvement in treatment except for relatively uncommon cancers. We expressed further concern that the lavishly funded establishment has "misled and confused the public and Congress by repeated claims that we are winning the war against cancer."

As recently as 1986, the NCI promised that annual cancer mortality rates would be halved by the year 2000. The establishment now belatedly admits that cancer rates are increasing sharply. However, with the enthusiastic support of the chemical industry, these are ascribed exclusively to smoking, dietary fat itself (ignoring the tenuous evidence relating this to colon, breast, and other cancers), and "mysterious" causes. Meanwhile, it discounts substantial evidence incriminating a wide range of chemical and radioactive carcinogens permeating the environment, air, water, food, and the workplace. Examples include occupational carcinogens causing lung cancer in nonsmoking workers, parental exposure to occupational carcinogens (implicated in more than 20 studies as causes of childhood cancer, which increased by 28 percent between 1950 and 1987), and carcinogenic pesticides in food, which are estimated to cause tens of thousands of excess cancers annually.

Non-mysterious causes of breast cancer, which the establishment ignores let alone investigates, include carcinogenic contaminants in dietary fat, particularly pesticides, PCBs, and estrogens (with extensive and unregulated use as growth-promoting animal feed additives).

Mammography, claimed as a diagnostic triumph, is an important and ominous cause. The high sensitivity of the breast, especially in younger women, to radiation-induced cancer was known by 1970. Nevertheless, the establishment then screened some 300,000 women with X-ray dosages so high as to increase breast cancer risk by up to 20 percent in women aged 40 to 50 who were mammogrammed annually. Women were given no warning whatever; how many subsequently developed breast cancer remains uninvestigated.

Mammography risks persist with lower X-ray doses at modern centers. This is evidenced by excess breast cancer mortality in younger women noted in a Canadian study, besides four other published studies, reported in a June 1991 editorial of *The Lancet*. Strangely, the NCI and ACS castigate my reference to this public information as "unethical and invalid." Moreover, there is no known benefit from screening of young, as opposed to post-menopausal, women— a warning endorsed by the American College of Physicians and Canadian Breast Cancer Task Force. Additionally, the establishment ignores safe and effective alternatives to mammography, particularly transillumination with infrared scanning.

While explaining away soaring cancer rates, the establishment, abetted by cheerleading science journalists, grossly exaggerates treatment success. Periodic announcements of dramatic advances are based on initial reduction in tumor size rather than on prolonged survival. For most cancers, survival has not changed for decades. Contrary claims are based on rubber numbers.

Furthermore, the establishment is financially interlocked with giant pharmaceutical companies (grossing $1 billion annually in cancer drug sales), with inherent conflicts of interest.

The establishment devotes minimal resources to research and education on cancer cause and prevention—only 5 percent of the $1.9 billion NCI budget. Furthermore, the establishment provides no scientific support for legislation and regulation to reduce avoidable exposures to industrial carcinogens.

As emphasized by critics of the cancer establishment, drastic reforms are needed.

DANGERS AND UNRELIABILITY OF MAMMOGRAPHY: BREAST EXAMINATION IS A SAFE, EFFECTIVE, AND PRACTICAL ALTERNATIVE

Contrary to popular belief and assurances by the U.S. media and the cancer establishment—the National Cancer Institute (NCI) and American Cancer Society (ACS)—mammography is not a technique for early diagnosis. In fact, a breast cancer has usually been present for about eight years before it can finally be detected. Furthermore, screening should be recognized as damage control, rather than misleadingly as "secondary prevention."

DANGERS OF SCREENING MAMMOGRAPHY

Mammography poses a wide range of risks of which women worldwide still remain uninformed.

Radiation Risks

Radiation from routine mammography poses significant cumulative risks of initiating and promoting breast cancer (1–3). Contrary to conventional assurances that radiation exposure from mammography is trivial—and similar to that from a chest X-ray or spending one week in Denver, about 1/1,000 of a rad (radiation-absorbed dose)—the routine practice of taking four films for each breast results in some 1,000-fold greater exposure, 1 rad, focused on each breast rather than the entire chest (2). Thus, premenopausal women undergoing annual screening over a ten-year period are exposed to a total of about 10 rads for each breast. As emphasized some three decades ago, the premenopausal breast is highly sensitive to radiation, each rad of exposure increasing breast cancer risk by

Coauthored with Rosalie Bertell and Barbara Seaman; published in *International Journal of Health Services,* Volume 31, Number 3, 2001.

1 percent, resulting in a cumulative 10 percent increased risk over ten years of premenopausal screening, usually from ages 40 to 50 (4); risks are even greater for "baseline" screening at younger ages, for which there is no evidence of any future relevance. Furthermore, breast cancer risks from mammography are up to fourfold higher for the 1 to 2 percent of women who are silent carriers of the A-T (ataxia-telangiectasia) gene and thus highly sensitive to the carcinogenic effects of radiation (5); by some estimates this accounts for up to 20 percent of all breast cancers annually in the United States (6).

Cancer Risks from Breast Compression

As early as 1928, physicians were warned to handle "cancerous breasts with care—for fear of accidentally disseminating cells" and spreading cancer (7). Nevertheless, mammography entails tight and often painful compression of the breast, particularly in premenopausal women. This may lead to distant and lethal spread of malignant cells by rupturing small blood vessels in or around small, as yet undetected breast cancers (8).

Delays in Diagnostic Mammography

As increasing numbers of premenopausal women are responding to the ACS's aggressively promoted screening, imaging centers are becoming flooded and overwhelmed. Resultingly, patients referred for diagnostic mammography are now experiencing potentially dangerous delays, up to several months, before they can be examined (9).

UNRELIABILITY OF MAMMOGRAPHY

Falsely Negative Mammograms

Missed cancers are particularly common in premenopausal women owing to the dense and highly glandular structure of their breasts and increased proliferation late in their menstrual cycle (10, 11). Missed cancers are also common in post-menopausal women on estrogen replacement therapy, as about 20 percent develop breast densities that make their mammograms as difficult to read as those of premenopausal women (12).

Interval Cancers

About one-third of all cancers—and more still of premenopausal cancers, which are aggressive, even to the extent of doubling in size in one month, and more likely to metastasize—are diagnosed in the interval between successive annual mammograms (2, 13). Premenopausal women, particularly, can thus be lulled into a false sense of security by a supposedly negative result on an annual mammogram and fail to seek medical advice.

Falsely Positive Mammograms

Mistakenly diagnosed cancers are particularly common in premenopausal women, and also in postmenopausal women on estrogen replacement therapy, resulting in needless anxiety, more mammograms, and unnecessary biopsies (14, 15). For women with multiple high-risk factors, including a strong family history, prolonged use of the contraceptive pill, early menarche, and nulliparity—just those groups that are most strongly urged to have annual mammograms—the cumulative risk of false positives increases to "as high as 100 percent" over a decade's screening (16).

Overdiagnosis

Overdiagnosis and subsequent overtreatment are among the major risks of mammography. The widespread and virtually unchallenged acceptance of screening has resulted in a dramatic increase in the diagnosis of ductal carcinoma-in-situ (DCIS), a pre-invasive cancer, with a current estimated incidence of about 40,000 annually. DCIS is usually recognized as micro-calcifications and generally treated by lumpectomy plus radiation or even mastectomy and chemotherapy (17). However, some 80 percent of all DCIS never become invasive even if left untreated (18). Furthermore, the breast cancer mortality from DCIS is the same— about 1 percent—both for women diagnosed and treated early and for those diagnosed later following the development of invasive cancer (17). That early detection of DCIS does not reduce mortality is further confirmed by the 13-year follow-up results of the Canadian National Breast Cancer Screening Study (19). Nevertheless, as recently stressed, "the public is much less informed about overdiagnosis than false positive results. In a recent nationwide survey of women, 99 percent of respondents were aware of the possibility of false positive results from mammography, but only 6 percent were aware of either DCIS by name or the fact that mammography could detect a form of 'cancer' that often doesn't progress" (20).

Quality Control

In 1992 Congress passed the National Mammography Standards Quality Assurance Act requiring the Food and Drug Administration (FDA) to ensure that screening centers review their results and performance: collect data on biopsy outcomes and match them with the original radiologist's interpretation of the films (21). However, the centers do not release these data because the Act does not require them to do so. It is essential that this information now be made fully public so that concerns about the reliability of mammography can be further evaluated. Activist breast cancer groups would most likely strongly support, if not help to initiate, such overdue action by the FDA.

FAILURE TO REDUCE BREAST CANCER MORTALITY

Despite the long-standing claims, the evidence that routine mammography screening allows early detection and treatment of breast cancer, thereby reducing mortality, is at best highly questionable. In fact, "the overwhelming majority of breast cancers are unaffected by early detection, either because they are aggressive or slow growing" (21). There is supportive evidence that the major variable predicting survival is "biological determinism—a combination of the virulence of the individual tumor plus the host's immune response," rather than just early detection (22).

Claims for the benefit of screening mammography in reducing breast cancer mortality are based on eight international controlled trials involving about 500,000 women (23). However, recent meta-analysis of these trials revealed that only two, based on 66,000 postmenopausal women, were adequately randomized to allow statistically valid conclusions (23). Based on these two trials, the authors concluded that "there is no reliable evidence that screening decreases breast cancer mortality—not even a tendency towards an effect." Accordingly, the authors concluded that there is no longer any justification for screening mammography; further evidence for this conclusion will be detailed at the May 6, 2001, annual meeting of the National Breast Cancer Coalition in Washington, D.C., and published in the July report of the Nordic Cochrane Centre.

Even assuming that high quality screening of a population of women between the ages of 50 and 69 would reduce breast cancer mortality by up to 25 percent, yielding a reduced relative risk of 0.75, the chances of any individual woman benefiting are remote (18). For women in this age group, about 4 percent are likely to develop breast cancer annually, about one in four of whom, or 1 percent overall, will die from this disease. Thus, the 0.75 relative risk applies to this 1 percent, so 99.75 percent of the women screened are unlikely to benefit.

THE UNITED STATES VERSUS OTHER NATIONS

No nation other than the United States routinely screens premenopausal women by mammography. In this context, it may be noted that the January 1997 National Institutes of Health Consensus Conference recommended against premenopausal screening (24), a decision that the NCI, but not the ACS, accepted (4). However, under pressure from Congress and the ACS, the NCI reversed its decision some three months later in favor of premenopausal screening.

The U.S. overkill extends to the standard practice of taking two or more mammograms per breast annually in postmenopausal women. This contrasts with the more restrained European practice of a single view every two to three years (4).

BREAST EXAMINATION IS A SAFE AND EFFECTIVE
ALTERNATIVE TO MAMMOGRAPHY

That most breast cancers are first recognized by women themselves was admitted in 1985 by the ACS, an aggressive advocate of routine mammography for all women over the age of 40: "We must keep in mind the fact that at least 90 percent of the women who develop breast carcinoma discover the tumors themselves" (25). Furthermore, as previously shown, "training increases reported breast self-examination [BSE] frequency, confidence, and the number of small tumors found" (26).

A pooled analysis of several 1993 studies showed that women who regularly performed BSE detected their cancers much earlier and with fewer positives nodes and smaller tumors than women failing to examine themselves (27); BSE would also enhance earlier detection of missed or interval cancers, especially in pre-menopausal women (28). There is a strong consensus that the effectiveness of BSE critically depends on careful training by skilled professionals, and that confidence in BSE is enhanced with annual clinical breast examinations (CBEs) by an experienced professional using structured individual training (29). The tactile sensitivity of BSE can be increased by the use of Mammacare techniques to enhance lump detection skills (30, 31), and by the use of FDA-approved and nonprescription thin and pliable lubricant-filled sensor pads (32, 33).

In a joint U.S. and Chinese large-scale trial based on 520 Chinese factories, women in half the factories were trained in and practiced BSE, while the other group of women served as controls (34). The five-year follow up results reported no reduction in breast cancer mortality in women in the BSE group. However, these findings are of little, if any, significance in view of the minimum of a 10- to 13-year period required before the efficacy of mammography is claimed to occur in premenopausal women (24), especially as some of the trial's participants were in their thirties (28).

The critical importance and reliability of CBE has been strikingly confirmed by the recent Canadian National Breast Cancer Screening Study (19). This reported the results of a unique individually randomized controlled trial on some 40,000 women, aged 50 to 59 on entry, followed by record linkage for 9 to 13 years, with active follow-up of cancer patients for an additional 3 years. Half the women performed monthly BSE, following instruction by trained nurses, had annual CBEs (taking approximately ten minutes) by trained nurses, and had annual mammograms, while the other half practiced BSE and had annual CBEs but no mammograms. It should be noted that the CBE performance by trained nurses had been shown to be as good as, if not better than, that of the study surgeons (35), a finding of particular interest in view of the growing perception among women that professional women are more sensitive than men to women's health issues (36). The results of this study provide clear evidence on the reliability of CBE, in association with BSE (19): "In women age 50–59 years, the addition of annual mammography screening to physical examination has no impact on breast cancer mortality." In other words, the mammographic detection of nonpalpable cancers failed to improve survival rates, as "the majority of the small cancers detected by mammography represent pseudo-disease or overdiagnosis" (37); confirmation of this explanation awaits a trial, a protocol of which is available, comparing mammography alone with physical examination alone. It should further be noted that the mammogram group had a three-fold increase in the number of false positives compared with the CBE and BSE group, resulting in unnecessary biopsies.

The effectiveness of CBE is further supported by the results of a new Japanese mass screening study (38). Breast cancer mortality was compared in municipalities with or without "high coverage" by CBE. The age-adjusted breast cancer mortality between 1986–1990 and 1991–1995 was reduced by over 40 percent in "high coverage" municipalities, in contrast to only 3 percent in controls.

In spite of such evidence, the ACS and radiologists persist in their dismissiveness of CBE and BSE particularly as "a substitute for screening practices that have a 'proven' benefit such as mammograms" (33). The NCI no longer prints a BSE guide in its breast cancer booklet, claiming that "no studies have clearly shown a benefit of using BSE"; similarly, the ACS no longer distributes information on BSE, such as shower-hanger cards.

There are immediate needs for a large-scale crash program for training nurses in how to perform annual CBE and how to teach BSE. This need is critical for underinsured and uninsured low-socioeconomic and ethnic women in the United States, and even more so for developing countries. Once well trained, women of all social and cultural classes could perform monthly BSE, at no cost or risk apart from false positives, which decrease with increasing practice, along with annual CBE screening. Clinics offering CBE and training in BSE could be established nationwide, and eventually worldwide, in a network of clinics, community hospitals, churches, synagogues, and mosques. These clinics could also act as a comprehensive source of reliable information on how to reduce the risks of breast cancer, about which women still remain largely uninformed by the cancer establishment (2). Besides lifestyle and reproductive risk factors, emphasis should be directed to the massive overprescription of carcinogenic hormonal drugs and the avoidable and involuntary exposures to petrochemical and radionuclear carcinogens in the totality of the environment (39–41).

COSTS OF SCREENING

The dangers and unreliability of mammography screening are compounded by its growing and inflationary costs; Medicare and insurance average costs (as of 2001) are $70 and $125, respectively. Inadequate Medicare reimbursement rates are now prompting fewer hospitals and clinics to offer mammograms, and deterring young doctors from becoming radiologists. Accordingly, Senators

Charles Schumer (D-NY) and Tom Harkin (D-IA) are introducing legislation to raise Medicare reimbursement to $100 (42).

If all U.S. premenopausal women, about 20 million according to the Census Bureau, submitted to annual mammograms, minimal annual costs would be $2.5 billion (4). These costs would be increased to $10 billion, about 5 percent of the $200 billion 2001 Medicare budget, if all postmenopausal women were also screened annually, or about 14 percent of the estimated Medicare spending on prescription drugs. Such costs will further increase some fourfold if the industry, enthusiastically supported by radiologists, succeeds in its efforts to replace film machines, costing about $100,000, with the latest high-tech digital machines, approved by the FDA in November 2000, costing about $400,000. Screening mammography thus poses major threats to the financially strained Medicare system. Inflationary costs apart, there is no evidence of the greater effectiveness of digital than film mammography (43), as confirmed by a study reported at the November 2000 annual meeting of the Radiological Society of North America (44). In fact, digital mammography is likely to result in the increased diagnosis of DCIS.

The comparative cost of CBE and mammography in the 1992 Canadian Breast Cancer Screening Study was reported to be 1 to 3 (45). However, this ratio ignores the high costs of capital items including buildings, equipment, and mobile vans, let alone the much greater hidden costs of unnecessary biopsies, specialized staff training, and programs for quality control and professional accreditation (46). This ratio could be even more favorable for CBE and BSE instruction if both were conducted by trained nurses. The excessive costs of mammography screening should be diverted away from industry to breast cancer prevention and other women's health programs.

CONFLICTS OF INTEREST

The ACS has close connections to the mammography industry (39). Five radiologists have served as ACS presidents, and in its every move, the ACS promotes the interests of the major manufacturers of mammogram machines and films, including Siemens, DuPont, General Electric, Eastman Kodak, and Piker. The mammography industry also conducts research for the ACS and its grantees, serves on advisory boards, and donates considerable funds. DuPont also is a substantial backer of the ACS Breast Health Awareness Program; sponsors television shows and other media productions touting mammography; produces advertising, promotional, and information literature for hospitals, clinics, medical organizations, and doctors; produces educational films; and, of course, lobbies Congress for legislation promoting availability of mammography services. In virtually all its important actions, the ACS has been and remains strongly linked with the mammography industry, while ignoring or attacking the development of viable alternatives (39).

ACS promotion continues to lure women of all ages into mammography centers, leading them to believe that mammography is their best hope against breast cancer. A leading Massachusetts newspaper featured a photograph of two women in their twenties in an ACS advertisement that promised early detection results in a cure "nearly 100 percent of the time." An ACS communications director, questioned by journalist Kate Dempsey, admitted in an article published by the Massachusetts Women's Community's journal *Cancer,* "The ad isn't based on a study. When you make an advertisement, you just say what you can to get women in the door. You exaggerate a point. . . . Mammography today is a lucrative [and] highly competitive business" (39) (see Chapter 5).

NEEDED REFORMS

Mammography is a striking paradigm of the capture of unsuspecting women by run-away powerful technological and pharmaceutical global industries, with the complicity of the cancer establishment, particularly the ACS, and the rollover mainstream media. Promotion of the multibillion dollar mammography screening industry has also become a diversionary flag around which legislators and women's product corporations can rally, protesting how much they care about women, while studiously avoiding any reference to avoidable risk factors of breast cancer, let alone other cancers.

Screening mammography should be phased out in favor of annual CBE and monthly BSE, as an effective, safe, and low-cost alternative, with diagnostic mammography available when so indicated. Such action is all the more critical and overdue in view of the still poorly recognized evidence that screening mammography does not lead to decreased breast cancer mortality (18, 21, 23).

Networks of CBE and BSE clinics, staffed by trained nurses, should be established internationally, including in developing nations. These low-cost clinics would further empower women by providing them with scientific evidence on breast cancer risk factors and prevention, information of particular importance in view of the continued high incidence of breast cancers, with an estimated 192,200 new U.S. cases predicted for 2001 (47), exceeding the number for any previous years. The multibillion dollar U.S. insurance and Medicare costs of mammography, besides those in other nations, should be diverted to outreach and research on prevention of breast and other cancers and on other women's health programs.

Chapter 4

EVALUATION OF THE NATIONAL CANCER PROGRAM AND PROPOSED REFORMS

A statement criticizing federal cancer policies, with particular reference to the National Cancer Institute (NCI), "Losing the 'War against Cancer': A Need for Public Policy Reforms," was released at a February 4, 1992, press conference in Washington, D.C. (1–3) (see Chapter 2, Part A). The statement was cosigned by Eula Bingham, former Assistant Secretary of Labor and Director of the Occupational Safety and Health Administration (OSHA); Irwin Bross, former Director of Biostatistics, Roswell Park Memorial Institute; David Rall, former Assistant Surgeon General and Director of the National Institute of Environmental Health Sciences (NIEHS); and myself. The statement was further endorsed by 64 other prominent experts in industrial medicine, carcinogenesis, epidemiology, and public health. The statement charged:

> Cancer now strikes one in three and kills one in four Americans, with over 500,000 deaths last year. Over the last decade, some 5 million Americans died of cancer and there is growing evidence that a substantial proportion of these deaths was avoidable.
>
> We express grave concerns over the failure of the "war against cancer" since its inauguration by President Nixon and Congress on December 23, 1971. This failure is evidenced by the escalating incidence of cancer to epidemic proportions over recent decades. Paralleling and further compounding this failure is the absence of any significant improvement in the treatment and cure of the majority of all cancers. Notable exceptions are the successes with some relatively rare cancers, particularly those in children.
>
> A recent report by the American Hospital Association predicts that cancer will become the leading cause of death by the year 2000 and the "dominant specialty" of American medicine. The costs in terms of suffering and death and the inflationary impact of cancer, now estimated at $100 billion annually (nearly 2 percent of the GNP), is massive. These costs are major factors in the

Published in *International Journal of Health Services,* Volume 23, Number 1, 1993.

current health care crisis, with per-case Medicare payments exceeding those of any other disease.

We express further concerns that the generously funded cancer establishment, the National Cancer Institute (NCI), and the American Cancer Society (ACS) and some twenty comprehensive cancer centers, have misled and confused the public and Congress by repeated claims that we are winning the war against cancer. In fact, the cancer establishment has continually minimized the evidence for increasing cancer rates, which it has largely attributed to smoking and dietary fat, while discounting or ignoring the causal role of avoidable exposures to industrial carcinogens in the air, food, water, and the workplace.

Furthermore, the cancer establishment and major pharmaceutical companies have repeatedly made extravagant and unfounded claims for dramatic advances in the treatment and "cure" of cancer. Such claims are generally based on an initial reduction in tumor size ("tumor response") rather than on prolongation of survival, let alone on the quality of life, which is often devastated by highly toxic treatments.

Reflecting such criticisms, the statement recommended specific and comprehensive drastic reforms in the priorities and policies of the NCI.

The cancer establishment, the NCI and ACS, responded with a media campaign of personal vilification akin to scientific McCarthyism. Furthermore, the NCI and ACS misrepresented the February 4 statement as exclusively mine (e.g., 4, 5) (see Chapter 2, Part F). Reacting to my responses (e.g., 6) (Chapter 2, Part G) and the ensuing publicity, the NCI invited me to present an "Evaluation of the National Cancer Program" at the May 5, 1992, meeting of the National Cancer Advisory Board, at which the President's Cancer Panel and NCI scientific and administrative staff were also present. This chapter is largely based on my May 5 evaluation of NCI policies (7, 8).

DISCREPANT NCI OBJECTIVES

The National Cancer Institute launched the cancer prevention awareness program in 1984 as part of the NCI's overall effort to reduce the rate of cancer mortality to one-half of the 1980 rate (from 168/100,000 to 84/100,000) by the year 2000 (9).

Within the next few years, however, the NCI made the poorly publicized and startling admission that its objective of reducing cancer mortality was totally unrealistic. The NCI now actually anticipates further increases, and not decreases, in cancer mortality rates, from 171/100,000 in 1984 to 175/100,000 by the year 2000 (10). This is a remarkable admission of the NCI's failure to even hold the line against increasing cancer mortality rates and the nation's second leading cause of death.

INCIDENCE AND MORTALITY TRENDS IN THE
GENERAL U.S. POPULATION

Cancer now strikes one in three and kills one in four, up from an incidence of one in four and a mortality of one in five in the 1950s. Age-standardized incidence rates in the overall U.S. population have increased sharply by 43.5 percent from 1950 to 1988 (11). Rates for some common cancers have increased more sharply: lung by 263 percent, prostate by 100 percent; and male colon and female breast by about 60 percent. Rates for some less common cancers have also increased more sharply: malignant melanoma, multiple myeloma, and non-Hodgkin's lymphoma by well over 100 percent, and testis and male kidney cancer by about 100 percent. The only major declines have been for stomach and cervix cancers (Table 1).

Increasing incidence rates have been accompanied by less sharply increasing mortality rates. From 1975 to 1984, overall age-standardized mortality rates increased by 5.5 percent from 162/100,000 to 171/100,000, while rates for those over 75 years increased by 9.0 percent from 1,212/100,000 to 1,351/100,000 (12). Americans 65 and over are now at a tenfold higher risk of developing cancer than younger age groups (11). The discrepancy between incidence and mortality trends probably reflects the overdiagnosis of benign as malignant neoplasms, especially for the breast and prostate (13, 14).

Contrary to their own data, both the NCI and ACS have insisted until very recently that cancer incidence and mortality rates, other than those due to tobacco, are not increasing: "We are not certainly experiencing an overall epidemic of cancer, except for that attributable to cigarette smoking" (15). Support for such unfounded assertions, however, persists from sources still relied on by the NCI as authoritative: "[The increase in mortality from cancer] can be accounted for in all industrialized countries by the spread of cigarette smoking" (16). Overwhelming contrary data have recently been summarized (17):

> In the USA and United Kingdom, mortality rates for lung cancer . . . have actually begun to decline in men, due in large part to reductions in smoking [18, 19]. Moreover, despite these reductions in lung cancer, incidence and mortality for many other types of cancer increased from 1969 to 1986 in 15 industrial countries, especially in persons over age 65 [20]. The causes of these recent increases in cancer cannot simply be explained by smoking, but appear to reflect other exposures to changing factors in the environment.

Furthermore, even assuming incorrectly that all lung cancer is due to smoking (see below), about 75 percent of the increased cancer incidence since 1950 is due to cancers at sites other than the lung (Table 1).

Table 1

Summary of changes in cancer incidence, United States, 1950–1988

Primary site	No. of new cases, all races, 1988[a]	Percent incidence changes in whites, 1950–1988
Stomach	24,800	−72.9
Colon/rectum	147,000	10.6
Larynx	12,200	58.7
Lung and bronchus	152,000	262.8
Males	100,000	222.5
Females	52,000	511.7
Melanoma of skin	27,300	303.3
Breast (females)	135,000	56.9
Cervix uteri	12,900	−77.7
Corpus uteri	34,000	−5.2
Ovary	19,000	2.9
Prostate gland	99,000	100.3
Testis	5,600	96.1
Urinary bladder	46,400	54.5
Kidney and renal pelvis	22,500	102.1
Hodgkin's disease	7,400	20.6
Non-Hodgkin's lymphoma	31,700	154.1
Leukemia	26,900	4.0
Childhood cancers	6,600	21.3
All sites, excluding lung	833,000	29.1
All sites	985,000	43.5

[a]NCI (11). Excluding basal and squamous skin cancers and all in situ cancers.

NEAR STATIC SURVIVAL RATES FOR COMMON CANCERS

Over the last two decades, the NCI and ACS leadership, with support of the cancer drug industry, have made overly optimistic and poorly founded claims for success with the latest anticancer drugs, based sequentially on cytotoxic chemotherapy, interferons, and recent biotechnology products including tumor necrosis factor, monoclonal antibodies, and interleukins. Responding to criticisms of such claims (21), the NCI asserted: "There is clear and striking evidence for improvements in cancer treatment, not only for the less common disease in younger age groups, but also for the common tumors that affect older age groups" (15).

The NCI's position is poorly supportable. The overall five-year survival rates for all cancers have not materially improved, with the notable exception of pediatric and other uncommon cancers, even in more recent years. From 1974 to 1987, survival rates increased marginally from 49.1 to 51.1 percent for all ages and races, and decreased from 38.6 to 38.4 percent for blacks (11).

The NCI and ACS claims for advances in ability to treat and cure cancer are meeting increasing skepticism (14, 22):

> For the majority of the cancers we examined, the actual improvements [in survival] have been small or have been overestimated by the published rates. . . . NCI does not systematically alert readers of its annual statistics reviews to potential sources of bias that affect changes in survival rates. . . . It is difficult to find that there has been much progress. . . . [For breast cancer], there was a slight improvement . . . [which] is considerably less than reported.

> The real survival rates [for the common cancers] have hardly changed since the sixties and seventies.

Based on a recent comprehensive review of the clinical oncology literature and a questionnaire survey of over 350 oncologists and research units worldwide, a leading German biometrician concluded (23):

> A least 80% of cancer deaths in Western industrial countries are due to advanced epithelial malignancies. Apart from lung cancer, particularly small-cell lung cancer, there is no direct evidence that chemotherapy prolongs survival in patients with advanced epithelial malignancies.
> The majority of publications equate the effect of chemotherapy with [tumor] response, irrespective of survival. Many oncologists take it for granted that response to therapy prolongs survival, an opinion which is based on a fallacy and which is not supported by clinical studies. To date there is no clear evidence that the treated patients, as a whole, benefit from chemotherapy as to their quality of life.
> With few exceptions, there is very little scientific basis for the application of chemotherapy in symptom-free patients with advanced epithelial malignancy. Although this is the opinion of a good number of well-known oncologists, the on-going studies do not take this fact into account.

The NCI's current claims for cancer cures are now more muted: "In patients with disseminated forms of the common epithelial tumors, both complete remissions and cures continue to elude us" (24).

PROFESSIONAL MINDSETS IN THE NCI

The key problem in the leadership of the cancer establishment is a professional mindset fixated on diagnosis, treatment, and research, coupled with

Table 2

Current (as of 1992) members of the National Cancer Advisory Board

Member	Date term ends	Scientific/Public	Expertise
Zora K. Brown	3/09/92	X (Public)	Public service, health policy
John R. Durant	3/09/92	X	Medical oncology, cytogenetics, immunology, university administration
Bernard Fisher	3/09/92	X	Surgery, surgical oncology
Phillip Frost	3/09/92	X (Public)	Civic leader, public service
Irene S. Pollin	3/09/92	X (Public)	Social work, counseling
Erwin P. Bettinghaus	3/09/94	X (Public)	Health education, communications
David G. Bragg	3/09/94	X	Radiology, radiologic technology, diagnostic oncology
Walter Lawrence	3/09/94	X	Surgery, oncologic surgery, cancer center administration, oncologic education
Howard M. Temin	3/09/94	X	Virology, oncology, carcinogenesis
Samuel A. Wells	3/09/94	X	Surgery, immunology, microbiology
Brenda L. Johnson	3/09/94	X (Public)	Public service, management
Frederick F. Becker	3/09/96	X	Carcinogenesis, pathology, tumor biology
Paul Calabresi (Chair)	3/09/96	X	Cancer research
Kenneth Chan	3/09/96	X	Drug metabolism, pharmacokinetics, preclinical and clinical pharmacology of anticancer drugs
Marlene A. Malek	3/09/96	X (Public)	Nursing, community programs
Deborah K. Mayer	3/09/96	X	Oncology nursing, public and professional education, public policy, clinical trials
Sidney Salmon	3/09/96	X	Medical oncology, immunology, hematology

Source: National Cancer Institute, March 12, 1992.

relative indifference to and ignorance of cancer cause and prevention. Critically, the current 18-member National Cancer Advisory Board (Table 2) "almost totally lacks expertise in occupational and environmental carcinogenesis" (25). This is clearly in violation of Section 407(a)(1)(B) of the National Cancer Act, which requires that no less than five members "shall be individuals knowledgeable in environmental carcinogenesis." Similarly lacking in such expertise is the three-member executive President's Cancer Panel.

CONFLICTS OF INTEREST IN THE NCI

Problems of professional mindsets in the NCI leadership appear further compounded by poorly recognized institutionalized conflicts of interest (26–28) (see also Chapter 1). For decades, the war on cancer has been dominated by powerful groups of interlocking professional and financial interests, with the highly profitable drug development system at its hub—and a background that helps explain why "treatment," not prevention, has been and still is the overwhelming priority, as indeed it is for most physicians. The members of the generously funded cancer establishment include the NCI, ACS, the comprehensive cancer centers such as New York's prototypical Memorial Sloan-Kettering, whose annual budget exceeds $350 million, NCI and ACS contractees and grantees at universities, and major pharmaceutical companies. Cancer care is big business, with annual cancer drug sales of approximately $1 billion.

The connections between the cancer establishment and the drug development industrial complex, chemical, pharmaceutical, and biotechnology companies, include Bristol-Myers Squibb, the nation's largest chemotherapy drug producer, which also controls key positions on Sloan-Kettering's board. Other board members have close affiliations with oil, steel, and various large corporations (Table 3); of particular additional interest is the interlocking relationship of Sloan-Kettering's board with the media giants. Another major component of the cancer drug industry is Sandoz Pharma Ltd., a huge pharmaceutical company, which recently signed a $100 million cancer drug development deal with Boston's Dana-Farber Cancer Institute. Furthermore, a "revolving door" operates among the NCI, the major cancer centers, and the drug companies. For example, Stephen Carter, head of drug research and development at Bristol-Myers Squibb, is a former director of NCI's Division of Cancer Treatment. Based on these concerns, I have requested the National Institutes of Health (NIH) Office of Scientific Integrity to investigate the NCI for possible conflicts of interest, with a view to minimizing any such future problems (29).

A more obvious conflict of interest has related to the three-member presidentially appointed Cancer Panel that controls NCI priorities and policies. The most long- standing past-chairman of the panel was Benno C. Schmidt, an investment banker, senior drug company executive, and member of the Board of Overseers of the Memorial Sloan-Kettering Comprehensive Cancer Center. He was followed by the late Armand Hammer, Chairman of Occidental Petroleum, a major polluting industry and manufacturer of carcinogenic chemicals. Congress has recently warned against such conflicts of interest in the Public Health Service (30): "The Secretary shall by regulation establish criteria for preventing, and for responding to the existence of, any financial interest . . . that (A) will create a bias in favor of obtaining results . . . that are consistent with financial interest; or (B) may be reasonably expected to create such a bias" (30).

Table 3

Potential conflicts of interest at the Memorial Sloan-Kettering
Comprehensive Cancer Center (MSKCC)

Ownership of cancer drug company securities by MSKCC, 1987

Security description	Shares	Market value (12/31/87)	Cancer drugs
American Home Products	1,800	$ 130,950	Cerubine
Bristol-Myers	13,500	561,938	Blenoxane, Cytoxan, etc.
IC Industries	10,000	329,877	Bolvadex
Eli Lilly	14,600	1,138,000	Oncovin, Velban, etc.
Merck & Co.	8,700	1,378,950	Cosmagen, Mustargen, etc.
Schering Plough Corp.	8,700	408,900	Intron A
Squibb	12,500	762,500	Hydrea, Teslac

Drug company ties of MSKCC overseers, 1988

Frederick R. Adler	Bio Technology General, Life Technologies, Inc., Scitex Corp., etc., director
Richard M. Furlaud	Squibb, president; Pharmaceutical Manufacturers Association, director
Richard L. Gelb	Bristol-Myers, chairman of the board
Louis V. Gerstner, Jr.	Squibb, director
Paul A. Marks, M.D.	Pfizer, director
John K. McKinley	Merck & Co., director
James D. Robinson, III	Bristol-Myers, director

Industrial ties of MSKCC overseers, 1988

Peter O. Crisp	Rockefeller Family & Associates
Richard M. Furlaud	Olin, director
Clifton C. Garvin, Jr.	Exxon, president
Louis V. Gerstner, Jr.	RJR Nabisco, Inc., chairman of the (tobacco company) board
Albert H. Gordon	Allen Group, Inc., director (automotive parts, etc.)
Elizabeth J. McCormack, Ph.D.	Philip Morris, director
John K. McKinley	Texaco, chairman of the board (ret.); Martin Marietta Corp., director
W. Earle McLaughlin	Algoma Steel, director
Thomas A. Murphy	General Motors, chairman of the board (ret.)
Ellmore C. Patterson	Bethlehem Steel Corp., director
John S. Reed	Philip Morris, United Technologies, director
Laurance S. Rockefeller	Exxon, Mobil, Standard Oil of Indiana, Standard Oil of California, etc., major shareholder
Robert V. Roosa	Owens-Corning Fiberglas, Texaco, director
Benno C. Schmidt	Freeport-McMoRan, Inc. (gas, oil, uranium oxide, etc. production), chairman of the executive committee
Fayez Z. Serafim	Pennzoil, etc., major investor
Frederick Seitz, Ph.D.	Ogden Corporation (waste incineration, aviation fueling, etc.), director
Virgil H. Sherrill	Reliance Electric Co., chairman

Table 3

(Cont'd.)

Media ties of MSKCC overseers, 1988	
Richard L. Gelb	New York Times Corp., director
Louis V. Gerstner, Jr.	New York Times Corp., director
George V. Grune	Reader's Digest, chief executive officer
Deane F. Johnson	Warner Communications, president
Laurance S. Rockefeller	Reader's Digest, director
Benno C. Schmidt	CBS, director (ret.)

Source: MSKCC Annual Financial Reports, 1987 and 1988.

QUESTIONABLE RELEVANCE OF SOME MAJOR BASIC RESEARCH PROGRAMS IN THE NCI TO CANCER IN GENERAL AND TO CANCER PREVENTION IN PARTICULAR

The NCI has traditionally maintained that basic research is one of its highest priorities to which major resources are allocated: "NCI has had a longstanding commitment to basic research" (31). The relevance of such research to the NCI's overall mission is, at best, questionable. There is no apparent evidence, or any basis for belief, for its relevance to cancer prevention. The views of some of the nation's leading molecular biologists and recipients of substantial NCI funding are illuminating (32–34):

I have no idea when we'll know enough to develop anything that's clinically applicable, and I don't know who's going to do it. . . . It's not a high priority in my thinking. I'm happy to work on the model systems we're working on. . . . [Responding to questions on the relevance of oncogene research, he replied], I think all of us would say honestly that it's the normal processes of the cell that are our real concern.

If you're giving me money, I'll talk about cures. Since you're not, I won't. Talking about cures is absolutely offensive to me. In our work, we never think about such things even for a second.

You can't do experiments to see what causes cancer. It's not an accessible problem, and it's not the sort of thing scientists can afford to do. You've got to live, and you've got to eat, you've got to keep your postdocs happy. Everything you do can't be risky.

Congressional skepticism on the NCI's high priority for basic research appears fully justified (35):

Research is serendipitous . . . and many of the important discoveries that enable us to fight cancer today originate at an institute other than the NCI. A number of them originated at [the National Institute of] General Medical Sciences, which devotes almost all of its budget to basic medical research, . . . [which] we starved [of funds]. . . . There will be a tremendous pressure on researchers who want to get dollars for their research grants to find some way to claim that they have a cancer angle in their research. . . . The fact is that from 1988 through this year, the NCI budget went up by 35%. Meanwhile heart-lung-blood [Institute's budget] went up 24%. Almost twice as many people die of those diseases as die of cancer. . . . [Yet] we would be funding 48% [of competitive grants] . . . at NCI, but we will be funding only half that research at heart-lung-blood.

THE NCI BUDGET FOR CANCER PREVENTION

Of an approximate $2 billion budget for 1992, the NCI allocates about $645 million, or 30 percent, to "cancer prevention," of which the Division of Cancer Etiology (DCE) receives about 82 percent and the Division of Cancer Prevention and Control (DCPC) the remainder (Table 4). Included in the "cancer prevention" budget is an allocation of some $335 million, 17 percent of the total budget, for "primary cancer prevention," defined as "those research activities

Table 4

1992 NCI budget on cancer prevention, in thousands of dollars

Total appropriation		$1,951,541
Cancer prevention (including primary prevention)		645,185
Division of Cancer Etiology (DCE)	$531,575	
Division of Cancer Prevention and Control (DCCP)	113,610	
As percent of total appropriations	30%	
"Primary cancer prevention"		334,693[a]
As percent of cancer prevention	52%	
As percent of total appropriations	17%	
Occupational cancer		19,000[b]
As percent of cancer prevention	3%	
As percent of total appropriations	1%	
NIOSH pass-through funds		500[b]
As percent of 1977 allocation (adjusted for inflation)	10%	

[a]Includes the total DCCP allocation of $113,610.
[b]Included in the "Primary Cancer Prevention" allocation.

designed to yield results that are directly applicable to the identification of risk and to interventions to prevent disease or the progression of detectable but asymptomatic disease" (31).

It should, however, be emphasized that the NCI has apparently never initiated any scientific or other "interventions" in legislative, regulatory, or public arenas (by a wide range of available mechanisms) designed to prevent or reduce avoidable exposures to any carcinogens other than tobacco.

The entire budget of DCPC is included in that of "primary cancer prevention," nearly half of which is allocated to investigator-initiated grants, with the remainder allocated to contracts and intramural research (Table 5). Included also is $19 million for research on occupational cancer—about 6 percent of the "primary prevention" budget and about 1 percent of the total NCI budget. Also included are pass-through funds of $500,000 to the National Institute of Occupational Safety and Health (NIOSH), only 10 percent of the $3 million 1977 allocation (adjusting for inflation). Review of the 1991 line item grant and contract obligations for "primary prevention" and for in-house DCPC programs (see Appendix, p. 74) reveals a predominant emphasis on smoking and nutrition. Also included are well-funded and highly questionable, if not hazardous, chemoprevention trials, particularly tamoxifen chemoprevention of breast cancer in healthy women, and studies on secondary cancers following treatment. With the exception of widely ranging anti-smoking programs, only minimal funding, $50 million at most, appears to be obligated for research on avoidable carcinogens in air, water, food, home, and the workplace. Furthermore, there is no evidence of any funding for interventions directed to reducing such avoidable exposures. Not surprising is the Congressional reaction: "A number of scientists have suggested that cancer prevention receives an even smaller percentage of the budget than what NCI considers primary prevention" (3).

The NCI leadership has misled and confused Congress as to its allocations for "cancer prevention," in general, and "primary cancer prevention," in particular,

Table 5

1992 NCI budget on "Primary Cancer Prevention,"
in thousands of dollars

Grants	$147.053
Contracts	45,660
Intramural research	28,370
Cancer prevention and control (DCPC)	113,610
Total	334,693

Source: National Cancer Institute, Letter to S. S. Epstein, June 2, 1992.

by a combination of budgetary manipulation and semantics. Illustrative is the following statement in the 1991 Congressional report on NCI authorization and appropriations, which relied on and quoted from NCI representations in its 1991 and 1992 budget estimates (30):

> NCI Director Samuel Broder has written, "Prevention is the most cost-effective way to deal with any disease or set of diseases; cancer is not an exception. Ultimately, the real gains in reducing cancer incidence and mortality will come from prevention." The prevention and control agenda outlined by the NCI in its proposed FY 1992 budget is comprehensive, scientifically valid and, most important, achievable. By increasing the percentage of the budget allocated to prevention from approximately 5 percent to 10 percent over two fiscal years, the Committee believes the real gains to which Dr. Broder referred can be achieved. . . . The cancer prevention and control program of NCI provides "the bridge between knowledge derived from basic and clinical research programs and its application in clinical and public health settings. . . . The primary focus of the Cancer Prevention Research Program is to develop and evaluate strategies for the prevention of cancer." The primary goal of cancer control "is to change personal behavior and patterns of practice to maximize the impact of cancer prevention and control regimens on cancer morbidity and mortality." For this reason, cancer prevention and control activities hold the greatest promise of achieving the goal of significantly reducing cancer incidence and mortality by the year 2000.

Particularly noteworthy is the NCI's equation of cancer prevention with "blame-the-victim" concepts of cancer causation, to the virtual exclusion of avoidable and unknowing exposures to industrial carcinogens in air, water, food, the home, and the workplace. This misrepresentation is further confounded by the NCI's failure to admit to Congress that it has totally abandoned its unrealistic objective of "significantly reducing cancer incidence and mortality by the year 2000."

It is furthermore clear that the NCI has no intention of making any substantial changes in its current policies and priorities. The NCI fiscal year 1993 "bypass" budget, which is presented directly to the President, circumventing the NIH and Department of Health and Human Services' bureaucracy, calls for an allocation of $2.7 billion. The bypass budget itemizes a total of $205 million for DCPC for the expansion of itemized current prevention programs, with no reference whatsoever to research and interventions relating to occupational cancer and other avoidable exposures to environmental carcinogens (36). The same reservations relate to the 1993 NIH reauthorization bill, which earmarks $325 million for research on breast cancer, besides $75 and $72 million for research on ovarian and prostate cancers, respectively.

NCI ESTIMATES ON THE CONTRIBUTION
OF LIFESTYLE AND ENVIRONMENTAL FACTORS
TO CANCER MORTALITY

Current (1991) NCI estimates on the causes of cancer (Table 6) are largely based on an obsolete analysis of trends in cancer mortality from 1933 to 1977 reported a decade ago (37). However, such estimates reflect a lack of recognition of the multiple causes of some, if not most, cancers. Thus, the true sum total of all "causes" should well exceed 100 percent. It is of further interest to note that the Doll and Peto (37) report concluded that "there is no evidence of any generalized increase [in cancer mortality] other than that due to tobacco." This conclusion, however, was reached by excluding consideration of blacks and of all people over the age of 65, just those groups in which more than half of all cancer deaths have been reported, and by incorrectly ascribing lung cancer almost exclusively to smoking. It should also be emphasized that the 1981 Doll and Peto estimates are devoid of any cited quantitative scientific data, apart from tobacco, for which the confounding variable of occupational exposures was ignored.

The basis of Doll and Peto's estimates is as follows: they assumed that diet causes 35 percent (even up to 70 percent) of cancers and that smoking causes 30 percent and that these together with other causes, such as alcohol and sunlight, total 96 percent. This leaves a balance of 4 percent. To bring these figures neatly up to 100 percent, Doll and Peto conveniently ascribed 4 percent to occupational causes. They attempted to dignify this tenuous hypothesis by circular references to other blame-the-victim advocates, including Higginson, Armstrong, and Wynder, who in turn cited earlier publications of Doll and Peto as their authority (37). Doll's continuing insistence on his obsolete blame-the-victim hypothesis, which trivializes the role of environmental and occupational exposure to

Table 6

NCI estimates on the contribution of "lifestyle
and environmental factors" to cancer mortality

Diet	35%
Tobacco	30%
Reproductive/sexual behavior	7%
Occupation	4%
Alcohol	3%
Geophysical factors	3%
Pollution	2%
Industrial products	1%
Medicine and medical procedures	1%
Total	86%

Source: U.S. DHHS/NCI (10).

industrial carcinogens (16), is scientifically unsupported (25). Doll's position is also consistent with his industrial interests, as illustrated by his position until recently as Warden and Director of the industry-financed Green College, Oxford. Green College was established in 1978 as a "special point of entry for industrial interests wishing to collaborate with University departments in research" (38).

THE NCI TRIVIALIZES CAUSES OF LUNG CANCER OTHER THAN SMOKING

Smoking is indisputably a leading cause of disease and death from cardiovascular disease and lung cancer, and cancers at other sites generally to a much lesser extent. However, the NCI leadership has trivialized the substantial evidence for a major role of occupational and urban causes of lung cancer. This evidence includes the following:

1. The incidence of lung cancer in nonsmokers has more than doubled over recent decades (39).

2. Lung cancer rates in black men are some 40 percent higher and have been increasing more rapidly than in whites over the last few decades. While more black men identify themselves as current smokers, they have in fact smoked less and started smoking later in life than white men (40–42).

3. The incidence of adenocarcinoma of the lung, which is less clearly related to smoking than are squamous and oat cell carcinoma (43), has increased sharply over recent decades (44). The most recent data (1983–1987) for the percentage of all lung cancer that is due to adenocarcinomas are 26.5 and 32.4 percent in whites and blacks, respectively (11).

4. The role of occupation as a major confounding variable was ignored in nearly all of the 30 or so retrospective studies associating lung cancer with smoking (45).

5. There are strong positive associations, largely independent of smoking habits, between lung cancer and occupational exposure to a wide range of carcinogenic products, such as arsenic, chrome, nickel, and BCME, and carcinogenic processes, such as copper smelting, uranium, zinc, and lead mining, spray painting, and tanning (17).

6. The high lung cancer rates in workers in casting areas of iron foundries are related to their daily inhalation of levels of polycyclic aromatic hydrocarbon carcinogens equivalent to 10 to 20 packs of cigarettes (46); these estimates ignore the incremental role of silica.

7. On the basis of studies linking urban air pollution and lung cancer (47), the 1970 "National Panel of Consultants on the Conquest of Cancer" concluded that "lung cancer [is] undoubtedly attributable to the air pollution in certain environments" (48). Subsequent studies, including those on diesel exhaust, have also incriminated air pollution as a significant cause of lung cancer (49–52). Other studies have demonstrated excess lung cancer rates in communities residing near

large petrochemical plants (53). Of clear relevance is evidence that U.S. industries in 1991 discharged into the environment some 3.6 billion pounds of chemicals, including a wide range of carcinogens (54).

8. Age-adjusted lung cancer death rates not attributable to smoking have recently been computed from published data on the proportion of active smokers, the proportion of former smokers, and the amounts smoked (55). Non-smoking attributable causes of lung cancer were found to range from 13 percent in white men to 28 percent in black women, and to be 67 percent higher in black than in white men and 16 percent higher in black than in white women (Table 7). "These residual rates place nonsmoking attributable lung cancers among the three or four most common cancers [in terms of mortality] in the U.S." (42).

Finally, it should be noted that until very recently, the NCI and ACS have tried to explain away increasing cancer incidence rates by ascribing them almost exclusively to smoking (e.g., 15).

THE NCI TRIVIALIZES OCCUPATIONAL CANCER AS A MAJOR CAUSE OF CANCER MORTALITY

The NCI's current estimate that occupational cancer is responsible for only 4 percent of total cancer mortality (10) is largely based on obsolete analyses of cancer trends from 1933 to 1977 (37). Contrary evidence includes the following:

1. Over the last decade or so (late 1970s to early 1990s), a plethora of new studies have identified a wide range of additional carcinogenic products and processes inducing cancers in a wide range of organs, particularly lung, brain, bladder, and kidney tumors and multiple myeloma (e.g., 17, 56–58).

Table 7

Smoking and non-smoking attributable causes of lung cancer

| | Age-adjusted lung cancer mortality rates, per 100,000, 1984 | | | |
| | Male | | Female | |
	White	Black	White	Black
Rate	71.8	101.0	25.2	24.1
Smoking attributed	62.5	85.5	19.4	17.3
Non-smoking attributed	9.3	15.5	5.8	6.8
Percent non-smoking attributed	13.0%	15.4%	23.0%	28.2%

Source: Schneiderman et al. (55).

2. Based on exposure data, NIOSH (59) has estimated that approximately 11 million workers are exposed to occupational carcinogens. Surveillance of these workers by the NCI and NIOSH is minimal, at best.

3. In the same year that Doll and Peto published their 4 percent estimate, which the NCI leadership regularly cites, Peto also admitted to divergent estimates of up to an order of magnitude greater (60): "Occupational factors are likely to account for . . . a "large" percentage (e.g., 20–40 percent) of all U.S. cancer. . . . [Even low estimates] represent large enough absolute numbers of deaths to justify both intensive research and political action. . . . A mere 2.5 percent of all U.S. cancer deaths would represent some 10,000 deaths per year."

4. Of 37,000 total cancer deaths each year in New York State, 10 percent (3,700) are estimated to be due to occupational exposures (61). Since the exposure patterns of the New York and national work forces have been shown to be similar, the annual U.S. mortality from occupational cancer would thus be approximately 50,000, or about 10 percent of all cancer deaths.

5. The relative risks for cancers induced in a wide range of organs following exposures to occupational carcinogens, such as aromatic amines, benzene, and BCME, are orders of magnitude greater than the risks for the general population.

6. Asbestos, clearly the single most important *known* occupational carcinogen, is estimated to cause some 300,000 cancer and other deaths by 2030, including 60,000 non-smoking-related mesotheliomas (62). As recently emphasized (20), such evidence negates continuing assertions by Doll—on whom the NCI still heavily relies for its low 4 percent estimate of occupational causes of total cancer mortality—that asbestos is only responsible for a "few cases of mesothelioma" (16).

7. Some 20 U.S. and international studies have incriminated parental exposures to occupational carcinogens as major causes of childhood cancer (63), whose incidence has increased by 21 percent since 1950.

8. Based on a recent analysis of cancer mortality trends in 15 industrialized countries from 1969 to 1986, it was concluded that "we have identified changes in the incidence and mortality rates for cancers at other sites [than those related to smoking] . . . in the middle and older age groups throughout the industrialized world" (19).

THE NCI ACCEPTS TENUOUS EVIDENCE FOR THE ROLE OF A HIGH-FAT DIET ITSELF AS A MAJOR "CAUSE" OF BREAST AND OTHER CANCERS

A high intake of fat has been associated with cancer of the breast, colon, rectum, and prostate, and possibly pancreas, uterus and ovary. Dietary factors are estimated to account for approximately 35% of cancers (10).

This "high-fat" hypothesis, however, is largely based on Doll and Peto (37) and related reports by other "blame-the-victim" advocates, which provide only weak and inconsistent supporting evidence. It should further be noted that Peto subsequently retracted this 35 percent estimate: "[Recommendations for reducing dietary fat] should chiefly be because they *will* help avoid heart disease, rather than because they *may well* avoid cancer, . . . the evidence in this respect is less secure" (64). "We'd like to have definitive evidence [on diet and cancer], but we don't have it. There is nothing in the league with smoking, which is a big and definite risk factor" (quoted in 65).

Furthermore, with reference to the role of dietary fat as a major cause of breast cancer, which NCI policy-makers explicitly accept, a recent review concluded: "The results of case-control and cohort studies [e.g., 66] have produced at best inconsistent results" (67).

THE NCI FAILS TO RECOGNIZE PREVENTABLE CAUSES OF BREAST CANCER

Despite expenditures of over $1 billion on breast cancer over the last two decades (68), "we must conclude that there has been no progress in preventing the disease" (69). NCI programs on breast cancer prevention reflect myopia and questionable science, as illustrated by emphasis on a high-fat diet by itself as the major cause. This is further compounded by neglect and by an apparent unfamiliarity with evidence incriminating a wide range of carcinogenic pesticides and other xenobiotic dietary contaminants. None of the NCI's past heavily funded nutritional studies claiming associations between dietary fat and breast cancer, besides colon and other cancers, have investigated or apparently even considered the confounding variable of carcinogenic contaminants. Less understandable is the NCI's failure to consider investigation of the role of dietary contaminants in its proposed multimillion dollar studies on the relation of diet and breast cancer. Evidence for the role of these contaminants includes the following (70) (see Chapter 2, Part B):

1. Carcinogenic pesticides, such as DDT, chlordane, and dieldrin, which concentrate in animal fats, induce breast cancer in rodents (71, 72). This creates a strong presumption for a causal role of such dietary contaminants in breast cancer in women, particularly as the sites of tumor induction are generally similar in experimental animals and humans (73).

2. Promotion by DDT of mammary tumors induced in rodents by the potent carcinogen acetamidophenanthrene "might be considered possible contributors to the high incidence of breast cancers" (74).

3. DDT and PCBs concentrate in human breast cancer itself in contrast to adjacent nonneoplastic tissue (75), and in breasts with cancer in contrast to those with fibrocystic disease (76).

4. Breast cancer mortality in premenopausal Israeli women declined by 30 percent following regulations reducing levels of DDT and other carcinogenic pesticides in dietary fat, in spite of increasing fat consumption and decreasing parity (77).

5. In view of the known carcinogenicity of exogenous estrogens, lifelong exposure to estrogenic contaminants in animal fat, due to their unregulated use as growth-promoting feed additives, is clearly a risk factor for breast cancer. Warnings of such breast cancer risks, including by the NCI's former leading expert in endocrinology, have gone unheeded by the cancer establishment (78).

6. Exogenous estrogens are synergists for the carcinogenicity of irradiation in the rodent breast (79, 80). Estrogens are also synergists in the induction of mammary cancer in rats by polynuclear hydrocarbon carcinogens (81).

Apart from ignoring the role of avoidable carcinogenic dietary contaminants, the NCI and ACS have also failed to investigate the carcinogenic hazards of mammography, particularly the relation between increasing breast cancer rates and the high-dose mammograms administered without warning to some 300,000 women in the 1970s Breast Cancer Detection and Demonstration Program (BCDDP). Based on a wide range of previously published epidemiological data, an authoritative international expert group in 1972 estimated incremental breast cancer risks of approximately 1 percent per rad of exposure (82). Thus, a premenopausal woman given one mammogram annually, for 10 years, with a conservative estimated dose of two rads per exposure, would be at a 20 percent excess risk. A confidential memo by a senior NCI physician in charge of the screening program (83) may explain why, in spite of warnings by the National Academy of Sciences in 1972 and by the NCI's own key scientific staff (84), women were not warned of this risk. The memo may also account for the cancer establishment's enthusiasm for the BCDDP program: "Both the [ACS] and NCI will gain a great deal of favorable publicity because they are bringing research findings to the public and applying them. This will assist in obtaining more research funds for basic research and clinical research which is sorely needed" (83).

It may be further noted that the NCI has also failed to adequately explore safe alternatives to mammography, particularly transillumination with infrared light scanning (85, 86). This is all the more serious in view of recent reports of excess breast cancer mortality in premenopausal women following mammography, together with accumulating evidence of its diagnostic ineffectiveness in younger women (87), including the recent large-scale Canadian study by Cornelia Baines and Anthony Miller: "There is no evidence to support introduction of service mammography for women under 50, and some may argue that there should be a moratorium on all mammography for symptom-free women in this age group outside randomized control trials" (88).

The NCI still ignores carcinogenic dietary contaminants and high-dose mammography in the 1970s as preventable causes of breast cancer (70). Meanwhile, the NCI designates its tamoxifen chemoprevention trial as "primary cancer prevention." In May 1992, the NCI initiated this trial on 16,000 healthy women at increased risk of breast cancer, for familial and more questionable reasons, including age over 60 years (89). The tamoxifen trial is a prospective experiment in human carcinogenesis whose scientific invalidity is compounded by a misleading patient consent form, trivializing risks and exaggerating benefits (90, 91); participating oncologists and institutions clearly risk future malpractice claims.

Tamoxifen, which is structurally related to DES, induces covalent DNA adducts in rodents, thus making "this drug a poor choice for the chronic preventative treatment of breast cancer" (92). Tamoxifen induced 15 percent of liver tumors in rats at doses equivalent to the daily 20-mg low dose in human adjuvant therapy, and 71 percent at the higher 40-mg dose (93, 94); these tumors were highly malignant (95). This experimental evidence of potent carcinogenicity is confirmed by two case reports of liver cancer among 931 women receiving 40-mg tamoxifen doses in the Stockholm adjuvant therapy trials (96), and more strikingly by several reports of endometrial cancer, particularly in the Stockholm trial documenting a 6.4 relative risk of endometrial cancer (97). It should further be emphasized that the median follow-up for all the seven reported tamoxifen trials was only 80 months (94); very few healthy women have taken the drug for more than five years (95). Thus, tamoxifen may well be a much more potent human carcinogen than is currently recognized.

THE NCI TRIVIALIZES ENVIRONMENTAL POLLUTANTS AS CAUSES OF AVOIDABLE CANCER

According to the NCI, "pollution" and "industrial products" are together responsible for only 3 percent of cancer deaths (Table 6). Estimates such as these fail to reflect an extensive body of evidence. This includes the exponential production and manufacture of a wide range of synthetic organic chemicals, particularly industrial carcinogens (26), from one billion pounds per annum in the 1940 dawn of the petrochemical era to over 400 billion pounds annually by the 1980s (40). Only some 10 percent of these new industrial chemicals have been adequately tested for carcinogenicity (98). More critically, of some 120 carcinogens identified in experimental animals over the last two decades, less than 10 percent have yet been subjected to epidemiological study by the NCI or by industry (99).

The role of environmental pollution as a substantial cause of increasing cancer rates is illustrated by reference to just one class of industrial chemicals, carcinogenic pesticides:

1. Some 53 carcinogenic pesticides are registered for use on major crops, such as apples, tomatoes, and potatoes, which become contaminated with detectable

residues. Consumption of common foods with residues of 28 of these pesticides has been associated with some 20,000 excess annual cancer deaths (100). It was further estimated that if then-current exposure levels were to continue, 6,000 preschool children would develop cancer from exposure to residues of carcinogenic pesticides in fruits and vegetables (101). Environmental Protection Agency (EPA) policies now allow residues of a single carcinogenic pesticide on a single food item at levels posing a "negligible cancer risk" of 1/100,000 excess cancers, equivalent to some 35 excess annual cancer deaths. However, based on EPA estimates, aggregate risks from consumption of about 30 food items contaminated by residues of 30 carcinogenic pesticides would thus result in about 30,000 excess cancers each year, assuming conservatively that risks are no more than additive (102, 103). It should be further stressed that the NCI has failed to undertake epidemiological studies on the great majority of pesticides known, in some instances for decades, to induce cancer in experimental animals and which are common dietary contaminants.

2. Some 34 pesticides are commonly used for professional lawn care treatment at application rates up to fivefold in excess of agricultural. Ten of these pesticides (29 percent) are known to induce cancer in rodents (104); this evidence has been confirmed for one of these pesticides, 2,4-D, in occupational studies by NCI epidemiologists (105, 106). Recent studies have also demonstrated major excesses of lymphomas in dogs living in homes with gardens that receive regular lawn care treatment (107). Infants and children are also clearly at major excess risk from such exposures. Of relevance in this connection is the EPA's recent report that the theoretical maximum levels of some dietary pesticide residues, including carcinogens, may exceed published standards by a factor of more than 10,000 (108).

3. Over the last three decades, tens of millions of U.S. homes have been treated for termites by subterranean application of the slowly degradable carcinogenic pesticides chlordane and heptachlor (109). These pesticides are a complex mix of some 150 components, including undisclosed potent carcinogenic contaminants, termed "inert" by the EPA and industry (110). The agricultural use of these pesticides was phased out after 1975 EPA suspension/cancellation hearings concluded that their food residues posed an "imminent hazard" of cancer (109). It was subsequently determined that routine termite treatment could result in persistent air contamination with exposure levels greater than those that the EPA had determined to pose an imminent cancer hazard on food, and which posed risks in the order of 300 to 3,000 excess annual cancer deaths. Commonplace misapplication of these pesticides resulted in higher air contaminant levels and still higher cancer risks. No epidemiological studies have ever been conducted on the very large number of people living in contaminated homes, in spite of repeated recommendations (111–113). While NCI scientists agreed, in principle, to conduct an epidemiological feasibility study on people living in chlordane-contaminated homes (114), this has not yet been undertaken.

REFORMING THE NCI

Obstacles

Drastic reforms of NCI policies, with their minimal priorities on "primary cancer prevention," are long overdue. However, a complex of powerful constraints limits the practical feasibility of implementing such reforms, particularly in the near future. These include: direct control of the NCI, uniquely and in contrast to all other National Health Institutes, by the President, who appoints the NCI's Director, executive Cancer Panel, and advisory National Cancer Board; the nearly total lack of expertise in environmental and occupational carcinogenesis in the NCI leadership, particularly the Cancer Panel, and in the Advisory Board, in violation of Section 407 of the National Cancer Act; professional mindsets of past and present directors and senior staff who are fixated on diagnosis, treatment, and basic research; powerful self-interested support for NCI priorities by a national network of cancer clinicians, basic researchers, and academic and clinical institutions; powerful support from the ACS, whose policies lockstep with the NCI; indifference to and poor comprehension of primary prevention, which is restrictedly focused on simplistic and obsolete blame-the-victim theories and chemoprevention; failure to recognize the relation between escalating cancer rates and avoidable exposure to carcinogens in air, water, food, the home, and the workplace; support from giant cancer drug pharmaceutical industries, with interlocking financial and personal interests; pressures from chemical industries in support of exclusionary blame-the-victim theories of cancer causation; an apparent conscious or subconscious duplicity of the NCI leadership in attempting to persuade the public and Congress that we are winning the war against cancer; the NCI's semantic and budgetary manipulations or fundamental misunderstanding, designating a wide range of unrelated and marginal programs as "primary prevention" programs in order to justify grossly inflated claims for primary prevention allocations; and the historic lack of effective scientific, Congressional, grassroots, and labor constituencies for primary cancer prevention.

Proposed Reforms

The group of 68 experts, signatories to the statement "Losing the 'War against Cancer'," proposed a series of reforms, not as a specific blueprint but as general guidelines for redefining the mission and priorities of the NCI. Most critically, they recommended that (2, pp. 456–458):

> 1. The NCI must give cancer cause and prevention at least equal emphasis, in terms of budgetary and personnel resources, as its other programs, including diagnosis, treatment, and basic research; NCI's current annual budget is $1.9 billion. This major shift in direction should be initiated immediately and

completed within the next few years. This shift will also require careful monitoring and oversight to prevent misleading retention of old unrelated programs under new guises of cancer cause and prevention.

2. A high priority for the cancer prevention program should be a large-scale and ongoing national campaign to inform and educate the media and the public, besides Congress, the Administration, and the industry, that much cancer is avoidable and due to past exposures to chemical and physical carcinogens in air, water, food, and the workplace, as well as to lifestyle factors, particularly smoking. It should, however, be noted that a wide range of occupational exposures and urban air pollution have been incriminated as causes of lung cancer, besides smoking. Accordingly, the educational campaign should stress the critical importance of identifying and preventing carcinogenic exposures and reducing them to the very lowest levels attainable within the earliest practically possible time.

3. The NCI should develop systematic programs for the qualitative and quantitative characterization of carcinogens in air, water, food, and the workplace, with particular emphasis on those that are avoidable. Such information should be made available to the general public, and particularly to subpopulations at high risk, by an explicit and ongoing "right to know" educational campaign, such as the specific labeling of food and consumer products with the identity and levels of all carcinogenic contaminants. While taking a lead in this program, the NCI should work cooperatively with federal and state regulatory and health agencies and authorities, industry, public health and other professional societies, labor, and community-based citizen groups.

4. The NCI should cooperate with the National Institute of Environmental Health Sciences (NIEHS), and other NIH institutes, in investigating and publicizing other chronic toxic effects induced by carcinogens, including reproductive, neurological, hematological, and immunological diseases, besides cancer.

5. The NCI should cooperate with the National Institute for Occupational Safety and Health and other agencies to develop large-scale programs for monitoring, surveillance, and warning of occupational, ethnic, and other subpopulation groups at high risk of cancer due to known past exposures to chemical or physical carcinogens.

6. In close cooperation with key regulatory agencies and industry, the NCI should initiate large-scale research programs to develop noncarcinogenic products and processes as alternatives to those currently based on chemical and physical carcinogens. This program should also include research on the development of economic incentives for the reduction or phase-out of the use of industrial carcinogens, coupled with economic disincentives for their continued use, especially when appropriate noncarcinogenic alternatives are available.

7. The NCI should provide expertise to Congress, federal and state regulatory and health agencies and authorities, and industry on the fundamental scientific principles of carcinogenesis including: the validity of extrapolation

to humans of data from valid animal carcinogenicity tests; the invalidity of using insensitive or otherwise questionable epidemiological data to negate the significance of valid animal carcinogenicity tests; and the scientific invalidity of efforts to set safe levels or thresholds for exposure to chemical and physical carcinogens. The NCI should stress that the key to cancer prevention is reducing or avoiding exposure to carcinogens, rather than accepting and attempting to "manage" such risk. Current Administration policies are, however, based on questionable mathematical procedures of quantitative risk assessment applied to exposures to individual carcinogens, while concomitant exposures to other carcinogens in air, water, food, and the workplace are ignored or discounted.

8. The NCI should provide Congress and regulatory agencies with scientific expertise necessary to the development of legislation and regulation of carcinogens. Illustrative of such need is the Administration's revocation in 1988 of the 1958 Delaney amendment to the Federal Food, Drug and Cosmetic Act, banning the deliberate addition to foods of any level of carcinogen. This critical law was revoked in spite of the overwhelming endorsement of its scientific validity by a succession of expert committees over the past three decades. Neither the NCI, nor others in the cancer establishment, provided any scientific evidence challenging the validity of this revocation, including its likely impact on future cancer rates.

9. The limited programs on routine carcinogenicity testing, now under the authority of the National Toxicology Program (NTP), should be expanded and expedited with the more active and direct involvement of the NCI. (On a cautionary note, it should be emphasized that this program, which is clearly the direct responsibility of the NCI, was transferred to the NTP in 1978 because of mismanagement and disinterest of the NCI). Underutilized federal resources, particularly national laboratories, should be involved in carcinogenicity testing programs. The costs of carcinogenicity testing of profitable, and potentially profitable, chemicals should be borne by the industries concerned, and not by NTP and the NCI and ultimately the taxpayer.

10. The NCI should undertake large-scale intramural and extramural research programs to characterize known carcinogenic exposures, both industrial and lifestyle, in terms of their estimated impact on cancer, and the practical feasibility of their avoidability or elimination within defined early periods.

11. The NCI should substantially expand its intramural and extramural programs on epidemiology research and develop large-scale programs on sensitive human monitoring techniques, including genetic and quantitative analysis of body burdens of carcinogens, and focus them specifically on cancer cause and prevention. The NCI should also take a key role in the design, conduct, and interpretation of epidemiological investigations of cancer by federal and state regulatory and health agencies and authorities.

12. The NCI should develop large-scale training programs for young scientists in all areas relating to cancer cause and prevention.

13. Continued funding by the NCI of its comprehensive cancer centers should be made contingent on their developing strong community out-reach programs in cancer cause and prevention, as opposed to their present and almost exclusive preoccupation with diagnosis and treatment. Centers should also establish tumor registries focused on identifying environmental and occupational carcinogens, and on the surveillance of occupational and other populations at high risk of cancer.

14. With Congressional oversight and with advice from the NIH Office of Scientific Integrity, the NCI should take early action to disclose information on any interlocking financial interests between its Panel, Advisory Board, advisory committees and others in the cancer establishment (including directors of comprehensive cancer centers), and major pharmaceutical companies involved in cancer drugs and therapy, and other industries. The NCI should also take the necessary precautions to prevent any such future conflicts.

15. The NCI should be enjoined from making or endorsing claims for new "cancer cures" unless these are clearly validated by data on reduced mortality rates and unless they conform to standard FDA regulations on claims for therapeutic efficacy.

Mechanisms

Recognizing the powerful complex of interlocking obstacles to their proposed reforms, the group of 68 experts concluded (2, p. 458):

> There is no conceivable likelihood that such reforms will be implemented without legislative action. The National Cancer Act should be amended explicitly to reorient the mission and priorities of the NCI to cancer cause and prevention. Compliance of the NCI should then be assured by detailed and ongoing Congressional oversight and, most critically, by House and Senate Authorization and Appropriation committees. However, only strong support by the independent scientific and public health communities, together with concerned grassroots citizen groups, will convince Congress and Presidential candidates of the critical and immediate need for such drastic action.

The emergence of the group of 68 experts poses a unique challenge to the current policies and priorities of the NCI, and a unique opportunity for developing appropriate drastic reforms. Of critical importance is the need for additional industrial medicine professionals to join this group, endorse its objectives, and actively participate in the planning and implementation of future strategies. Endorsement should also be solicited from other scientific and public health professionals. Tens of thousands of avoidable cancer deaths each year should prove an adequate stimulus to abandon customary scientific reticence and proceed instead with aggressive action programs, including media campaigns and the enrollment of support from organized labor and from nationwide grassroots citizen groups.

Equally critical is the need for active support for Congress, particularly members of NCI appropriations and authorization committees who have demonstrated concern for setting high priorities for primary cancer prevention. They should be encouraged to develop initiatives, including the following: encouraging the NCI to accept a realistic definition of primary cancer prevention (excluding both important but irrelevant programs on chemoprevention and scientifically questionable programs, such as nutrition per se), based on research and interventions for reducing or eliminating exposure to avoidable carcinogens in air, water, food, the home, and the workplace; requiring the NCI to submit a detailed annual report on all primary prevention programs, with abstracts and line item budget allocation for each; developing appropriate mechanisms for the scientific evaluation of NCI primary prevention programs by qualified independent experts; developing progressive "set-aside" appropriations, such as 10 percent of the total budget each year, for primary prevention, until they reach parity with all other NCI programs combined, ideally within a five-year period; complying with the National Cancer Act requirement that at least five members of the NCI's Advisory Board should be scientists with recognized authority in environmental and occupational carcinogenesis; requiring NCI scientists to provide expertise to Congress, Federal and regulatory agencies, and local authorities concerned with legislation and regulation of avoidable exposures to environmental and occupational carcinogens; and amending the National Cancer Act as follows (2, p. 458): "The NCI should be removed from direct Presidential authority, and reintegrated within NIH, and thus made directly responsive to the scientific community at large and the advice and consent of Congress."

POSTSCRIPT

The NCI has ignored the concerns expressed by the independent group of experts released on February 4, 1992, the critique of its programs and policies presented at the May 5, 1992, meeting (on which this chapter is based), and a series of subsequent communications. Further illustrative of the NCI's intransigence is its September 4, 1992, endorsement of recent proposals by the National Institute of Environmental Health Sciences to scuttle the attenuated carcinogenicity testing of industrial and other chemicals by the National Toxicology Program. These proposals have been sharply condemned by an independent group of some 60 experts (*Food Chemical News*, October 19, 1992, p. 10). Such reckless indifference to cancer prevention further emphasizes the need for drastic reforms and new leadership of the NCI.

APPENDIX: IN-HOUSE PROGRAMS—
FISCAL YEAR 1991 OBLIGATIONS FOR PRIMARY PREVENTION

DCPC In-House

The Division of Cancer Prevention and Control (DCPC) of the National Cancer Institute (NCI) has as its mandate the conduct of research on cancer prevention, cancer control, and the surveillance and monitoring of the incidence, mortality, and morbidity of cancer. Priorities include research to develop and evaluate cancer prevention regimens, research on special populations, and research to effect the full translation of research into applications. The Division is comprised of four Programs and includes the Cancer Prevention Research Program, the Cancer Control Science Program, the Early Detection and Community Oncology Program, and the Surveillance Program. The overall goal of these efforts is to achieve significant reductions in cancer incidence, mortality, and morbidity with a concomitant increase in cancer survival.

The Office of the Director (OD) is responsible for the coordination and direction of DCPC's programs. Total in-house costs for the OD in Cancer Control were $2,209,000.

The research in the Cancer Prevention Research Program (CPRP) is divided into two broad categories, chemoprevention, and diet and nutrition, that are pursued through both extramural and intramural mechanisms. The aim of chemoprevention research is to identify specific chemical substances that demonstrate anti-cancer activity in humans. Ultimately, these specific substances may be prescribed for high-risk individuals through dietary supplementation. A wide variety of pharmacological and chemical substances are being investigated, for example, tamoxifen, ibuprofen, and calcium. The goals of the diet and nutrition program are to conduct research in nutritional and molecular regulation, prevention-related epidemiology, clinical trials and nutrition studies; identify and validate cancer-preventive dietary patterns; and—through NCI's information dissemination channels—encourage and change the dietary patterns of the public. Total in-house costs for Cancer Control in the CPRP were $3,429,000.

The Cancer Control Science Program (CCSP) is designed to identify the most effective strategies for bringing cancer prevention and control methods to the public and to the nation's health care providers. The Program identifies and develops strategies to surmount the barriers limiting the full transfer of new scientific results to practice. It also fosters cancer control research across the country and works with state and local health organizations/agencies on developing cancer control plans for their regions and making maximal use of existing data on cancer. Total in-house costs for Cancer Control in the CCSP were $3,997,000.

The Early Detection and Community Oncology Program is responsible for the identification and evaluation of technologies for early detection, biomarker research, rehabilitation for cancer patients, and community-based clinical trials in prevention, control, and treatment. The goal of early detection research is to increase the effectiveness of early detection practices that could lead to a reduction in cancer morbidity and mortality. Emphasis is also placed on the application of early cancer detection in medical practice. Research initiatives on new methods and approaches in early detection are undertaken with the goal of extending this research to comparative trials in high-risk groups, and in other defined populations.

In addition, research is aimed at finding intermediate endpoints of cancer prevention that can be used as markers of cancer risk or as early detection tests prior to the development of cancer. Such markers would also be validated in clinical trials so that they can be used to measure the success of prevention strategies.

Another mission of the Program is to train the next generation of scientists and practitioners in order to provide the field with qualified people to advance all facets of cancer prevention and control. Total in-house costs for EDCOP in Cancer Control were $5,515,000.

The Surveillance Program monitors the cancer burden on the population of the United States through the measurement of cancer incidence, mortality, and survival and the assessment of individual and societal factors that mediate these cancer measures both directly and indirectly. The ultimate purpose of cancer surveillance is to guide future programmatic and resource allocation decisions of the National Cancer Program.

The surveillance effort includes the development of information and statistical analysis systems, such as population-based registries and national probability surveys, and conduct of a broad series of studies focused on specific cancer control indicators. Programmatically and operationally, cancer surveillance requires a strong interface between methodologic techniques and cancer control initiatives in prevention, early detection, and treatment. Total in-house costs for Cancer Control in the SP were $1,670,000.

The research program in epidemiology spans a variety of areas and includes secondary data analysis from the cancer control supplement of the National Health Interview Survey as well as the Surveillance, Epidemiology and End Results (SEER) program. Total in-house costs for Epidemiology were $2,720,000.

The Physical and Chemical research categories include support to NCI's Smoking, Tobacco and Cancer Program, the evaluation of the "Working Well," a worksite-based cancer prevention and control program, and support related to research on oncologic pain. Total in-house costs were $73,000.

The Nutrition research category includes support for activities related to the retinoid skin cancer trial as well as a beta-carotene skin cancer trial in albinos, a computer-based dietary intervention program for worksites, and general support for nutrition-related activities. Total in-house costs were $292,000.

DCE In-House

The Division of Cancer Etiology (DCE) of the National Cancer Institute is responsible for planning and directing a national program of basic research including laboratory, epidemiologic, and biometric research on the cause and natural history of cancer and means for preventing cancer. The DCE evaluates mechanisms of cancer induction and promotion by chemicals, viruses, and environmental agents and serves as the focal point for the federal government on the synthesis of clinical, epidemiological, and experimental data relating to cancer causation. Division staff participate in the evaluation of program-related aspects of other basic research activities as they relate to cancer cause and prevention. The DCE is comprised of three research program organizations: the Epidemiology and Biostatistics Program; the Chemical and Physical Carcinogenesis Program; and the Biological Carcinogenesis Program.

The Epidemiology and Biostatistics Program plans, directs, manages, and evaluates a program of epidemiologic, demographic, statistical, and mathematical research activities, and provides statistical and relevant automatic data-processing services to support the research programs throughout the NCI. The Program is comprised of four intramural branches and one extramural branch; Clinical Epidemiology Branch; Environmental Epidemiology Branch; Radiation Epidemiology Branch; Biostatistic Branch; and the Extramural Programs Branch. The total in-house costs for prevention activities in FY 1991 were $13,243,000.

The Chemical and Physical Carcinogenesis Program (CPCP) plans, develops, directs, and evaluates a national program of basic and applied research in which agents known or suspected to have carcinogenic and/or tumor-promoting activity are evaluated from the standpoint of mechanism of action, metabolism, interactions with biologically important macromolecules, and related areas. The Program also supports basic research involving the development of effective agents to prevent or reverse the process of carcinogenesis. A significant portion of the activities of the CPCP intramural laboratories listed below involves primary prevention and nutrition studies.

The Laboratory of Chemoprevention plans, develops, and implements a research program on the use of pharmacological agents for the prevention of cancer; studies molecular mechanisms of action of chemopreventive agents such as retinoids; studies polypeptide growth factors, including their isolation, characterization, and mechanism of action; and develops new methods to control the activity of peptide growth factors, utilizing techniques of molecular genetics and immunology. Total in-house prevention expenditures in FY 1991 were $1,535,000.

The Laboratory of Human Carcinogenesis plans, develops, and conducts a research program assessing mechanisms of carcinogenesis in epithelial cells from humans and experimental animals; experimental approaches in biological systems for the extrapolation of carcinogenesis data and mechanisms from experimental animals to the human situation; and host factors that determine differences in carcinogenic susceptibility among individuals. The total in-house prevention expenditures in FY 1991 were $2,733,000.

The Laboratory of Cellular Carcinogenesis and Tumor Promotion plans, develops, and implements a comprehensive research program to determine the molecular and biological changes that occur at the cellular and tissue level during the process of carcinogenesis. For FY 1991, the total in-house prevention expenditures for physical and chemical carcinogenesis were $1,250,000 and for nutrition research, $400,000.

The Laboratory of Comparative Carcinogenesis plans, develops, and conducts a research program to compare effects of chemical carcinogens in rodents and non-human primates; identifies determinants of susceptibility and of resistance to carcinogenesis; identifies, describes, and investigates mechanisms of interspecies differences and of cell and organ specificity in carcinogenesis; investigates the perinatal age period and pregnancy in modifying susceptibility to chemical carcinogens; and conducts biologic and morphologic studies on the pathogenesis of naturally occurring and induced tumors in experimental animals. The total in-house prevention expenditures in FY 1991 were $1,783,000.

The Laboratory of Experimental Carcinogenesis plans, develops, and implements a research program aimed at elucidating mechanisms of malignant transformation in human and animal cells by chemical carcinogens and other cancer-causing agents; to determine critical cellular and genetic factors involved in initiation, promotion, and progression of these transformed cells; and to apply, whenever possible, the knowledge obtained from these studies toward effective prevention of cancer in humans. For FY 1991, the total in-house prevention expenditures for physical and chemical carcinogenesis were $1,250,000 and for nutrition, $610,000.

The Laboratory of Molecular Carcinogenesis plans, develops, and conducts a research program designed to clarify the molecular biology of carcinogenesis; elucidate the fundamental nature of the interactions of carcinogenic agents, especially chemical, with biological systems in the induction of cancer; define those environmental and endogenous factors that relate to and modify the carcinogenic process; and clarify the metabolic regulatory processes that are related to carcinogenesis. The total in-house prevention expenditures in FY 1991 were $770,000.

The Laboratory of Biology plans, develops, and conducts in vitro and in vivo investigations aimed at elucidating the role of chemical, physical, and biological agents in the modulation of carcinogenesis. Coordinated biochemical and biological studies utilizing human and animal cell models are used to characterize the cellular alterations associated with carcinogenesis. These include assessment of the effect of physiologic host mediating factors; determination of cell surface changes; and evaluation of the relationships between differentiation, chromosome alterations, and carcinogenesis. The total in-house prevention expenditures in FY 1991 were $260,000.

The Laboratory of Experimental Pathology plans, develops, and implements research on the experimental pathology of carcinogenesis, especially concerned with the induction of neoplasia by chemical and physical factors in epithelial tissues. The total in-house prevention expenditures in FY 1991 were $100,000.

Note — This chapter is based on an invited presentation to the NCI on May 5, 1992, later published in the *American Journal of Industrial Medicine*.

Chapter 5

AMERICAN CANCER SOCIETY:
THE WORLD'S WEALTHIEST "NONPROFIT"
INSTITUTION

The American Cancer Society (ACS) is accumulating great wealth in its role as a "charity." According to James Bennett, professor of economics at George Mason University and recognized authority on charitable organizations, in 1988 the ACS held a fund balance of over $400 million with about $69 million of holdings in land, buildings, and equipment (1). Of that money, the ACS spent only $90 million—26 percent of its budget—on medical research and programs. The rest covered "operating expenses," including about 60 percent for generous salaries, pensions, executive benefits, and overhead. By 1989, the cash reserves of the ACS were worth more than $700 million (2). In 1991, Americans, believing they were contributing to fighting cancer, gave nearly $350 million to the ACS, 6 percent more than the previous year. Most of this money comes from public donations averaging $3,500, and high-profile fund-raising campaigns such as the springtime daffodil sale and the May relay races. However, over the last two decades, an increasing proportion of the ACS budget comes from large corporations, including the pharmaceutical, cancer drug, telecommunications, and entertainment industries.

In 1992, the American Cancer Society Foundation was created to allow the ACS to actively solicit contributions of more than $100,000. However, a close look at the heavy-hitters on the Foundation's board will give an idea of which interests are at play and where the Foundation expects its big contributions to come from. The Foundation's board of trustees included corporate executives from the pharmaceutical, investment, banking, and media industries. Among them:

Published in *International Journal of Health Services,* Volume 29, Number 3, 1999.

- David R. Bethune, president of Lederle Laboratories, a multinational pharmaceutical company and a division of American Cyanamid Company. Bethune is also vice president of American Cyanamid, which makes chemical fertilizers and herbicides while transforming itself into a full-fledged pharmaceutical company. In 1988, American Cyanamid introduced Novatrone, an anti-cancer drug. And in 1992, it announced that it would buy a majority of shares of Immunex, a cancer drug maker.
- Multimillionaire Irwin Beck, whose father, William Henry Beck, founded the nation's largest family-owned retail chain, Beck Stores, which analysts estimate brought in revenues of $1.7 billion in 1993.
- Gordon Binder, CEO of Amgen, the world's foremost biotechnology company, with over $1 billion in product sales in 1992. Amgen's success rests almost exclusively on one product, Neupogen, which is administered to chemotherapy patients to stimulate their production of white blood cells. As the cancer epidemic grows, sales for Neupogen continue to skyrocket.
- Diane Disney Miller, daughter of the conservative multi-millionaire Walt Disney, who died of lung cancer in 1966, and wife of Ron Miller, former president of the Walt Disney Company from 1980 to 1984.
- George Dessert, famous in media circles for his former role as censor on the subject of "family values" during the 1970s and 1980s as CEO of CBS, and now chairman of the ACS board.
- Alan Gevertzen, chairman of the board of Boeing, the world's number one commercial aircraft maker with net sales of $30 billion in 1992.
- Sumner M. Redstone, chairman of the board, Viacom Inc. and Viacom International Inc., a broadcasting, telecommunications, entertainment, and cable television corporation.

The results of this board's efforts have been very successful. A million here, a million there—much of it coming from the very industries instrumental in shaping ACS policy, or profiting from it.

In 1992, *The Chronicle of Philanthropy* reported that the ACS was "more interested in accumulating wealth than in saving lives." Fund-raising appeals routinely stated that the ACS needed more funds to support its cancer programs, all the while holding more than $750 million in cash and real estate assets (3).

A 1992 article in the *Wall Street Journal,* by Thomas DiLorenzo, professor of economics at Loyola College and veteran investigator of nonprofit organizations, revealed that the Texas affiliate of the ACS owned more than $11 million worth of assets in land and real estate, as well as more than 56 vehicles, including 11 Ford Crown Victorias for senior executives and 45 other cars assigned to staff members. Arizona's ACS chapter spent less than 10 percent of its funds on direct community cancer services. In California, the figure was 11 percent, and under 9 percent in Missouri (4):

Thus for every $1 spent on direct service, approximately $6.40 is spent on compensation and overhead. In all ten states, salaries and fringe benefits are by far the largest single budget items, a surprising fact in light of the characterization of the appeals, which stress an urgent and critical need for donations to provide cancer services.

Nationally, only 16 percent or less of all money raised is spent on direct services to cancer victims, like driving cancer patients from the hospital after chemotherapy and providing pain medication.

Most of the funds raised by the ACS go to pay overhead, salaries, fringe benefits, and travel expenses of its national executives in Atlanta. They also go to pay chief executive officers, who earn six-figure salaries in several states, and the hundreds of other employees who work out of some 3,000 regional offices nationwide. The typical ACS affiliate, which helps raise the money for the national office, spends more than 52 percent of its budget on salaries, pensions, fringe benefits, and overhead for its own employees. Salaries and overhead for most ACS affiliates also exceeded 50 percent, although most direct community services are handled by unpaid volunteers. DiLorenzo summed up his findings by emphasizing the hoarding of funds by the ACS (4):

> If current needs are not being met because of insufficient funds, as fund-raising appeals suggest, why is so much cash being hoarded? Most contributors believe their donations are being used to fight cancer, not to accumulate financial reserves. More progress in the war against cancer would be made if they would divest some of their real estate holdings and use the proceeds—as well as a portion of their cash reserves—to provide more cancer services.

Aside from high salaries and overhead, most of what is left of the ACS budget goes to basic research and research into profitable patented cancer drugs.

The current budget of the ACS (as of 1998) is $380 million and its cash reserves approach $1 billion. Yet its aggressive fund-raising campaign continues to plead poverty and lament the lack of available money for cancer research, while ignoring efforts to prevent cancer by phasing out avoidable exposures to environmental and occupational carcinogens. Meanwhile, the ACS is silent about its intricate relationships with the wealthy cancer drug, chemical, and other industries.

A March 30, 1998, Associated Press Release shed unexpected light on questionable ACS expenditures on lobbying (5). National vice president for federal and state governmental relations Linda Hay Crawford admitted that the ACS was spending "less than $1 million a year on direct lobbying." She also admitted that over the last year, the society used ten of its own employees to lobby. "For legal and other help, it hired the lobbying firm of Hogan & Hartson, whose roster includes former House Minority Leader Robert H. Michel (R–IL)."

The ACS lobbying also included $30,000 donations to Democratic and Republican governors' associations. "We wanted to look like players and be players," explained Crawford. This practice, however, has been sharply challenged. The Associated Press release quotes the national Charities Information Bureau as stating that it "does not know of any other charity that makes contributions to political parties."

Tax experts have warned that these contributions may be illegal, as charities are not allowed to make political donations. Marcus Owens, director of the IRS Exempt Organization Division, also warned that "The bottom line is campaign contributions will jeopardize a charity's exempt status."

TRACK RECORD ON PREVENTION

Marching in lockstep with the National Cancer Institute (NCI) in its "war" on cancer is its "ministry of information," the ACS (6, pp. 306–314). With powerful media control and public relations resources, the ACS is the tail that wags the dog of the policies and priorities of the NCI (7, 8) (see Chapters 1 and 4). In addition, the approach of the ACS to cancer prevention reflects a virtually exclusive "blame-the-victim" philosophy. It emphasizes faulty lifestyles rather than unknowing and avoidable exposure to workplace or environmental carcinogens. Giant corporations, which profit handsomely while they pollute the air, water, and food with a wide range of carcinogens, are greatly comforted by the silence of the ACS. This silence reflects a complex of mindsets fixated on diagnosis, treatment, and basic genetic research together with ignorance, indifference, and even hostility to prevention, coupled with conflicts of interest.

Indeed, despite promises to the public to do everything to "wipe out cancer in your lifetime," the ACS fails to make its voice heard in Congress and the regulatory arena. Instead, the ACS repeatedly rejects or ignores opportunities and requests from Congressional committees, regulatory agencies, unions, and environmental organizations to provide scientific testimony critical to efforts to legislate and regulate a wide range of occupational and environmental carcinogens. This history of ACS unresponsiveness is a long and damning one, as shown by the following examples (6, pp. 306–314):

1. In 1971, when studies unequivocally proved that diethylstilbestrol (DES) caused vaginal cancers in teenaged daughters of women administered the drug during pregnancy, the ACS refused an invitation to testify at Congressional hearings to require the FDA (U.S. Food and Drug Administration) to ban its use as an animal feed additive. It gave no reason for its refusal.

2. In 1977 and 1978, the ACS opposed regulations proposed for hair coloring products that contained dyes known to cause breast and liver cancer in rodents. In so doing, the ACS ignored virtually every tenet of responsible public health as these chemicals were clear-cut liver and breast carcinogens.

3. In 1977, the ACS called for a Congressional moratorium on the FDA's proposed ban on saccharin and even advocated its use by nursing mothers and babies in "moderation" despite clear-cut evidence of its carcinogenicity in rodents. This reflects the consistent rejection by the ACS of the importance of animal evidence as predictive of human cancer risk.

4. In 1978, Tony Mazzocchi, then senior representative of the Oil, Chemical, and Atomic Workers International Union, stated at a Washington, D.C., round-table between public interest groups and high-ranking ACS officials: "Occupational safety standards have received no support from the ACS."

5. In 1978, Congressman Paul Rogers censured the ACS for doing "too little, too late" in failing to support the Clean Air Act.

6. In 1982, the ACS adopted a highly restrictive cancer policy that insisted on unequivocal human evidence of carcinogenicity before taking any position on public health hazards. Accordingly, the ACS still trivializes or rejects evidence of carcinogenicity in experimental animals, and has actively campaigned against laws (the 1958 Delaney Law, for instance) that ban deliberate addition to food of any amount of any additive shown to cause cancer in either animals or humans. The ACS still persists in an anti-Delaney policy, in spite of the overwhelming support for the Delaney Law by the independent scientific community.

7. In 1983, the ACS refused to join a coalition of the March of Dimes, American Heart Association, and the American Lung Association to support the Clean Air Act.

8. In 1992, the ACS issued a joint statement with the Chlorine Institute in support of the continued global use of organochlorine pesticides—despite clear evidence that some were known to cause breast cancer. In this statement, Society vice president Clark Heath, M.D., dismissed evidence of this risk as "preliminary and mostly based on weak and indirect association." Heath then went on to explain away the blame for increasing breast cancer rates as due to better detection: "Speculation that such exposures account for observed geographic differences in breast cancer incidence or for recent rises in breast cancer occurrence should be received with caution; more likely, much of the recent rise in incidence in the United States . . . reflects increased utilization of mammography over the past decade."

9. In 1992, in conjunction with the NCI, the ACS aggressively launched a "chemoprevention" program aimed at recruiting 16,000 healthy women at supposedly "high risk" of breast cancer into a 5-year clinical trial with a highly profitable drug called tamoxifen. This drug is manufactured by one of the world's most powerful cancer drug industries, Zeneca, an offshoot of the Imperial Chemical Industries. The women were told that the drug was essentially harmless, and that it could reduce their risk of breast cancer. What the women were not told was that tamoxifen had already been shown to be a highly potent liver carcinogen in rodent tests, and also that it was well-known to induce human uterine cancer (6, pp. 145–151).

10. In 1993, just before PBS *Frontline* aired the special entitled "In Our Children's Food," the ACS came out in support of the pesticide industry. In a damage-control memorandum sent to some 48 regional divisions, the ACS trivialized pesticides as a cause of childhood cancer, and reassured the public that carcinogenic pesticide residues in food are safe, even for babies. When the media and concerned citizens called local ACS chapters, they received reassurances from an ACS memorandum by its vice president for Public Relations (9):

> The primary health hazards of pesticides are from direct contact with the chemicals at potentially high doses, for example, farm workers who apply the chemicals and work in the fields after the pesticides have been applied, and people living near aerially sprayed fields. . . . The American Cancer Society believes that the benefits of a balanced diet rich in fruits and vegetables far outweigh the largely theoretical risks posed by occasional, very low pesticide residue levels in foods.

11. In September 1996, the ACS together with a diverse group of patient and physician organizations filed a "citizen's petition" to pressure the FDA to ease restrictions on access to silicone gel breast implants. What the ACS did not disclose was that the gel in these implants had clearly been shown to induce cancer in several industry rodent studies, and that these implants were also contaminated with other potent carcinogens such as ethylene oxide and crystalline silica.

This abysmal track record on prevention has been the subject of periodic protests by both independent scientists and public interest groups. A well-publicized example was a New York City, January 23, 1994, press conference, sponsored by the author and the Center for Science in the Public Interest. The press release stated: "A group of 24 scientists charged that the ACS was doing little to protect the public from cancer-causing chemicals in the environment and workplace. The scientists urged ACS to revamp its policies and to emphasize prevention in its lobbying and educational campaigns." The scientists—who included Matthew Meselson and Nobel laureate George Wald, both of Harvard University; former OSHA director Eula Bingham; Samuel Epstein, author of *The Politics of Cancer;* and Anthony Robbins, past president of the American Public Health Association—criticized the ACS for insisting on unequivocal human proof that a substance is carcinogenic before it will recommend its regulation.

This public criticism by a broad representation of highly credible scientists reflects the growing conviction that a substantial proportion of cancer deaths are caused by exposure to chemical carcinogens in the air, water, food supply, and workplace, and thus can be prevented by legislative and regulatory action. Calling the ACS guidelines an "unrealistically high-action threshold," a letter to ACS executive vice president Lane Adams states that "we would like to express our hope that ACS will take strong public positions and become a more active force to protect the public and the work force from exposure to carcinogens."

ACS's policy is retrogressive and contrary to authoritative and scientific tenets established by international and national scientific committees, and is in conflict with long-established policies of federal regulatory agencies. Speakers at the conference warned that unless the ACS became more supportive of cancer prevention, it would face the risk of an economic boycott. Reacting promptly, the ACS issued a statement claiming that cancer prevention would become a major priority. However, ACS policies have remained unchanged. More recently, the author has issued this warning again, a warning echoed by activist women's breast cancer groups.

In *Cancer Facts & Figures—1998,* the latest annual ACS publication (as of early 1999) designed to provide the public and medical profession with "Basic Facts" on cancer—other than information on incidence, mortality, signs and symptoms, and treatment—there is little or no mention of prevention (10). Examples include: no mention of dusting the genital area with talc as a known cause of ovarian cancer; no mention of parental exposure to occupational carcinogens as a major cause of childhood cancer; and no mention of prolonged use of oral contraceptives and hormone replacement therapy as major causes of breast cancer. For breast cancer, ACS states: "Since women may not be able to alter their personal risk factors, the best opportunity for reducing mortality is through early detection." In other words, breast cancer is not preventable in spite of clear evidence that its incidence has escalated over recent decades, and in spite of an overwhelming literature on avoidable causes of this cancer (6, Chapt. 6). In the section on "Nutrition and Diet," no mention at all is made of the heavy contamination of animal and dairy fats and produce with a wide range of carcinogenic pesticide residues, and on the need to switch to safer organic foods.

CONFLICTS OF INTEREST

Of the members of the ACS board, about half are clinicians, oncologists, surgeons, radiologists, and basic molecular scientists—and most are closely tied in with the NCI. Many board members and their institutional colleagues apply for and obtain funding from both the ACS and the NCI. Substantial NCI funds go to ACS directors who sit on key NCI committees. Although the ACS asks board members to leave the room when the rest of the board discusses their funding proposals, this is just a token formality. In this private club, easy access to funding is one of the "perks," and the board routinely rubber-stamps approvals. A significant amount of ACS research funding goes to this extended membership. Such conflicts of interest are evident in many ACS priorities, including their policy on mammography and their National Breast Cancer Awareness campaign (6, pp. 311–314).

Mammography

The ACS has close connections to the mammography industry. Five radiologists have served as ACS presidents, and in its every move, the ACS reflects the interests of the major manufacturers of mammogram machines and films, including Siemens, DuPont, General Electric, Eastman Kodak, and Piker. In fact, if every woman were to follow ACS and NCI mammography guidelines, the annual revenue to health care facilities would be a staggering $5 billion, including at least $2.5 billion for premenopausal women. Promotions of the ACS continue to lure women of all ages into mammography centers, leading them to believe that mammography is their best hope against breast cancer. A leading Massachusetts newspaper featured a photograph of two women in their twenties in an ACS advertisement that promised early detection results in a cure "nearly 100 percent of the time." An ACS communications director, questioned by journalist Kate Dempsey, responded in an article published by the Massachusetts Women's Community's journal *Cancer:* "The ad isn't based on a study. When you make an advertisement, you just say what you can to get women in the door. You exaggerate a point. . . . Mammography today is a lucrative [and] highly competitive business."

In addition, the mammography industry conducts research for the ACS and its grantees, serves on advisory boards, and donates considerable funds. DuPont also is a substantial backer of the ACS Breast Health Awareness Program; sponsors television shows and other media productions touting mammography; produces advertising, promotional, and information literature for hospitals, clinics, medical organizations, and doctors; produces educational films; and, of course, lobbies Congress for legislation promoting availability of mammography services. In virtually all of its important actions, the ACS has been strongly linked with the mammography industry, ignoring the development of viable alternatives to mammography.

The ACS exposes premenopausal women to radiation hazards from mammography with little or no evidence of benefits. The ACS also fails to tell them that their breasts will change so much over time that the "baseline" images have little or no future relevance. This is truly an American Cancer Society crusade. But against whom, or rather, for whom?

National Breast Cancer Awareness Month

The highly publicized National Breast Cancer Awareness Month campaign further illustrates these institutionalized conflicts of interest. Every October, ACS and NCI representatives help sponsor promotional events, hold interviews, and stress the need for mammography. The flagship of this month-long series of events is National Mammography Day, on October 17 in 1997.

Conspicuously absent from the public relations campaign of the National Breast Cancer Awareness Month is any information on environmental and other avoidable causes of breast cancer. This is no accident. Zeneca Pharmaceuticals— a spin-off of Imperial Chemical Industries, one of the world's largest manufacturers of chlorinated and other industrial chemicals, including those incriminated as causes of breast cancer—has been the sole multimillion-dollar funder of National Breast Cancer Awareness Month since its inception in 1984. Zeneca is also the sole manufacturer of tamoxifen, the world's top-selling anticancer and breast cancer "prevention" drug, with $400 million in annual sales. Furthermore, Zeneca recently assumed direct management of 11 cancer centers in U.S. hospitals. Zeneca owns a 50 percent stake in these centers known collectively as Salick Health Care.

The link between the ACS and NCI and Zeneca is especially strong when it comes to tamoxifen. The ACS and NCI continue aggressively to promote the tamoxifen trial, which is the cornerstone of its minimal prevention program. On March 7, 1997, the NCI Press Office released a four-page "For Response to Inquiries on Breast Cancer." The brief section on prevention reads:

> Researchers are looking for a way to prevent breast cancer in women at high risk. . . . A large study [is underway] to see if the drug tamoxifen will reduce cancer risk in women age 60 or older and in women 35 to 59 who have a pattern of risk factors for breast cancer. This study is also a model for future studies of cancer prevention. Studies of diet and nutrition could also lead to preventive strategies.

Since Zeneca influences every leaflet, poster, publication, and commercial produced by National Breast Cancer Awareness Month, it is no wonder these publications make no mention of carcinogenic industrial chemicals and their relation to breast cancer. Imperial Chemical Industries, Zeneca's parent company, profits by manufacturing breast cancer–causing chemicals. Zeneca profits from treatment of breast cancer, and hopes to profit still more from the prospects of large-scale national use of tamoxifen for breast cancer prevention. National Breast Cancer Awareness Month is a masterful public relations coup for Zeneca, providing the company with valuable, if ill-placed, good will from millions of American women.

The Pesticide Industry

Just how inbred the relations between the ACS and the chemical industry are became clear in the spring of 1993 to Marty Koughan, a public television producer. Koughan was about to broadcast a documentary on the dangers of pesticides to children for the Public Broadcasting Service's hour-long show, *Frontline*. Koughan's investigation relied heavily on an embargoed, ground-breaking report issued by the National Academy of Sciences in June of 1993 entitled "Pesticides in the Diet of Children." This report declared the nation's food supply "inadequately protected" from cancer-causing pesticides and a significant threat to the health of children.

An earlier report, issued by the Natural Resources Defense Council in 1989, "Intolerable Risk: Pesticides in our Children's Food," had also given pesticide manufacturers failing marks. The report was released in high profile testimony to Congress by movie actress Meryl Streep. A mother of young children, Streep explained to a packed House chamber the report's findings, namely, that children were most at risk from cancer-causing pesticides on our food because they consume a disproportionate amount of fruits, fruit juices, and vegetables relative to their size, and because their bodies are still forming. Shortly before Koughan's program was due to air, a draft of the script was mysteriously leaked to Porter-Novelli, a powerful public relations firm for produce growers and the agri-chemical industry. In true Washington fashion, Porter-Novelli plays both sides of the fence, representing both government agencies and the industries they regulate. Its client list in 1993 included Ciba-Geigy, DuPont, Monsanto, Burroughs Wellcome, American Petroleum Institute, Bristol-Meyers-Squibb, Hoffman-LaRoche, Hoechst Celanese, Hoechst Roussel Pharmaceutical, Janssen Pharmaceutical, Johnson & Johnson, the Center for Produce Quality, as well as the U.S. Department of Agriculture, the NCI, plus other National Institutes of Health.

Porter-Novelli first crafted a rebuttal to help the manufacturers quell public fears about pesticide-contaminated food. Next, Porter-Novelli called up another client, the American Cancer Society, for whom Porter-Novelli had done pro bono work for years. The rebuttal that Porter-Novelli had just sent off to its industry clients was faxed to ACS Atlanta headquarters. It was then circulated by e-mail on March 22, 1993, internally—virtually verbatim from the memo Porter-Novelli had crafted for a backgrounder for 3,000 regional ACS offices to have in hand to help field calls from the public after the show aired.

"The program makes unfounded suggestions . . . that pesticide residue in food may be at hazardous levels," the ACS memo read. "Its use of 'cancer cluster' leukemia case reports and non-specific community illnesses as alleged evidence of pesticide effects in people is unfortunate. We know of no community cancer clusters which have been shown to be anything other than chance grouping of cases and none in which pesticide use was confirmed as the cause."

This bold, unabashed defense of the pesticide industry, crafted by Porter-Novelli, was then rehashed a third time, this time by the right-wing group, Accuracy in Media (AIM). AIM's newsletter gleefully published quotes from the ACS memo in an article with the banner headline: "Junk Science on PBS." The article opened with "Can we afford the Public Broadcasting Service?" and went on to disparage Koughan's documentary on pesticides and children. "In Our Children's Food . . . exemplified what the media have done to produce these 'popular panics' and the enormously costly waste [at PBS] cited by the *New York Times.*"

When Koughan saw the AIM article he was initially outraged that the ACS was being used to defend the pesticide industry. "At first, I assumed complete ignorance on the part of the ACS," said Koughan. But after repeatedly trying, without success, to get the national office to rebut the AIM article, Koughan began to see what was really going on. "When I realized Porter-Novelli represented five agrichemical companies, and that the ACS had been a client for years, it became obvious that the ACS had not been fooled at all," said Koughan. "They were willing partners in the deception, and were in fact doing a favor for a friend—by flakking for the agrichemical industry."

Charles Benbrook, former director of the National Academy of Sciences Board of Agriculture, worked on the pesticide report by the Academy of Sciences that the PBS special would preview. He charged that the role of the ACS as a source of information for the media representing the pesticide and produce industry was "unconscionable" (11). Investigative reporter Sheila Kaplan, in a 1993 *Legal Times* article, went further: "What they did was clearly and unequivocally over the line, and constitutes a major conflict of interest" (12).

Cancer Drug Industry

The intimate association between the ACS and the cancer drug industry, with current annual sales of about $12 billion, is further illustrated by the unbridled aggression which the Society has directed at potential competitors of the industry (13).

Just as Senator Joseph McCarthy had his "black list" of suspected communists and Richard Nixon his environmental activist "enemies list," so too the ACS maintains a "Committee on Unproven Methods of Cancer Management" which periodically "reviews" unorthodox or alternative therapies. This Committee is comprised of "volunteer health care professionals," carefully selected proponents of orthodox, expensive, and usually toxic drugs patented by major pharmaceutical companies, and opponents of alternative or "unproven" therapies which are generally cheap, nonpatentable, and minimally toxic (13).

Periodically, the Committee updates its statements on "unproven methods," which are then widely disseminated to clinicians, cheerleader science writers, and the public. Once a clinician or oncologist becomes associated with "unproven methods," he or she is blackballed by the cancer establishment. Funding for the accused "quack" becomes inaccessible, followed by systematic harassment.

The highly biased ACS witch-hunts against alternative practitioners is in striking contrast to its extravagant and uncritical endorsement of conventional toxic chemotherapy. This in spite of the absence of any objective evidence of improved survival rates or reduced mortality following chemotherapy for all but some relatively rare cancers.

In response to pressure from People Against Cancer, a grassroots group of cancer patients disillusioned with conventional cancer therapy, in 1986 some 40 members of Congress requested the Office of Technology Assessment (OTA), a Congressional think tank, to evaluate available information on alternative innovative therapies. While initially resistant, OTA eventually published a September 1990 report that identified some 200 promising studies on alternative therapies. OTA concluded that the NCI had "a mandated responsibility to pursue this information and facilitate examination of widely used 'unconventional cancer treatments' for therapeutic potential" (14).

Yet the ACS and NCI remain resistant, if not frankly hostile, to OTA's recommendations. In the January 1991 issue of its *Cancer Journal for Clinicians* ACS referred to the Hoxsey therapy, a nontoxic combination of herb extracts developed in the 1940s by populist Harry Hoxsey, as a "worthless tonic for cancer." However, a detailed critique of Hoxsey's treatment by Dr. Patricia Spain Ward, a leading contributor to the OTA report, concluded just the opposite: "More recent literature leaves no doubt that Hoxsey's formula does indeed contain many plant substances of marked therapeutic activity" (13).

Nor is this the first time that the Society's claims of quackery have been called into question or discredited. A growing number of other innovative therapies originally attacked by the ACS have recently found less disfavor and even acceptance. These include hyperthermia, tumor necrosis factor (originally called Coley's toxin), hydrazine sulfate, and Burzynski's antineoplastons. Well over 100 promising alternative nonpatented and nontoxic therapies have already been identified (15). Clearly, such treatments merit clinical testing and evaluation by the NCI using similar statistical techniques and criteria as established for conventional chemotherapy. However, while the FDA has approved approximately 40 patented drugs for cancer treatment, it has still not approved a single nonpatented alternative drug.

Subsequent events have further isolated the ACS in its fixation on orthodox treatments. Bypassing the ACS and NCI, the National Institutes of Health in June 1992 opened a new Office of Alternative Medicine for the investigation of unconventional treatment of cancer and other diseases. Leading proponents of conventional therapy were invited to participate. The ACS refused and still (as of early 1999) refuses. The NCI grudgingly and nominally participates while actively attacking alternative therapy with its widely circulated *Cancer Information Services*. Meanwhile, the NCI's police partner, the FDA, uses its enforcement authority against distributors and practitioners of innovative and nontoxic therapies.

In an interesting development, the Center for Mind-Body Medicine in Washington, D.C., held a two-day conference on Comprehensive Cancer Care: Integrating Complementary and Alternative Medicine. According to Dr. James

Gordon, president of the Center and chair of the Program Advisory Council of the NIH Office of Alternative Medicine, the object of the conference was to bring together practitioners of mainstream and alternative medicine, together with cancer patients and high-ranking officials of the ACS and NCI. Dr. Gordon warned alternative practitioners that "they're going to need to get more rigorous with their work—to be accepted by the mainstream community" (16). However, no such warning was directed at the highly questionable claims by the NCI and ACS for the efficacy of conventional cancer chemotherapy. As significantly, criticism of the establishment's minimalistic priority for cancer prevention was effectively discouraged.

THE ROLE OF THE ACS IN THE
WAR AGAINST CANCER

The launching of the 1971 War Against Cancer provided the ACS with a well-exploited opportunity to pursue it own myopic and self-interested agenda. Its strategies remain based on two myths—that there has been dramatic progress in the treatment and cure of cancer, and that any increase in the incidence and mortality of cancer is due to aging of the population and smoking, while denying any significant role for involuntary exposures to industrial carcinogens in air, water, consumer products, and the workplace.

As the world's largest nonreligious "charity," with powerful allies in the private and public sectors, ACS policies and priorities remain unchanged. Despite periodic protests, threats of boycotts, and questions on its finances, the Society leadership responds with powerful public relations campaigns reflecting denial and manipulated information and pillorying its opponents with scientific McCarthyism.

The verdict is unassailable. The ACS bears a major responsibility for losing the winnable war against cancer. Reforming the ACS is, in principle, relatively easy and directly achievable. Boycott the ACS. Instead, give your charitable contributions to public interest and environmental groups involved in cancer prevention. Such a boycott is well overdue and will send the only message this "charity" can no longer ignore. The Cancer Prevention Coalition (chaired by the author) in April 1999 formally announced a nationwide campaign for an economic boycott of the ACS (http://www.preventcancer.com).

Note — Samuel Epstein received the Project Censored Award, popularly known as the Alternative Pulitzer Prize, for this chapter, as originally published in *IJHS*. The chapter is modified from Chapters 16 and 18 of *The Politics of Cancer—Revisited,* East Ridge Press, New York, 1998.

LEGISLATIVE PROPOSALS FOR REVERSING THE CANCER EPIDEMIC AND CONTROLLING RUN-AWAY INDUSTRIAL TECHNOLOGIES

LOSING THE WINNABLE WAR AGAINST CANCER

We are losing the winnable war against cancer (1, 2). Over recent decades, the age-standardized incidence of cancer in industrialized nations has escalated to epidemic proportions, with lifetime cancer risks in the United States now approaching one in two for men and one in three for women. The overall increase of all cancers in the United States from 1950 to 1995 was 55 percent, of which lung cancer, primarily attributed to smoking, accounted for about 12 percent. Over the same period, non-smoking-related cancers increased as follows: prostate cancer, non-Hodgkin's lymphoma, and multiple myeloma, 200 percent; testicular cancer, 110 percent; brain and nervous system cancer, 80 percent; breast and male colon cancer, 60 percent; and childhood cancer, 20 percent. Similarly, a survey of 15 other major industrialized nations has shown that non-smoking-related cancers are responsible for about 75 percent of the overall increased incidence of cancer since 1950.

While cancer rates have escalated, our ability to treat and "cure" most cancers, with the notable exception of the relatively rare childhood and testicular cancers, has, contrary to general impressions, remained largely unchanged for decades.

The modern cancer epidemic cannot be explained away on the basis of increasing longevity, because incidence and mortality rates are adjusted (age-standardized) in cancer registries to reflect this trend. Nor can the epidemic be largely attributed to faulty personal lifestyle factors. Although smoking is clearly the single most important cause of cancer, the incidence of lung cancer in men, but not women, is declining because of a reduction in smoking, while the incidence of a wide range of non-smoking-related cancers is increasing at proportionately greater rates. Nor can the role of high-fat diets be incriminated as a major cause of

Published in *International Journal of Health Services*, Volume 30, Number 2, 2000.

cancer, in sharp contrast to heart disease. Illustratively, not only are breast cancer rates in Mediterranean countries low despite diets with up to 40 percent olive oil fat, but epidemiological studies over the past two decades have consistently failed to establish any causal relationship between breast cancer and the consumption of fat per se, excluding consideration of meat and dairy fats heavily contaminated with carcinogenic pesticides and industrial pollutants (2). Finally, increasing cancer rates cannot be attributed to genetic factors, which are directly implicated in, at most, well under 10 percent of all cancers; the genetics of human populations cannot possibly have changed within the last few decades.

What, then, is the predominant cause of the modern cancer epidemic? The answer is based on a strong body of scientific evidence pointing to the role of run-away industrial technologies, particularly in the petrochemical and radio-nuclear industries, whose explosive growth since the 1940s has, to varying degrees in different nations, outstripped the development of social control infrastructures and mechanisms. As a result, our total environment—air, water, consumer and medicinal products, and the workplace—has become pervasively contaminated with a wide range of often persistent industrial carcinogens. Thus the public at large is unknowingly exposed to avoidable chemical and radionuclear carcinogens from conception to death.

How have those institutions charged with responsibility for fighting the war against cancer responded to this crisis? In the United States, the predominant complex of responsible institutions, the "cancer establishment," is comprised of the governmental National Cancer Institute (NCI) and the private "charity," the American Cancer Society (ACS), together with their national network of funded university scientists and Comprehensive Cancer Centers. The cancer establishment has massive resources at its disposal. The 1999 budget of the NCI was $2.8 billion, up from $220 million in 1971 when President Nixon declared the "War Against Cancer" in response to cancer establishment pressures and demands for increased funding, with the highly misleading promise that this would enable the conquest of cancer by 1987. With ACS support, the NCI is now (as of early 2000) aggressively lobbying to increase its budget still further, to $5 billion by 2003. The current budget of the ACS is about $580 million, with cash reserves and other assets of $800 million.

The policies and priorities of the cancer establishment are narrowly fixated on damage control—diagnosis and treatment—and basic molecular research with indifference, not always benign, to cancer prevention. For the ACS, this indifference reaches the level of overt hostility (3, 4) (see also Chapter 5). These and other concerns relating to fiscal malpractice have led the *Chronicle of Philanthropy,* the authoritative U.S. charity watchdog, to charge that the ACS is "more interested in accumulating wealth than saving lives." The NCI's budgetary allocation for occupational cancer, the most avoidable of all cancers—which according to conservative estimates is responsible for about 10 percent of all U.S. cancer deaths, besides being a major cause of childhood cancer—is only 1 percent.

The budget for research and outreach on African-American and other ethnic minorities, with their disproportionately high cancer rates, is also only 1 percent of the NCI's $2.8 billion annual funding. Allocations for all primary prevention activities, smoking apart, are well under 5 percent.

The cancer establishment's professional mindset and priorities are compounded by disturbing conflicts of interest, particularly for the ACS, with the cancer drug and other industries. As the NCI's previous director Dr. Samuel Broder recently admitted, the NCI has become "what amounts to a governmental pharmaceutical company." The establishment's myopic mindset is further illustrated by a succession of widely publicized misleading claims to have turned "the tide against cancer" and for the latest "miracle" or "magic bullet" cancer drugs, claims that have rarely been subsequently substantiated over the last four decades.

Most seriously, the poorly accountable U.S. cancer establishment has failed to provide Congress, regulatory agencies, and the public with available scientific information on a wide range of avoidable carcinogenic exposures. As a result, corrective legislative and regulatory action has still not been taken, and the public has been and still is denied its right to know of such information and the opportunity to take action to reduce its risks of cancer. At the same time, the U.S. and other cancer establishments, explicitly relying on obsolete evidence and biased claims by industry-indentured academic and institutional apologists in the United States and United Kingdom, particularly Sir Richard Doll (1, 5), still seek to trivialize escalating cancer rates and to explain them away on the virtually exclusive basis of "blame-the-victim" or faulty lifestyle causation, coupled with "guesstimates" to the effect that "pollution [and] industrial products" account for only 3 percent of cancer mortality. The reliability of Doll as the alleged leading international expert on public health and cancer causation is even more strikingly challenged by his invidiously unique insistence that neither leaded petroleum nor low-level radiation nor dioxin pose any public health hazards (5).

Based on a fully documented, published analysis of such evidence, the U.S. and U.K. cancer establishments have recently been charged with major responsibility for losing the winnable war against cancer (1). This serious charge against the NCI and ACS comes as no surprise, having first been raised at a February 4, 1992, press conference held in Washington, D.C., by an ad hoc coalition of some 65 leading U.S. experts in public health, preventive medicine, and cancer prevention, including past directors of three major federal agencies (see Chapter 2, Part A). These concerns are all the more serious in view of the strong influence exerted by U.S. cancer establishment policies on those of Canada, the United Kingdom, and other nations worldwide, and their mutually reinforcing and interlocking relationships. As disclosed at a September 13, 1999, London press conference, the policies of the U.K. cancer charities are as gravely derelict as those of the United States (6). We are thus faced with an unparalleled crisis of international proportions and one that will be further exacerbated with the growing industrialization of relatively underdeveloped European nations, such as Greece, Spain, and Portugal, besides "lesser developed" Asiatic and other nations.

A series of six legislative proposals has been developed to address these critical concerns. While one or two of these are under consideration, to varying degrees, in some Parliaments worldwide, most appear unprecedented. These proposals form an interlocking complex, the whole of which is greater than the sum of its parts.

While these proposals are primarily directed to cancer and avoidable and involuntary carcinogenic exposures, we should keep in mind that the majority of carcinogens also induce other chronic toxic effects—including reproductive, endocrine disruptive, neurotoxic, and immunotoxic—for which there are no comparable systematic data on incidence trends, thus limiting correlative analysis. Cancer in effect thus represents a quantifiable paradigm of the adverse public health effects of run-away industrial technologies, as well as a paradigm of failed democratic decision making. A reduction of cancer rates per se will most likely be paralleled by a reduction in the incidence of other chronic, environmentally induced diseases.

It should come as no surprise that these legislative proposals are also highly applicable to the potential and poorly predictable, untested public health and environmental impacts of unrelated emerging industrial technologies, particularly genetically engineered food production.

PROHIBITION OF AUTHORIZATION OF NEW CARCINOGENIC PRODUCTS AND UNTESTED NEW TECHNOLOGIES

Under the terms of the 1948 U.N. Universal Declaration of Human Rights, the right to life and its corollary right to health are the first and most important of all fundament rights recognized by many international conventions. Thus, implementary legislation is needed to mandate that considerations of life and health take absolute precedence over economics and trade.

The first line of defense against risks from avoidable carcinogenic and otherwise toxic exposures is an absolute prohibition of further increasing the burden of current exposures due to the authorization of new carcinogenic products and processes. Such a prohibition is based on the obvious "Precautionary Principle" that preventing new risks and following zero-risk policies are essential for public and environmental protection. As such, this "Principle" is particularly relevant to genetically engineered food, for which industry claims of safety are based on "trust us" assurances rather than published scientific data.

The Precautionary Principle was first politically invoked by the German government, at the Second North Sea Conference in 1994, in relation to marine dumping of toxic wastes (7). Such policies are clearly preferable to deliberately accepting risks and then attempting to "manage" them by reducing exposures to levels claimed "acceptable" by self-interested industry or complicit regulatory agencies. While recognizing the sovereign rights of each nation to set its own levels of sanitary protection, zero-risk policies must constitute the standard principle and not the rare exception, as is current practice. In this connection, it may be noted that French President Jacques Chirac, at a 1998 meeting of the World Conservation Union, proposed increasing the powers of the U.N. Environment Program to avoid sovereignty disputes that hamper the global fight against pollution. President Chirac warned that countries were holding on to an outdated idea of sovereignty, while environmental pollution ignored national borders.

The Precautionary Principle would thus mandate the categorical responsibility of industry to provide unequivocal evidence on the safety of any new product and process, thereby ensuring that it does not pose potential or recognized human or environmental risks. This principle further absolves citizens and regulatory agencies from the heavy burden of proving risks in response to industry challenges, and allows the banning of suspect products in circumstances of scientific uncertainty. The raw data on which industry claims of safety are based, apart from their interpretation, must be fully disclosed and evaluated at industry's expense by an independent agency with qualified representation of nongovernmental organizations (NGOs). This is essential to exclude bias or manipulation, for which there is a well-documented and decades-old track record in a wide range of petrochemical and other industries (8). An illustrative recent example is afforded by the review of 161 studies in the National Library of Medicine files on four heavily regulated industrial chemicals—formaldehyde, perchloroethylene, atrazine, and alachlor. While only 14 percent of industry studies reported toxic or carcinogenic effects, such effects were disclosed in 71 percent of independent studies (9). The recent announcement by the U.S. Chemical Manufacturers Association of a new, $1 billion safety testing program merits skepticism rather than reassurance, compounded by the program's being headed by Dr. Roger McLennan. Over the last decade, McLennan has worked hard to disprove the overwhelming evidence on the cancer risks of diesel exhaust, and before that he worked for the Chemical Industry Institute of Toxicology, whose major function was to challenge or attempt to explain away evidence on the carcinogenicity of profitable industrial chemicals.

REDUCTION OF TOXICS IN USE

The second line of defense against avoidable carcinogenic exposures is the reduction or phase-out of toxics in use in the wide range of petrochemical and other carcinogenic products and processes already established in commerce. Strategies based on reduction in the use of toxics—phasing out the manufacture, use, and disposal of carcinogenic and otherwise toxic chemicals, coupled with their replacement by safe alternative technologies—are not only practical but cost-effective. The effectiveness of such strategies clearly depends on the establishment of an explicitly defined, strict schedule for the shortest feasible phase-out time and for monitoring industry compliance.

Such initiatives were strongly endorsed at the February 4, 1992, press conference. Among recommendations for reforming the U.S. cancer establishment and reorienting its priorities to cancer prevention, major emphasis was directed to a reduction in toxics use (1):

> In close cooperation with key regulatory agencies and industry, the NCI should initiate large scale research programs to develop non-carcinogenic products and processes as alternatives to those currently based on chemical and physical carcinogens. This program should also include research on the development of economic incentives for the reduction or phase out of the use of industrial carcinogens, coupled with economic disincentives for their continued use, especially when appropriate non-carcinogenic alternatives are available.

It should be stressed that toxics use reduction is based on the principle of risk prevention, in sharp contrast to the "risk management" strategies strongly favored by industry; a growing battery of handsomely funded industry think tanks, such as the Harvard Center for Risk Analysis and the International Life Sciences Institute, specializing in "risk assessment"; and complicit regulatory agencies. Risk management accepts the inevitability of risk from industrial processes and products while claiming that such risks can be managed to levels variously described as "acceptable" or "insignificant" or "minimal." These claims are derived from highly dubious, if not manipulated, risk-assessment mathematical formulas, shaped by predetermined financial or regulatory interest, claiming to predict minimal deaths expected from any particular carcinogenic exposure.

Following a well-organized political campaign by environmental groups, the Commonwealth of Massachusetts unanimously passed the Toxics Use Reduction Act in 1989, which created the Massachusetts Toxics Use Reduction Program (10). The Act is a specific form of pollution prevention that focuses on reducing the use of toxic chemicals and generation of hazardous waste by improving and redesigning industrial products and processes. The Toxics Use Reduction Institute of the University of Massachusetts, Lowell, played an important role in developing the Act by providing education, training, research on new materials and processes, a technical library and information source, and specialized laboratories for evaluating alternative safe technologies. The achievements of this Act include reducing the generation of toxic wastes from 1989 to 1997 by 50 percent by reducing toxics use by 20 percent; establishing toxics use reduction as the preferred means for achieving compliance with federal and state environmental statutes; promoting reduction in the production and use of toxic chemicals; enhancing and strengthening the enforcement of existing environmental laws; promoting coordination between state agencies administering toxics-related programs; and sustaining and promoting the competitiveness of Massachusetts industry (11).

The Massachusetts Act could also serve as a useful model for national and state U.S. and international legislation. The active interest of mainstream industry in such initiatives could well be encouraged by granting tax incentives for the urgent development of safe alternatives to toxic-based conventional technologies, and assessing tax penalties for failure to adopt available safe alternative technologies.

The relatively new trend to voluntary and economy-driven corporate environmentalism, however, may prove more potent than ideologically and legislatively driven toxics use reduction (12). A major development in this trend is the selling of services and functions rather than products (13, 14). For instance, the Atlanta-based U.S. company Interface Inc. leases floor-covering services and recycles old carpets rather than selling carpets that otherwise must eventually be incinerated or dumped in landfills. Similarly, Xerox now leases copiers and recycles old models. A parallel development is Eco-efficiency and Pollution Prevention (E2 P2), typified by the growing investment of Royal Dutch Shell, Amoco, and British Petroleum in renewable, sustainable energy sources, including wind, solar power, and fuel cells, and in extending product ranges to improved gasoline mixes (15). While cynicism from citizen groups may be reasonably anticipated, given the past environmental track record of these companies, these initiatives should nevertheless be welcomed. In addition, the potential mutually reinforcing role of legislative and marketplace pressures should be fully recognized.

A further example of the role of marketplace pressures that merits legislative recognition and support relates to consumer products—food, cosmetics and toiletries, and household products. The growth of organic and nontoxic non-mainstream products in U.S. markets has reached double-digit annual figures over the last decade. A 1995 published rating of some 4,000 conventional mainstream and safe non-mainstream products for undisclosed carcinogenic ingredients and contaminants resulted in a significant market shift away from hazardous to safe products, which are becoming increasingly price competitive (1, Appendix XIV; 16). Clearly, such health-driven marketplace pressures depend on a fully informed public that recognizes its right to know of involuntary and avoidable exposures to carcinogens in consumer products, as well as in the air, water, and workplace. Such knowledge and concerns have recently been reflected by the success of expensive safe products. Illustrative are the booming sales of a leading sportswear manufacturer, Patagonia, which has completely converted to organic cotton by using well-established integrated pest management strategies (12); this is particularly important as cotton is the most pesticide-intensive U.S. crop, accounting for 10 percent of all national pesticide use. These concepts have recently been amplified and extended into a new paradigm for a system called "natural capitalism," which has set a landmark agenda for a rational and ecologically sound concept of industrial development (17).

RIGHT TO KNOW

The right to know is, or should be, an inalienable and fundamental demo-cratic principle, with the probable exception of national security concerns. Industry claims of confidentiality and trade secrecy are often a serious deterrent to the recognition of potential risks from carcinogenic and otherwise toxic products. There is thus an urgent need to develop international rules to restrict claims of confidentiality to what is unarguably essential to protect independently validated proprietary information, exclusive of any health considerations. All other information on the carcinogenic and otherwise toxic risks of a product, drug, or process must be automatically and fully released and made fully avail-able to the public. It should be emphasized, however, that with limited exceptions, the right to know in most nations is more honored in the breach than in the observance.

The greatest incentive to reducing toxics use is public knowledge of their identity and routes of avoidable exposure, particularly when safe alternatives are available. Right-to-know initiatives are thus among the most practical and potent political strategies in the war against cancer and against untested new products and technologies. Critical steps in this direction have already been developed in Europe with recent requirements for the labeling of genetically engineered foods.

However, labeling per se is inadequate unless accompanied by an explicit "Red Flag" warning of recognized cancer and other health, environmental, and occupational risks and also of poorly defined or potential risks, as is the case with genetically engineered foods. Furthermore, labeling should not be used as a justifi-cation for authorizing new carcinogens or for the continuing use of carcinogenic products already in commerce. Labeling is no substitute for a moratorium or a ban. Labeling not only discriminates against uneducated and lower socioeconomic population groups, but may encourage industry to target such groups and penetrate national markets by price-regulation strategies.

Consumer Products

Mainstream industry consumer products—foods and beverages, cosmetics and toiletries, and household products including home, lawn, and garden pesticides—contain a wide range of undisclosed carcinogens (ingredients, contaminants, and precursors) that pose major, but generally unrecognized, avoidable risks of cancer.

Examples of carcinogens in 12 common consumer products, "The Dirty Dozen," none of them labeled with any cancer warning, are listed in Table 1, (on page 102) (1, Table 17.4 and Appendix XIV). The gravity of these risks is illus-trated by the following few examples:

- Beef frankfurters: Children eating up to about a dozen each month are at an approximately fourfold risk of brain cancer and sevenfold risk of leukemia.
- Talc: Women, in the reproductive years, regularly dusting their genital area with talc after bathing or showering are at about a threefold risk of developing ovarian cancer.
- Permanent hair color: Women using permanent or semi-permanent black or dark brown hair dyes are at increased risk for non-Hodgkin's lymphoma, multiple myeloma, chronic leukemia, and breast cancer. In fact, growing evidence suggests that use of these hair dyes accounts for about 20 percent of all non-Hodgkin's lymphomas in U.S. women.

Consumer product legislation is well overdue. All foods grown with the application of carcinogenic pesticides should be clearly labeled with a cancer warning, the name of each carcinogenic pesticide, and the concentrations of its residues. Of particular concern are the high residues of multiple carcinogenic pesticides in grains, vegetables, and fruit. Recent estimates indicate that by the age of one, cancer risks from residues of just eight common pesticides in 20 infant foods exceed lifetime "acceptable" cancer risks estimated by the U.S. Environmental Protection Agency. The complete chemical composition of all cosmetics and toiletries should be clearly labeled, and all carcinogenic ingredients, contaminants, and precursors should be identified, together with a cancer warning against each. The complete composition of all household cleaning and other products, including home, lawn, and garden pesticides, should also be clearly labeled, together with "Red Flag" cancer warnings for each listed carcinogenic ingredient. Consumer product legislation should require data and affidavits in support of claims of safety for organic or other products. Consideration should also be given to the granting of tax incentives to the manufacturers of safe alternative products.

Prescription Drugs

A recent survey of 241 high-volume U.S. prescription drugs reported that nearly half posed cancer risks based on carcinogenicity tests designed by their manufacturers to prove safety (18). Many carcinogenic drugs have been identified at low-test dosages, near or at therapeutic levels. These risks are compounded because carcinogenic drugs are often administered individually or in various combinations to tens of millions of patients, sometimes for decades and starting in childhood. One leading authority has claimed that prescription drugs may pose the single most important class of unrecognized and avoidable carcinogenic risks for the entire U.S. population (18).

To argue that such risks are more than justified by the very real benefits of these drugs is to posit a false dilemma, especially given that patients are rarely affirmatively and explicitly informed of these risks and of the availability of safer and effective alternatives. Legislation is urgently required to ensure that the

Table 1

The "Dirty Dozen" consumer products

FOOD

Beef frankfurters (e.g., Oscar Mayer Foods Corporation)
Unlabeled toxic ingredients: *benzene hexachloride,* carcinogenic; *dacthal,* carcinogenic (can be contaminated with dioxin); *dieldrin,* carcinogenic; *DDT,* carcinogenic;
heptachlor, carcinogenic; *hexachlorobenzene,* carcinogenic; *lindane,* carcinogenic;
hormones, carcinogenic and feminizing; *antibiotics,* some are carcinogenic, e.g.,
sulfamethazine.
Labeled toxic ingredient: nitrite, interacts with meat amines to form carcinogenic
nitrosamines
NOTE: Substantive evidence of causal relation to childhood cancer.

Whole milk (e.g., Borden or Lucerne)
Unlabeled toxic ingredients: *DDT,* carcinogenic; *dieldrin,* carcinogenic; *heptachlor,*
carcinogenic; *hexachlorobenzene,* carcinogenic; *antibiotics,* some are carcinogenic;
recombinant bovine growth hormone and IGF-1, evidence of breast, prostate, and
colon cancer promotion.

COSMETICS and TOILETRIES

Talcum powder (e.g., Johnson & Johnson, Inc.)
Labeled toxic ingredient: *talc,* carcinogenic.
NOTE: Substantive evidence of causal relation to ovarian cancer.

Cover Girl Replenishing Natural Finish Make-up (Foundation) (Procter &
Gamble, Inc.)
Labeled toxic ingredients: *BHA,* carcinogenic; *talc,* carcinogenic; *titanium dioxide,*
carcinogenic; *triethanolamine (TEA),* interacts with nitrites to form carcinogenic
nitrosamines; *lanolin,* often contaminated with DDT and other carcinogenic
pesticides.

Crest Tartar Control Toothpaste (Procter & Gamble, Inc.)
Labeled toxic ingredients: *FD & C Blue #1,* carcinogenic; *saccharin,* carcinogenic;
fluoride, possible carcinogen.

Alberto VO5 Conditioner (Essence of Neutral Henna) (Alberto-Culver USA, Inc.)
Labeled toxic ingredients: *formaldehyde,* carcinogenic; *polysorbate 80,* can be contaminated with the carcinogen 1,4-dioxane; *FD & C Red #4,* carcinogenic.

Clairol Nice 'n Easy (Permanent Haircolor) (Clairol, Inc.)
Labeled toxic ingredients: *quaternium-15,* formaldehyde releaser, carcinogenic;
diethanolamine (DEA), interacts with nitrites to form a carcinogenic nitrosamine;
phenylene-diamines, include carcinogens and other ingredients inadequately tested
for carcinogenicity.
NOTE: Substantive evidence of causal relation to lymphoma, multiple myeloma, and
other cancers.

Table 1

(Cont'd.)

HOUSEHOLD PRODUCTS

Ajax Cleanser (Colgate-Palmolive, Inc.)
Unlabeled toxic ingredient: *crystalline silica,* carcinogenic.

Zud Heavy Duty Cleanser (Reckitt & Colman, Inc.)
Unlabeled toxic ingredient: *crystalline silica,* carcinogenic.

Lysol Disinfectant Spray (Reckitt & Colman, Inc.)
Labeled or unlabeled toxic ingredient: *orthophenylphenol (OPP),* carcinogenic.

Zodiac Cat & Dog Flea Collar (Sandoz Agro, Inc.)
Labeled toxic ingredient: *propoxur,* carcinogenic.

Ortho Weed-B-Gon Lawn Weed Killer (Monsanto Co.)
Labeled toxic ingredient: *sodium 2,4-dichlorophenoxyacetic acid (2,4-D),* carcinogenic.
NOTE: Substantive evidence of causal relation to lymphoma, soft tissue sarcoma, and other cancers.

---

pharmaceutical industry provides clear and explicit information on carcinogenic prescription and nonprescription drugs, which should also be labeled with clear warnings of such risks. Physicians should also be required to endorse these warnings, provide patients with information on safe and effective alternatives, and be held accountable for failure to do so.

Occupational Cancer

In addition to the use of controlled production and closed-system technologies and other control systems including local exhaust ventilation, workers and their representatives have inalienable rights to full information on the identity of all carcinogens, including raw materials, intermediates, impurities, and final products, to which they are exposed, provided by explicit labeling and posting. Additionally, they are entitled to quantitative information on levels of inhalation and skin exposure for each carcinogen. All such information should be made available to workers daily and should be reported to the responsible regulatory authorities.

Environmental Cancer

Citizens are entitled to full access to information from local and national government on their avoidable carcinogenic exposures from air and water. Such information is likely to encourage industry to reduce environmental emissions and discharges of carcinogenic and toxic pollutants and also to encourage more stringent governmental regulation.

Every regional municipal authority should be required to provide consumers with a complete list of carcinogenic contaminants and their concentrations in drinking water, enclosed with each water bill. Similarly, every chemical, mining, and nuclear industry should be required to disclose to local communities and regional and national governments a complete listing of all carcinogens, including intermediates and products, that they use, process, manufacture, and dispose of. They should also be required to disclose the amounts of each carcinogen they discharge into surrounding air and water. No industry should be allowed to operate unless it provides ongoing quantitative information on smokestack and other atmospheric emissions of carcinogens in the air of its perimeter and in the local community.

DECISION MAKING ON CANCER AND RELATED PUBLIC HEALTH EFFECTS

Key governmental decisions and policies are generally determined by recommendations of cancer institutions, designated expert scientific committees, and regulatory bodies. The independence, integrity, expertise, and accountability of these groups are thus matters of critical concern.

All institutions comprising the cancer establishment and receiving government or other tax-exempt funds should be required to provide clear and audited budgetary statements defining their sources of funding and their expenditures on basic molecular research, diagnosis and treatment, and primary prevention.

Budgetary information on prevention should specify allocations for the following: (*a*) research primarily directed to investigating avoidable causes of cancer; (*b*) research on all possible risk factors for each type of cancer whose incidence has increased substantially over recent decades; (*c*) research on cancer risks from carcinogens identified in well-designed animal tests and/or listed by the International Agency for Research on Cancer; (*d*) activities directed toward the development of a comprehensive registry for all carcinogens to which general populations and populations at high risk may be exposed; and (*e*) outreach activities providing Congress or Parliament, governmental agencies, and the public with available information on all avoidable carcinogenic exposures and the actions that may be taken to reduce or avoid such exposures.

Legislation to ensure full accountability and transparency of all cancer institutions involved in cancer research and related activities is long overdue. Legislation is also needed to ensure that cancer institutions direct the highest priorities, with at least half their budgets specifically allocated to research and outreach on primary cancer prevention. As an examination of the track records of the U.S. and U.K. cancer establishments makes clear, only drastic reforms of their policies, priorities, and leadership will achieve such objectives and belatedly restore an overdue sense of mission and balance to winning the losing war against cancer.

The 1972 U.S. Federal Advisory Committee Act requires that the composition of regulatory agency advisory committees reflect balanced and qualified representation of all concerned interests, and meetings be publicized in advance and open to the public (19). However, in practice, these requirements are generally honored more in the breach than the observance.

In a 1997 U.S. and Canadian challenge against the E.U. ban on hormonal meat before the World Trade Organization, the 134-nation trade regulatory authority, I served together with other international scientists as public health consultant to the European Union in defense of its ban. Apart from documenting the scientific evidence on the cancer and other risks from high residues of unmonitored sex hormones in meat, I analyzed the reports and composition of the relevant Food and Agriculture/World Health Organizations (FAO/WHO) committees, particularly the 1988 Joint Expert Committee on Food Additives (JECFA) on whose authority the U.S. and Canadian legal action was largely based, all of which had claimed that hormonal meat was safe. On the basis of this analysis, I concluded (1, Appendix XI):

> The membership of these committees reflects disproportionate representation of U.S. senior regulatory officials and of veterinary and food scientists, with minimal if any involvement of independent experts in preventive medicine, public health and carcinogenesis. The European Commission Scientific Conference of November 29–December 1, 1995 also reflects such imbalanced representation. While Conference participation of "scientists directly employed" by industry was "generally refused," no apparent attempt was made to identify or exclude industry consultants, contractees or grantees. Furthermore, the Conference based its findings and conclusions largely on unpublished industry data.

The FAO/WHO advisory committees thus clearly represent a sanitized front for powerful industry interests and predetermined regulatory decisions, rather than sound science and consumer safety (20). Similar concerns relate to the February 1998 JECFA committee report and the September 1998 Codex Committee on Veterinary Drugs in Foods report, both of which concluded that genetically engineered (rBGH/rBST) milk is safe in spite of strong published evidence to the contrary (1, Appendix XII).

Clearly, legislation is needed to require that expert scientific committees, such as JECFA, and regulatory agencies, such as the Codex Alimentarius, International Office of Epizootics, FAO, and WHO/International Labor Organization (ILO), that deal with health and environmental concerns conform to basic requirements to ensure unbiased and sound scientific findings and appropriate subsequent regulatory decisions (20, 21). Examination of the structure of the WHO/ILO committee on asbestos over recent years is illustrative of extreme pro-industry representation, bias, and reckless indifference to occupational safety and health. Past experience clearly confirms that scientists appointed to expert committees exclusively by administrative or regulatory agencies are rarely, if ever, impartial and objective, apart from serious questions on their competence, qualifications, and standing in the independent scientific community. These considerations apply particularly to the World Trade Organization, the current global regulatory authority.

Absolute rights should be given by law to grant consumer, environmental, occupational, cancer prevention, and other concerned NGOs full membership on scientific and advisory committees. They should also be given full right to participate in the evaluation and selection of scientists performing risk assessment, and also financial support to appoint their own experts to work with scientific and regulatory committees charged with safety evaluation of industrial products and processes, medicinal drugs, consumer products, and emerging technologies, notably genetically engineered foods.

Similar and equally rigorous legislation is needed for executive, advisory, and scientific committees of all cancer institutions (governmental, charitable, and academic) to ensure full accountability and transparency of their deliberations and to ensure that maximal priority is directed to cancer prevention, rather than virtually exclusively to damage control—diagnosis and treatment—and basic molecular research.

Transparency of all scientific and regulatory proceedings should be further ensured by providing advanced public information on scheduled committee meetings that should be open without restriction to the public.

WHITE-COLLAR CRIME

There is an overwhelming disparity between the full force of criminal law and punishment directed at perpetrators of theft, property damage, or personal violence and the lenient civil proceedings against industry managers and executives and their consultants who knowingly manipulate, distort, or suppress information on the environmental, occupational, and consumer hazards of their products and processes. As Ralph Nader has aptly commented, there are two standards of justice in modern industrialized society: "jail for crime in the streets, but bail for crime in the suites." This flagrant inequity in our dual system of justice is exacerbated by major socioeconomic differences between the two classes of offenders, notably the differences in opportunity, education, income, and social standing. Furthermore, the obvious one-to-one direct and immediate impact of blue-collar crime on a single victim is generally in striking contrast to white-collar industry crime, the effects of which are largely sanitized by the nonpersonal and indirect relationship between the criminal and the multiple victims, often numbering in the many thousands, and by the usually long latency between crime and effect.

Over two decades ago, Congressman John Conyers, the distinguished Democratic chairman of the U.S. Congress House Committee on the Judiciary, invited me to assist in drafting legislation and to testify on white-collar crime, as defined by "nondisclosure of certain matters by certain business entities and personnel," in relation to environmental and health concerns (22). Congressman Conyers's bill, which urged criminal penalties including imprisonment for such corporate crimes, was presented to Congress on July 26, 1979. However, its passage was blocked by Republican committee members, and it has not since been reintroduced.

In testimony on this proposed legislation, I stated (22):

> In my activities in the interface between science and public policy, I have had occasion to undertake detailed investigations of the regulatory data base of a wide range of consumer products and industrial chemicals. These investigations have revealed a pattern of constraints, including gross negligence, manipulation, distortion, suppression and destruction of data, which are so frequent as to preclude their dismissal as exceptional aberrations. Besides the businesses concerned, involved in the generation and interpretation of such constrained data are a complex of commercial testing and consulting laboratories and organizations and academic consultants, supported by a network of industry front organizations and quasi-professional societies. Such constrained data have served as the basis for the past and continuing successful strategies of some segments of the industry which have minimized or denied risk to workers and the public-at-large, and have maximized product or process efficacy and the apparent preoccupations with short term economic growth to the detriment of considerations of long term adverse public health and environmental impacts, have resulted in a burgeoning toll of cancer and other preventable diseases.
>
> These grave charges, including "knowing (acts of) nondisclosure," are not made lightly or speculatively. They pose fundamental questions of legal equity, besides reflecting the subversion of democratic decision making processes by special interests.
>
> The thrust of this bill is consistent with the finest traditions of American business. It offers business the timely opportunity to explicitly reassert its highest ethical standards and, by policing itself, to preclude or limit the need for further regulatory policing. Clearly, the bill imposes no unreasonable restraints on commerce or on technological innovation, but merely seeks to encourage honest disclosure of 'lethal defects,' and to deter and punish those who knowingly commit criminal acts on 'nondisclosure.' In so doing, the bill will discourage the introduction into commerce of products and processes with 'lethal defects,' with attendant major economic, dislocation following their subsequent withdrawal once these defects become belatedly recognized. Successful self-policing by business will act as a major brake to burgeoning product liability suits, such as those we are now experiencing for asbestos products. Finally, the bill offers a unique opportunity to restore the eroding public confidence in big business, in general, and the chemical industry, in particular, and thus to reverse the growing and nationally damaging trend of polarization and confrontation between business, and the general public and labor. Recognition of these various considerations and the overall favorable impact of this bill on business has been clearly recognized by Irving S. Shapiro, Chairman of E.I. DuPont de Nemours & Co. who, speaking on behalf

of the Business Roundtable, agreed in hearings of September 13, 1979 that
the same standard of criminal law should be applied to business executives
and corporations as for the general public and who, with the Justice Department, on November 28 [1979], approved a tough package of white collar
crime proposals.

In the absence of such legislative disincentives, white-collar crime affecting environmental and health safety has continued unabated and extended into global
markets. Such misconduct, which I have investigated over three decades and
have reported on in peer-reviewed scientific journals and otherwise publicized,
includes:

- Suppression and manipulation by Vesicol Chemical Company of data on the
  carcinogenic and other chronic toxic effects of the pesticides chlordane and heptachlor, which have been extensively used for termite treatment of wood (23).
- Monsanto's suppression and denial of clear evidence of adverse veterinary
  and public health effects of genetically engineered milk hormone (rBGH/
  rBST) and of excess levels of a growth factor, IGF-1, in hormonal milk, which
  poses serious cancer and other risks to consumers (1, Appendix XII).
- The undisclosed cancer risks of a wide range of consumer products.
- The cancer risks of silicone gel breast implants, particularly those coated with
  polyurethane foam, long-standing evidence of which has been suppressed
  by Dow Corning Company, Bristol-Myers Squibb, and other manufacturers, as well as by plastic surgeons and their professional associations
  (1, Appendix V; 24).
- Suppression by Eli Lilly Company of its own evidence on the grave risks of
  ovarian cancer from its aggressively promoted and advertised new drug
  Evista (raloxifene), used for the prevention of postmenopausal osteoporosis
  (1, Appendix V).

A 1990 publication, "Corporate Crime: Why We Cannot Trust Industry-Derived
Safety Studies" (23) (see Chapter 16), details evidence illustrating the gravity
and commonplace nature of these concerns, and warns:

> The control of pesticides, as of all synthetic chemicals, in most industrialized
> countries relies heavily or even entirely on safety data supplied by the manu-
> facturers. Such a regulatory system can only be effective if the companies
> conducting and reporting the studies honestly disclose any adverse findings.
> The record shows, however, that all too often company executives and their
> scientists knowingly suppress or manipulate information that could affect the
> licensing and sale of their products.

Among more recent examples of corporate misconduct is the reckless behavior
of the tobacco industry, now the subject of multiple federal, state, and civil
litigations. The most egregious of such conduct has been detailed in extensive

secret documents obtained from R. J. Reynolds Company in the course of civil litigation and released to the public in January 1998 (25). The Company's "Joe Camel" advertising campaign deliberately targeted underage smokers in calculated efforts to recruit lifetime adult smokers, most of whom start smoking or become addicted by the age of 18. With huge promotional expenditures from 1987 to 1998, R. J. Reynolds recruited about 560,000 underage U.S. smokers. No criminal charges have yet been brought against this industry despite the devastating scourge of future disease and death we can expect from the Camel campaign, including cancers of the lung and other sites, cardiovascular disease, stroke, chronic obstructive lung disease, and adverse complications of pregnancy, apart from inflationary medical costs and loss-of-productivity costs.

More serious than such corporate crime is professional white-collar crime of the U.S. and other cancer establishments. Despite mandated and avowed responsibility in all areas relating to cancer, and despite massive resources and the nation's misplaced trust, the NCI and ACS have failed for decades to inform the public, let alone Congress and national and global regulatory agencies, of well-documented scientific data on a wide range of avoidable cancers caused by undisclosed carcinogenic exposures, such as those in common consumer products (Table 1). Equally serious concerns extend to the irresponsible policies of the U.K. cancer establishment, notably the Cancer Research Campaign and the Imperial Cancer Research Fund (6). Another blatant example of the U.S. cancer establishment's grossly derelict conduct relates to its failure to warn healthy women aggressively recruited for chemoprevention trials for breast cancer with the highly profitable cancer drug tamoxifen—although evidence for such prevention is at best highly arguable—that the drug is a very potent liver carcinogen (1, Appendix V; 26). The willful suppression of this information poses major risks of cancer to healthy women and raises grave ethical and legal concerns that extend well beyond medical malpractice.

Clearly, white-collar environmental and health crime legislation is critically needed and well overdue worldwide. Congressman Conyers's 1979 bill could well serve as a useful model. Consideration should also be directed to the establishment of an International Public Health Crimes Court or Tribunal, modeled along the lines of the International War Crimes Tribunal, for the investigation and indictment of transnational corporations whose products and processes pose recognized or potential dangers to public health and environmental integrity.

Apart from criminal prosecution of white-collar crime, legislation is also needed to empower citizens who become aware of undisclosed carcinogenic hazards in consumer products to take civil action to enjoin their distribution and sale and to receive as a benefit a share of past illegal sales together with some type of mandatory financial sanctions. Precedents for such initiatives have been embodied in the Proposition 65 law passed by California in 1986. Similar laws have been enacted in other U.S. states.

INDEPENDENT CITIZEN SAFETY AGENCY

There are critical and long overdue needs for the establishment of an Independent Citizen Safety Agency. This agency should be given wide powers to police the effectiveness of current health and safety regulations and to act as intermediary between consumers, workers, and their NGOs on the one hand, and regulatory authorities and industry on the other. The agency should be empowered to establish a clearinghouse for receiving and evaluating complaints from individual consumers, workers, and their interest groups on all health-related issues; to collect, systematize, and evaluate new scientific data and assess their implications for current and proposed new regulations; and to publish and disseminate information, in explicit and simple language, on possible health and environmental risks from regulated products and processes and from the proposed authorization of new products and processes.

The agency should be fully independent and responsible only to Congress or Parliament. It should be established on the models of antitrust and cartel agencies, with wide powers of investigation, decision making, and fining of violators. The agency should be a public watchdog, an ombudsman with teeth, directly accountable only to Congress or Parliament.

Note — This chapter is largely based on a December 9, 1998, address to the Swedish Parliament on the occasion of my receipt of the 1998 Right Livelihood Award, popularly known as the Alternative Nobel Prize.

Chapter 7

THE CRISIS IN U.S. AND INTERNATIONAL CANCER POLICY

LOSING THE WINNABLE WAR AGAINST CANCER

Pressured by leading representatives of the cancer establishment, the National Cancer Institute (NCI) and the American Cancer Society (ACS), the U.S. Congress passed the National Cancer Act in 1971. The act launched the National Cancer Program, under the direction of the NCI, to attack and eradicate cancer and "to disseminate cancer information to the public." President Nixon enthusiastically embraced the act, and increased the NCI's budget from $149 to $223 million. Since then, the NCI's budget has increased nearly 30-fold, to $4.2 billion in 2002, with $4.6 billion authorized for 2003 (Table 1). In spite of these massively increased allocations, we are losing the winnable war against cancer.

Escalating Incidence of Cancer

Over recent decades, the incidence of cancer in the United States has escalated to epidemic proportions (1), now striking nearly one in two men (44 percent) and more than one in three women (38 percent). This increase translates into approximately 56 percent more cancer in men and 22 percent more cancer in women over the course of a single generation (2). As admitted by recent NCI and ACS estimates, the incidence of cancer will increase still further, doubling by 2050, with grave inflationary consequences (3).

From 1973 to 1999, based on the latest available data (1), the overall incidence of cancer rates at all sites, adjusted to reflect the aging population, increased approximately 24 percent (Table 2). Although the overall incidence of lung cancer increased 30 percent, it decreased 6 percent in men and increased 143 percent in women, reflecting major changes in smoking practices, apart from the well-recognized risks of passive smoking. Unquestionably, smoking remains the single most important cause of cancer. Particularly striking, however, was the increase of

Published in *International Journal of Health Services,* Volume 32, Number 4, 2002 (based on the Cancer Prevention Coalition "Stop Cancer Before It Starts Campaign" report.

Table 1

Growth of the National Cancer Institute budget from 1970 to 2002

Year	Budget, billions of dollars	Percent increase over previous period[a]
1970	0.149	
1971	0.223	49.7
1979	0.94	321.5
1992	1.8	91.5
1998	2.6	44.4
2002	4.2	61.5
2003	4.6 (authorized)	9.5

[a]Approximately 30-fold increase from 1970 to 2002.

predominantly non-smoking-related cancers, notably: malignant melanoma, 156 percent; liver cancer, 104 percent; non-Hodgkin's lymphoma, 87 percent; thyroid cancer, 71 percent; testicular cancer, 67 percent; postmenopausal breast cancer, 54 percent; brain cancer, 28 percent; and acute myeloid leukemia, 16 percent. Childhood cancers (age 0 to 14 years) increased 26 percent overall: acute lympho-cytic leukemia, 62 percent; brain, 50 percent; bone and joint, 40 percent; and kidney, 14 percent. Childhood cancers remain the number one killer of children other than accidents. The median age for the diagnosis of cancer is now 67 for adults and 6 for children.

During recent years, the incidence of lung cancer in men has decreased still more sharply, while that of non-smoking-related cancers has continued its steady increase (1). From 1992 to 1999, increasing rates included: thyroid cancer, 22 percent; malignant melanoma, 18 percent; acute myeloid leukemia, 13 percent; and postmenopausal breast cancer, 7 percent (Table 3). Childhood cancers increased 7 percent overall: bone and joint, 20 percent; leukemia, 18 percent; acute lymphocytic leukemia, 16 percent; and kidney, 14 percent.

These increasing U.S. cancer rates, particularly of non-smoking-related cancers, are also reflected in other major industrialized nations (4).

Misleading Assurances by the NCI and ACS

Despite the escalating incidence of overall and site-specific cancer rates from 1973 to 1999, and despite massively increased resources, the NCI and ACS have continued to make empty claims about major progress in the war against cancer.

In 1984, reacting to growing concerns about increasing cancer mortality rates, blamed on lack of funding and Congressional support, the NCI launched the "Cancer Prevention Awareness Program," claiming that this would halve the 1980 overall cancer mortality rate of 160 per 100,000 to 84 per 100,000 by 2000. This was followed by a 1986 NCI document, *Cancer Control Objectives,* which similarly claimed that the overall mortality rate of 167 per 100,000 would be halved by 2000. In fact, this rate has remained unchanged, other than a minor reduction due to the decrease in lung cancer resulting from reduced smoking by men.

On March 1998, at a heavily promoted Washington, D.C., press briefing, the NCI and ACS released their *Report Card* announcing a recent "reversal of an almost 20-year trend of increasing cancer cases, and deaths" (5). "These numbers are the first proof that we are on the right track," enthused then NCI director Dr. Richard Klausner. Media coverage was extensive and uncritical. The next day, a *New York Times* headline supportively announced "a sharp reversal of the incidence [of cancer, and that] the nation may have reached a turning point" in the war against cancer (6). The news could not have come at a better time for cancer researchers. Just as Congress began working on the 1999 biomedical budget, a group of experts announced that the U.S. had "turned the corner" in the war on cancer (6).

In fact, the "reversal" in the overall incidence of cancer from 1992 to 1998 was manipulated and minimal (about 7 percent). The decline was largely due to the reduction of lung cancer in men following their decreased smoking. Furthermore, any true decline would have been considerably less had incidence, as well as mortality, rates been more appropriately age-adjusted to the age distribution of the current population, rather than that of the 1970 population as misleadingly calculated by the NCI, with its relatively higher representation of younger age groups (7). Even the reduction of prostate cancer is highly questionable, as the *Report Card* authors admitted: "The decreased incidence rates [of prostate cancer] may be the result of decreased utilization of PSA screening tests" (5). The incidence of "prostate cancer" decreased approximately 20 percent (from 196 to 155 per 100,000) from 1992 to 1998. Moreover, the incidence rates for many non-smoking-related cancers continued to escalate sharply (Table 3) and to outweigh the decline in the incidence of lung cancer in men (1, 8).

Ignoring these criticisms, the cancer establishment persisted in making empty promises about winning the cancer war. The NCI's *Cancer Progress Report* for 2001 claimed that rates of new cancers and deaths were falling overall, while admitting that these declines largely reflected a reduction in smoking-related deaths in men (9). However, the report again ignored the sharply increased incidence rates, both overall and for a wide range of non-smoking-related cancers, from 1973 to 1999. As a leading critic on the politics and finance of science recently commented, "The good news about cancer must be emphasized and, if need be, manufactured, to keep up public spirits and support . . . for more money . . . without public interference in the use of the money" (10).

Table 2

Age-adjusted incidence rates (all races), per 100,000, 1973–1999

Primary site	1973	1999	Percent change
Oropharynx	13.1	10.3	−21.4
Esophagus	3.9	4.9	25.6
Stomach	13.1	8.4	−35.9
Colorectal	57.8	54.3	−6.1
Liver	2.7	5.5	103.7
Pancreas	12.3	10.7	−13.0
Larynx	5.1	4.1	−19.6
Lung	49.0	63.5	29.6
Males	85.9	81.1	−5.6
Females	20.9	50.7	142.6
Breast (all ages)	98.5	139.1	41.2
Under 50 years	39.1	43.0	10.0
Over 50 years	254.0	390.8	53.9
Cervix	17.2	8.0	−53.5
Uterus	31.7	25.1	−20.8
Ovary (all ages)	16.5	17.0	3.0
Under 65 years	11.5	11.1	−3.5
Over 65 years	50.4	57.8	14.7
Testis	3.3	5.5	66.7
Kidney	7.9	11.1	40.5
Bladder	18.1	21.2	17.1
Prostate	85.3	174.8	104.9
Brain	5.3	6.8	28.3
Thyroid	4.2	7.2	71.4
Malignant melanoma	6.8	17.4	155.9
Hodgkin's disease	3.4	2.8	−17.6
Non-Hodgkin's lymphoma	10.2	19.1	87.3
Multiple myeloma	4.6	5.0	8.7
Leukemias	12.5	11.2	−10.4
Acute myeloid	3.1	3.6	16.1
Childhood (0–14 years)[a]			
All sites	11.5	14.5	26.0
Bone and joint	0.5	0.6	20.0
Brain	2.3	3.4	50.2
Hodgkin's disease	0.7	0.4	−32.7
Kidney	0.7	0.8	14.2
Leukemias	3.3	4.7	44.5
Acute lymphocytic	2.2	3.6	61.7
Non-Hodgkin's lymphoma	1.0	0.8	−21.7

Table 2

(Cont'd.)

Primary site	1973	1999	Percent change
All sites, excluding lung	336.0	412.6	22.8
Males	362.6	474.7	30.9
Females	328.6	371.6	13.1
All sites	385.0	476.1	23.7
Males	448.5	555.8	23.9
Females	349.5	422.3	20.8

[a]Based on 1975–1999 data.

In May 2002, in a stunning reversal, the NCI and ACS suddenly abandoned their long-standing promises about winning the war against cancer. In their "Annual Report to the Nation," they admitted that *the incidence of cancer is expected to double by 2050 due to the aging population* (3). They made no reference, however, to the sharply increasing incidence, over the last three decades, of cancers in younger age groups, such as childhood and testicular cancers (Table 2).

MINIMAL RESEARCH ON PRIMARY PREVENTION

The research policies and priorities of the cancer establishment remain dominated by professional mindsets fixated on damage control (screening, diagnosis, and treatment) and molecular research. High priority for screening, or "secondary prevention," persists in spite of long-standing challenges (which have finally received headline coverage; see 11) to its questionable effectiveness for cancers such as prostate, lung, premenopausal breast cancers, and childhood neuroblastoma. Minimal emphasis on (and even indifference to) primary prevention remains, particularly research on avoidable causes of cancer other than those attributed to smoking and other lifestyle factors. This is in striking contrast to the cancer establishment's high priority for "secondary prevention," defined as screening, diagnosis, and "chemoprevention" by the use of vitamins or drugs such as tamoxifen, in generally futile attempts to reduce the effects of prior carcinogenic exposures. For the ACS, this indifference to primary prevention even includes hostility (see Appendix I, p. 136; see also Chapter 5).

Compounding these problems of professional mindsets are poorly recognized institutionalized conflicts of interest, particularly for the ACS. For decades, powerful groups of interlocking corporate interests, with the highly profitable cancer drug industry at their hub, have dominated the losing war against cancer.

Table 3

Age-adjusted incidence rates (all races), per 100,000, 1992–1999

Primary site	1992	1999	Percent change
Oropharynx	12.2	10.3	−15.6
Esophagus	4.6	4.9	6.5
Stomach	9.2	8.4	−8.7
Colorectal	58	54.3	−6.4
Liver	4.0	5.5	37.5
Pancreas	10.7	10.7	0.0
Larynx	5.0	4.1	−18.0
Lung	69.6	63.5	−8.8
Males	97.4	81.1	−16.7
Females	49.9	50.7	1.6
Breast (all ages)	132	139.1	5.4
Under 50 years	43.4	43	−0.9
Over 50 years	363.9	390.8	7.4
Cervix	10.0	8.0	−20.0
Uterus	24.8	25.1	1.2
Ovary (all ages)	17.6	17.0	−3.4
Under 65 years	11.8	11.1	−5.9
Over 65 years	58.0	57.8	−0.3
Testis	5.2	5.5	5.8
Kidney	10.7	11.1	3.7
Bladder	21.2	21.2	0.0
Prostate	235.9	174.8	−25.9
Brain	7.0	6.8	−2.9
Thyroid	5.9	7.2	22.0
Malignant melanoma	14.8	17.4	17.6
Hodgkin's disease	2.9	2.8	−3.4
Non-Hodgkin's lymphoma	18.6	19.1	2.7
Multiple myeloma	5.9	5.0	−15.3
Leukemias	12.8	11.2	−12.5
Acute myeloid	3.2	3.6	12.5
Childhood (0–14 years)[a]			
All sites	13.5	14.5	7.4
Bone and joint	0.5	0.6	20.0
Brain	3.2	3.4	6.2
Hodgkin's disease	0.5	0.4	−20.0
Kidney	0.7	0.8	14.3
Leukemias	4.0	4.7	17.5
Acute lymphocytic	3.1	3.6	16.1
Non-Hodgkin's lymphoma	0.8	0.8	0.0

Table 3

(Cont'd.)

Primary site	1992	1999	Percent change
All sites, excluding lung	441.6	412.6	−6.6
Males	558.1	474.7	−14.9
Females	367.5	371.6	1.1
All sites	511.2	476.1	−6.9
Males	655.5	555.8	−15.2
Females	417.4	422.3	1.2

In a surprisingly frank statement, Dr. Samuel Broder, NCI director from 1989 to 1995, stated the obvious: "The NCI has become what amounts to a government pharmaceutical company" (quoted in 12). Broder resigned from the NCI to become chief scientific officer of Ivax, subsequently moving to become chief medical officer of Celera Genomics; both companies are major manufacturers of cancer drugs. By linking their interests with those of major cancer drug companies, both the NCI and ACS have directed their priorities away from research on primary prevention toward a virtually exclusionary emphasis on damage control (see 13, for an extensive range of primary scientific and policy citations).

The cancer establishment has long insisted that faulty lifestyle, particularly smoking, inactivity, and fatty diet—excluding any recognition of contamination of animal fat with carcinogenic pesticides—is the predominant cause of cancer. This exclusionary or predominant lifestyle emphasis, also known as "blaming the victim," has been strongly reinforced by U.S. and international reliance on a biased and inept report on U.S. cancer mortality by U.K. epidemiologists Dr. Richard Doll and his protégé Richard Peto, published in 1981 (14). Over the last three decades, Doll's track record on primary prevention reveals strong pro-industry bias and conflicts of interest (see Appendix II, p. 139). In the absence of cited scientific data, Doll and Peto *guesstimated* that lifestyle factors are responsible for some 95 percent of all cancer mortality. This left a balance of 5 percent, which they arbitrarily assigned to occupation, pollution, and "industrial products," a belief to which they remain largely fixated. Strangely excluded from their guesstimates was any consideration of mortality of people over the age of 65 and African Americans—just those groups disproportionately affected by cancer—and any consideration of cancer incidence. Also excluded was any recognition of the substantial evidence that exposures to a wide range of carcinogenic occupational products and processes are, besides smoking, major causes of lung cancer (13). There is also clear evidence of additive or synergistic interactions between carcinogenic occupational exposures and smoking. Nevertheless, the NCI and

ACS continue to direct minimal research and emphasis to occupational and environmental causes of cancer, despite substantial data relating these factors to the escalating incidence of overall and site-specific cancers.

The cancer establishment's continued trivialization of the major impact of occupational cancer is particularly egregious. Based on National Institute of Occupational Safety and Health surveys, some 11 million men and 4 million women are involuntarily exposed to a wide range of occupational carcinogens, representing the single largest cause of avoidable cancer. A 1979 confidential report by consultants to the chemical industry trade association (the American Industrial Health Council) admitted that exposures to occupational carcinogens were responsible for at least 20 percent of all cancers and that they posed a "public health catastrophe" (15). Although this report was widely leaked, Doll and Peto ignored it. A more recent limited and conservative estimate concluded that occupational exposures are responsible for 10 percent of cancer mortality, about 55,000 avoidable annual deaths in the United States (16). Poorly recognized is the increased incidence of mesotheliomas, uniquely induced by asbestos, doubling and quadrupling in white and African-American men, respectively, from 1977 to 1999 (1). Additionally, paternal and maternal exposures to occupational carcinogens have been implicated as significant causes of childhood cancer, the overall incidence of which has increased by 26 percent since passage of the 1971 National Cancer Act (Table 2). Furthermore, lower-level exposures to occupational carcinogens such as asbestos and benzene often extend from the industrial plants into local communities and, to a lesser extent, to the entire U.S. population.

The cancer establishment ignores or rejects the basic fundamental of the widely accepted *precautionary principle.* For example, it has failed to undertake research based on nationwide community concerns about clusters of adult and childhood cancers in the vicinity of nuclear power plants, petrochemical industries, and Superfund hazardous waste sites—areas disproportionately and discriminatorily located in low-socioeconomic African-American and other ethnic communities. Worse still, despite the increased availability of data on air and water pollutants from large chemical industries and hazardous waste sites, following the Environmental Protection Agency's creation of the National Toxic Release Inventory in 1987, and the more detailed and user-friendly right-to-know exposure data at the state level, particularly in Massachusetts and New Jersey (17), both the NCI and ACS remain silent on or even dismissive of such concerns. And the NCI's silence persists despite substantial data incriminating avoidable undisclosed exposures of the population at large to ionizing radiation and industrial carcinogens, particularly persistent organic pollutants, that contaminate the entire environment: air, water, soil, the workplace, and consumer products such as food, household products, cosmetics, and toiletries. Such exposures have been incriminated, to varying degrees, in the escalating incidence of overall and site-specific cancers over recent decades.

Blatant examples of the NCI's dismissiveness include the assertion by then NCI director Dr. Richard Klausner at Rep. Nancy Pelosi's (D-CA) town hall meeting on July 26, 1996, that "low level (therapeutic) ionizing radiation does not demonstrate an increased risk." This was contrary to the conclusions of two NCI staffers involved in the U.S. Scoliosis Control Study that the relatively low cumulative breast dose was responsible for 70 percent excess breast cancer mortality (18). Furthermore, a hearing by the U.S. Senate Permanent Subcommittee on Investigations on September 16, 1998, revealed that the NCI had suppressed the results of its iodine-131 "Thyroid Cancer Study" for more than a decade, a delay resulting in several hundred deaths.

The NCI's minimal priorities on primary prevention research are further exemplified by its dismissal or trivialization of the significance of evidence derived from valid carcinogenicity tests in rodents; the ACS is even more dismissive. An illustration of this is a September 1992 statement by Dr. Richard Adamson, past director of the NCI's Division of Cancer Epidemiology, that trivialized the risks posed by food contaminated with pesticides such as Alar, shown to be carcinogenic in validated rodent tests (13, p. 495). Further illustrative is senior NCI staffer Dr. Leslie Ford's dismissal (19) in June 1995 of well-documented evidence on the potent hepatocarcinogenicity in rats (with formation of irreversible DNA adducts) of tamoxifen, a drug used in breast cancer chemoprevention trials in healthy women (20). Ford dismissed this evidence, of which women are still uninformed, as "premature," claiming that carcinogenic effects were seen only at "high doses," although these doses were similar to those used in the trial. She further attempted to discredit this evidence on the remarkable grounds that no women in the trial had developed liver cancer over the preceding few years. The same logic would exculpate most unequivocal carcinogens, such as asbestos, benzene, and vinyl chloride, which rarely, if ever, induce cancer with such brief latency.

The relation of environmental factors to risks of breast cancer is supported by a 1995 report on immigrants from high-risk nations such as the United States and Canada to low-risk nations such as Japan, and also the reverse migration (21). Slowly but surely, the immigrants, no matter at what age they moved from their country of origin, assumed breast cancer risks similar to those experienced by native-born women. More striking confirmation comes from a 2000 report on a large-scale study of identical twins in Sweden, Denmark, and Finland: "The overwhelming contribution to the causation of cancer in the population of [90,000] twins that we studied was the environment" (22). A recent study stresses the critical significance of these findings: "Thus the conclusion from twin studies is consistent with the conclusion from migrant studies: *the majority, probably the large majority, of important cancers in western populations are due to environmental rather than genetic factors.* Overly enthusiastic expectations regarding genetic research for disease prevention have the potential to distort research priorities for spending and health" (23, emphasis added).

We should also note that most carcinogens also induce other chronic toxic effects, notably genetic, endocrine-disruptive reproductive, hematological, and immunological effects, for which no incidence trend data comparable to those for cancer are available. Cancer, in effect, likely represents a quantifiable paradigm of a wide range of adverse public health effects resulting from run-away industrial technologies.

MINIMAL FUNDING OF PRIMARY PREVENTION

The cancer establishment grossly exaggerates its alleged allocations for research and advocacy on primary prevention, while trivializing the role of industrial carcinogens as avoidable causes of cancer.

The National Cancer Institute

The NCI claimed that $350 million (17 percent) of its approximately $2 billion 1992 budget was allocated to primary prevention. However, primary prevention expenditures (based on published independent estimates, unchallenged by the NCI) were less than $50 million (2.5 percent), of which $19 million (0.9 percent) was allocated to occupational cancer (24) (see Chapter 4). Only $15 million (0.03 percent) of the $4.2 billion 2002 budget is allocated to intramural occupational research. These trivial allocations strikingly illustrate the NCI's past and current reckless neglect of primary cancer prevention.

The NCI leadership has used manipulation and semantics to mislead and confuse Congress about its claimed allocations for primary cancer prevention. The institute massively exaggerates such allocations by including unrelated "secondary prevention" screening, diagnosis, and chemoprevention by the use of dietary "nutraceuticals" or drugs such as tamoxifen in questionable efforts to reduce susceptibility to prior carcinogenic exposures. Not surprising was the reaction by Rep. David Obey (D-WI) at hearings before a House Subcommittee of the Committee on Appropriations on March 16, 1992: "A number of scientists have suggested that cancer prevention receives an even smaller percentage of the budget than what NCI considers primary prevention." This skepticism is further detailed in later exchanges between Rep. Obey and Dr. Klausner. Rep. Obey's questions and Dr. Klausner's responses of May 1, 1998, are summarized below, followed by my comments on Klausner's responses (13).

Question: "Provide a breakdown of NCI's cancer prevention funding by categories—where prevention is the primary purpose of the grant."
Answer: "Funding for primary prevention in 1997 was over $480 million, almost 50 percent [of which] was directed towards environmental exposures, 19 percent was directed towards nutrition research, 14 percent involved smoking, and 2 percent was related to occupational exposures. . . . Opportunities in cancer

prevention are emerging and we anticipate fully to take advantage of these opportunities."

Comment: The claimed $480 million primary prevention expenditures, approximately 20 percent of the budget, are inconsistent with the NCI's February 1997 budget for "research dollars by various cancers," listing an allocation of $249 million for "cancer prevention and control." Furthermore, no information was provided on the alleged 50 percent expenditure on "environmental exposures." The 19 percent for nutrition research was allocated to chemoprevention, in attempts to protect against avoidable exposures to environmental carcinogens, and to the "protective effects" of low-fat, high fruit and vegetable diets, while ignoring evidence on the role of dietary contamination with carcinogenic pesticides. As disturbing was the less than 2 percent allocated to occupation, the single most important cause of avoidable carcinogenic exposures. The balance of 15 percent of the alleged $480 million primary prevention expenditures was unaccounted for. In response to a later request for information from the House Committee on Government Reform and Oversight, Klausner responded by simply doubling this figure to approximately $1 billion.

Question: "Other than tobacco and exposure to sunlight, do you think that the general public has been adequately informed about avoidable causes of cancer?"

Answer: "The NCI and other organizations including the ACS . . . have worked for years to inform the public about lifestyle choices that could increase or decrease the risks of cancer—through NCI's Cancer Information Services—and through distribution of millions of publications. In addition, when testing shows that chemicals cause cancer, NCI and other agencies including the National Toxicology Program (NTP) and the International Agency for Research on Cancer (IARC) publicize the test results."

Comment: This response illustrates the NCI's fixation on personal responsibility for cancer prevention. The NCI still takes no responsibility for public dissemination of scientific information on avoidable risks from involuntary and unknowing exposures to a wide range of carcinogenic chemicals, including those identified and systematized by the IARC and, on a more limited basis, by the NTP. And senior NCI scientists are on record as denigrating the human relevance of carcinogenicity test data. Furthermore, the NCI has rarely, if ever, testified before Congress on the validity of published evidence on avoidable carcinogenic exposures, nor has it provided such information to regulatory agencies.

Question: "Should the NCI develop a registry of avoidable carcinogens and make this information widely available to the public?"

Answer: "Such information is already available from NCI's Cancer Information Service—and also from IARC and the NTP."

Comment: The IARC and the NTP have not developed such registries, nor is it their mission.

Question: "During the hearing, you stated that NCI could effectively spend $5 billion by 2003. Provide a budget mechanism table that shows how you would allocate this level of spending in 2003, compared to 1998."

Answer: "NCI envisions a three-pronged approach:

1. Sustain at full measure the proved research programs that have enabled us to come this far.
2. Seize 'extraordinary opportunities' to further progress brought about by our previous successes. Our goals in these areas are: Cancer genetics; pre-clinical models of cancer; and imaging technologies, defining the signatures of cancer cells.
3. Create and sustain mechanisms that will enable us to rapidly translate our findings from the laboratory into practical applications that will benefit everyone."

Comment: This response is as broad in generalization as it is sparse in detail.

The most revealing evidence of the NCI's highly restricted policies on primary prevention is detailed in its *Cancer Progress Report* of 2001 (9). The report compares past "progress with the cancer-related targets set forth in the Department of Health and Human Services Objectives for the first decade of the 21st century." The report states that "behavioral factors," detailed in nineteen pages, are responsible for as much as 75 percent of all cancer deaths in the United States, while recognizing that "certain chemicals in the environment are known to cause cancer." However, these carcinogenic chemicals, summarily dealt with in three pages, are restricted to secondhand smoke; benzene in the air, particularly from smoking and occupational exposures; and radon in the home.

An even more limited comprehension (or greater neglect) of prevention is revealed in the "Highlights" of the NCI's *Cancer Facts* of May 2001, which begins "Cancer prevention is a major component and current priority—to reduce suffering and death from cancer. Research in the areas of diet and nutrition, tobacco cessation, chemoprevention, and early detection and screening are the NCI's major cancer prevention programs" (25). No mention is made of environmental and occupational carcinogens.

The American Cancer Society

In 1998, the ACS claimed that it funded nineteen large research grants on "Environmental Carcinogenesis," at a cost of $2.6 million—0.4 percent of its $678 million revenues, apart from $873 million assets. However, the great majority of these grants were in molecular biology; only three, funded for a total of $330,000 (less than 0.1 percent of revenues), reasonably qualified as environmental cancer research. The ACS also claimed that it funded 92 "Prevention" grants, with $23 million. Again, these largely dealt with molecular biology, with $2.4 million allocated to tobacco and diet, excluding any consideration of contamination with carcinogenic (besides other toxic) pesticides. A recent report has confirmed that concentrations of toxic and carcinogenic pesticide residues, including DDT, are three times higher in conventional foods than in organic foods (26). The ACS is even more dismissive than the NCI in its understanding of and priorities on primary cancer prevention. In *Cancer Facts and Figures 2002,* the ACS blandly reassures readers that cancer risks from dietary pesticides, hazardous waste sites, ionizing radiation from "closely controlled" nuclear plants, and nonionizing radiation are all at such low levels as to be "negligible" (27).

In striking contrast to the ACS's indifference to cancer prevention, in February 2002, the Canadian Cancer Society unequivocally affirmed the precautionary principle "to develop our cancer prevention and risk reduction messages" (28). However, in its September 2001 "Discussion Document," the Canadian government effectively rejected this principle, as recently criticized by the Canadian Environmental Law Association, in favor of a cost-benefit and scientific risk-based framework (29).

The Canadian Cancer Society has also joined with the Sierra Club of Canada in demanding a ban on the "cosmetic" use of carcinogenic pesticides for the home, garden, lawn, and recreational facilities (30). The Minister of Health, Anne MacLellan, promptly rejected this demand, claiming that "there is no evidence to support such a case. Pesticides are registered only if their risks have been determined to be acceptable when used according to instructions" (31). Note that such pesticide uses are being withdrawn in the United States, in part because of requirements of the 1996 Food Quality Protection Act and, in considerable part, because Canada has no U.S.-type legal liability deterrents.

FAILURE OF OUTREACH AND ADVOCACY
ON PRIMARY PREVENTION

Both the NCI and ACS have instant access to the highly receptive media, close contacts with Congress, and powerful public relations operations. Fully using these outreach resources, the cancer establishment issues a prodigious ongoing stream of information, press releases, databases, and public educational materials—the latter including the Comprehensive Public Cancer Database System, dealing with screening, diagnosis, clinical research, and the latest claimed advances in treatment. In sharp contrast, the cancer establishment makes little or no effort to warn the public of well-documented risks, based on experimental or epidemiological evidence, from involuntary exposure to a wide range of industrial carcinogens, including those in consumer products—food, cosmetics, toiletries, and household products. As importantly, the cancer establishment has also failed to warn of potential carcinogenic risks on the basis of incomplete or suggestive, although not definitive, evidence and has failed to direct high priority to research and advocacy on such risks. Such failure is a blatant disregard of the fundamental principles of public health and of the scientific basis of the precautionary principle.

The cancer establishment has shown reckless failure to warn the public, the media, Congress, and regulatory agencies of *experimental* evidence on a wide range of avoidable risk factors or causes of cancer, including (13):

- High concentrations of multiple residues of carcinogenic pesticides in non-organic fruits and vegetables (26), of particular significance in the diets of infants and young children.
- Irradiation of meat, with 300,000 times the ionizing radiation (or more) of a chest X-ray, inducing the formation of unique radiolytic products and increased benzene levels that pose carcinogenic and genotoxic risks and causing major vitamin depletion (32) (see Chapter 14).
- The fluoridation of drinking water, of highly questionable effectiveness in preventing dental caries in children, despite evidence that oral administration of fluoride induces a dose-related incidence of bone cancer in male rats.
- The use of raloxifene (Evista) by women for the prevention of osteoporosis and alleged prevention of breast cancer, despite Eli Lilly's own unpublicized experimental evidence that the drug induces ovarian cancer in mice and rats at about one-third of the recommended therapeutic dose. This is seriously compounded by Lilly's admission, unpublicized in its full-page newspaper advertisements and elsewhere, that the "clinical relevance of these tumor findings is unknown" (33).
- The use of tamoxifen, strongly promoted by the NCI and ACS, in breast cancer chemoprevention trials in healthy women, despite evidence that its effectiveness is highly questionable and that the drug is a potent liver carcinogen in rats (20), in addition to the absence of informed consent regarding this grave danger.
- Employment of some one million U.S. women in industries that expose them to more than 50 carcinogens incriminated as causes of breast cancer in rodent tests or in epidemiological studies.
- The overprescribed use of Ritalin for "attention deficit disorders" in children, despite evidence that it induces liver cancer and rare aggressive hepatoblastomas in mice at doses similar to the "therapeutic" (34) and in the absence of informed parental consent.
- The presence in mainstream industry cosmetics and toiletries of a wide range of frank carcinogenic ingredients, such as phenyl-*p*-phenylenediamine, diethanolamine, and hydroquinone. These products also contain "hidden" carcinogens from precursors such as diazolidinyl urea and quaternium 15, which break down to release formaldehyde; polyethylene glycol, which is contaminated with two carcinogens, ethylene oxide and 1,4-dioxane; and diethanolamine, which, apart from evidence of its carcinogenicity following skin application to mice, interacts with nitrites to form the potent carcinogen

nitrosodiethanolamine. Such exposures to multiple carcinogens is of particular concern in view of the virtual lifelong use of such ingredients in common cosmetics and personal care products, their application to large areas of skin, and the concomitant presence of detergents in these products, notably sodium lauryl sulfate, which facilitate skin absorption.

- The use of the highly potent and volatile 1,4-dichlorobenzene as a room and toilet deodorizer and moth repellant.

The cancer establishment has shown reckless failure to warn the public, the media, Congress, and regulatory agencies, particularly the Food and Drug Administration, Occupational Safety and Health Administration, and Environmental Protection Agency, of *epidemiological* evidence on a wide range of avoidable and involuntary risk factors or causes of cancer, including (13):

- Exposure of the entire U.S. population, to varying degrees, to a wide range of industrial carcinogens, particularly dioxin, PCBs, and agricultural pesticides, which have polluted the entire environment: air, water, and food.
- Extensive use of the herbicide atrazine in the United States, while banned in most European nations. This is the most common pollutant in rainwater, snow runoff, groundwater, and drinking water. A series of epidemiological studies over the last decade have incriminated atrazine as a cause of non-Hodgkin's and Hodgkin's lymphoma and ovarian cancer. And atrazine has also been shown to induce breast cancer in rodents, associated with endocrine-disruptive effects (35). Against this background of the NCI's silence is a 2002 news story (36) and a research paper describing how atrazine induces multiple sex-organ abnormalities in frogs at levels as low as 0.1 parts per billion in water (37). Humans have now become "canaries" for frogs!
- Highly suggestive epidemiological evidence for a relationship between fluoridation of drinking water with industrial fluorosilicate wastes (contaminated with carcinogenic heavy metals) and bone cancer in young men. Fluoride is added to the water supply of about 60 percent of the U.S. population, in contrast to only 2 percent of the European population, which has much lower rates of dental caries (13).
- The commonplace recycling of toxic wastes, including heavy metals, dioxins, and radionuclides, into common plant food and farm fertilizers. These wastes bioaccumulate in soil and contaminate food, water, and air (38).
- Excess blood levels of the natural insulin-like growth factor one (IGF-1), strongly associated with major excess occurrences of breast, colon, and prostate cancers. Unlabeled milk and other dairy products from cows injected with Monsanto's genetically engineered growth hormone (rBGH) are contaminated with high levels of IGF-1, and their consumption thus poses increased risks of these cancers (39).

- High levels of estradiol and other natural and synthetic sex hormones in U.S. meat from cattle implanted with sex hormones to increase carcass weight, posing risks of breast and other hormonal cancers. Other risks include endocrine-disruptive effects, approximately 10,000 times more potent than those associated with pesticides such as DDT, and hormonal contamination of water by runoff from feedlots.
- The relationships (with varying degrees of strength) between breast cancer and avoidable carcinogenic exposures such as prolonged use of estrogen and progesterone hormone replacement therapy, as now aggressively and misleadingly promoted on national television and in full-page advertisements in major national newspapers; premenopausal mammography; proximity of residence to Superfund sites; and exposure of some one million women to occupational carcinogens, particularly methylene chloride, benzene, ethylene oxide, and phenylenediamine dyes.
- The relationship between hormone replacement therapy and ovarian cancer.
- The relationship between perineal dusting with talcum powder by premenopausal women and ovarian cancer.
- The relationship between non-Hodgkin's lymphoma, multiple myeloma, and bladder and breast cancers and prolonged used by some 20 million women of permanent and semi-permanent black or dark brown hair dyes.
- The relationship between non-Hodgkin's lymphoma and exposure to herbicides, particularly, 2,4-D, in male agricultural workers.
- Exposure of some 11 million men and 4 million women to industrial chemicals and radiation, well recognized as causes of occupational cancer.
- The relationship between paternal and maternal exposure to occupational carcinogens and childhood cancers.
- The relationship between frequent consumption of nitrite-dyed hot dogs and childhood leukemia and brain cancer.
- The strong associations between childhood cancers, particularly brain cancer, non-Hodgkin's lymphoma, and leukemia, and domestic exposure to pesticides from uses in the home, including pet flea collars and lawn and garden pesticides. Another major exposure is commonplace use in schools.
- The relationship between the widely prescribed use of lindane for treatment of lice and scabies and childhood brain cancer.
- The suggestive relationship between childhood cancer and radioactive emissions from 103 aging nuclear power plants. Notorious among these is the Indian Point complex, with its worst safety rating and its location in a densely populated region (within a 50-mile radius encompassing 7 percent of the U.S. population). Findings of high and increasing levels of radioactive strontium-90 in baby teeth support this evidence (40).
- The suggestive relationship between malignant melanoma and the use of sunscreens (particularly in children) that fail to block UV radiation.

In spite of these widely ranging examples, the NCI and ACS have never attempted to develop a systematic reader-friendly, comprehensive registry of avoidable carcinogenic exposures and make it available to the public. This silence effectively denies U.S. citizens their fundamental democratic right to know about avoidable causes of a wide range of cancers, which could empower them to reduce their own risks of disease and death.

The NCI also fails to provide federal and state agencies with the scientific carcinogenicity data on which regulatory decisions are based, claiming that this is not their responsibility. Regulatory agencies are charged with a wide range of other responsibilities, but they lack the authority and the wealth of scientific and educational resources specifically directed to cancer, which are heavily invested in the cancer establishment. Moreover, the NCI and ACS have failed to provide such data to Congress as a basis for developing appropriate legislation and regulatory authority (41) (see Chapter 6).

The NCI's silence is also largely responsible for the faulty science on the basis of which regulatory decisions are becoming increasingly subverted by special interests. A battery of industry-funded think tanks, notably the Cato, Hudson, and International Life Sciences Institutes, support industries responsible for avoidable carcinogenic exposures; they claim that particular carcinogens do not pose a significant hazard. Also responsible are indentured academics and academic think tanks, notably the Harvard Center for Risk Analysis, whose past director, Dr. John Graham, is now the administrator of the Office of Information and Regulatory Affairs of the Office of Management and Budget. These no-hazard claims are based on a complex of "risk management" models, "risk-benefit analysis," and highly questionable "risk assessment" of individual carcinogens that ignore additive or possibly synergistic interactions with other carcinogenic exposures. These claims are also based on the spurious insistence upon uncovering common mechanisms of action before data from carcinogenicity tests can be extrapolated to humans. Guidelines developed by Dr. Graham and incorporated in the December 2000 "Data Quality Act" effectively challenge and sharply limit the regulation of carcinogens, as well as a wide range of other public health hazards.

The NCI's silence on primary cancer prevention is in frank violation of the 1971 National Cancer Act's specific charge "to disseminate cancer information to the public." This silence is also in flagrant denial of the 1988 Amendments to the National Cancer Program (Title 42, Section 285A), which call for "an expanded and intensified research program for the prevention of cancer caused by occu-pational or environmental exposure to carcinogens."

The ACS's silence on primary prevention is in striking contrast to claims for advocacy, as emphasized in its *Cancer Facts and Figures 2002*: "Cancer is a political, as well as medical, social, psychological, and economic issue. Every day, legislators make decisions that impact the lives of millions of Americans who have been touched by cancer. To affect those decisions positively, the Society has identified advocacy as part of its mission and as one of its top corporate priorities and works nationwide to promote beneficial policies, laws, and regulations for those affected by cancer" (27).

Finally, the cancer establishment's massive funding of a nationwide network of research institutes and hospitals virtually ensures the silence of their epidemiologists and other scientists on primary prevention. These constraints were strikingly exemplified in a recent widely publicized television program, "Kids and Chemicals," on the relationship between chemical exposures and childhood cancer and other diseases (42). The program featured progressive and well-qualified experts, some funded by the NCI, who expressed strong concerns while stressing the alleged inadequacy of current information. One expert stated, "We suspect that children who are exposed to pesticides are at greater risk of childhood cancer than other children. But mostly we don't know." Another maintained, "We have a very serious lack of information of how to go about preventing these diseases, because we haven't had enough information." For these reasons, the experts called for the National Children's Study over the next 20 years, at a cost of $50 million annually. This proposal trivializes the available information on avoidable causes of childhood cancer, of which the public has an overdue and undeniable right to know. Such information should have been made widely available over the last two decades so that the escalating incidence of childhood cancer could have been curbed. Moreover, no mention whatsoever was made in the TV program of the primary responsibility of the NCI, whose funding is more than adequate to undertake further needed research on avoidable causes of childhood cancer.

SURRENDER OF CANCER POLICY TO SPECIAL INTERESTS

On February 27, 2002, Sen. Dianne Feinstein (D-CA) introduced the National Cancer Act of 2002 (S. 1976). Cosponsored by thirty bipartisan senators, including majority leader Tom Daschle (D-SD), the bill is a new version of the 1971 act that launched the National Cancer Program. The bill adds $1.4 billion to the $4.6 billion 2003 budget authorized by President Bush, with extra funds coming from the new federal cigarette tax increase, and adds a further 50 percent annual increase to $7 billion by 2007, reaching a grand total of $14 billion. Feinstein said her goal is to "form our new battle plan to fight cancer." The legislation (as of mid-2002) has been referred to the Committee on Health, Education, Labor, and Pensions, chaired by Sen. Edward M. Kennedy (D-MA).

The Senate bill establishes a national network of twenty "translation" centers to combine basic and clinical research and commercialize promising findings. The bill also mandates insurance coverage for cancer screening, smoking cessation, genetic testing, and quality care standards.

Regrettably, this well-intentioned bill will not achieve its objectives, as it unwittingly surrenders the National Cancer Program to special interests while virtually ignoring primary prevention. The legislation has been strongly criticized by survivor coalitions, headed by the Cancer Leadership Council, and also by the American Society for Clinical Oncology (ASCO). Of major concern, bill S. 1976 shifts control of cancer policy from the public to the private sector (from the federal NCI to the "nonprofit" ACS) and creates confusing duplication and overlapping responsibilities.

More disturbing is the bill's background. Meeting secretly behind closed doors in September 1998, the ACS created, funded, and promoted the National Dialogue on Cancer (NDC). This was cochaired by former President George Bush and Barbara Bush, with Senator Feinstein as vice-chair and former governors Tom Ridge of Pennsylvania and Tommy Thompson of Wisconsin as "collaborating partners" (43). Included also were a hundred representatives from survivor groups and the giant cancer drug industry. The NDC leadership then, without informing its NDC participants, unilaterally spun off its own Legislative Committee, cochaired by Dr. John Seffrin, CEO of the ACS, and Dr. Vincent DeVita, former NCI director, to advise Congress on the proposed new National Cancer Act.

The ACS track record raises grave concerns about special interests and conflicts of interest, in sharp opposition to the public interest (Appendix I). Dr. John Durant, former ASCO executive, president (awarded the 2002 ASCO Presidential U.S. Cancer Fighter of the Year award), charged: "It has always seemed to me that this was an issue of control by the ACS over the cancer agenda. They are protecting their own fundraising capacity" from competition by survivor groups (quoted in 43). These conflicts of interest extend to the personal. The NDC Legislative Committee cochair, Dr. DeVita, is board chair of CancerSource.com, a Web site promoting the ACS *Consumers' Guide to Cancer Drugs*; other Legislative Committee members also serve on the board. These members have thus developed their own special interests in a publicly funded forum.

An increasing proportion of ACS revenues come from the pharmaceutical, cancer drug, mammography film and machine, and biotechnology industries. This is reflected in generous ACS allocations for research on highly profitable patented cancer drugs and aggressive promotion of premenopausal mammography. In striking contrast, less than 0.1 percent of revenues are allocated to environmental, occupational, and other avoidable causes of cancer. Not surprisingly, and unambiguously, the authoritative U.S. charity watchdog, the *Chronicle of Philanthropy,* warned against the transfer of money from the public purse to private hands: "The ACS is more interested in accumulating wealth than saving lives" (quoted in 44) (see Chapter 5).

More seriously, ACS policies on primary cancer prevention extend from a decades-long track record of indifference to frank hostility, compounded by pro-industry bias (Appendix I). This even extends to the tobacco industry. Shandwick International, representing R. J. Reynolds, and Edelman Worldwide, representing Brown & Williamson Tobacco Company, have been major public relations firms for the NDC Legislative Committee in rewriting the National Cancer Act (45).

The highly politicized and nontransparent agenda of the ACS is troubling. This is further exemplified by its direct governmental lobbying. Equally troubling are questionably legal donations to Democratic and Republican governors' associations: "We wanted to look like players and be players," an ACS representative admitted (quoted in 44, p. 568).

The ACS has clearly disqualified itself from any future leadership role in the National Cancer Program, which should remain under NCI control. Furthermore, *Feinstein's $14 billion five-year funding proposal should be amended and specifically redirected from generously funded damage control (screening, diagnosis, and treatment) and related basic research to primary cancer prevention. This could then be funded with $2.8 billion annually over the next five years.*

Additional funding for prevention should be provided by the private sector. Individual petrochemical and radionuclear industries should be held directly liable for direct and indirect costs relating to research and advocacy on their suspect or known carcinogens. This includes rodent testing, monitoring, epidemiology, surveillance, and full disclosure of all relevant information to the public, the media, federal and state regulatory agencies, and Congress.

As stressed by the statement "Losing the War against Cancer," released on February 4, 1992 (see Chapter 2, Part A), the long overdue new funding for prevention from both the public and private sectors "will require careful monitoring and oversight [of the NCI] to prevent misleading retention of old unrelated programs, particularly 'secondary prevention,' under the new guises of primary prevention." This precaution is critical in view of the NCI's track record of budgetary manipulation, as illustrated in the 1988 exchanges between Rep. Obey and former NCI director Klausner quoted earlier.

If more funding for clinical and basic research on cancer treatment could be justified, this could be made available from the private sector by reinstating the "reasonable pricing" clause from agreements between the NCI and the cancer drug industry that were intended to protect against exorbitant profiteering from the sale of drugs developed with taxpayers' dollars (46). These agreements were struck in 1995 at the insistence of former director of the National Institutes of Health, Harold Varmus, a past major recipient of NCI funds for basic cancer research. Unprotected by these restraints, the NCI paid for the research and development and for subsequent expensive clinical trials on the cancer drug Taxol. The NCI then gave Bristol-Myers Squibb the exclusive right to market and sell Taxol at the exorbitant price of approximately $5.00 per milligram, more than twenty times the manufacturing price. Taxol has been a blockbuster for the industry, posting sales of more than $3 billion since its approval in 1992. *So, the taxpayers pay twice:* first with their tax dollars for NCI drug research, and second by buying cancer drugs from the industry at grossly inflated prices. This is the rule rather than the exception for drugs developed by the NCI, a rule that should be revoked as soon as feasible.

HOW TO WIN THE LOSING WAR

The policies and priorities of the U.S. cancer establishment have remained unchanged for decades, despite periodic challenges from the independent scientific community, activist groups, and labor. Preeminent among these challenges was a Washington, D.C., press conference held on February 4, 1992, when a group of sixty-eight scientists, including leading national experts in cancer prevention and public health, released the statement "Losing the War Against Cancer" (see Chapter 2, Part A). These experts included past directors of three federal agencies: Dr. Eula Bingham, former Assistant Secretary of Labor, Occupational Safety and Health Administration; the late Dr. David Rall, former Assistant Surgeon General, U.S. Public Health Service, and director of the National Institute of Environmental Health Sciences; and Dr. Anthony Robbins, past director of the National Institute for Occupational Safety and Health.

Expressing strong concerns over the failure of the "War Against Cancer," the statement emphasized that "this failure is evidenced by the escalating incidence of cancer to epidemic proportions over recent decades" and expressed "further concerns that the generously funded cancer establishment, the NCI and ACS, have misled and confused the public and Congress by repeated claims that we are winning the war against cancer. In fact, the cancer establishment has continually minimized the evidence for increasing cancer rates which it has largely attributed to smoking and dietary fat, while discounting or ignoring the causal role of avoidable exposures to industrial carcinogens in air, food, water, and the workplace."

The 1992 statement proposed a comprehensive series of reforms as general guidelines for redefining the mission and priorities of the NCI. These were largely directed to correcting the overwhelming imbalance in priorities and funding between research and advocacy on primary cancer prevention and on damage control (screening, diagnosis, and treatment), besides molecular biology. However, none of these recommended reforms were considered, let alone implemented.

More than a decade later, and commemorating the 30th anniversary of President Nixon's inauguration of the "War Against Cancer," we more urgently warn of its continuing failure. Notwithstanding an approximate thirty-fold increase of the NCI's budget over the last three decades (Table 1) and prior insistence about winning the cancer war, the NCI and ACS have admitted that *the incidence of cancer is expected to increase dramatically due to the aging population, doubling by 2050* (3). Conspicuous by its absence is any recognition of the increasing incidence of cancer in childhood and younger age groups or that most cancers at all ages reflect prior avoidable carcinogenic exposures and could thus be prevented.

Equally disturbing is the increasing and powerful influence of the ACS, in view of its frank hostility to cancer prevention and its conflicts of interest (Appendix I). The ACS's influence will, effectively and perhaps irreversibly, consolidate special agenda interests and corporate influence over future national cancer policy.

For these reasons, we urge the critical need to mobilize broad Congressional and public recognition of this national crisis and to develop urgent corrective public policy reforms. While active support by independent experts in cancer prevention and public health remains critical, at this late stage the cancer war can most realistically and effectively be waged at a grassroots level. The essential basis for such a strategy is three-fold:

1. Self-interest. The incidence of cancers, particularly non-smoking-related cancers, has escalated to epidemic proportions over recent decades, now striking nearly one in two men and more than one in three women in their lifetimes; few families remain unaffected. So, any scientifically documented practical basis for reducing avoidable risks of cancer caused by involuntary exposures to industrial carcinogens in the environment is likely to receive widespread national support.
2. Insistence on citizens' inalienable democratic right to know. An overwhelming body of critical public health information about a wide range of involuntary and avoidable carcinogenic exposures still remains buried in industry and government files or in the relatively inaccessible scientific literature. This effectively deprives citizens of their ability to take personal action to reduce their own risks of cancer and to take political action, at the local, state, and national levels, in efforts to ensure Congressional response.
3. Insistence on environmental justice. Cancer disproportionately affects disadvantaged socioeconomic and ethnic population subgroups.

The successful implementation of such strategies would decrease the incidence of cancer and save lives. It would also pose poorly defensible challenges to both the NCI and ACS for their long-standing minimal priorities for research and advocacy on primary prevention. Citizen-based strategies would also challenge the near total failure of the cancer establishment to inform citizens, as well as Congress and regulatory agencies, of well-documented scientific evidence of involuntary exposures to a wide range of industrial carcinogens; for the ACS, this failure even extends to hostility to such primary prevention. Recognition of ACS policies would thus fully justify a national economic boycott and diversion of charitable funding to citizen activist groups dedicated to cancer prevention.

Public disclosure of the decades-long track record of the ACS on primary prevention, including conflicts of interest with the giant cancer drug industry, ties to the tobacco industry, and nontransparency, would also challenge the fundamental basis of the recent Senate initiative (S. 1976) to shift substantial control of future cancer research and policy to the ACS. Clearly, hearings on this initiative by the Senate Committee on Health, Education, Labor, and Pensions are critical and overdue. These hearings should focus on the disturbing background to S. 1976, to the continuing minimalist policies and priorities on primary prevention by the NCI and ACS, and to the special agenda interests of the ACS. Essential to the credibility of such hearings is testimony from the wide range of independent scientific experts and citizen activist groups who have endorsed this document (see Appendix, pp. 299–305). This could well lead to recognition of the essential need to redirect national and international policies to ensure maximal emphasis on primary prevention and to correct the overwhelming imbalance in priorities and resources between primary prevention and damage control. This redirection of public policy should be immediate and not held hostage to alleged inadequacies of information, the need for "conclusive science," and long-term future research, as recently advocated (42).

We further emphasize that *our public policy concerns are truly global.* The policies of U.S. cancer institutions and associations, with their minimal priorities and allocations for research and advocacy on primary prevention, remain the gold standard for the policies of Europe and other industrialized nations and, even more critically, for those of "lesser developed" countries. Continuing reliance by the NCI and ACS on the discredited claim by Doll that "occupation, pollution, and industrial products" are trivial causes of cancer (14) poses a serious global threat; this claim has recently been supported in a widely publicized book by an unqualified author (47). Doll's guesstimates encourage the reckless and poorly regulated rush by powerful national and multinational corporations to industrialize impoverished Third World and other developing countries.

Particularly egregious is Canada's continued export of virtually all the asbestos it mines, 97 percent of all asbestos mined worldwide, to Asia and other developing nations. Canada is the world's largest asbestos exporter and has exerted powerful influence to protect asbestos from being condemned by the World Health Organization, International Program on Chemical Safety, and International Labor Organization (48). Asiatic workers are dying because of Canada's claims about the safety of the "controlled use" of asbestos and its unwillingness to close its Quebec mines. The Canadian government persists in this fatal trade, despite the recent World Trade Organization ruling in favor of national bans of asbestos imports (48).

Whether against cancer or terrorism, war is best fought by preemptive strategies based on prevention rather than based reactively on damage control. As importantly, the war against cancer must be waged by leadership accountable to the public interest and not to special agenda private interests.

SUMMARY

Since passage of the 1971 National Cancer Act, the overall incidence of cancer has escalated to epidemic proportions, now striking nearly one in two men and more than one in three women in their lifetimes. While smoking is the single largest cause of cancer, the incidence of lung and other smoking-related cancers in men has declined sharply. In striking contrast, there has been a major increase in the incidence of predominantly non-smoking-related cancers in men and women and in the incidence of childhood cancers.

Nevertheless, the National Cancer Institute and American Cancer Society, the cancer establishment, have given misleading assurances of major progress in the war against cancer. These culminated in their 1998 *Report Card* claiming a recent "reversal of an almost 20-year trend of increasing cancer cases." In fact, the "reversal" was minimal and artifactual. In May 2002, the NCI and ACS finally admitted that *the incidence of cancer is expected to double by 2050.*

The escalating incidence of cancer does not reflect lack of resources. Since 1971, the NCI's budget has increased almost thirty-fold, reaching $4.2 billion by 2002, while annual ACS revenues are approximately $800 million. The cancer establishment's mindset remains fixated on damage control (screening, diagnosis, and treatment) and basic molecular research. This is coupled with an indifference to preventing avoidable causes of cancer, other than faulty lifestyle—smoking, inactivity, and fatty diet. This exclusionary claim remains based on a scientifically discredited 1981 report by British epidemiologists Richard Doll and Richard Peto, who guesstimated that lifestyle factors are responsible for 95 percent of all cancers, with the 5 percent balance arbitrarily assigned to environmental and occupational causes. For the ACS, this indifference to primary prevention includes a long track record of hostility, compounded by conflicts of interest with the giant cancer drug and other industries. Not surprisingly, the *Chronicle of Philanthropy,* the nation's leading charity watchdog, has charged that the ACS is "more interested in accumulating wealth than in saving lives."

The cancer establishment's funding for primary prevention research is trivial. While the NCI has made wildly varying estimates for prevention research—up to 50 percent of its budget—independent estimates are closer to 2.5 percent; the NCI's current intramural research funding on occupational cancer is only $15 million. The ACS's "Environmental Research" funding is less than 0.1 percent of revenues.

The cancer establishment conducts minimal research on avoidable exposures to a wide range of occupational and environmental industrial carcinogens, including nationwide cancer clusters in the vicinity of nuclear power plants, petrochemical industries, and Superfund hazardous waste sites that are disproportionately located in ethnic and low-socioeconomic communities, and exposures to ionizing radiation and persistent organic pollutants contaminating the entire environment: air, water, soil, the workplace, and consumer products. Besides conducting minimal research, the cancer establishment fails to warn the public, media, Congress, and regulatory agencies of avoidable exposures to a wide range of carcinogens identified in rodent tests. These include commonly prescribed drugs such as Ritalin and Evista; carcinogenic ingredients in cosmetics and personal care and household products; residues of carcinogenic pesticides in non-organic fruit and vegetables; the commonplace recycling of industrial wastes, containing a wide range of carcinogens, into common plant food and farm fertilizers; and exposure of one million women working in industries to more than 50 carcinogens incriminated as causes of breast cancer in rodents, in some instances reinforced by epidemiological evidence.

The cancer establishment also fails to warn of epidemiological evidence on a wide range of avoidable causes of cancer. These include exposure of the entire population to a wide range of industrial carcinogens that have permeated the entire environment—air, water, and food; exposures to carcinogenic pesticides from use in the home, garden, schools, recreational facilities, and agriculture; causes of childhood cancer such as parental occupational exposure to carcinogens during pregnancy, consumption of hot dogs contaminated with nitrosodiethanolamine from the use of nitrite coloring agents, and use of lindane for treatment of childhood scabies and lice; and risks of ovarian cancer from perineal dusting with talc.

The cancer establishment's failure to warn of disease and death from avoidable exposures to industrial carcinogens is in striking contrast to its stream of press releases, briefings, and media reports claiming the latest advances in screening and treatment. This silence flagrantly violates the 1988 Amendments to the National Cancer Program, calling for "an expanded and intensified research program for the prevention of cancer caused by occupational or environmental exposure to carcinogens."

In February 2002, Sen. Dianne Feinstein introduced the 2002 National Cancer Act. As of mid-2002, this legislation has been referred to the Senate Committee on Health, chaired by Sen. Edward Kennedy. The bill authorizes $14 billion in funding over a five-year period to establish a new version of the 1971 National Cancer Act and shifts major control of cancer policy from the public (NCI) to the private (ACS) sector, creating confusing duplication and conflicting responsibilities.

The background of the Senate bill is disturbing, having been developed by the ACS under conditions of nontransparency and behind closed doors. This is more disturbing in view of the ACS's highly politicized agenda, including possibly illegal donations to political parties. Clearly, hearings on the bill are critical. Feinstein's $14 billion five-year funding proposal should be amended and redirected from generously funded damage control (screening, diagnosis, and treatment) and related basic research to primary prevention. This could then be funded with $2.8 billion annually over the next five years. Congressional hearings should also focus critically on the continuing minimalist policies on primary prevention by the NCI and ACS and on the special agenda interests of the ACS. Essential to the credibility of such hearings would be testimony from independent scientific experts and representatives of activist citizen groups.

Control of the National Cancer Program must remain in the public sector. National cancer policies are now threatened more than ever before by the intransigent indifference of the cancer establishment to primary prevention. This silence reflects a denial of citizens' democratic right to know and a rejection of basic environmental justice and the Precautionary Principle. Citizen activist groups nationwide, supported by independent scientists, must be mobilized if the losing war against cancer is ever to be won.

Most carcinogens induce other toxic effects, including genetic, endocrine-disruptive, and immunological effects. Cancer thus represents a quantifiable paradigm of a wide range of adverse health effects resulting from run-away industrial technologies.

These public policy concerns are truly global. Current U.S. policies of indifference to primary cancer prevention and fixation on damage control remain based on the discredited 1981 assertions of Doll and Peto. U.S. policies are the gold standard for major industrialized nations and even more so for "lesser developed" nations, which are particularly vulnerable to the reckless rush toward unregulated industrialization.

Whether against cancer or terrorism, war is best fought by preemptive strategies based on prevention rather than based reactively on damage control. As importantly, the war against cancer needs to be waged by leadership accountable to the public interest and not to special agenda interests.

POSTSCRIPT

Since 1994, strong direct and indirect industry pressures, conflicts of interest, and procedural nontransparency have seriously jeopardized the independence and integrity of the World Health Organization's International Agency for Research on Cancer (IARC) programs for the evaluation of human carcinogenic risks. "Evidence for carcinogenicity provided by results of experimental bioassays have been disregarded on the basis of unproven mechanistic hypotheses,—very serious consequences for public health may follow" (63; see also Chapter 9, Table 5).

Note — This chapter is based on the report *The Stop Cancer Before It Starts Campaign: How to Win the Losing War Against Cancer,* released at a Washington, D.C., press conference on February 20, 2003. For listing of endorsers, see p. 301.

APPENDIX I: THE AMERICAN CANCER SOCIETY'S TRACK RECORD ON CANCER PREVENTION[1]

• In 1971, when studies unequivocally proved that diethylstilbestrol (DES) caused vaginal cancers in teenaged daughters of women taking the drug during pregnancy, the ACS refused an invitation to testify at Congressional hearings

---

[1] Information here is mainly from Epstein (13).

requiring the Food and Drug Administration (FDA) to ban use of DES as an animal feed additive.

• In 1977 and 1978, the ACS opposed regulations proposed for hair coloring products containing dyes known to cause breast and liver cancer in rodents, despite clear evidence of human risk.

• In 1977, the ACS called for a Congressional moratorium on the FDA's proposed ban on saccharin and even advocated its use by nursing mothers and babies in "moderation," despite clear-cut evidence of its carcinogenicity in rodents.

• In 1978, Tony Mazzocchi, then senior representative of the Oil, Chemical and Atomic Workers International Union, stated at a Washington, D.C., roundtable meeting between public interest groups and high-ranking ACS officials, "Occupational safety standards have received no support from the ACS."

• In 1978, Rep. Paul Rogers censured the ACS for doing "too little, too late" in failing to support the Clean Air Act.

• In 1982, the ACS adopted a highly restrictive cancer policy that insisted on unequivocal epidemiological evidence of carcinogenicity before taking any position on public health hazards. Accordingly, the ACS still trivializes or rejects evidence of carcinogenicity in experimental animals and has actively campaigned against laws (e.g., the 1958 Delaney Law) that ban deliberate addition to food of any amount of any additive shown to cause cancer in either animals or humans.

• In 1983, the ACS refused to join a coalition of the March of Dimes, American Heart Association, and American Lung Association to support the Clean Air Act.

• In 1984, the ACS created October National Breast Cancer Awareness Month, funded and promoted by Zeneca, an offshoot of the U.K. Imperial Chemical Industry, a major manufacturer of petrochemical products. The ACS leads women to believe that mammography is their best hope against breast cancer. A recent ACS advertisement promised that "early detection results in a cure nearly 100 percent of the time." Responding to questions from a journalist, an ACS communications director admitted, "The ad is based on a study. When you make an advertisement, you just say what you can to get women in the door. You exaggerate a point. . . . Mammography today is a lucrative [and] highly competitive business." There are close and intimate associations between the ACS and this giant "business," mammography film and machine industries, which constitute clear conflicts of interest. Even more seriously, Awareness Month publications and advertisements studiously avoid any reference to the wealth of information on avoidable causes and prevention of breast cancer.

• In 1992, the ACS supported a statement by the Chlorine Institute defending the continued global use of organochlorine pesticides, despite clear evidence of their persistence and carcinogenicity. The ACS's vice president Clark Heath, M.D., dismissed evidence of this risk as "preliminary and mostly based on weak and indirect associations."

• In 1992, the ACS, in conjunction with the NCI, launched the breast cancer "chemoprevention" program aimed at recruiting 16,000 healthy women at supposedly "high risk" into a five-year clinical trial with the highly profitable drug tamoxifen, manufactured by Zeneca. Evidence of the claimed effectiveness of tamoxifen is, at best, arguable. Furthermore, promoters trivialize evidence of the drug's life-threatening adverse effects on healthy women. More seriously, information that tamoxifen poses grave risks of liver cancer, as it is a highly potent liver carcinogen in rats (in which it also induces irreversible DNA adducts), remains suppressed.

• In 1993, just before PBS aired the *Frontline* special "In Our Children's Food," the ACS came out in support of the pesticide industry. In a damage-control memorandum sent to some 48 regional divisions, the ACS trivialized pesticides as a cause of childhood cancer and reassured the public that food contaminated with residues of carcinogenic pesticides is safe, even for babies. When the media and concerned citizens called local ACS chapters, they received reassurances: "The primary health hazards of pesticides are from direct contact with the chemicals at potentially high doses, for example, farm workers who apply the chemicals and work in the fields after the pesticides have been applied, and people living near aerially sprayed fields. . . . The American Cancer Society believes that the benefits of a balanced diet rich in fruits and vegetables far outweigh the largely theoretical risks posed by occasional, very low pesticide residue levels in foods."

• In February 1994, the ACS published a study designed to reassure women on the safety of dark permanent hair dyes and trivialize risks of fatal and nonfatal cancers as documented in over six prior reports. However, the ACS study was based on a group of some 1,100 women with an initial age of 56 who were followed up for seven years only. The ACS concluded that "women using permanent hair dyes are not generally at increased risk of fatal cancer." However, for women over 63, risks of cancer are increased up to 20-fold for non-Hodgkin's lymphoma and multiple myeloma, 34-fold for bladder cancer, and 8-fold for breast cancer. As designed, the ACS study would have missed the great majority of these cancers and ruled out dark hair dyes as important risks of avoidable cancers.

• In September 1996, the ACS, together with patient and physician organizations, filed a "citizens' petition" to pressure the FDA to ease restrictions on access to silicone gel breast implants. What the ACS did not disclose was that several industry rodent studies had shown the gel in these implants to induce cancer and that these implants were also contaminated with other potent carcinogens, such as ethylene oxide and crystalline silica.

• In 1998, the ACS allocated $330,000, less than 0.1 percent of its $678 million revenues, to research on environmental carcinogenesis, while claiming allocations of $2.6 million, 0.4 percent of its revenues.

• In May 1999, the ACS issued a statement trivializing cancer risks from consumption of genetically engineered, rBGH/BST milk containing high levels of the growth factor IGF-1. This reassurance was in striking contrast to substantial published scientific evidence that elevated blood levels of IGF-1 are strongly associated with excess risks of breast, colon, and prostate cancers.

• In January 2000, *Cancer Letter* revealed that the ACS has clear ties to the tobacco industry. Shandwick International, representing R. J. Reynolds Holdings, and Edelman, representing Brown & Williamson Tobacco Company, have been major public relations firms for the ACS in its attempts to rewrite the 1971 National Cancer Act and in conducting voter education programs in the past-presidential campaign.

• In 2002, the "Environmental Cancer Risk Section" of the ACS *Cancer Facts and Figures 2002* dismissively states that carcinogenic exposures from dietary pesticides, "toxic wastes in dump sites," ionizing radiation from "closely controlled" nuclear power plants, and nonionizing radiation are all "at such low levels that risks are negligible."

APPENDIX II: RICHARD DOLL'S TRACK RECORD ON CANCER PREVENTION

Sir Richard Doll is still generally considered the most influential and authoritative cancer epidemiologist worldwide. In 1954, together with Dr. Bradford Hill, Doll warned that, besides smoking, exposure to nickel, asbestos, gas-production tars, and radioactivity were major causes of cancer (13). In 1955, he published a landmark report warning of high cancer rates in asbestos workers (49). In 1967, in the prestigious Rock Carling Fellowship lecture, Doll further warned that an "immense" number of substances were known to cause cancer and that prevention of cancer was a better strategy than cure (50). In the late 1960s Doll could have been considered a radical.

Over subsequent decades, however, Doll drastically changed his views and gradually emerged as a major defender of corporate industry interests. This role has been reinforced by his key influence in prestigious U.K. governmental and nongovernmental committees and charities, particularly the Imperial Cancer Research Fund. In these overlapping roles, Doll has trivialized or dismissed industrial and occupational factors as causes of cancer, which he predominantly attributes to faulty lifestyle, particularly smoking. Furthermore, as the leading spokesman for U.K. charities, Doll has insisted that they should focus exclusively on scientific research and not become involved in prevention research and education (13).

• In 1976, despite well-documented concerns about the risks of fluoridating drinking water with industrial wastes (13), Doll declared that it was "unethical" not to do so (51).

• In 1981, in his report on causes of cancer in the United States (14), Doll claimed that occupation was responsible for 4 percent of cancer mortality rather than 20 percent, as previously admitted by consultants to the American Industrial Health Council of the Chemical Manufacturers' Association (15).

• In 1982, as a long-standing consultant to Turner & Newall, the leading U.K. asbestos corporation, Doll gave a speech to workers at one of its largest plants (52); this speech was in response to a TV exposé that forced the government to reduce occupational exposure limits to an allegedly low level (1 fiber/cc). Doll reassured the workers that the new exposure limit would reduce their lifetime risk of dying from cancer to "a pretty outside chance" of 1 in 40 (2.5 percent). This, however, is an extremely high risk. Doll has also declined to testify on behalf of dying plaintiffs or their bereaved families in civil litigation against asbestos industries. Furthermore, Doll has filed a misleading sworn statement in U.S. courts on behalf of Turner & Newall (52).

• In 1983, in support of U.S. and U.K. petrochemical companies, Doll claimed that lead in petroleum-vehicle exhaust was not correlated with increased lead levels in blood and learning disabilities in children (53). Doll's research has been generously funded by General Motors.

• In 1985, the U.K. Society for the Prevention of Asbestos and Industrial Disease criticized Doll for manipulating scientific information in order to assure us that only one in 100,000 people working in an office containing undamaged asbestos risk asbestos-related disease and death (54).

• In 1985, in a letter to the judge of an Australian Royal Commission that was investigating claims of veterans who had developed cancer following exposure to the herbicide Agent Orange in Vietnam, Doll expressed strong support for the defense claims of its major manufacturer, Monsanto. He stated that "TCDD [dioxin], which has been postulated to be a dangerous contaminant of the herbicide, is at the most, only weakly and inconsistently carcinogenic in animal experiments" (55). In fact, dioxin is the most potent tested carcinogen, apart from confirmatory epidemiological evidence. Doll's defense, resulting in denial of the veterans' claims, was publicized by Monsanto in full-page advertisements in major newspapers worldwide.

• In 1987, Doll dismissed evidence of childhood leukemia clusters near 15 U.K. nuclear power plants (56). Faced with evidence of a 21 percent excess of lymphoid leukemia in children and young adults living within ten miles of these plants, Doll advanced the novel hypothesis that the "over clean" homes of nuclear plant workers rendered their children susceptible to unidentified leukemia viruses (57).

• In 1988, Doll claimed that the excess mortality from leukemia and multiple myeloma among servicemen exposed to radiation from atom bomb tests was a "statistical quirk" (58). (In the London *Times* of January 29, 1988, Doll is reported as saying that the statistical difference was curious.)

• In 1988, in a review on behalf of the U.S. Chemical Manufacturers' Association, Doll claimed there was no significant evidence for an association between occupational exposure to vinyl chloride and brain cancer (59). However, this claim was based on an aggregation of several studies, some of which provided evidence of a statistically significant association.

• In 1992, in a letter to a major U.K. newspaper, Doll exhorted the public to trust industry and scientists and to ignore warnings by the "large and powerful anti-science mafia" of risks from dietary residues of carcinogenic pesticides (60).

• In January 2000, Doll admitted in a deposition to donations by the chemical industry to Green College, Oxford, where he had been the presidential "Warden" (61). He also admitted that the largest "charitable" donation (£50,000) came from Turner & Newall, the leading U.K. asbestos multinational, "in recognition of all the work I had done for them."

Doll's persisting dominance in U.K. cancer policy is exemplified by a 1999 letter from the Ministry of Health stating that, based on Doll's 1981 report (14), "Relatively little of the cancer burden (5–10 percent) is attributed to occupational, environmental or consumer exposure to specific chemicals" (62). (*Note* — See Doll's retraction of these statements, Chapter 9, Table 8.)

Chapter 8

STRATEGIES FOR THE
STOP CANCER CAMPAIGN

THE STRATEGY MEETING

The Cancer Prevention Coalition (CPC) has convened a meeting of leading scientists, and representatives of physician, consumer, environmental, and environmental justice groups, the Congressional Black Caucus, labor, and socially responsible business, to an *invitation-only* April 28, 2003, conference in Washington, D.C. The goal of this meeting is to develop a complex of broadly based collaborative strategies for implementing the Stop Cancer Before It Starts Campaign. This Campaign, launched in February 2003, is based on a CPC report on preventable causes of cancer, reviewed, sponsored, and endorsed by some 100 leading cancer prevention scientists and representatives of leading activist groups (this report is the basis for Chapter 7). The purpose of the April 28 meeting is to follow up on this report with the next logical steps to implement strategies for a national cancer prevention campaign.

BACKGROUND

Since passage of the 1971 National Cancer Act, the incidence of cancer has escalated to epidemic proportions, now striking about 1.3 million and killing about 550,000 annually. Nearly one in two men and more than one in three women now develop cancer in their lifetimes. While smoking is unquestionably the single largest cause of cancer, the incidence rates of lung and other smoking-related cancers in men have declined sharply; these rates are "age-adjusted" to exclude the influence of longevity. In striking contrast, there have been major increases in rates of predominantly non-smoking-related adult cancers, which are disproportionately higher among African Americans, and also of childhood cancers.

Prepared by the Cancer Prevention Coalition as a position paper for an April 28, 2003, strategy meeting on its Stop Cancer Before It Starts(see Chapter 7).

Nevertheless, the cancer establishment, the National Cancer Institute (NCI) and American Cancer Society (ACS), have repeatedly made long-standing assurances of major progress in the war against cancer. Illustratively, the NCI's 1998 *Report Card* claimed a recent "reversal of an almost 20-year trend of increasing cancer case"; this "reversal," however, was minimal and artifactual. Against this background, the February 2003 "pledge" by NCI Director Andrew von Eschenbach to "eliminate the suffering and death due to cancer . . . and to do it by 2015" is disingenuous.

The escalating incidence of cancer does not reflect lack of resources. Since 1971, the NCI's budget has increased approximately 30-fold, reaching $4.6 billion this year (2003). Paradoxically, NCI's escalating budget over the last three decades is paralleled by the escalating incidence of cancer.

Apart from basic research, the cancer establishment's mindset remains fixated on "secondary" prevention or damage control—screening, diagnosis, chemoprevention (the use of drugs or nutrients in efforts to reduce risks from prior avoidable carcinogenic exposures)—and treatment; this mindset is compounded by interlocking relations between the NCI and ACS and the cancer drug industry. It is coupled with indifference to primary prevention—that is, preventing a wide range of avoidable industrial causes of cancer—other than predominantly faulty lifestyle, smoking, inactivity, and fatty diet. This exclusionary claim remains based on a scientifically discredited 1981 report by British epidemiologist Drs. Richard Doll and Richard Peto. They "guesstimated" that lifestyle factors are responsible for up to 90 percent of all cancers, with the balance arbitrarily assigned to environmental and occupational causes. However, following recent damaging revelations on conflicts of interest, Doll admitted, in June 2002, that environmental exposures are major causes of cancer.

In spite of Doll's recent admission, his long-standing emphasis on lifestyle factors as the predominant cause of cancer has been strongly supported by a World Health Organization (WHO) April 3, 2003, report. The report warns that "cancer rates are set to increase by 15 percent . . . by 2020." In a detailed press release accompanying the report, it was further stated that "Researchers will demonstrate that successful behavioral changes in tobacco, alcohol, and diet will prevent far more cancers than the elimination of toxins such as industrial pollution, car exhaust and dioxins." It may be noted that the report was coedited by Dr. Paul Kleihues, director of the WHO's International Agency for Research on Cancer (IARC). Dr. Kleihues has recently been charged with lack of transparency in his Agency's activities, with particular regard to industry influence.

The indifference of the ACS to primary prevention extends to hostility, compounded by conflicts of interest with the giant cancer drug and other industries. Not surprisingly, the *Chronicle of Philanthropy*, the nation's leading charity watchdog, has charged that the ACS is "more interested in accumulating wealth than in saving lives." These considerations are particularly critical in view of the increasing domination of NCI policies by the ACS.

In 1992, the NCI claimed that funding for prevention research was $350 million, 17 percent of its approximately $2 billion budget; this claim manipulatively included funding for "secondary" prevention. However, independent estimates, unchallenged by the NCI, were under $50 million, 2.5 percent of its budget. In the NCI's $1.7 billion 2001 budget, 12 percent was allocated to "Cancer Prevention and Control," without any reference to primary prevention. ACS "Environmental Research" 1998 funding was $330,000, less than 0.1 percent of its $678 million revenues, apart from $873 million assets.

The U.S. cancer establishment conducts minimal research on avoidable exposures. These include a wide range of petrochemical, ionizing radiation, and other industrial carcinogens contaminating the totality of the environment—air, water, soil, and the workplace; carcinogenic contaminants and ingredients in consumer products; and carcinogenic prescription drugs and "low-dose" radiation diagnostic procedures. More critically, the NCI and ACS have failed to warn the public, media, Congress, and regulatory agencies of such avoidable exposures to industrial and other carcinogens incriminated in rodent tests and/or epidemiological studies. The ACS goes further by trivializing such risks. In its *Cancer Facts and Figures 2000,* the ACS dismissively reassures that carcinogenic exposures from dietary pesticides, "toxic wastes in dump sites," ionizing radiation from "closely controlled" nuclear power plants, and non-ionizing radiation are all "at such low levels that the risks are negligible." These concerns are heightened by the February 2002 appointment of NCI Director Dr. Andrew von Eschenbach, past president-elect of the ACS, who advocates privatization of national cancer policy by shifting its major control from the NCI to the ACS.

This failure to warn the public of avoidable cancer risks is in stark contrast to NCI's prodigious stream of press releases, briefings, and media reports claiming the latest miracle drugs and breakthroughs in treatment. These claims are also in striking contrast to increasing cancer mortality rates, increasing by 2 percent for whites and 9 percent for African Americans, from 1973 to 1999. This silence also violates National Cancer Act amendments, calling for "an expanded and intensified research program for the prevention of cancer caused by occupational or environmental exposure to carcinogens."

The decades-long silence of the cancer establishment on a wide range of avoidable causes of cancer, other than personal lifestyle, has tacitly encouraged powerful industries that manufacture carcinogenic products, and corporate polluters. Such misconduct has been characterized as "white-collar crime" by Rep. John Conyers' 1979 and 1984 bills, imposing criminal penalties for economically motivated corporate misconduct with adverse public health or environmental consequences. By its silence on avoidable causes of cancer, the cancer establishment is complicit in these adverse consequences and thus bears heavy responsibility for the current cancer epidemic.

National cancer policies are now threatened more than ever before by the cancer establishment's indifference to primary prevention and by its silence on avoidable causes of cancer, other than personal lifestyle. As seriously, this silence denies citizens their democratic "Right to Know" and empowerment to reduce their own cancer risks, and rejects environmental justice by sacrificing public health to powerful corporate interests.

This silence has facilitated, and is further compounded by, strategies of the current U.S. administration's Office of Management and Budget to trivialize the significance of avoidable carcinogenic exposures and thus effectively deregulate them.

The war against cancer can only be waged by collaborative strategies based on primary prevention, rather than on "secondary" prevention or damage control. As importantly, this war must be waged by leadership accountable to the public rather than special interests.

STRATEGIES

As proposed in its report, the Campaign is based on a series of interlocking and mutually reinforcing strategies. These include:

- Developing grassroots national support based on the right to know, empowerment, and environmental justice
- Publicizing a critique of the cancer establishment
- Legislative initiatives
- State initiatives
- Expansion of the Campaign's support base

Developing Grassroots National Support

The most realistic strategy for developing grassroots national support, a prerequisite for the Campaign's success, is that based on self-interest, rather than abstractions or ideology. Cancer is thus unique in this regard as it affects virtually every family in the nation. However, the devastating impact of cancer is likely to be met with passivity or even denial, unless the public is provided with practical information on how to reduce their own risks. Of obvious importance is the prevention of smoking, particularly prior to addiction in late adolescence. Less well-recognized, however, is the critical need for user-friendly information on avoidable cause of a wide range of non-smoking-related cancers whose incidence has dramatically escalated over recent decades.

Right to Know. The public's right to know of avoidable cancer risks is fundamental to the Campaign, and is the basis for building a national grassroots coalition. The continuing failure of the NCI and ACS to provide the public, and also Congress and regulatory agencies, with such information is a flagrant denial of this right. Information on such denial should be focused on four target groups, each affording practical methods of empowerment, as follows:

1. *Consumers:* Consumers have the right to be provided with information and explicit label warnings on carcinogenic ingredients and contaminants in their food, cosmetics and toiletries, and household products. This will enable consumers to boycott mainstream companies selling unsafe products, and reward smaller non-mainstream companies marketing safe alternatives. With increasing demand for the latter, economies of scale will reduce their higher prices, and thus gradually reflect environmental justice concerns.

2. *Patients:* Patients should be advised to exercise their right to know by requesting full information on cancer and other risks of prescription drugs, particularly as detailed in the Precautions section of the *Physicians Desk Reference* (PDR). For the wide range of common prescription drugs posing cancer risks, safer alternatives should be requested, in accordance with legal and ethical requirements for informed patient consent. Patients should also be made aware of the carcinogenic risks of high-dose X-ray procedures, particularly pediatric CT scans, and fluoroscopy. Patients should then seek those currently few radiologists and clinics practicing dose-reduction techniques, and request dosage records for each examination.

3. *Citizens:* Citizens have increasing opportunities for empowerment on an individual or community basis. By plugging their zip codes into the Environmental Defense Scorecard (www.scorecard.org), citizens can obtain basic information on toxic and carcinogenic pollutants to which they are exposed. They can then organize to alert the media, and join with regional or national environmental groups to publicize their concerns to local and state health authorities, and to their state governors.

4. *Workers:* Workers are at particularly high risk for cancers because of exposures, at work or in the course of work, to a wide range of occupational carcinogens. For example, two of the fastest rising cancers in the United States, melanoma of the skin and non-Hodgkin's lymphoma, are associated with sunlight exposure in those who work outdoors, and pesticide and solvent exposures, respectively. Workers can act to reduce these exposures through their unions and health and safety committees if they are empowered by knowledge of the risks and their right to have a say in reducing their exposures. Continued and increased emphasis on primary prevention of carcinogenic exposures at work is essential to any cancer prevention campaign.

It should be stressed that the long-standing denial of citizens' right to know disproportionately affects low-income African Americans, raising serious concerns about environmental justice. These population groups are at particularly high risk of cancer in view of their common discriminatory location near petrochemical plants, hazardous waste sites, municipal incinerators, and nuclear reactors. The NCI and ACS should be pressured to conduct epidemiological cluster analyses to investigate concerns about excess cancer rates in these locations. Critical to the credibility of such investigations would be involvement in their design and monitoring by independent epidemiologists, nominated by minority groups, funded by the cancer establishment.

National Grassroots Offices. Over the past three years, the CPC has developed a national network of some 100 grassroots offices. These are provided with information on a wide range of aspects of cancer prevention and public policy, and are encouraged to make this available to their local communities and the media. Contact between the local offices and the Chicago-based parent organization is further maintained by bimonthly hourly conference calls, each presenting information on topics such as food irradiation or carcinogenic prescription drugs, followed by a question and answer period. These contacts are now being expanded.

Publicizing a Critique of the Cancer Establishment

A critique of the cancer establishment is well overdue. It is essential to interest the mainstream media in a close examination of the cancer establishment's policies that have gone largely unchallenged, and should have been justifiably criticized, for decades. Conceivably, this situation could be reversed, provided there was substantial foundation funding for expensive ads and a national PR campaign. More realistically, however, would be a mounting series of articles and reports, coordinated and authored by the Campaign endorsers and others, formerly acting individually, in smaller independent newspapers and radio stations nationwide. These reports should be focused on hot-button topics such as local or regional exposures to environmental carcinogens, concerns about cancer clusters, the escalating rates of cancers in children and retirees, and the known causes of such cancers.

Key to all such media activities would be emphasis on the escalating rates of non-smoking-related cancers, which cannot be explained away by longevity; on the minimal priority and funding of the NCI and ACS for research and public information on the prevention of avoidable exposures to carcinogens; and on the cancer establishment's denial of the public's fundamental democratic right to know about such avoidable exposures. It should be emphasized that the NCI's silence and minimal priorities on avoidable causes of cancer violate amendments to the National Cancer Program, calling for "an expanded and intensified research program for the prevention of cancer caused by occupational or environmental exposures to carcinogens."

It might be argued that regulatory agencies, or industry itself, should be targets of our prevention campaign. However, given the responsibility and control of fundamental information on cancer prevention by the multibillion-dollar funded cancer establishment, primary emphasis must be the establishment's respon-sibility for non-information and, more seriously, misinformation. An egregious example of the latter is, as noted earlier, the reassurance by the ACS, in its *Cancer*

Facts and Figures 2002, that cancer risks from dietary pesticides, "toxic wastes in dump sites," ionizing radiation from "closely controlled" nuclear plants, and non-ionizing radiation are "all at such low levels that the risks are negligible."

Legislative Initiatives

Legislative initiatives should be based on the scientific data detailed in the Campaign report. Responsibility should also be shared among national environmental, consumer, and health groups, particularly those with substantial Congressional expertise. These groups should develop and nurture a cadre of supporters on Capitol Hill for a bevy of bipartisan investigative and legislative initiatives, and as spokespersons in the media and press events.

Congressional committees have the authority to initiate investigations and direct relevant agencies to conduct them. Such investigations will confirm the NCI's minimal budgetary allocations for prevention, contrary to its insistence otherwise; the ineffectiveness of present policies on cancer prevention; and the practical feasibility of primary prevention. The optimal strategy would be to create multiple investigations to develop a drumbeat for prevention. Also, irrespective of their committees, individual members of Congress can initiate any such investigations.

An overdue initiative would be to join with the International POPs Elimination Network of non-governmental organization (NGOs) in obtaining support for implementary Senate legislation for endorsing the May 2001 Stockholm Convention. This treaty mandates the global elimination of 12 organochlorine petrochemicals (in the first instance), which are readily disseminated worldwide and which bioaccumulate in the food chain. So far, 24 nations have endorsed the Convention, nearly half of the 50 needed to ratify it. U.S. ratification would virtually ensure its enactment.

Recent Developments. Two recent initiatives have been developed in support of CPC's Stop Cancer Campaign. Rep. Jan Schakowsky (D-IL), member of the Committee on Energy and Commerce, has requested the General Accounting Office (GAO) to investigate the NCI's claimed funding for primary cancer prevention, with requests for the following information:

1. Funding for Research on Prevention: For programs whose primary objective is focused on prevention, rather than research in which prevention is incidental to other primary objectives.
a. Intramural
b. Extramural: by grants and contracts
2. Funding for Outreach: Providing the public, and also Congress and regulatory agencies, with a scientifically documented comprehensive registry of avoidable causes of cancer, and avoidable exposures to carcinogens in: air,

water, the workplace, and consumer products (food, cosmetics and toiletries, and household products); prescription drugs; and diagnostic radiation.

This request for a GAO investigation has been supported by Rep. Donna Christian-Christensen (D–Virgin Islands), member of the House Committee on Resources and chair of the Congressional Black Caucus Health Brain Trust. Rep. Christensen will be attending the Campaign meeting.

Rep. John Conyers, Jr. (D-MI), dean of the Congressional Black Caucus and ranking member of the House Judiciary Committee, has expressed strong concerns about the indifference of the NCI to cancer prevention, and on the disproportionate impact of cancer in minority communities.

State Initiatives

Political, and a wide range of other, initiatives should be developed at the state and local levels. Since the 2002 mid-term elections, Congress remains divided and gridlocked. Accordingly, leadership and innovative policies on domestic agendas are likely to shift further from the national to state, county, and city levels. The short- and long-term impacts of this shift are likely to exceed any marginal Congressional domestic initiatives. Priority should thus be directed to working with state governors who are likely to be particularly sensitive to broadly based grassroots domestic concerns, of which the escalating and avoidable incidence of cancer is surely a major priority. It should be noted that Democratic governors now (as of April 2003) control 24 states, an increase from 21. These include 13 of the largest states representing 53 percent of the population, including Pennsylvania, Illinois, and Michigan, and also Republican strongholds like Kansas and Wyoming.

Toxics Use Reduction. Of immediate priority is implementing state-level toxics reduction. With the active cooperation of environmental groups and socially responsible business, all states should be pressed to enact the equivalent of the Massachusetts 1989 Toxics Use Reduction Act. This Act requires statewide industries to disclose the chemicals they use, what they are doing to reduce use of toxic chemicals, and what they could be doing to reduce their emissions through reduction of pollution at its source. Since passage of the Act, the most toxic environmental emissions in the state decreased by 73 percent, from 20.6 to 5.5 million pounds, through improvement and redesign of manufacturing processes and products.

Additionally, 25 noncompliant states will be urged to stop exempting pesticides from taxes. City and county actions on cancer prevention, such as toxics-free procurement, should also be implemented. Media training should be organized for local activist groups in order to provide high-profile coverage in numerous media outlets.

The Minnesota Initiative. On April 8, 2003, consumer and environmental groups in the state of Minnesota enthusiastically agreed to initiate a Stop Cancer Campaign, in collaboration with the CPC. Certainly the logistics of organizing such a statewide campaign offer benefits of ease of communication and integration and cohesiveness, and may well create a unique model for developing a practical basis for national strategies. The Minnesota initiative is also further facilitated by the state's well-developed strong reputation and track record for social and human rights concerns. The importance of this initiative cannot be overstressed.

Expansion of the Campaign's Support Base

While representatives of a wide range of groups and individual activists have sponsored or endorsed the Campaign, the membership and outreach of each group should be expanded by its own representatives. It is anticipated that individual Campaign groups will also develop initiatives primarily reflecting their own agendas, including adverse public health effects other than carcinogenic. It should, however, be recognized that most carcinogens are intertwined with and also induce other chronic toxic effects of growing concern. These include hormonal (endocrine disruptive), multiple chemical sensitivity, and immunological dis-orders, for which there are no incidence data comparable to those for cancer. Cancer thus represents a uniquely quantifiable sentinel indicator for other adverse public health impacts of poorly regulated industrial technologies and products.

REACH: AN UNPRECEDENTED SCIENCE-BASED EUROPEAN INITIATIVE FOR REGULATING INDUSTRIAL CHEMICALS

THE PRECAUTIONARY PRINCIPLE AS THE BASIS FOR REACH

Under the terms of the 1948 U.N. Universal Declaration of Human Rights, the right to life and its corollary, right to health, are the first and most important of all fundamental rights recognized by many international conventions. Thus, implementary legislation is needed to mandate that considerations of life and health take absolute precedence over economics and trade (1) (see Chapter 6).

One of the earliest scientific and legal expressions of this concept is the "Precautionary Principle," embodied in the 1992 Rio Declaration (2): "In order to protect the environment, the precautionary approach shall be widely applied by States according to their capabilities. Where there are threats of serious or irreversible damage, lack of full scientific certainty shall not be used as a reason for postponing cost-effective measures to prevent environmental degradation." In the same year, the U.N. Conference on Environment and Development (UNCED) also invoked the Precautionary Principle in its Biodiversity Convention treaty (3) and in its Agenda 21 report on risks of environmental degradation (4). In 1993, the European Commission (EC), the European Union's administrative body, established the Precautionary Principle as a fundamental basis of environmental law (5). This was subsequently accepted as a "full fledged and general principle of international law" (6).

The Precautionary Principle was first invoked by the German government at the 1994 Second North Sea Conference, in relation to marine dumping of toxic wastes. Such policies were accepted as clearly preferable to deliberately accepting risks and then attempting to "manage" them by reducing exposures to levels claimed "acceptable" by self-interested industry and complicit regulatory

Published in *International Journal of Health Services*, Volume 35, Number 1, 2005.

agencies. Recognizing the sovereign rights of each nation to set its own levels of sanitary protection, it was emphasized that precautionary policies should constitute the standard principle, and not the current rare exception (Table 1).

By the 1990s, Sweden had established itself as the most environmentally responsible European nation. In 1997, the Swedish Chemicals Policy Committee published a revolutionary document entitled "Towards a Sustainable Chemicals Policy," which embraced the fullest implementation of the Precautionary Principle ever proposed. This was approved by the Swedish Parliament in 2001. These policies shifted the burden of proof of safety away from the public to industry. Industry was required to produce detailed evidence that all new chemicals

Table 1

The Precautionary Principle (PP) as the basis for REACH

1948: U.S. Declaration of Human Rights

Created the impetus for implementary legislation, mandating that life and death concerns should take absolute precedence over economics and trade.

1992: Rio Declaration

The earliest scientific and legal expression of the PP, stressing that action to prevent environmental degradation should not be contingent on "full scientific certainty."

1992: U.S. Conference on Environment and Development (UNCED)

Invoked the PP in its Biodiversity Convention treaty and reports on risks of environmental degradation.

1993: The EC establishes PP as a fundamental basis of environmental law

1994: Second North Sea Conference

Established the PP in relation to marine dumping of toxic wastes.

1997: Swedish Chemicals Policy Committee, "Towards a Sustainable Chemicals Policy"

Embraced the fullest implementation of the PP ever proposed. It was approved by Parliament in 2001. The law banned persistent organic pollutants, and very persistent chemicals, and set short time limits for their testing and phase-out.

1998: World Conservation Union

President Chirac proposed increasing the powers of the U.N. Environment Program to avoid sovereignty disputes in the global fight against pollution.

2001: REACH 2001

Incorporated the PP as its basis for risk assessment and management. However, as REACH is primarily directed to regulating chemicals for which there are substantive scientific data on adverse effects, the term "Precaution and Prevention Principle" is clearly more appropriate than "Precautionary Principle."

---

proposed for use would pose no carcinogenic, mutagenic, or reproductive effects, or adverse environmental impacts, particularly persistence and bioaccumulation. The law also banned persistent organic pollutants and other persistent chemicals, such as lead, and required the phasing out of chlorinated paraffins, such as plasticizers and flame retardants. Swedish companies were given five years to test an estimated 2,500 chemicals used in quantities of more than 1,000 tons/year for such effects. By 2010, chemicals used in lesser amounts will also have to be tested.

At a 1998 meeting of the World Conservation Union, President Jacques Chirac proposed increasing the powers of the U.N. Environment Program to avoid sovereignty disputes that hamper the global fight against pollution. President Chirac warned that countries were holding on to outdated concepts of sovereignty, while environmental pollution ignores national borders.

REACH

In the European Union, only the EC has the authority to initiate legislation. Responsibility for chemicals management is shared by the Directorate General Environment and the Directorate General Enterprise. In 1998, the two directorates began to draft legislation on industrial chemicals. Contrary to general understanding, tile impetus for this initiative was not the Precautionary Principle. Instead, it was the fundamental inconsistency between the absence of regulations for industrial chemicals and, in striking contrast, the detailed regulations for "substances," including pesticides, food additives, and pharmaceuticals. Most of the latter regulations had already been passed, and were in fact completed by the end of 2000. The draft legislation was thus responsive to World Trade Organization (WTO) rules for nondiscriminatory regulations for the manufacture of chemicals (producers) and substances (products).

In a February 2001 "White Paper: Strategy for a Future Chemicals Policy" (7), the EC recommended that regulations known as REACH (Registration, Evaluation, Authorization of CHemicals) be administered by a European Chemicals Bureau (ECB). The regulations were intended to replace some 40 existing directives on the manufacture and import of industrial chemicals in the originally 15 countries of the European Union, currently an amalgam of the highly diverse 25 nations of the "new European Union." The procedures, detailed by REACH, embody the Precautionary Principle as the basis for risk assessment and management (8), and for assessing and balancing the externalized costs of industry and the internalized benefits to the public of regulation.

It should, however, be stressed that the Precautionary Principle, historically and scientifically, is and should be restricted to new technologies and new chemicals for which there are no available data on their public health and environmental impacts. Under these circumstances, it is the responsibility of the industry concerned to generate and publish such data, as an essential precaution before any regulation can be considered (1). However, this is clearly not the case for REACH, which relates to the assessment of substantive data on adverse effects. In these circumstances, as is the case for REACH, the term "Prevention Principle" is more appropriate than the "Precautionary Principle," even recognizing the fact that the latter has become embodied in the E.U. regulatory process (Table 1).

The expectation was that the REACH proposals would be formally presented to the European Parliament and Council of Ministers after the May 2004 elections, and that the current Parliament would get a "first reading" prior to that date. This would tend to solidify Parliament's position on REACH in its subsequent second and third readings. The E.U. Parliament tends to be more "green" than the EC and would thus be likely to approve or even strengthen REACH. Final approval by the Council of Ministers from E.U. nations was expected in 2005. Individual nations would then have to incorporate REACH into their own national laws. It should be noted that the majority of the EC's legislative proposals eventually become E.U. law.

The E.U. chemical industry is concentrated in four nations. Germany is the largest, accounting for 26 percent of E.U. production in 2000, followed by France (17 percent), the United Kingdom (14 percent), and Italy (12 percent).With the exception of France, output growth in the large E.U. producers remains less than in the United States. Small manufacturing enterprises, with less than 250 employees, account for 28 percent of production value in the E.U. chemical industry. The aggregate European chemical industry remains competitive internationally, with the United States as its single biggest competitor.

Principles

REACH recommended that the European Union adopt an unprecedented complex of regulations for industrial chemicals. These were designed to "make a major contribution to achieve safe use of chemicals at a global level." E.U. Environment Commissioner Margot Wallström hailed these proposed regulations: "The new policy introduces a radical paradigm shift. It is high time to place the responsibility where it belongs, with industry."

While stressing these critical safety concerns, the REACH proposals were also designed to stimulate industrial innovation, particularly the development of cost-effective, safe, substitute technologies and products. Another important objective was to encourage "the *substitution* of dangerous by less dangerous substances where suitable alternatives are available."

REACH proposed that the following generic classes of industrial chemicals should be regarded as of "very high concern" (VHC):

• Category 1 or 2 *C*arcinogens, *M*utagens, or *R*eproductive toxins (CMRs), which are known (category 1) or are very likely (category 2) to induce such toxic effects in humans.

- Chemicals that can become widely disseminated in the environment, and which are *P*ersistent, *B*ioaccumulative, and *T*oxic (PBT), with particular reference to *P*ersistent *O*rganic *P*ollutants (POPs).
- Chemicals that are *v*ery *p*ersistent and *v*ery *b*ioaccumulative (vPvB) in humans and wildlife, and for which toxicity data are still unavailable.

It should also be recognized that many of these chemicals are ingredients or contaminants in pesticides and in consumer products, including food, cosmetics, and household products.

Registration. Industry is required to notify the ECB, which is responsible for the "Classification and Labeling of Dangerous Substances," of intent to produce or import new and existing chemicals in a Chemical Safety Report (CSR) dossier. The dossier includes the following information: data on the identity of each chemical; toxicological and ecotoxicological properties of intended uses; estimated human and environmental exposures; production quantity; proposed classification and labeling; safety data sheet; preliminary risk assessment; and proposed risk management. This information is to be entered into a publicly available database to be managed by the ECB; industry is required to pay fees for each submission. Registration of basic information is required for the following:

- About 30,000 high production volume (HPV) chemicals manufactured or imported by any industry in excess of 1 ton/year; about 80 percent of these would only require registration before 2013.
- "Articles": finished articles classified as dangerous, or that release dangerous substances in excess of 1 ton/year.
- Experimental or R&D chemicals produced by any company in amounts less than 1 ton/year; waived for at least 5 years.

In an attempt to reduce registration costs, the European Union encouraged industry to form consortia and to share CSR data. REACH would require manufacturers and importers to pre-register their chemicals at least 18 months prior to the registration deadline. Companies that pre-register the same chemical can participate in a Substance Information Exchange Forum where they can share testing and related information, whose costs are estimated to range from €75,000 to €125,000 per chemical. REACH would also impose penalties to discourage "free riding" by companies refusing to pay their fair share of testing costs.

Evaluation. Testing of HPV chemicals is tiered on the basis of marketed volumes in excess of 1 ton/year, as follows:

- 1 to 10 tons: physicochemical, toxicological, and ecotoxicological data are required; testing should generally be limited to *in vitro* methods.

- 10 to 100 tons: "base-set" testing is required, on a "case by case basis," for chemicals that are suspected, for reasons including quantitative structure-activity relationship, to be PBT and CMRs.
- 100 to 1,000 tons: "Level 1" substance-tailored testing for long-term effects is required, based on information including physicochemical properties, uses, and exposures.
- More than 1,000 tons: "Level 2" additional, more comprehensive, long-term testing is required.

Testing requirements for an estimated 5,000 chemicals exceeding a production volume of 100 tons are critical in view of the gross inadequacy of current test data on HPV chemicals. A 1999 review of about 2,500 HPV chemicals, based on the International Uniform Chemical Information Database, revealed that no data were available for 21 percent, less than the required "base-set" data were available for 65 percent, and "base-set" data were available for only 14 percent (9). Moreover, a 1998 review revealed that internationally accepted Screening Information Data-Sets were available for only 8.5 percent of all U.S. HPV chemicals (10).

Authorization. Authorization will be granted for an estimated 1,400 VHC chemicals, including those produced in volumes below 100 tons/year, estimated at 5 percent of registration chemicals. This will be granted subject to specific conditions and strict deadlines. The following categories of VHCs are specified:

- 850 chemicals currently classified as category 1 or 2 CMRs; an additional 500 or so CMRs may be identified through future testing.
- Chemicals with POP characteristics.
- Endocrine-disruptive chemicals that have been associated with reproductive cancers, hormonal effects (including congenital disease and male infertility), and impaired immune and nervous system development, and also endocrine abnormalities in wildlife.

Objectives

- Reducing poorly recognized adverse public health and environmental impacts, and their poorly recognized major economic costs, particularly those resulting from avoidable exposures to toxic industrial chemicals.
- Reducing industry's concerns about costs from anticipated toxic tort litigation, on behalf of citizens and workers, and civil liability for environmental damage (11). However, these costs are of limited deterrence, as awards by E.U. courts are still lower than in the United States.
- Reducing industry's liability from anticipated claims based on human rights jurisprudence (11).

- Reducing poorly recognized adverse environmental impacts, besides their poorly recognized externalized major economic costs, resulting from avoidable contamination of air, water, food, and the workplace with VHC chemicals.
- Stimulating industry innovation by encouraging "the substitution of dangerous by less dangerous substances where suitable alternatives are available."
- Increasing transparency: making industry responsible for "providing full information to the public—so creating pressure on industry to develop safe substances."
- Encouraging progressive industry and downstream users to further expand current safe-product markets, and stimulating the development of new safe substitute products and markets.

Estimated Industry Costs

- Registration: €300 million.
- Testing of 30,000 HPV chemicals: €2.1 billion.
- Total: €2.4 billion.
- Administrative costs: approximately €0.4 billion; these will be recovered on a fee-based system.

Spread over 11 years, these costs are approximately 0.05 percent of the E.U. chemical industry's €417 billion turnover in 2000. REACH also indicates that some of these costs may be passed on to downstream companies, presumably these costs would then be shared by the public. Furthermore, these costs are likely to be dwarfed by costs of poorly recognized public health and environmental impacts, to which REACH makes the briefest reference. These include the "significantly increased . . . incidence of testicular cancer in young men, and allergies over the last decades, for which the underlying reasons have not yet been identified." REACH also fails to make any reference to legal costs and human rights liabilities resulting from failure to regulate the E.U. chemical industry (11).

Transparency and Right to Know

In principle, REACH recognizes the need for increasing transparency, for avoiding conflicts of interest in advisory committee members, and for providing full information to the public. "The public has a right to access to information about the chemicals to which they are exposed. This will enable them to make [industry] develop safer substitutes." Nevertheless, REACH states that the EC "believes that industry . . . should mainly be responsible for providing information on health and environmental effects to consumers." REACH also assures industry that "commercially sensitive information will be suitably protected."

Reactions to REACH

The principles of REACH have received strong support from E.U. and U.S. cancer-prevention and public health scientists and physicians. These include those represented by the Association Française pour la Recherche Thérapeutique Anti-Cancéreuse and the Cancer Prevention Coalition, representing approximately 100 leading cancer-prevention and public health scientists, and also representatives of NGOs and citizen activist groups. In the European Union, these groups include the European Environmental Bureau, a coalition of 146 NGOs, the World Wildlife Fund–U.K. (WWF-U.K.), Pesticide Action Network, and the European Trade Union Technical Bureau. In the United States, these groups include the Science and Environmental Health Network, Physicians for Social Responsibility, the Alliance for Safe Alternatives, the Lowell Center for Sustainable Production, the Environmental Health Fund, the Environmental Working Group, and the Natural Resources Defense Council.

A few industries have welcomed REACH. BP Chemicals–Europe greeted the five-year registration waiver for experimental substances as "good news." More broadly, Bayer AG emphasized that REACH would encourage innovation, by forcing companies to develop substitutes for hazardous chemicals. However, the REACH proposals have met with overwhelming resistance from other European and American chemical industries and trade associations, including the European Chemical Industrial Council (CEFIC; 12), the American Chemistry Council (ACC; 13), and the American Chamber of Commerce to the European Union. They claimed that REACH requirements would stifle innovation, result in major job losses, pose inflationary costs, disrupt global trade, and violate trade secrecy and WTO Rules (14).

At the root of these claims is a fundamental ideological opposition to the Precautionary Principle, as exemplified in REACH. This requires governments to base regulatory policies proactively on the probability, or reasonable possibility, of risk. However, the position of industry, supported by U.S. regulatory policy, is insistence that regulations should be imposed only retroactively in response to "credible evidence of unreasonable risk" of disease, death, or environmental degradation, and then only following a cost-benefit analysis (15).

In striking contrast to E.U. governments, which have maintained neutral positions, the Bush administration has encouraged industry to take aggressive opposition to REACH (15–17). Secretary of State Colin Powell, in a March 2002 U.S. "Nonpaper on E.U. Chemical Policy," warned that the Precautionary Principle would result in "politically motivated bans" of U.S. chemical products (15), which account for more than 20 percent of all U.S. exports (14). Dr. John Graham, administrator of the U.S. Office of Information and Regulatory Affairs, and former director of the industry-funded Harvard University Center for Risk Analysis, in a May 18, 2003, speech to E.U. regulators, stated that the administration considers the Precautionary Principle "to be a mythical concept, perhaps like a unicorn" (16).

Confidential documents obtained under the U.S. Freedom of Information Act have revealed that the U.S. State and Commerce Department, Environmental Protection Agency, and Office of the U.S. Trade Representative have formed an alliance with Dow Chemical to fight REACH (18, 19). These tactics, however, may backfire. Senator Frank Lautenberg (D-NJ), with other influential Congressional democrats, is drafting a proposal to overhaul U.S. regulations to resemble the European Union's proposed reforms (20, 21).

The mainstream industry opposition has been mobilized by the ACC and the CEFIC, each accounting for approximately 30 percent of the world's chemical production. The Trans-Atlantic Business Dialogue (22) has been established to coordinate industry opposition to REACH. A leaked ACC memo has revealed aggressive and well-funded plans to fight laws and regulations based on the Precautionary Principle (23). ACC's public relations campaign is being handled by Nichols-Dezenhall, which has hired former FBI and CIA agents to create phony front groups and to spy on environmental activists, including digging through their trash in efforts to smear them.

These behind-the-scenes tactics are in striking contrast to industry's initiatives to sanitize its public image. The ACC has announced a "Reputation Initiative," advocating a "High Production Volume (HPV) Chemical Testing Program" and a "Long-Range Research Initiative on Testing Chemical Hazards" (24). Along similar lines, the Chemical Manufacturers Association has launched a "Responsible Care Campaign.—We are not asking the public to trust us. We are asking everyone to track us" (24).

In its May 2002 preliminary comments, CEFIC requested exemption of the following from REACH requirements: all chemicals that "are adequately controlled by other legislation"; R&D chemicals; "substances" marketed below 1 ton/year per manufacturer; and polymers and their intermediates (12). The request for polymer exemption has been strongly reinforced by other industries, notably Hydro Polymers, which insisted that polymers "including PVC present a low level of harm." This industry also insisted that it was unreasonable to be concerned about endocrine disruptive phthalates, in view of the EC's failure to take action against contamination of water with natural or contraceptive estrogen.

The first formalized critique of REACH was detailed by the ACC on July 10, 2003 (13): "REACH is impractical and too costly and should be replaced by a 'risk-based approach': REACH is trade restrictive and incompatible with WTO objectives, and international chemical regulations; the European Union should instead rely on existing registration and risk management, rather than REACH; and the high costs of REACH would impose a negative impact on innovation and competitiveness of E.U. industry."

The ACC's more specific criticisms include the following: the "duty of care" base-set CSR (Chemical Safety Report) data requirements are impractical and too costly, and should be replaced by tailored testing requirements, based on use and exposure patterns; polymers should be exempted from registration requirements in "view of the low risk to health and the environment"; the high-priority regulatory requirements for VHC chemicals should be authorized only if warranted by "use and exposure patterns"; endocrine disruption is "a mode of action and not a health effect," and thus inappropriate for authorization; and authorization would force industry to "develop and submit socioeconomic substitution."

The opposition to REACH by E.U. and U.S. industry was so strong that the European Union was forced to make substantial concessions. These were jointly developed by the Swedish Environment Commissioner Margot Wallström, and Enterprise Commissioner Erkki Liikanen. Key among these was the reduction from 30,000 to 10,000 HPV chemicals for which comprehensive safety testing would be required, in spite of the minimal available test data on most of them. Among other major concessions was the exemption from requirements for data on reproductive toxicity and environmental persistence of chemicals produced in amounts from 1 to 10 tons.

THE 2003 WEAKENED VERSION
OF REACH

In May 2003, the European Commission issued its revised legislative proposals as a Staff Working Paper, which was finalized in October 2003 (25). These revisions reflect strong pressure by E.U. and U.S. industries and by the U.S. administration. To a lesser extent, these proposals also reflect political and economic differences between E.U. member states. The Working Paper was adopted as the final basis for regulations in October 2003 (25).

Principles

The stated objectives of the Staff Paper are similar to those of REACH. However, the latter requirements have been sharply cut back in response to heavy pressure to reduce the allegedly high costs of regulation to industry. This is paralleled by the EC's limited recognition of the much higher, poorly quantifiable health and environmental costs of past and current failure to regulate, let alone future costs. It is also paralleled by inadequate recognition by industry of the increasing likelihood of toxic tort and other legal and human rights liabilities. Reflecting these perspectives, the revised REACH proposals have drastically curtailed their earlier objectives. This has been achieved by "lightening," waiving, or even exempting most registration and other requirements (Table 2).

Table 2

Summary comparison of REACH 2001 and its 2003 version

	REACH 2001	2003 REACH Version
Registration		
Chemical safety reports	Required	Exempted
HPV chemicals	Required for > 1 ton	Lightened for 1–10 tons
Polymers	Required	Exempted
Imports	Required	Exempted
Downstream users	Required	Exempted
Transparency	Required	Exempted
Evaluation		
HPV chemicals	30,000	10,000
Authorization		
VHC chemicals	Required	May be waived
CMRs 1 and 2	Required	May be waived
PBTs	Required	May be waived
vPvB	Required	May be waived
EDCs	Required	May be waived

Note: Abbreviations: HPV, high production volume; VHC, very high concern; CMR, carcinogens, mutagens, reproductive toxins; PBT, persistent, bioaccumulative, toxic; vPvB, very persistent, very bioaccumulative; EDC, endocrine-disruptive chemical.

"May be waived" in 2003 version on the basis of "socio-economic grounds," or claims that risks can be "adequately controlled," or that there is "no right to concern."

Registration. Industry is exempt from any requirements to submit Chemical Safety Reports, and most other requirements are lightened or even waived.

- HPV chemicals manufactured or imported in amounts below 10 tons/year: waived for at least six years, and then subject to review.
- Chemicals manufactured or imported in amounts below 1 ton/year: exempted.
- Intermediates: unspecified "lighter requirements."
- R&D chemicals: exempted for up to ten years.
- Polymers: exempted.
- "Articles": exempted, unless they contain a chemical that is classified as dangerous and can be released from the products.
- Imports: exempted, unless they contain chemicals that are classified as dangerous and can be released from the products.
- Downstream users: exempted.
- Transparency: breached by a "practical formula" provision for protecting confidential business information.

Evaluation

- CSR testing requirements for HPV chemicals: reduced from 30,000 to 10,000.
- CSRs for downstream users: replaced by "Safety Data Sheets."
- Chemicals manufactured or imported in "the sensitive 1 to 10 tons/year range:": "lower test requirements."
- R&D chemicals: testing threshold increased from 10 kg to 1 ton/year.
- Testing requirements for chemicals: waived if "unnecessary," or if "information can be obtained by other means," or "if profile of use does not require it."
- Polymers: exempted from any testing requirements.
- Intermediates: drastic reduction for any testing requirements.
- Downstream users: exempted from any testing requirements.
- For any amount of any chemical: CSRs could be waived by encouraging development of computer-based qualitative or quantitative structure-activity relationships (QSARs) that may "permit the prediction of . . . environmental or health effects without the need for further animal tests."

However, in spite of numerous studies on such short-term QSAR tests over the past four decades, there is minimal if any evidence on their reliability and ability to predict synergistic interactions and complex metabolic processes. In sharp contrast, the validity of extrapolating carcinogenicity evidence from rodent tests to human risk has been overwhelmingly supported for decades by independent scientists, blue-ribbon expert federal and nonfederal committees, and the World Health Organization's International Agency for Research on Cancer (IARC). Additionally, positive evidence from numerous rodent tests has been confirmed epidemiologically, generally decades later (26). Of striking relevance is the December 2002 report of the International Consortium's Mouse Genome Project, which reported that roughly 99 percent of mouse genes have a functional equivalent in the human genome, that their biological programming is amazingly similar, and that the mouse is thus an ideal laboratory animal for investigating the molecular basis of human disease (24, 26).

Furthermore, in view of industry's decades-long attempts, on a variety of spurious grounds, to challenge the validity and human relevance of rodent carcinogenicity data, it is unlikely that industry would accept any positive QSAR data on carcinogenicity. It is equally likely that industry would claim negative QSAR data as exculpatory.

Authorization. The Staff Paper offers industry the opportunity to avoid authorization costs for VHC chemicals, either "on socio-economic grounds" or by presenting a plan for "adequate control" and future R&D on safe substitutes for hazardous chemicals. These loopholes fail to reflect the current availability of a wide range of such cost-competitive substitutes.

Public Information. It is claimed that "the public at large will benefit from the information gathered because of REACH, as they will be better informed about potential risks from specific substances." Apart from this single reassuring sentence, there is no indication whatsoever about how any such information will be made available to the public and to industry workers (27). Furthermore, there is no evidence that the public and labor, and their NGO and other representatives, have been consulted in the development of the finalized 2003 proposals.

The 2003 Proposals Underestimate the Benefits of Regulation

Based on selected or unreferenced sources, the 2003 proposals understate the benefits of regulation. Examples include the following:

- Ninety percent of the health benefits associated with chemicals are related to historical exposures, or will not be identified by REACH, or cannot be tackled.
- "The proportion of all diseases due to agro-industrial chemicals and chemical pollution from diffuse sources is between 0.6 percent and 2.5 percent in developed market economies" (28).
- "For occupational cancer in developed countries—there would be an equivalent of 4,500 lives saved per year due to REACH."

Reactions to the Revised 2003 Proposals

In contrast to their overwhelming support of REACH, the Association Française pour la Recherche Thérapeutique Anti-Cancéreuse (ARTAC), the Cancer Prevention Coalition (CPC), scientists from Technical Working Groups of the SCALE initiative, and a wide range of citizen and labor groups and NGOs have strongly criticized the 2003 proposals.

REACH SHOULD BE STRENGTHENED, NOT WEAKENED

The European Commission must be strongly commended for developing REACH. However, these proposals have been weakened by the EC's capitulation to pressure from E.U. and U.S. industries, strongly reinforced by the U.S. administration. These concessions are also responsive to exaggerated claims of the costs of REACH, which in fact are only 0.05 percent of the chemical industry's €417 billion turnover in 2000. In striking contrast, the 2003 Staff Paper fails to recognize the much higher public health and environmental costs of its drastically weakened regulations. Clearly, REACH should be strengthened, not weakened (Table 3).

Table 3

How to strengthen REACH

Mandatory substitution of VHC chemicals

Authorization to be denied if safe alternatives are available.

Transparency: Citizens' right to know

Independent audit of industry's chemical safety dossiers prior to registration.

Independent audit of industry's claims for waiving authorization of VHC chemicals based on no "right to concern" or that risks can be " adequately controlled."

Comprehensive information on air and water emissions of industries handling VHC chemicals.

Comprehensive information on industrial contaminants in air, water, the workplace, and consumer products—food, cosmetics, and household products.

Assurances that downstream users will be fully informed, other than by industry, of identity, volume, and dangers of registered and unregistered chemicals.

All advisory committees to include representatives of independent expert stakeholders, and meetings to be open to the public; all committee members to fully disclose their conflicts of interest.

Evaluation of benefits

Estimated health benefits, €50 billion over 30 years, do not reflect the escalating incidence of non-smoking-related cancers, nor early life exposures due to industrial chemicals.

Environmental benefits to be estimated and recognized.

Industry benefits from technological innovation stimulated by REACH to be estimated and recognized.

Evaluation of costs

Independent audit of industry's claims of high costs of REACH as the basis of aggressive industry opposition.

Reckless industry practices are violations of human rights, and white-collar crime

Incorporation of the 2003 European Environment and Health Strategy Work Plan (SCALE)

Incorporation of the 2004 European Pollutant Emission Register

Incorporation of the 2004 Rotterdam Convention on Prior Informed Consent (PIC) for Import of Industrial Chemicals

Prohibition of import of all HPV and VHC chemicals that have not been registered and evaluated under the terms of REACH.

Evaluation

REACH's minimal requirement for in vitro test data for 1 to 10 tons/year HPV chemicals is scientifically untenable. It ignores the highly questionable validity and relevance of such data, apart from concerns about carcinogenic and endocrine-disruptive potency. More importantly, REACH focuses on the carcinogenic and other toxic effects of individual chemicals, particularly VHC chemicals, to the exclusion of well-documented evidence on additive and unpredictable synergistic interactions between individual carcinogens (26). Of additional concern is extensive evidence on the effects of lipophilic chemicals in increasing percutaneous and inhalation absorption and synergizing the toxicity of a wide range of individual chemicals, such as formaldehyde, styrene, and atrazine (29).

Authorization

The proposed REACH ban on or restriction of HPV chemicals is flawed by the exemption permitting their continued use if industry claims that their risks can be "adequately controlled." This qualification is an open invitation to claims for exemption, based on definitional grounds. For this reason, all claims for "adequate control" should be subject to mandatory evaluation by an independent advisory committee, appointed by the European Chemicals Bureau and funded by the applicant industry. The composition of such a committee should reflect balanced representation of a wide range of qualified stakeholders, including independent scientific and technical experts and NGO and labor representatives.

Toxics Use Reduction

Industries manufacturing or processing HPV chemicals should be required to implement toxics use reduction programs. These should be modeled on the requirements of the Commonwealth of Massachusetts 1989 Toxics Use Reduction Act, as a precedent-setting legislative statement on the Precautionary Principle (30). The Act created the Massachusetts Toxics Use Reduction Program, focused on reducing the use of toxic chemicals and the generation of hazardous wastes by improving and redesigning industrial products and processes. Within 10 years of the Act's passage, its achievements included reducing the use of toxic chemicals by 40 percent, toxic wastes by 58 percent, and toxic emissions by 80 percent. Additionally, a cost-benefit analysis revealed a savings of $11.1 million to the 550 industries and companies involved. The program is ongoing and has recently been expanded to incorporate toxics substitution (31).

The continued use by industry of VHC chemicals should be made subject to mandatory requirements by the ECB for routine monitoring for point source and fugitive air emissions and water discharges. The continued use of these chemicals should also be subject to requirements for material balance studies in order to match outputs to inputs, and thus to quantify environmental losses and enable prompt process remediation. In this connection, the E.U. chemical industry has claimed that there have been major reductions in air and water emissions over recent years. However, these reductions have been largely offset by major increases in productivity (Table 4).

The Substitution Principle

REACH states that an "important objective is to encourage the *substitution* of dangerous by less dangerous substances where suitable alternatives are available." However, REACH fails to mandate this principle as an obligate requirement for authorization. Substitution is a critical basis for risk prevention, in contrast to industry's continued emphasis on "risk management" (32). Recognition of this fundamental principle has recently been emphasized by the Swedish Government, which explicitly stated that authorization of hazardous chemicals should be granted only if industry can demonstrate that safe substitutes are unavailable (33). Similarly, the U.K. Royal Commission has "recommended that the U.K. Government adopt substitution as a central objective of chemicals policy" (34).

Allowing for reasonable phase-in time, substitution should be a routine requirement for the authorization of VHC chemicals, particularly those that are persistent, bioaccumulative, and toxic (PBT). Exceptions to this requirement should be

Table 4

E.U. chemical industry: Recent
changes in emissions and productivity

	Change, percentage
Atmospheric emissions, 1990–2001	
Greenhouse gases (e.g., nitrous oxide)	−50
Acidifying gases (e.g., sulfur dioxide)	−48
Ozone precursors (e.g., non-methane volatile organic chemicals)	−38
Water emissions, 1996–2000	
Chemical oxygen demand	−17
Nitrogen compounds	−25
Heavy metals	−43
Productivity, 1990–2001	+33

Sources: Atmospheric and water emissions, based on industry data (12); productivity based on EC data (25).

contingent on confirmation by the Chemical Bureau, in transparent decision-making proceedings, that safe substitutes are neither available nor pending.

Over the last decade, an increasing number of progressive industries and retailers have made major advances in substitution for a very wide range of VHC chemicals, based on substantial developments in Green Chemistry and Clean Production technologies (35, 36). Examples include:

- Substitution of the use of lead in soldering and electronic products by tin, silver, copper, bismuth, and zinc. This has been implemented by industries including IBM, NEC, Phillips, Panasonic, Fujitsu, Matsushita, and Hitachi.
- Substitution of PBDE flame retardants by internal metal-framed casings or by polycarbonate resin retardants, particularly in printed wire circuit electronic boards. This has been implemented by industries including IBM, Motorola, Hewlett Packard, NEC, Apple, Great Lakes Chemicals, Sumitomo Dow, Matsushita, and Bayer, and by retailers including Marks & Spencer and H&M.
- Substitution of alkylphenol ethoxylate (APE) surfactants by alcohol ethoxylates in textile and leather finishing treatments, water-based paints, and cosmetics. This has been implemented by industries including Colgate-Palmolive and Procter & Gamble, and by major retailers including Boots.
- Substitution of chlorinated solvents by supercritical carbon dioxide in microelectronics, paints, paint coatings, manufacture of polymers such as Teflon, and dry-cleaning processes. This has been implemented by industries including Dow Chemical, DuPont, Micell Technologies, and Global Technologies.
- Substitution of agricultural, municipal, and domestic uses of synthetic pesticides by well-developed and cost-effective integrated Pest Management (IPM) techniques.

It should further be emphasized that the substitution principle will also avoid and solve the "current paralysis by analysis" that is inherent in REACH's requirements for comprehensive testing of HPV chemicals (32).

The Economic Benefits of Regulation

REACH should be strengthened by explicit reference to the very high and increasingly recognized public health and environmental costs of under-regulation. A recent economic study has stressed that "Caution can be costly, but indifference to serious risks can be disastrous. . . . Furthermore, the costs of mitigation often are far less than initially projected, because of induced technical changes; delaying mitigation can therefore increase costs" (37). Examples include estimates by the U.S. Environmental Protection Agency (EPA) of $22 trillion net human health benefits of the 1970 Clean Air Act over a 20-year period (38), and the estimated 300,000 deaths averted by the control of chlorofluorocarbons

(39). Such major benefits for the European Union are in striking contrast to exaggerated industry claims of the high costs of REACH's proposals.

The Right to Know

REACH should be strengthened by an emphasis that the right to know is an inalienable democratic principle, with the exception of sensitive national security concerns. This right clearly extends to information on avoidable risks of disease and death, and environmental contamination, due to industry practices. As such, these rights override claims of trade secrecy and confidentiality. It should, however, be recognized that the right to know in the European Union, besides other nations, is more honored in the breach than in the observance. REACH should explicitly acknowledge this right and detail the mechanism for its widest implementation.

Public Exposure to HPV Chemicals. Recognizing these rights, REACH should mandate that all industries manufacturing or processing HPV, particularly VHC, chemicals develop routine automated monitoring of point source, of fugitive toxic emissions to air, and of discharges to water. Such monitoring data should be made contemporaneously available to the public and to the ECB. Requirements for atmospheric monitoring should also be extended to municipal solid waste incinerators, in view of their emissions of high levels of dioxins and furans from the combustion of plastics, chlorinated organic chemicals, and other downstream products based on HPV chemicals and household trash (40, 41).

The public and farmers should also be explicitly warned of cancer risks from the use of common pesticides, such as phenoxyacetic acid and chlorophenols. Since their 1978 ban in Sweden, the incidence of non-Hodgkin's lymphoma, which had been increasing in previous decades, has decreased sharply. In contrast, the incidence of this cancer in France and the United States has approximately doubled over the last two decades (42, 43).

The public's right to know should also extend to consumer products, the ultimate downstream source of public exposure to toxic industrial chemicals, particularly carcinogens, mutagens, and reproductive toxins. It should be stressed that food, household products, and cosmetics and toiletries contain a wide range of undisclosed CMRs. Notable among these: carcinogenic pesticides in household products; carcinogenic pesticide residues in grains, vegetables, and fruits; carcinogenic ingredients and contaminants in cosmetics; and endocrine-disruptive phthalates and other ingredients in cosmetics. These should be clearly labeled with explicit "red flag" warnings, and with the name and concentration of each CMR in each product. The ECB should consolidate all such data, publish them on a regular basis, and make them contemporaneously available, in a computerized toxic release inventory database, to local communities nationwide.

Occupational Exposure to HPV Chemicals. Workers are at the highest risk of high-level exposure to HPV, particularly VHC, chemicals. Industry must recognize workers' right to know of information on all such life-threatening dangers. These include specific information on the chemical and common name of each carcinogen and information on each carcinogenic process. Additionally, each industry must provide workers and their representatives with specific information on precautions taken to avoid inhalation and skin exposures. These include the use of closed-system technologies; exhaust ventilation; continuing and sensitive automated air monitoring; surface monitoring; and personal respiratory and skin protection. All such information must be made contemporaneously available to workers and their representatives.

Body Burdens of HPV Chemicals. Considering the wide range of exposure of the public to HPV chemicals, it is not surprising that many of these chemicals have been identified, particularly in the United States, as "body burden" contaminants in the fat and blood of the general population. This information would be likely to mobilize large-scale national support for strong regulatory action to protect against such unarguable evidence of reckless industry practices.

Over the last three decades, the Environmental Protection Agency and the Centers for Disease Control and Prevention (CDC) have issued a series of reports on body burdens of persistent organic pollutants, including DDT, aldrin, dieldrin, chlordane, heptachlor, and their metabolites. These reports include:

- National Human and Nutrition Examination Surveys 1970–1998. This identified high concentrations of eight POPs in 4,600 serum samples from the general population; 99 percent of these were contaminated with average DDT levels of 14 ppb.
- National Human Milk Study, 1977–1983. This was based on analyses of 1,850 breast milk samples; 55 percent were found to be contaminated with average heptachlor epoxide levels of 77 ppb.
- The CDC's January 2003 National Report on Human Exposure to Environmental Chemicals. This survey identified 116 contaminants in the serum and urine of more than 2,000 volunteers, selected as representative of the U.S. population from 1999 to 2000. These contaminants were grouped as follows: dioxin and furans; polychlorinated biphenyls (PCBs); polycyclic aromatic hydrocarbons; pesticides—organochlorine, organophosphate, carbamate, and herbicides; phthalates; heavy metals; and phytoestrogenic endocrine-disruptive chemicals.

Not surprisingly, similar results have been reported from the European Union. In their November 2003 National Biomonitoring Survey, the WWF-U.K. reported on analyses of serum from 155 U.K. volunteers for 78 industrial chemicals, in three major groups: organochlorines, including DDT and lindane; PCBs; and polybrominated diphenyl ether (PBDE) flame retardants. Every single volunteer was found to be contaminated with chemicals from each group. The median to maximum concentration ranges were as follows: total organochlorines, 130 to 2,700 ppb; total PCBs, 17 to 670 ppb; and PBDEs, 6 to 420 ppb. As stressed in the report, all contaminants in each group are very persistent and very bioaccumulative (vPvB); many are also CMRs.

The E.U. Environment Commissioner Margot Wallström also participated in this survey. The median concentrations of contaminants in her serum were as follows: PCBs, 166 ppb; organochlorines, 133 ppb; DDT, 103 ppb; hexachloro-cyclohexane, 15 ppb; and PBDEs, 6 ppb.

Responsibility of REACH. REACH should stress that only limited information is currently available to the public on avoidable environmental contaminants, with multiple HPV chemicals, and on their heavy body burdens with these contaminants. This would encourage national support for strengthening REACH and would also ensure public demand for its right to know of all such information.

The European Pollutant Emission Register. A recent landmark development in citizens' right to know is the EC's February 23, 2004, launch of a European Pollutant Emission Register. This public register is required to report on 90 percent of point-source emissions to air and water by the largest and most polluting industrial facilities. These include industries manufacturing chemicals, metals, ceramics, cement, and leather; oil refineries, power stations, and waste-disposal plants; and intensive livestock-rearing facilities. Such information is intended to stimulate industry to reduce pollutant emissions. The register contains a wealth of data on pollutant emissions, readily available to the public (www.eper.cec.eu.int). In protest, the European Chemical Industry Council claims that this register presents threats to industrial confidentiality and competition.

Transparency

REACH is flawed by giving industry responsibility for transparency. REACH goes even further by breaching transparency with an unqualified provision ensuring that "commercially sensitive information will be suitably protected." Furthermore, REACH falls to recognize that regulatory decisions are generally based on recommendations by national scientific institutes and expert advisory committees. Their expertise, independence, integrity, and accountability are thus of critical concern, as is the transparency of their deliberations.

The composition of advisory committees should reflect balanced representation of qualified stakeholders, particularly scientists and technical representatives of citizen groups, NGOs, and labor. The transparency of such proceedings should be further ensured by providing advanced public notice on scheduled meetings, which should be open to the public.

The EC has recently implemented a new policy of openness, by requiring declarations of interest by advisory committee members (44). The EC has claimed that these members act independently, make declarations of interest, and declare conflicts of interest at each meeting. Even if that were the case, such information has never been open to public scrutiny. Moreover, the EC maintains that contacts between committee members and commercial organizations are "part of normal and professional life" and should not be treated as "undesirable" (44).

The overdue need to avoid conflicts of interest is exemplified by clear evidence of corporate influence in the IARC, the WHO's designated cancer research institute. The IARC grades industrial and other chemicals for their carcinogenicity, also evaluating evidence for hormonal (endocrine-disruptive) and genetic toxicity. A letter co-signed by 30 prominent independent scientists has charged that, for nearly two decades, the IARC has downgraded the carcinogenicity of a wide range of industrial carcinogens (45); this information has recently been detailed by a previous IARC director, a well-recognized international authority on chemical carcinogens (46). Such downgrading has exculpated some major carcinogenic chemicals from REACH's regulatory requirements (Table 5). Furthermore, there is evidence that the IARC not only has invited industry representatives and consultants to its meetings, but has even paid their expenses (44). Additionally, numerous industry employees and consultants have attended IARC meetings as "observers," to the exclusion of independent experts.

Even more flagrant conflicts of interest are inherent in the recent recommendations of the ECB's Commission Working Group of industry consultants, which would drastically alter the criteria of the IARC's categorization of carcinogens, besides also trivializing evidence on mutagens and reproductive toxins (47). These recommendations would virtually ensure that all carcinogens identified by standard testing procedures would be downgraded to IARC group 3 and would be exculpated from REACH's regulatory requirements on the following grounds: "Appearance of tumors especially at high dose levels, only in particular organs of certain species known to be susceptible to a high spontaneous tumor formation; appearance of tumors, only at the site of application, in very sensitive test systems, if the particular target is not relevant to man; lack of genotoxicity in short term tests *in vivo* and *in vitro;* existence of a secondary mechanism of action with the implication of a practical threshold above a certain dose level; existence of a species-specific mechanism of tumor formation irrelevant to man." The Commission Working Group has detailed these proposals, particularly those based on "policy considerations." However, these proposals have not been included in Directive 67/548/EC amendments, relating to REACH's regulation of CMRs.

It may be noted that a leading Working Group consultant is the geneticist Bruce Ames. Ames has been discredited for his insistence that there is no evidence for the increased incidence of cancer in the United Kingdom and United

Table 5

Downgrading of carcinogenicity ratings by IARC

Carcinogen	Use	Year	Carcinogenicity rating
Saccharin	Artificial sweetener	1987	2B
		1999	*3*
Amitrole	Herbicide	1986	2A
		1987	*2B*
Atrazine	Herbicide	1991	2B
		1999	*3*
1,3-Butadiene	Plastics, synthetic rubber	1986	1
		1988	*2A*
Di-(2-ethylhexyl)-phthalate	Plasticizer	1987	2B
		2000	*3*
Glasswool (fiberglass)	Insulation	1988	2B
		2002	*3*
Ethylene thiourea	Vulcanization of rubber and contaminant in EBDC fungicides	1987	2B
		2000	*3*

Note: Carcinogenicity ratings: group 1, known; group 2A, probable; group 2B, possible; group 3, not classifiable.

States other than due to tobacco, and for his dismissal of any risks from residues of carcinogenic pesticides in food (26, chap. 14).

There is also substantial evidence of major conflicts of interest in other WHO advisory groups, particularly those with responsibility for the safety of consumer products, notably meat and milk. These groups include the Food and Agricultural Organization and the Codex Alimentarius. On examination, these groups "reflect minimal expertise in public health, high representation of United States Department of Agriculture (USDA) and Food and Drug Administration (FDA) officials, and industry consultants, and reliance on unpublished industry information" (26, app. XI and app. XII).

It should also be recognized that recommendations of advisory committees are ostensibly based on scientific research reports. However, "there is growing evidence of conflicts of interest in private research submitted for regulation. For example, there are reports of a 'funding effect,' with sponsorship associated with favorable findings. There are also accounts of improper sponsor control over the design and reporting of results, and sponsor suppression or termination of research showing adverse effects" (48). For these reasons, personal and institutional requirements for transparency and disclosure of conflicts of interest should be extended to published research, whether federally or privately funded.

Even more serious conflicts of interest are well recognized in regulatory policies of the U.S. administration. A February 19, 2004, Knight Ridder newspaper article reported that an open letter from "more than 60 scientists, including 20 Nobel laureates and several science advisors to Republican presidents . . . accused the Bush Administration of suppressing, distorting or manipulating the work done by scientists at federal agencies . . . and [establishing] political litmus tests for scientific advisory boards."

White-Collar Industry Crime

White-collar crime is generally defined as crimes of economic motivation with adverse economic consequences. It has also been defined as crimes of economic motivation with adverse public health consequences, including cancer and other preventable disease, homicide, and environmental contamination. Examples of such crimes, with specific reference to the chemical industry, have been detailed in the author's 1979 Congressional testimony as follows (49):

Knowing Acts of Nondisclosure
• Suppression of carcinogenicity and other toxicity data on vinyl chloride by vinyl chloride/polyvinylchloride industries, and by the Chemical Manufacturers Association.
• Suppression of carcinogenicity data on bischloromethylether by Rohm & Haas.
• Suppression of carcinogenicity data on the pesticide kepone by Allied Chemical.
• Suppression of mutagenicity data on benzene by Dow Chemical.

Reckless Acts
• Gross exaggeration by Arthur D. Little, Inc. (under contract to the Society of the Plastics Industry, Inc.), and by Foster D. Snell, of data on the economic impact of compliance with a proposed occupational standard for vinyl chloride.
• Marketing of acrylonitrile plastic Coke bottles by Monsanto prior to its carcinogenicity testing.
• Falsification of test data on the drug aldactone and the artificial sweetener aspartame by Hazleton Laboratories, under contract to G.D. Searle.
• Destruction of epidemiological data on occupational carcinogens by Dow and DuPont.

• Destruction of test data on drugs, food additives, pesticides, and industrial chemicals by Industrial Biotest Laboratories, a subsidiary of Nalco Chemical (under subcontract to the Chemical Industry Institute of Toxicology).

It was recommended that responsibility for such crimes should be primarily directed to corporate directors and managers, and extended to other "knowing parties," including plant physicians and industrial hygienists and outside consulting companies and scientists (48). As an important incentive to "disclosure," it was also recommended that any "whistle blowing" worker or other personnel who reported "serious" dangers should be protected from retaliation or dismissal.

Recent disasters in the European Union have resulted in renewed interest in white-collar public health crime. In November 2001, criminal charges were filed against managers of Celtica, an Italian petrochemical company plant in Brindisi (50). About 70 current managers of the plant, and former owners, including Montedison, Enichem, and EVC, have been accused of environmental disaster, mass manslaughter for the leukemia deaths of 14 workers, and the sickness of a further 83 workers as a result of exposure to vinyl chloride and other toxic chemicals. While the first cases of leukemia were reported 23 years ago, investigation was delayed until prompted by a worker who has since died of cancer. The plant was closed by the police in November 2000.

Apart from criminal sanctions, the increasing likelihood of toxic tort and environmental litigation is likely to act as a growing deterrent to reckless industry practices. Consideration should also be given to the feasibility of obtaining redress from the European Court of Human Rights (11). Furthermore, personal rights to effective judicial remedy have long been established by the European Convention for the Protection of Human Rights and Fundamental Freedom (51). These issues are also within the jurisdiction of the European Court of Human Rights at Strasburg. It should further be noted that various networks of environmental enforcement agencies have recently been established, including the European Network on the Implementation and Enforcement of Environmental Law. Of related interest is the nonprofit Geneva and Washington, D.C., Center for International Environmental Law, which is focused on global environmental concerns.

Cancer Due to Industrial Carcinogens

REACH stressed the need for regulating HPV industrial carcinogens. However, explicit reference should be made to their role as major avoidable causes of cancer, as a poorly recognized result of inadequate regulation (26). Cancer is now a leading cause of disease and death in France and the United States (Table 6), now striking nearly one in two men and more than one in three women in their lifetimes. Over recent decades, and contrary to public perception, the overall incidence of cancer in France and the United States has escalated to epidemic

Table 6

Cancer cases and deaths in 2001, France and United States

	France		U.S.	
	No. of cases	% population	No. of cases	% population
Male	161,000	0.26	643,000	0.22
Female	117,200	0.19	625,000	0.21
Total	278,200	0.46	1,268,000	0.43
	No. of deaths	% population	No. of deaths	% population
Male	92,300	0.15	286,000	0.10
Female	57,700	0.10	267,000	0.09
Total	150,000	0.25	553,000	0.19

Sources: France: G. Pison, *Popul. Soc.* 366, March 2001; United States: U.S. Census Bureau.
Note: Population data for France as of January 1, 2001.

proportions (Table 7) (43, 52). This hardly justified the July 28, 2003, British Broadcasting Corporation Headline article, "Europe Winning Cancer Battle." It should be emphasized that the major increases in overall cancer incidence are accounted for by a wide range of predominantly non-smoking-related cancers (Table 7), and that these increases, and to a lesser extent for nonhormonal cancers, are related to a wide range of carcinogenic environmental exposures.

Furthermore, the virtually exclusionary fixation of E.U. and U.S. cancer institutions and governments on smoking and other lifestyle factors as the predominant cause of cancer remains based on undocumented 1981 "guesstimates" by Sir Richard Doll (Table 8). However, faced with mounting evidence and revelations of his major conflicts of interest as an undisclosed industry consultant, Doll has recently recanted and admitted the major importance of non-smoking-related causes of cancer. Notable among these are childhood cancers, for which lifestyle factors cannot be attributed and which have clearly been related to environmental exposures (Table 9).

Regional Cancer Clusters. Cancer clusters in regions adjacent to chemical industry plants and hazardous waste sites have long been recognized in the United States (26). Examples include Salem County, New Jersey, with the highest national incidence of bladder cancers in men and women; Love Canal, Niagara Falls, New York, with an excess of leukemia, breast cancer, and birth defects; and childhood leukemia in Woburn, Massachusetts—and in Sellafield in the United Kingdom. Such regional variations in cancer incidence prompted the

Table 7

Percentage changes in age-standardized cancer incidence rates, France and United States

	France, 1980–2000	U.S., 1975–2000
Prostate cancer	198%	88%
Malignant melanoma	171	124
Thyroid cancer	149	54
Non-Hodgkin's lymphoma	103	71
Breast cancer		
Overall	60	29
Premenopausal	N.A.	6
Postmenopausal	N.A.	37
Brain cancer	57	14
Multiple myeloma	55	12
Testicular cancer	46	54
Acute leukemia	36	15 (myeloid)
Childhood (0–14) cancers		
Overall	N.A.	31
Acute lymphocytic leukemia	N.A.	59
Brain cancer	N.A.	48
Kidney cancer	N.A.	43
Bone cancer	N.A.	20
Lung cancer		
Overall	19	19
Male	10	−11
Female	132	103
All sites		
Overall	28	18
Male	27	20
Female	31	13

Sources: France, based on Remontet et al. (43); United States, National Cancer Institute (52).

National Cancer Institute to publish "cancer maps" showing clusters of excessive cancer rates in regions of heavy industrialization, and concentrations of chemical plants (53).

Similar clusters have recently been recognized in Italy. Citing WHO data, the environmental group Legambiente reported that cancer rates in industrial areas of Brindisi are a record of 48 percent higher than the regional average, and the highest of all areas of Italy (54). Regional excesses in other highly industrialized areas and cities include 46 percent in Crotone; 22 percent in Taranto; and 21 percent in Massa-Carrara. It has been estimated that as many as 11 million Italians are at increased risk from such exposures.

Table 8

Sir Richard Doll's track record on prevention

1950–1970: Major contributions to cancer prevention
Precedent-setting research on smoking, nickel, gas-production tars, asbestos, and
radioactivity as causes of cancer.
Warning that an "immense" number of substances were known to cause cancer.
Warning that cancer prevention is a better strategy than cure.

1970–2001: Undisclosed industry consulting
  1976: Claimed that it was "unethical" not to treat drinking water with fluoridated
  industrial wastes.
  1981: Undocumented claims ("guesstimates") that lifestyle factors are responsible for
  95 percent of cancer mortality, and that only 5 percent are due to "pollution" and
  occupation.
  1982: As a long-standing consultant to Turner & Newall, the leading U.K. asbestos
  industry, reassured its workers that low-level asbestos exposure was safe; also refused
  to testify on behalf of dying workers or their bereaved families in litigation against the
  industry.
  1983: As a consultant to General Motors, denied that exposure to lead from leaded
  petroleum was hazardous to children.
  1985: Supported Monsanto in trivializing cancer risks of dioxin and denying claims of
  compensation by Australian veterans exposed to Agent Orange in the Vietnam War.
  1987: Dismissed evidence of excess rates of leukemia in children living near U.K.
  nuclear power plants.
  1998: Claimed that excess mortality from leukemia and multiple myeloma in
  servicemen exposed to atom bomb test radiation was "a statistical quirk."
  1998: On behalf of the U.S. chemical industry, denied evidence relating occupational
  exposure to vinyl chloride and brain cancer.
  2000: Admitted to "charitable donations" from Dow Chemical, "in recognition of all
  the work I had done for them."

2002: Retraction
Admitted that most cancers, other than those related to smoking and hormones, "are
induced by exposure to chemicals, often environmental."

Source: Epstein et al. (24, Appendix VII).

Community Cancer Clusters Related to Municipal Solid Waste (MSW) Inciner-
ators. Since 1997, yearly measurements of dioxin and furan emissions from
MSW incinerators that process over 6 million tons of wastes hourly have become
compulsory nationwide; high dioxin emissions were identified in 15 of 71 such
incinerators (40). Reflecting these considerations, the authors stressed that the
absence of a nationwide cancer registry precludes systematic analysis of cancer
incidence and clusters around highly polluting MSW incinerators. Nevertheless,

Table 9

Environmental risk factors for childhood cancer

Industrial pollutants in drinking water

Exposure to pesticides from urban spraying, and uses in schools, homes, gardens, and
  pet flea collars

Contamination of fruits and vegetables, particularly in baby foods, with carcinogenic
  pesticides

Exposures to wood playground sets treated with chromated copper arsenic

Maternal and paternal pre-conception exposure to occupational carcinogens

Proximity of residence to nuclear energy plants

---

highly significant clusters of soft tissue sarcoma and non-Hodgkin's lymphoma
have been reported from 1980 to 1995 among men and women living in the
vicinity of the Besançon (France) incinerator (41). Based on these results, local
authorities have upgraded the combustion chamber of the MSW and planned
the construction of a modernized facility. A case-control study confirmed the
high risk for non-Hodgkin's lymphoma in the highest-exposure zone surrounding
the Besançon MSW. The authors stressed that emissions from MSW incinerators
are one of the major environmental sources of dioxins, and are causally related
to non-Hodgkin's lymphoma and other health risks (41).

Community Cancer Clusters Related to Nuclear Plants. Nuclear plants represent
another major source of exposure to industrial carcinogens. However, in the
European Union they are regulated by the Directorate-General Environment
(55), rather than by REACH.

A case-control study has demonstrated a statistically significant increased
incidence of leukemia in people under the age of 25 living in the vicinity of
LaHague (France), one of the world's largest nuclear reprocessing plants. This
was attributed to routine atmospheric emissions of particulate radionuclides,
environmental marine contamination, the use of local beaches, and consumption
of local fish (56). The excess incidence of childhood leukemia in the Nord-
Cotentin region of France, where the LaHague reprocessing and other nuclear
installations are located, has been independently confirmed (57); excess incidences of childhood leukemia have also been reported in the vicinity of the
Sellafield reprocessing plant in the United Kingdom (58). These findings are
consistent with the excess incidences of childhood leukemia in proximity to
U.S. nuclear power plants (59). Further supportive is evidence of high levels of
strontium-90 in baby teeth of children living near U.S. nuclear plants (59).

In striking contrast, a well-designed investigation of people age 0 to 64 years
in some 500 communes near 13 main French nuclear plants reported no excess

cancer mortality (60). The authors, however, emphasized that their reliance on mortality, rather than incidence, data was due to the absence of a national cancer registry, and that local cancer registries did not include the area studied. "The availability of incidence data would represent a substantial increase in power, particularly when studying cancers of the thyroid and breast, Hodgkin's disease, and childhood leukemia, for which survival is fairly good" (60).

The French government has recognized risks of thyroid cancer in people living near its 19 nuclear power plants, and has supplied them with stable iodine tablets as a precaution against the accidental release of iodine isotopes (61). This seems prudent in view of the major increase in the incidence of thyroid cancer in men and women from 1975 to 1995, which cannot be associated with the Chernobyl nuclear accident (62). Major excesses in the incidence of thyroid cancer have also been reported in the United Staes following exposure to iodine-131 from radioactive fallout following atom bomb tests in Nevada in the late 1950s (26).

Apart from jurisdictional considerations, there is a clear relation between exposure to radiation and chemical carcinogenesis. Exposure to radionuclides is known to depress the immune response and thus enhance susceptibility to chemical carcinogens (63). Illustratively, radiation has been shown to synergize the carcinogenic effects of diethylstilbestrol in the breast (64).

Occupational Cancer. Specific provisions of the French Labor Code on the prevention of occupational cancer, based on a 1990 European Directive (65), apply to some chemicals, products, and processes defined as human carcinogens (IARC category 1) and probable human carcinogens (IARC category 2). Workers developing cancer following exposure to these carcinogens and carcinogenic processes (such as the manufacture of auramine and isopropyl alcohol, and the roasting of cupro-nickel mattes) should be entitled to compensation.

It should, however, be emphasized that only minimal priority and concern have been given to occupational cancer. Most critical is the virtually exclusive responsibility of industry for all aspects of occupational health and safety, including compensation (through social security), with inherent major conflicts of interest. Not surprisingly, more and more workers are now suing their current employers or former employers to increase compensation or to obtain any compensation. Related considerations include the underreporting of occupational cancer by poorly informed workers, and physicians without occupational expertise, particularly pneumologists (66, 67), and that most cancers are diagnosed after retirement, when their occupational causation tends to be unrecognized (66–69).

Entitlements to compensation are still highly limited, and extend only to a few malignancies: lung, nasosinus, bladder, liver, and skin cancers, leukemia, mesotheliomas, and osteogenic sarcomas. These restrictions also exclude other cancers for which there is valid evidence of occupational causation, such as brain cancer in farmers and vineyard workers exposed to pesticides (70), and non-Hodgkin's lymphoma in workers exposed to benzene and agrichemicals (71).

Moreover, compensation is restricted to male workers in some sectors, and it excludes self-employed workers (including farmers and agricultural workers).

Based on highly conservative and undocumented estimates that occupation is responsible for only 4 percent cancer mortality (72), the number of compensable cases in France in 1999 should have been approximately 7,000 (66). However, the 4 percent estimate was based on just a guess by a prominent U.K. epidemiologist, an undisclosed industry consultant (Table 8), and contrary to prior confidential industry estimates of more than 20 percent (69). Nevertheless, less than 1,000 male workers received compensation in 2001 (67).

In 1998, the French Ministry of Health created a new public agency, the Institut de Veille Sanitaire, with a Health and Work Department headed by an occupational physician and epidemiologist. Based on prevalence data from other appropriately matched nations, the Institut estimated that the number of annually compensable occupational cancers is much higher than previously recognized, and about 8,500 (69). Furthermore, apart from mesotheliomas, lung cancer, following exposures to eight carcinogens and carcinogenic processes, accounted for more than 50 percent of these cancers (69).

A recent authoritative report on occupational cancer in males, based on a wide range of cancers and carcinogens, estimated that the impact is substantially higher than previously recognized (68), with 20,000 annual cases and 13,000 deaths, corresponding to incidences of 12 percent and 14 percent, respectively (Table 10). Of additional, but largely unrecognized, concern is the fact that some 20 U.S. and international studies have clearly incriminated parental occupational exposures to carcinogens as major causes of childhood cancer (26).

Responsibility for ensuring the health and safety of workers involved in the manufacture and processing of carcinogenic and other VHC chemicals should be removed from industry and transferred to a responsible government agency. This agency should be staffed by highly qualified industrial hygienists and occupational physicians, and supervised by the Institut de Veille Sanitaire, or a designated agency in close collaboration with the Institut.

Table 10

Compensable occupational cancers
in French males

1999 estimates	7,000
2001 estimated compensated cases	<1,000
2002 estimates	8,500
2003 estimates	20,000

Sources: 1999, Aubrun et al. (66); 2001 and 2002, Imbernon (69); 2003, Goldberg (68).

Additionally, health and safety and other labor representatives should actively participate in corporate governance. Under a 1976 German *Mitbestimmung* co-determination law, industries with more than 2,000 workers are required to allocate to labor half of the seats on supervisory boards, whose key decisions must be endorsed by top management. Reaffirmation of this two-tier system of corporate governance was urged by the DGB, Germany's national trade union federation, at a recent conference in Berlin (73). It should be further noted that a 2002 study by the Cologne-based Max Planck Institute for the Study of Societies concluded that co-determination had not hindered industry interests, restructuring, and globalization. Of particular interest is President Chirac's March 2003 speech in which he stressed the need to "strengthen the fight against cancers of occupational origin" (74).

Prior Informed Consent

On February 23, 2004, the Rotterdam Convention on Prior Informed Consent (PIC) Procedure for Certain Hazardous Chemicals and Pesticides in International Trade became international law; the Convention established the principle that the import of any industrial chemical be subject to PIC. Sixty State Parties, including the United States, have signed the Convention, although the United States has not ratified it. Clearly, REACH should stipulate that the import of all VHC chemicals, and of HPV chemicals that have not been registered and evaluated, be prohibited under the terms of PIC.

The PIC requirement would act as a powerful and overdue deterrent to the import of hazardous chemicals and products from developing countries where environmental and occupational regulatory controls are minimal.

SCALE: The European Environment and Health Strategy Work Plan

In October 2003, following regional conferences in Brussels, Rome, and Warsaw, E.U. Environment Commissioner Wallström launched the European Environment and Health Strategy Work Plan. Known as SCALE, this initiative, which is independent of REACH, is based on *s*cientific evidence, focused on *c*hildren, enhanced *a*wareness, *l*egal and political remedies, and dynamic *e*valuation of progress. It must be stressed that SCALE is politically unrelated to REACH. However, it strengthens REACH conceptually by stressing the critical importance of early life sensitivity to industrial chemicals.

SCALE has established three Technical Working Groups, focused on the following priorities:

1. Indicators and Priority Diseases: environment and health indicators; respiratory and neurodevelopmental diseases; childhood cancer

2. Integrated Monitoring of Children: pilot studies on dioxins, PCBS, heavy metals, and endocrine-disruptive chemicals
3. Research Needs

While such research is obviously important, there is already substantial evidence of the increasing prevalence of a wide range of childhood diseases (75–78). There is also substantial evidence of these children's known, or suspected, exposures to HPV chemicals and other environmental contaminants, especially in utero and early life exposures. These include:

- Neurodevelopmental disorders, including autism, attention deficit disorders, dyslexia, and mental retardation. These have been linked to neurotoxicants, including lead, mercury, and POPs, particularly PCBs.
- Hormonal disorders, including cryptorchidism, hypospadias, altered sex ratios at birth, sperm abnormalities, and premature puberty. These have been linked to endocrine-disruptive chemicals, particularly POPs—PCBs, poly-brominated biphenyls, and furans.
- Respiratory diseases, including asthma and allergies. These have been linked to ambient and indoor air pollutants, including fine particulates, diesel exhaust, and ozone.
- Cancer. While there is clear evidence of the sharply escalating incidence of a wide range of childhood cancers over recent decades in the United States, no such comparable data are available in the European Union (Table 7). Moreover, these cancers have been linked to a wide range of environmental causes, including proximity of residence to nuclear energy plants; exposures to pesticides from urban spraying; uses in schools, particularly wood playground sets treated with chromated copper arsenate preservatives; industrial pollutants in drinking water; and maternal and paternal exposures (pre- and post-conception) to occupational carcinogens (Table 9).

It should be further stressed that *in utero* and early life exposures are significant determinants of reproductive abnormalities and other diseases, including cancer, manifesting in adult life. The relation between treating pregnant women with diethylstilbestrol and the rare vaginal cancers in their post-pubertal daughters, besides urogenital abnormalities in their adult sons, has been well recognized for over three decades (26). Even more relevant is recent evidence that testicular cancer, whose incidence rates in France and the United States have increased by more than 40 percent in recent decades (Table 7), can be initiated during fetal life following exposure to endocrine-disruptive chemicals (79). Blood levels of a wide range of POPs, including chlordanes, PCBs, and hexachlorobenzene, were shown to be three to four times higher in mothers of men diagnosed with testicular cancer than in matched controls.

In addition to focusing on early life exposures and childhood disease, SCALE should direct highest priority to the overwhelming discrepancies between child health in western and eastern Europe. Illustratively, infant mortality rates in western Europe are in the range of 3 to 6 per 100,000 while those in eastern Europe range up to 17 per 100,000, reaching as high as 37 per 100,000 in Turkey (80).

Based on these widely ranging concerns, SCALE has developed an Action Plan with defined goals and actions for the period 2004 to 2010. This Action Plan will be the EC's major contribution to the Fourth Ministerial Conference on Environment and Health, convened by the WHO's Regional Ministerial Conference, in Budapest, in June 2004.

It should, however, be recognized that more than adequate scientific data are currently available to implement SCALE's objectives. In fact, emphasis on further research needs could be counterproductive and could be exploited by industry for continued regulatory inaction. Clearly, the objectives of the SCALE initiative should be incorporated into REACH in order to emphasize the importance of early life exposure to VHC chemicals. This would also ensure that REACH's proposals reflect evolving information on toxic exposures in early life and would identify critical research gaps. Clearly, a wide range of considerations afford a more than adequate basis for strengthening REACH (Table 3).

THE GLOBAL IMPACT OF REACH

Despite major concessions, the fundamental principles of REACH remain intact and represent a unique and unprecedented complex of regulations for controlling the chemical industry and reducing its major adverse public health and environmental impacts. This was emphasized by E.U. Environment Commissioner Margot Wallström in a November 15, 2003, letter to the *Financial Times:* "The chemicals reform is a test case for the principle of sustainable development. To be sustainable, any policy has to reconcile economic, social and environmental concerns. Achieving this balance is particularly important in the case of chemicals, where the stakes are so high on all three sides. It is high time that European citizens got the high level of protection for environment and health they have the right to expect. This is why we need a new strategy for chemicals management, and we should never forget this."

In fact, the changes needed to restore the integrity of REACH require relatively few modifications, just a few paragraphs or so, in the 1,200-page 2003 legislative proposals. These changes could readily be made by the European Parliament in its second and third readings of the proposals.

Even more critically, Europe, as the world's largest chemical market, has the ability to set a precedent for drastic reform of global legislative policies on the regulation of industrial chemicals. Furthermore, European regulations have far exceeded those of the United States since the 1990s (Table 11). REACH has dramatically emphasized the inadequacies of the 1976 U.S. Toxic Substances Act, whose regulations still require testing of only about 5 percent of chemicals in commerce (21). Reflecting such concerns, which have been exacerbated by

Table 11

Comparison of health and environmental regulations in
Europe and the United States

Up to 1970s
  Regulation of risk was more vigorous in the United States.

Up to 1990s
  The EC made great progress in regulation, and nearly closed the gap with the United States.

From 1990s
  Regulation of risk in the European Union has far exceeded that in the United States.

Source: Christoforou (81).

the deregulation policies of the Bush administration, progressive Congressional Democrats are now drafting a proposal to overhaul U.S. regulations to conform with those of REACH. These initiatives are likely to extend to the state level, and have already been effected at the city level by San Francisco.

Note — This chapter was released at a press conference and was summarized as a keynote address delivered at the International Colloquium—Cancer, Environment, and Society, UNESCO, Paris, May 2004.

PART II

Hidden
Carcinogens in Food

Chapter 10

DEBATE ON SAFETY OF RECOMBINANT BOVINE GROWTH HORMONE

In early 1990, the *International Journal of Health Services* published my report on the potential health hazards of the use of synthetic (recombinant) bovine growth hormone (BGH) in dairy cattle, in which I included criticisms of the U.S. Food and Drug Administration's regulatory activities (the report is presented as Part A of this chapter). This report, in the words of Ann Gibbons in *Science* in August 1990, "had consequences." In her News & Comment article (included here as Part B), Gibbons introduced a review, in the same issue of *Science,* by two FDA researchers, which purported to show that use of recombinant BGH presents "no increased health risk to consumers." At the end of Part B, I've added a note on some of the flaws in this FDA review. In her comments, Gibbons also referred disparagingly to publication of my report in *IJHS,* to which Vicente Navarro, Editor-in-Chief of the journal, quickly responded (Part C).

A. POTENTIAL PUBLIC HEALTH HAZARDS OF RECOMBINANT BOVINE GROWTH HORMONE

TRACK RECORD OF THE FOOD AND DRUG ADMINISTRATION AND THE U.S. DEPARTMENT OF AGRICULTURE

The Food and Drug Administration (FDA) is responsible for approving the registration and use of animal drugs and issuing residue tolerances. Section 512 of the 1968 Animal Drug Amendments to the 1938 Federal Food, Drug, and

Part A published in *International Journal of Health Services,* Volume 20, Number 1, 1990.

Cosmetic Act (FFDCA) mandates the FDA to require manufacturers submitting new animal drug applications to provide "a description of practical methods" for analysis and monitoring of drug residues in food. The U.S. Department of Agriculture (USDA) is responsible for monitoring food animals and their products by FDA-approved methods in order to detect and prevent the occurrence of illegal food residues.

The granting by the FDA of an Investigative New Animal Drug (INAD) exemption for the synthetic hormones on the basis of allegedly confidential data and their allowing the sale of unlabeled hormonal milk and meat reflects the agency's highly relaxed view of its responsibilities. As stated in a recent FDA Talk Paper, and elsewhere, sponsors have not been required to measure the increase of bovine growth hormone (BGH) in milk of treated cattle over that in milk from untreated cattle. Rather, the safety of BGH is allegedly based on the limited quantity of the hormone administered on a daily basis and the fact that BGH is not biologically active in humans or other primates (1). Furthermore, in granting the INAD exemption, the FDA is in apparent violation of the 1968 FFDCA amendments mandating that the agency must have a "prescribed and approved" test method, which the industry is required to provide, for determining whether the drug is being improperly used, with resulting illegal residues in food.

Of additional concern is the fact that the FDA has inappropriately relied on standard protocols that are largely irrelevant for the safety evaluation of biosynthetic milk hormones. In fact, the only reported evidence of adverse effects has emerged from incidental findings in efficacy trials based on Technical Advisory Document (TAD) protocols designed primarily for milk production trials. In particular, the agency has failed to require evaluation of the toxicological effects of the milk hormones in large-scale multigenerational and multilactational tests, and evaluation of the safety of milk and dairy products, with regard to a wide range of critical public health concerns.

The conduct of the regulatory agencies in the matter of milk hormones is consistent with their track record. As evidenced in an extensive series of Government Accounting Office investigations and Congressional hearings, USDA and FDA regulation is in near total disarray, aggravated by denials and cover-ups. A 1986 Congressional report concluded: "FDA has consistently disregarded its responsibility, . . . repeatedly put what it perceives are interests of veterinarians and the livestock industry ahead of its legal obligation to protect consumers, . . . jeopardizing the health and safety of consumers of meat, milk, and poultry" (2). Further illustrative is the April 1989 USDA proposal to end inspection of the nation's 6,300 meat and poultry processing plants and instead to rely on voluntary compliance. The proposed plan, originally entitled "Discretionary Inspections," and then euphemistically renamed "Improved Processing Inspection System," has met with a storm of criticism from sources including the American Meat Institute and major meat packers.

It should be noted that an earlier draft of this report was submitted to FDA Commissioner Young on July 19, 1989. A reply of August 11, 1989, from Dr. G. Guest (Director of the Center for Veterinary Medicine) alleges, in the total absence of supporting data, that the report "contains many misstatements of scientific fact," although none are specified. Dr. Guest also offered the irrelevant assurance that the FDA is preparing a report on the scientific basis of its decision to allow the sale of unlabeled dairy products from hormone-treated cows to the general public. As of September 6, 1989, the FDA has failed to provide a documented scientific critique of the report. It may also be noted that in an internal memorandum of July 18, 1989, Dr. Guest admitted "the likely problems with cattle safety" in cows on clinical trials, and questioned whether "some sense of security to the consumer" would be gained by allowing use of synthetic hormones only as a prescription drug.

INDUSTRY CLAIMS ON MILK HORMONES

The industry claims, as exemplified in a recent promotional report by the Animal Health Institute (3), are highly misleading. It is claimed that the synthetic hormones increase milk yields by an average of 10 to 25 percent, that milk quality is unchanged, that increased hormone levels are not found in milk, that there are no adverse reproductive or other effects in treated cows, and that the synthetic hormones are safe because they are not biologically active in humans. The Animal Health Institute report quotes from a milk hormone production trial conducted by Cornell University to the effect that "it appeared that the cows were simply unaffected," and emphasizes that "subsequent studies at more than 20 universities confirm many of these observations." The report omits reference to the wide range of adverse effects noted in about half the limited number of methionyl-BGH (met-BGH) production trials (see "Adverse Veterinary Effects") and makes no reference to met-BGH, except incidentally in an efficacy graph. Finally, the report makes no reference to the highly variable and inconsistent yields in the milk production trials.

Apart from misrepresentations, the industry claims are usually restrictedly based on small numbers of cows (seven to ten per test group), reflecting TAD efficacy protocols in which adverse veterinary effects were only incidentally noted. Claims that increased hormone levels are not found in milk are suspect since they do not reflect anticipated dose-response relationships and do not reflect increased plasma levels noted in several studies (see "Potential Adverse Public Health Effects").

The industry claims for the synthetic hormones are based on a complex of strategies. These exaggerate efficacy; omit reference to, trivialize, or dismiss documented adverse veterinary effects; and reflect misleading manipulation of data. Furthermore, these claims fail to reflect the absence of critical studies that could elicit further information on adverse veterinary effects and, even more critically, on adverse public health effects. The past success of the industry strategies also reflects suppression of data, on the alleged grounds of trade secrecy, and the unbalanced and indentured nature of in-house and academic research on synthetic milk hormones. Certainly, the documented evidence of adverse veterinary effects of milk hormones justifies the highest index of suspicion as to undocumented industry claims on human safety.

ADVERSE VETERINARY EFFECTS

Available data on adverse veterinary effects in cows hyperstimulated by daily injections of the synthetic hormones are sparse and are largely based on incidental findings in small-scale milk production trials, in the absence of multilactational and multigenerational toxicological studies. The significance of these findings, to which no reference is made in industry promotional literature, is emphasized by the small size of the trial groups, ranging from seven to 47 cows for each treatment group. The gross statistical insensitivity of such trials has recently been emphasized. "At least 2,423 cows would be needed in each group to detect an increase in disease frequency from 5 to 10 percent, and at least 11,773 cows in each group for a change from 1 to 2 percent" (4). The importance of stress-related diseases associated with prolonged elevation in plasma levels of BGH has been strikingly confirmed in transgenic pigs in which there were "significant improvements in both daily weight gain and feed efficiency." However, these pigs also developed "a high incidence of gastric ulcers, arthritis, cardiomegaly, dermatitis, and renal diseases" (5). It should be noted that these scientists, unlike their indentured dairy science counterparts, carefully investigated adverse veterinary effects as well as productivity.

Negative Energy Balance

Biosynthetic milk hormones induce a prolonged negative energy balance, similar to that in the rising phase of lactation, for at least eight weeks, during which increased milk production is paralleled by "reduced total body fat," excessive tissue loss, and hypertrophy of foregut tissue (6). This sustained negative energy balance appears to be associated with increased stress, susceptibility to infectious disease, and measurable changes in the composition of milk.

Increased Incidence of Infectious Diseases

In the Cyanamid-Pennsylvania met-BGH trial, mastitis developed in four of eight cows at 12.5 mg/day and in two of seven at 50 mg/day. High somatic cell counts were observed at all dosages in the Monsanto-Missouri trial, and at 25 mg/day in the Cyanamid-Missouri trial (4). Additionally, a high level of unspecified infectious disease was noted in one of nine trials. An increased incidence of unspecified (and unpublished) infectious disease has recently been confirmed (7).

Reduced Fertility

Evidence of reduced fertility has been noted incidentally in four of nine milk production trials (4, 8). Such evidence is further supported by evaluation of the results of 59 industry or industry-sponsored trials recently reported in two supplements of the *Journal of Dairy Science* (Volume 70, Supplement 1, 1987, and Volume 71, Supplement 1, 1988). Reproductive data were cited in six of these 59 trials—only two of which involved second lactations—all of which uniformly demonstrated significant adverse reproductive effects (9). The overall conception or pregnancy rates of controls in these six trials were 89 percent versus 59 percent in injected cows. More marked effects were noted in one study with pregnancy rates of 82 percent in controls versus 41 percent in high-dose-level cows, although conception rates were similar in all groups (10). In general, these adverse reproductive effects were ignored or trivialized. Illustratively, in one of the six trials it was claimed that "reproductive performance did not differ from contemporary herdmates," although conception rates in controls were 100 percent versus 50 percent in injected cows (11). Again, another study claimed that "health measurements were not consistently altered by sometribove" (met-BGH), although conception rates were 95 percent in controls versus 79 percent in injected cows (12).

In addition to the inhibition of conception rates noted in some of the six trials, one of these demonstrated reduction in pregnancy rates in the absence of effects on conception (10). As recently recognized (in 1989), "BST [bovine somatotropin, i.e., BGH] may affect embryo survival. In one study, the conception rate of BST-treated cows was not influenced. However, there was evidence that BST-treated cows particularly those receiving high doses maintained fewer pregnancies" (13).

Thus, even from a narrowly focused economic perspective, and ignoring costs of other adverse veterinary effects, increased productivity from the use of synthetic milk hormones could be more than offset by economic losses due to reproductive impairment (9).

Heat Intolerance

Heat intolerance was noted at two dosage levels in one of nine trials (4). Such intolerance could pose particular problems for uses of biosynthetic hormones in tropical climates.

Changes in Nutritional Quality of Milk

Available data on the effects of hormones on the nutritional status and composition of milk, including protein subtractions, vitamins, and minerals, are minimal. However, it is clear that the hormones induce a wide range of measurable changes in milk composition. Increased fat yields and concentrations have been noted (14). Additionally, there is a statistically significant increase in long-chain fatty acids and decrease in short-chain fatty acids (15); this is associated with reduction in casein, in relation to both total and true protein, which is likely to decrease cheese yields. Such significant changes in the composition of milk in hormonally treated cattle are becoming increasingly recognized (e.g., 8).

Questionable Efficacy of Milk Hormones

The adverse veterinary effects so far noted are not necessarily offset by improved milk production. Contrary to promotional claims, the effects of synthetic hormones on milk production are highly variable and inconsistent. In nine met-BGH trials, outstanding responses were obtained in two herds and very poor responses in another two herds. "About one-third of all BST-treated herds would be predicted to fall between the consensus low limit of 10 percent more milk and my estimate of minus 1 percent based on the nine trials" (16). In spite of strident industry denials, burnout or lactational crash has been noted in hormone-treated cattle, particularly at high dose levels (7, 9), although no data have as yet been made available on its incidence.

Other Growth Hormones in Milk

Apart from unresolved questions on incremental levels of synthetic hormones in milk, somatomedins such as insulin-like growth factors (IGF-1), whose endogenous production is stimulated by milk hormones, have been detected in the milk of cows treated with synthetic hormones. Based on the very limited available data, the milk of treated cows appears to sustain high levels of IGF-1, similar to those found in untreated cows after the first week of lactation (17, 18). Additionally, the normal inverse relationship between endogenous growth hormone and blood insulin levels is disturbed following BGH treatment (19).

Misuse of Milk Hormones

Apart from concerns about overdosage of lactating cows, the off-label use of synthetic BGH as a growth-promoting hormone in calves and sheep has also been reported. Such misuses are all the more likely in view of the absence of practical and sensitive methods for detecting and monitoring hormonal levels in milk and meat. Also, the documented record of extensive misuse of growth-promoting animal sex hormones does not inspire confidence that milk hormones will be handled any more responsibly.

Critical Data Gaps

It should be stressed that no information is available from large-scale multilactational and multigenerational dose-response tests with synthetic hormones on a wide range of veterinary and related concerns. These include: milk production efficacy; alterations in the detailed biochemical composition of milk, its nutritional quality, and its suitability for cheese production; alterations in reproduction and fertility; detailed studies on the growth and health of calves of injected cows; endocrinological effects; biochemical, endocrine, and metabolic evidence of stress; stress-induced susceptibility to and increased incidence of viral infections, including bovine leukemia; increased levels in milk of antibiotics necessitated by increased bovine infections; allergenicity and immunogenicity of hormonal milk; response of hormone-treated cattle to vaccines; mobilization in milk of fat-soluble carcinogens from depot fat by the sustained lipolytic action of milk hormones; and identification and measurement in milk and meat of synthetic hormone residues and of incremental levels of IGF-1 and other somatomedins.

POTENTIAL ADVERSE PUBLIC HEALTH EFFECTS

An editorial in a highly conservative British medical journal recently (in 1988) warned that before the use of BGH can be considered commercially, "one would need to be completely reassured that the appropriate tests have been carried out thoroughly and professionally and that there is not the slightest hazard to human health" (20). In fact, the use of milk hormones poses serious risks of adverse public health effects that have not been adequately considered (7, 8), in spite of continued unfounded but strident industry and industry contractee assurances of safety. Apart from a wide range of information gaps that negate such assurances, there are some highly suggestive contrary data.

Relationship of Biosynthetic to Natural Milk Hormones

Industry claims that synthetic BGH is "natural" are false. Both BGH and met-BGH are xenobiotics (8). Natural BGH consists of 191 amino acid residues in linear sequence. The Elanco BGH, however, has a series of eight additional amino acid residues, known as linker proteins, at one end of the molecule (21); the more potent met-BGH has an alien methionyl terminal residue. In addition to such chemical differences, synthetic BGH is synthesized on a bacterial rather than a mammalian ribosome and its bacterial links have not been clipped off, resulting in possibly different biological activities from natural BGH. The FDA has recently admitted that biosynthetic milk hormones "are about 0.5 to 3 percent different in molecular structure" from the natural hormone (22).

Biological Activity of Milk Hormones

The industry initially claimed that BGH was "species-specific" to cattle, and thus could not possibly have any effects in humans. However, BGH is now known to be active in a wide range of species, including goats, pigs, sheep, mice, and even fish. Accordingly, the industry has changed its position and now claims that BGH is "species-limited" (23).

Natural BGH derived from pituitary glands was shown in the 1950s to have "no effect on human growth, sexual development or well-being" (24). Natural BGH is immunologically different from the human hormone and differs structurally in some 30 percent of its amino acid residues. While natural BGH is inactive in all primates, it should be noted that human growth hormone is only active in humans when given in high (milligram) doses. Additionally, some human dwarfs, Laron-type, are resistant to the treatment with human growth hormone unless it is administered together with androgens (25). Moreover, no studies on humans have been conducted with the synthetic hormones, especially the more potent met-BGH. Furthermore, it was demonstrated some 30 years ago that chymotrypsin digests of natural BGH are biologically active in humans, in whom they induce nitrogen retention (26); these considerations prompted unheeded recommendations to Monsanto some 26 years ago to undertake detailed studies on the biological activity of peptide fragments of synthetic milk hormones (7). Thus, the synthetic hormones could be biologically active in humans following absorption of novel peptides, formed during pasteurization or during proteolytic digestion in the alimentary canal. Also, the intact hormone molecule could be absorbed into the blood from the digestive tract, particularly in newborn infants prior to closure time and in infants or adults with impaired protein digestion in diseases such as cystic fibrosis; absorption of intact protein molecules has been demonstrated in newborn babies and some adults (7, 8). The industry recently (in 1987) admitted that "some proteins are absorbed into the blood stream without being fully digested" (24).

Industry claims that increased levels of synthetic hormones are not found in the milk of injected cows (3) using radioimmune assays. However, there are no available data on the comparative sensitivity and specificity of these assays for natural as opposed to synthetic hormones. Additionally, it is likely that administration of synthetic hormones will inhibit endogenous production of natural BGH and its levels in milk (25). In a recent (1988) publication purporting to confirm these claims, the upper range of levels in cows treated with 25 mg/day of synthetic BGH was more than 50 percent in excess of controls (27). Furthermore, dose-response relationships for plasma levels of synthetic BGH in the range of 5–30 ppb (ng/ml) have been reported (28). Up to 700 percent increased plasma levels have been reported following synthetic BGH dosing in late lactation (29); others have confirmed such elevations (e.g., 30). Paradoxically, excess levels of synthetic hormones have not been reported in milk assays by industry and its contractees. Clearly, the milk of treated cows should be assayed by independent scientists using techniques that have yielded clearcut results with plasma.

Biological Activity of Growth Factors

There is a growing consensus that the mechanism of action of the pituitary growth hormone is through the induction of somatomedin growth factors, particularly IGF-1 (31). From all criteria, bovine and human IGF-1 appear identical (31, 32). Most of the specific activities of natural BGH, including milk production, gluco-neogenesis, diabetogenesis, nitrogen retention, lipolysis, mitogenesis, and adipose tissue and bone growth, are mediated through somatomedins. Moreover, mammary gland receptors for IGF-1 have been identified (33).

Increased IGF-1 levels have been reported in goat's milk following synthetic BGH treatment (17). As subsequently briefly reported, high levels of IGF-1 are found in normal cow's milk immediately after calving, falling to 1-5 ng/ml by 200 days (18). However, levels induced by daily injections of BGH were sustained at 6-20 ng/ml. Thus, irrespective of the possible activity in humans of synthetic BGH digestion products, mitogenic effects could be indirectly induced in humans by sustained incremental levels of IGF-1 and other somatomedins following absorption of their intact molecules or biologically active fragments from the gastrointestinal tract. Such effects could include premature growth stimulation in infants, gynecomastia in young children, and breast cancer in women.

A recent publication insisting that BGH technology is sound nevertheless warned that (31): "Investigation of IGFs requires attention, particularly where animal health and food residues are concerned since they possess many biological activities and are immunologically and biologically similar among species. . . . Some concerns arise as to the possibility of abnormal levels of IGF-1 in the milk of BGH-treated cows and, with it, consumer health." Another publication warns (18): "The implications of IGF-1 in milk for the human infant cannot be determined until we know more about the activity and function of milk IGF-1 in the newborn. However, total growth factor activity in cow's milk, as assessed by a cell proliferation test *in vitro* which also detects components other than IGF-1, is not altered by BST treatment."

In addition to detailed studies on IGF-1 levels in the milk of BGH-treated cows, the effects in humans of increased levels should be studied with priority, particularly since some consumers have already and unknowingly been exposed to BGH milk; this population at risk should be identified and subjected to long-term surveillance. Systematic studies on IGFs should include dose-response in vitro investigations with human cells and tissues and dose-response studies in infant and adult primates, with a view to defining the effects of incremental milk levels in humans.

Activity of Hormonally Induced Stressor Metabolites

The levels in milk of stressor metabolites induced by synthetic hormones and somatomedins, such as epinephrines, catecholamines, and cortisol, should be determined by sensitive and specific assays. The stressing action in humans of these metabolites should be investigated.

Infectivity of Hormonal Milk

The stressing effect in cows of synthetic hormones and somatomedins may induce immunosuppression and activate latent viruses, such as bovine leukosis virus (BLV) and bovine immunodeficiency virus (BIV), which may well increase susceptibility to other infectious agents. Levels of such viruses in hormonally treated milk and their human infectivity should be investigated with particular reference to risks of immunosuppression and leukemia. The relationship between these viruses and the AIDS (acquired immune deficiency syndrome) complex is of further concern, particularly in view of the high level of homogeneity between BIV and human immunodeficiency virus type 1, and the infectivity of BLV to chimpanzees.

Antibiotics in Hormonal Milk

The increased incidence of infectious diseases, which has been noted in efficacy trials and which is presumably stress induced, is likely to result in increased antibiotic treatment and antibiotic levels in milk. Accordingly, the incidence of infectious diseases and of antibiotic levels in milk should be investigated with particular reference to the risks of induction of antibiotic resistance in the general population.

Allergenicity of Hormonal Milk

The allergenic and immunogenic effects in humans of met-BGH in milk, and of novel peptides resulting from its pasteurization or digestion, should be investigated. This is of particular concern in view of the substantial evidence on the high incidence of antibody development in humans treated with methionyl human growth hormone, rather than with the natural hormone (34).

Fat-Soluble Carcinogens in Hormonal Milk

The fat and milk of cattle are contaminated with a wide range of carcinogens, including pesticides such as heptachlor epoxide and dieldrin and xenobiotics such as polychlorinated biphenyls (PCBs) and tetrachlorodibenzodioxin. The lipolytic effect of hormonal treatment is likely to mobilize carcinogens from body fat and increase their milk levels, a matter of particular concern to young infants. For these reasons, possible incremental levels of fat-soluble carcinogens in hormonal milk should be determined.

Nutritional Quality of Hormonal Milk

The nutritional quality of hormonal milk should be investigated in multilactational and multigenerational tests. As recently emphasized, such data "on'detailed components of milk, e.g., casein fractions, are not available" (27). Available data, however, demonstrate major increases in long-chain saturated fatty acids relative to medium and short-chain saturated fatty acids, and up to 27 percent higher fat levels in hormonal milk (14). Dose-response relationships between milk fat and synthetic BGH have also been reported (28).

Misuse of BGH and Met-BGH

In the event that registration should ever be granted to these biosynthetic hormones, there would be no practical method to prevent their extensive off-label misuse, as is well documented for sex growth hormones, or to detect and even monitor for such misuse. It is thus highly likely that these hormones would be administered at excessive dosages to lactating cows and as growth stimulants to calves, sheep, and other cattle, increasing still further the exposure of the general public to these highly potent biological agents.

PUBLIC POLICY RECOMMENDATIONS

1. The manufacture, domestic sale, and export, including foreign licensing agreements, of biosynthetic milk hormones should be banned immediately. This ban should remain effective until a wide range of concerns on public health and veterinary safety have been posed and fully resolved.

2. The sale of milk, milk products, and meat from hormone-treated cows should be embargoed immediately. To ensure compliance, industry and its academic contractees must be required to immediately identify all past and currently treated herds.

3. Attempts should be made to identify and place under long-term medical surveillance all consumers, especially infants, who are at potential risk from having consumed hormonally contaminated milk, milk products, and meat.

4. The industry and its academic contractees must be required to make immediate full disclosure of all unpublished data and reports; claims for confidentiality must be legally preempted on the grounds of overriding concerns about public health and welfare.

5. The conduct of industry and of its academic contractees with regard to suppression and manipulation of data should be subject to Congressional investigation.

6. The conduct of the FDA in granting an INAD exemption for the testing of synthetic hormones in cows and approving the sale of hormonal milk, in apparent violation of the 1968 FFDCA amendments, together with its unfounded assurances of safety, should be subject to legal challenge and Congressional investigation.

7. The industry must be required to develop and undertake multilactational and multigenerational dose-response and other protocols appropriate for the investigation of potential adverse public health effects from hormonally contaminated milk, milk products, and meat. Such research should be subject to ongoing independent review. These protocols must include: specific and sensitive assays for synthetic hormones and somatomedins; investigation of the biological activity of these hormones and growth factors in milk; analysis of milk for stressor chemicals; investigation of the biological activity of such stressor chemicals at levels expected in hormonal milk; analysis of milk for antibiotics necessitated by treatment of stress-induced infections in lactating cows; analysis of milk for stress-induced or activated viral agents; analysis of milk for increased levels of fat-soluble carcinogens mobilized by synthetic hormones; investigation of the allergenicity and immunogenicity of synthetic hormones and of any derived novel peptides; investigation of the response to vaccines of treated cows; and detailed analysis of the nutritional quality of hormonal milk.

8. The industry must also be required to fund research in accordance with independently approved protocols, which should be awarded, supervised, and otherwise administered by a neutral, independent intermediary such as the National Institutes of Health or the National Science Foundation.

9. Pending action at the federal level, state legislatures should take immediate initiatives including labeling milk, dairy products, and meat from cows treated with synthetic BGH and banning the state sale of these products. State legislatures should also investigate the conduct of state universities in their contractual relations with industry, their involvement in the sale of unlabeled hormonal milk, and their misleading assurances of the safety of synthetic milk hormones.

POSTSCRIPT

The following effects in BGH-treated cows have received striking recent confirmation: increased incidence of infectious diseases (35); reduction in fertility (36); and increased levels of IGF-1 in milk (37). On August 23, 1989, the Foundation on Economic Trends, in association with farm, animal welfare, consumer, and environmental groups, petitioned FDA to ban sales of dairy products from BGH-treated cattle; the petition was based on a draft of this report. Simultaneously, national supermarkets banned dairy products from BGH-treated cows.

The author's September 6 Wisconsin State testimony triggered a large-scale defensive reaction and public relations blitz by the industry. Illustrative is a Consumer Information Program by Elanco, Monsanto and Upjohn entitled, "You've had BST and Cookies All Your Life," which, apart from gross misrepresentations, falsely equates synthetic with natural BGH.

Note — This chapter is based in part on Testimony on Assembly Bill 200, "Relating to Bovine Growth Hormones," Wisconsin State Assembly Committee on Agriculture, State Capitol, Madison, September 6, 1989.

B. FDA PUBLISHES BOVINE GROWTH HORMONE DATA

Ann Gibbons

In an unprecedented move, the U.S. Food and Drug Administration (FDA) is publishing data on the safety of a drug before it has been approved for use. The drug, recombinant bovine growth hormone (rBGH), has been the subject of a hot controversy over health effects. But in this issue of *Science* [volume 249, 1990] (see page 875), two FDA researchers publish a review of 30 years of studies on the hormone by its manufacturers and independent scientists and conclude that it presents "no increased health risk to consumers."

In spite of the fact that the FDA isn't expected to rule on use of rBGH for a year, the agency felt it couldn't wait to publicize the data. "There's this public concern about the safety and economics, and a lot of Congressional interest," says Gerald Guest, director for the FDA's Center for Veterinary Medicine and the man who will decide whether to approve the drug for use in dairy cows. "We'd like to get our side of the story out, to show why we're comfortable with the safety. We'd like for people to know that it's a thoughtful process, and we want it to be open and credible."

Both the Congressional scrutiny and the consumer pressure are intense. The FDA is undergoing two Congressionally mandated audits of the 10-year process by which it evaluated the health and safety effects of rBGH, which is intended to make cows produce more milk. At the same time, consumer groups are threatening to boycott milk from the cows that will be given the hormone if the drug is approved.

Part B was published by an editor in *Science,* 249: 852–853, 1990.

So it's understandable that the FDA wants to calm the waters. But the move may not get them what they want. Critics charge that publishing the article makes the agency a backer of the drug rather than a neutral evaluator. To Samuel S. Epstein, a physician and professor of occupational and environmental medicine at the University of Illinois College of Medicine, what's "unprecedented" about the FDA action is that the agency is acting "as a booster or advocate for an animal drug that hasn't yet been approved."

Epstein, a vocal environmentalist, has joined ranks with genetic engineering critic Jeremy Rifkin to criticize the FDA and the four companies that make rBGH: American Cyanamid, Elanco (a subsidiary of Eli Lilly), Monsanto, and Upjohn. Earlier this year Epstein published a paper in the little known (and non-peer-reviewed) *International Journal of Health Services* charging that the FDA had abdicated its regulatory responsibility by relying on research done by industry and industry's "indentured academics."

Epstein has done no experimental studies on rBGH, but reviewing studies by others convinced him, he says, that there are unresolved questions, including whether rBGH stimulates premature growth in infants and breast cancer in women. He wants the FDA to require studies of the toxicological effects of milk hormones in large-scale tests on cows for several years to make sure there are no adverse effects on them or their offspring.

Another Epstein charge is that the rBGH manufacturers have manipulated published data on human health effects and failed to disclose data showing the drug causes ill effects in cows including lesions and a higher incidence of infectious disease. Epstein is calling for a full-scale investigation of the FDA and the hormone's makers.

Both the FDA and the companies believe they have good answers for all of Epstein's points. More than 130 studies have been done on rBGH by industry and independent scientists, and no definitive health effects have been found, industry and FDA spokesmen say. "Everyone in the whole science world except for Dr. Epstein would not think [rBGH] ever would be active in humans," says C. Greg Guyer, an FDA pharmacologist and one of the authors of the current review.

That review concludes that rBGH is very unlikely to be biologically active in human beings. For one thing, the hormone is known not to be active when injected intravenously into children suffering from dwarfism due to a lack of growth hormone. And in the review, Guyer and his colleague cite findings that even in rats—which are known to respond to intravenous doses—oral dosages don't produce biological effects.

As for safety effects on animals, Monsanto spokesman Larry O'Neill concedes that some cows given the hormone did develop mastitis, an inflammation of the udder, and other symptoms. But, O'Neill adds, those cows were given five times the normal dose of rBGH in toxicology studies that are now being reviewed by the FDA—not covered up, as Epstein has suggested.

Yet Epsteins report has had consequences. It caused four grocery chains and several food-processing companies to refuse milk from treated herds while the hormone remains under FDA review. And although the all-out blitz on the FDA he asked for hasn't happened, his criticisms did prompt the General Accounting Office and the Inspector General of the Department of Health and Human Services to begin audits of the agency's regulatory process for rBGH.

But those audits have begun to take on a routine character to the FDA, which has been looking into the health effects of rBGH since 1982. "You almost have to take a number to decide who's going to review our process next, but we feel comfortable about it," says Guest. "I suspect this will be the most extensively studied product we've ever handled."

Epstein's note — The FDA publication referred to by Ann Gibbons (J. C. Juskevich and C. G. Guyer, *Science* 249: 875–884, August 1990) is a scientific travesty for reasons including the following:

- The principal reviewer was Dr. Dale Bauman, Monsanto's lead academic consultant, who has been clearly shown to have manipulated and suppressed evidence of adverse veterinary effects of rBGH.
- A major, behind-the-scenes, acknowledged contributor to the publication was Susan Sechen, a graduate student of Bauman, who flagrantly violated FDA conflict-of-interest regulations by publishing articles in support of Monsanto and rBGH while still an FDA employee.
- The references for all FDA' s claims of safety of rBGH and rBGH milk were based on some 16 unpublished confidential industry studies.
- Contrary to previously published data, FDA claimed that there were no biological differences between rBGH and BGH, and between rBGH and BGH milk.
- Contrary to standard regulatory requirements for new animal drugs, no reference was made to the fact that the standard (two year) chronic oral toxicity tests were not undertaken by Monsanto or the other biotech industries; nine studies were acute (less than one month duration) and one study was subchronic (90 days duration).
- Contrary to FDA's claims, based on Monsanto's confidential data subchronic rat toxicity data in FDA' s possession, rBGH is absorbed into blood following short-term oral administration to rats and induces specific antibody formation, thus strengthening further the need for chronic toxicity tests.
- The FDA fraudulently misrepresented Monsanto's claims that the weight of organs of rats dosed orally with rBGH or IGF-1 were unchanged, rather than in fact increased, by presenting the data in absolute values rather than relative to whole body weights. Furthermore, as detailed in my 1990 *International Journal of Health Services* publication (Part A of this chapter), FDA uncritically presented a summary of Monsanto's unpublished gerrymandered data, claiming that IGF-1 had no growth-promoting effects in organs of rats in short-term feeding tests.

C. Rebuttal of Gibbons's Article in *Science* Discrediting the Epstein Publication

Vicente Navarro

Ann Gibbons, in her article "FDA publishes bovine growth hormone data" (News & Comment, 24 Aug., p. 852), aims at discrediting Samuel S. Epstein's critique of the Food and Drug Administration's regulatory policies by referring to the *International Journal of Health Services*—where the article by Epstein was published—as a little known (and non-peer-reviewed) journal. Gibbons's article is wrong on both counts. *The* International Journal of Health Services *is one of the largest health policy journals in the United States, with the largest international readership among journals of this nature. Its board and editorial consultants include leading figures on health policy in this and other industrialized nations. It is also a peer-reviewed journal. An international body of referees guarantees its quality. All papers—including Epstein's—are reviewed by at least two referees.* The ratio of rejected versus accepted articles is one of the highest among scientific journals.

The *International Journal of Health Services* does not support or reject any of the conclusions reached by its contributors. Two well-regarded scientists who refereed Epstein's paper advised its publication. We will soon publish Monsanto's response and responses from other contributors regarding the issues raised in Epstein's article.

Epstein's note — Monsanto failed to accept the above invitation to publish a critique of my (Part A) article.

Part C was published as a letter to the editor of *Science,* October 19, 1990, p. 359.

Chapter 11

QUESTIONS AND ANSWERS ON SYNTHETIC BOVINE GROWTH HORMONES

Natural bovine growth hormone (BGH) is a protein hormone that controls bovine growth and lactation. Synthetic bovine growth hormones (rBGH) are manufactured by recombinant DNA biotechnology by the Agriculture Chemicals Division of Eli Lilly and Company (Elanco) in conjunction with the Dow Chemical Company, the Upjohn Company, American Cyanamid, and Monsanto.

Six years ago, the Food and Drug Administration approved the use of rBGH in large-scale productivity trials, and the sale to the public of unlabeled milk and meat from these trials. The FDA has announced that it proposes to approve the commercial use of BGH in the near future. The industry expects national and international sales of approximately $500 million annually.

THE DATABASE ON rBGH

Question: What is the source of the available database on rBGH?

Answer: The data on which the FDA review and approval process is based have been generated and interpreted exclusively by industry and by its academic contractees and consultants in some 22 U.S. university dairy science departments, to the exclusion of any input by independent scientists. Additionally, no independent scientists have been directly or indirectly involved at any stage of the FDA review process. A detailed independent scientific review, with full supportive references, has recently documented substantive evidence of adverse veterinary effects, besides raising critical questions on public health hazards to consumers from consumption of dairy products and meat from animals treated with rBGH (1) (see Chapter 10, Part A).

Published in *International Journal of Health Services,* Volume 20, Number 4, 1990.

Q: Does the track record of the BGH industry justify confidence in the validity of its database on toxic chemical products that the industry has attempted to market or has marketed in the past?

A: No. There is fully documented evidence that the database of these industries and their indentured academics has been self-interested and highly unreliable, reflecting manipulation, suppression, distortion, and destruction of data on a wide range of products, including animal feed additives and drugs, pesticides, detergents, plastics, and other industrial chemicals (2–6) (see also Chapter 1). The track record of these industries is thus fully reflected in their misconduct in emerging fields of commercial biotechnology.

EFFICACY OF rBGH AND BENEFITS TO THE DAIRY INDUSTRY

Q: Does the evidence support industry claims that administration of rBGH increases milk production by 10 to 25 percent and that this will result in substantial benefits to dairy farmers?

A: No. Independent analysis demonstrates that increases in milk yields are highly inconsistent and variable (7–9). Taking into account the costs of rBGH (estimated to be in the range of 25 to 75 cents per cow, per day) and extra feed—apart from the currently poorly recognized adverse veterinary effects, particularly reproductive—these data challenge the validity of industry claims on efficacy and benefits. Furthermore, available evidence indicates that increased milk production, contributing further to the national surplus and thus leading to a reduction in milk prices, is likely to result in a severe economic impact on the dairy farming industry, particularly on small dairy farms. Additionally, the reduction in casein levels noted in milk from rBGH-treated cows may adversely affect the cheese industry.

VETERINARY EFFECTS OF rBGH

Q: Does evidence support industry claims, endorsed by the FDA, that rBGH administration is safe for cattle?

A: No. Industry claims of safety are based on data derived only incidentally from inherently insensitive productivity trials, based on small numbers of cows, as opposed to appropriate and statistically valid toxicological tests, including multi-lactational and multi-generational studies, based on larger numbers of animals. Nevertheless, available data from these trials clearly demonstrate a high incidence of adverse effects, particularly clinical or subclinical mastitis and impaired reproductive performance (1, 7–9); also reported are severe and persistent injection site reactions, and lameness in heifers and cows. However, with the acquiescence of the FDA, the BGH industry has discounted, trivialized, or misinterpreted its own data on such adverse effects. There are also informal reports on other adverse effects including burnout or "lactational crash," and deaths associated with fatty degeneration of the liver. In view of this substantive evidence on adverse veterinary effects, it is critical that Investigational New Animal Drug Application (INADA) industry data be made available for detailed review by the independent scientific community.

The increased incidence of infectious disease in cows hyperstimulated by daily injections of rBGH, apart from other toxic effects such as heat intolerance, is highly suggestive of stress reactions. Nevertheless, there are no available data on the investigation of stress in rBGH-treated cows, immune function, and the activation of latent viruses. The absence of such data is critical in view of recent evidence on serious and lethal stress diseases associated with elevated BGH levels in transgenic pigs (1). Also, there are no available data on a wide range of other metabolic endocrine and biochemical functions in rBGH-treated cows.

PUBLIC HEALTH EFFECTS OF rBGH

Q: Does evidence support promotional industry claims equating or implying the identity of natural BGH and rBGH?

A: No. There are significant chemical and molecular differences between rBGH and natural BGH. rBGH contains up to eight additional amino acid groups at one end of the molecule; the FDA has recently admitted that there are some 3 percent structural differences between these hormones. It is well known that apparently minor structural variations—for example, involving only one or two amino acid groups in a protein molecule—can profoundly alter biological activity.[1] Additionally, there is no available information on the presence of nucleic acid and other bacterial contaminants in rBGH.

Q: Can current industry analytical tests detect rBGH in milk?

A: No. Industry has recently admitted that its current test procedures do not differentiate between natural BGH and rBGH. Also, no information is available as to whether industry has yet developed sensitive tests capable of specifically differentiating between these hormones, and what, if any, the results of such tests are; there is a critical need for the disclosure of these data. In addition, rBGH administration is likely to reduce normal (endogenous) production of BGH, so that most BGH in milk of treated cows is likely to be rBGH rather than natural BGH.

Q: Does evidence support the industry and FDA claims that milk and meat from rBGH-treated cows are safe for humans?

---

[1] For instance, sickle cell anemia is associated with the substitution of a single amino acid group (a glutamate is replaced by a valine) in a hemoglobin molecule; retinitis pigmentosa, an inherted disorder leading to blindness, is associated with the substitution of a single amino acid group in the rhodopsin or visual purple molecule.

A: No. The evidence is based on the following: studies in the 1950s showing that administration of BGH to human dwarfs did not result in increased growth; claims that there are no increased BGH levels in milk from rBGH-treated cows; and claims that any rBGH consumed by humans would be digested and inactivated. The human dwarf data are irrelevant because they were based on tests with natural BGH and not rBGH, apart from other considerations including the need to administer androgenic steroids together with human growth hormones to obtain any effects on growth in some clinical categories of dwarfs. Furthermore, proteolytic digests of natural BGH are metabolically active when injected in humans and induce metabolic effects in hypopituitary humans similar to those following administration of human growth hormone. Thus, peptide fragments of rBGH, formed during pasteurization or in the human alimentary tract, could be absorbed and induce a wide range of potential adverse effects, particularly allergic and inununogenic; also, absorption of intact protein molecules is well recognized, particularly in infants. It should be emphasized that no data are available on gastrointestinal absorption of rBGH and its peptide fragments in humans, or on the biological activity in humans of these synthetic molecules.

Similarly, there are no valid data on the detection and analysis of rBGH in milk and meat products, although increases in plasma levels of up to 700 percent have been reported. Very high levels of rBGH would also be expected in meat as a result of persistent injection site reactions. Concerns on the potential hazards of rBGH in milk and meat are further heightened by the failure of the FDA to require a preslaughter withdrawal period, even though this was strongly recommended by its own scientists in 1982 and 1983.

Other potential public health concerns for which no data are available relate to the presence of potent and potentially toxic contaminants in milk and meat from rBGH–treated cows. These include elevated levels of IGF-1, a species cross-reactive cell-stimulating growth factor; absorption of intact molecules or active peptide fragments of IGF-1 could possibly induce premature growth in infants and adverse cell-stimulating effects, such as promoting breast cancer. Also, abnormalities in the biological behavior of IGF-1 could be induced by rBGH (10). Other possible contaminants include stressor chemicals; antibiotics used in the treatment of cattle with infections induced by rBGH; and viruses, particularly leukemia/lymphoma and AIDS-like viruses, activated by rBGH. Whether or not any of these potential concerns pose real public health hazards can only be determined by detailed long-term investigations by qualified and independent scientists.

Q: Did the FDA require the industry, in accordance with 21CFR 514.1, to submit full reports of adequate tests by all methods reasonably applicable to show whether or not rBGH is safe for human use as suggested in the proposed labeling?

A: No. The extensive laboratory animal safety studies necessary to establish drug withdrawal times and human food safety of new drugs were not required.

FDA APPROVAL OF rBGH

Q: What was the basis of the FDA decision, some six years ago (as of 1990), to allow large-scale investigational trials on rBGH by industry and its academic contractees and to allow the sale to the uninformed public of unlabeled milk, milk products, and meat from unidentified herds?

A: The FDA action was largely based on its statement that humans are normally exposed to BGH in milk, falsely implying the identity of natural BGH and rBGH, and its unsupported claim that rBGH is not biologically active in humans.

Q: Has the FDA stated its position on the future commercial approval of rBGH?

A: Yes. The FDA has stated that rBGH will be commercially approved in the near future, prior to which the FDA will submit a summary of its scientific findings to a peer-reviewed journal. However, there is no indication as to whether such peer review will be conducted by independent scientists, as opposed to industry scientists or its academic contractees or consultants.[2]

Q: Has the FDA determined whether the conditions of use, recommended or prescribed in the proposed rBGH label, are reasonably certain to be followed in practice?

A: No. Once rBGH is approved, the FDA will lose control over its use with regard to dosage for dairy cattle and off-label use in dairy and meat animals.

Q: Does the proposed labeling for rBGH include reference to indications, dosages, route, methods, frequency and duration of administration, and any adverse veterinary effects, apart from unresolved questions on human safety?

A: No. Adequate labeling cannot be written for the use of rBGH under over-the-counter regulations. This labeling requires that adequate directions for use must be understandable to laypersons. The management, genetic, and other variables encountered in dairy farming cannot be adequately described on a label. Furthermore, no reference to human safety concerns has been proposed.

Q: Is the proposed labeling adequate to ensure the safe veterinary use of rBGH?

A: No. The use of rBGH would require monitoring of multiple variables to achieve increased production, particularly superior management; many small

---

[2] As of July 1990, an FDA manuscript was in press in *Science*. The chief editor of *Science* is considered by this author to be prejudiced and biased against environmental and consumer concerns (see Chapter 15), besides being an enthusiastic proponent of the commercial applications of biotechnology. The key reviewer of the FDA manuscript was Dale Baumann of Cornell University, who has been Monsanto's major contractee and consultant on BGH for nearly a decade.

dairy farms cannot accommodate such requirements. If the directions are not followed, problems arising from use of the product could be attributed to misuse, for which neither the FDA nor industry would admit responsibility.

Q: Has the FDA proposed the labeling of rBGH as a prescription drug in order to reduce consumer concerns on safety?
A: Yes. This, however, is not a valid or legal reason for labeling a production drug for prescription uses. Furthermore, a prescription drug would require a veterinary–client relationship that could not possibly be followed in large-scale commercial uses.

THE FDA REVIEW PROCESS

Q: Has the FDA Center for Veterinary Medicine (CVM) conducted the BGH review process in compliance with the Federal Food Drug and Cosmetic Act, the current regulations and requirements of 21 CFR 514.1, published guidelines, and unpublished policies, with regard to efficacy, veterinary safety, and human safety?
A: No. For details, see below (11, 12).

Q: Does the CVM have inappropriate contacts with the regulated industries, and is there evidence of inappropriate industry influence?
A: Yes. the CVM director has met regularly with personnel of the Animal Health Institute, a trade organization representing the regulated industries. There is, however, no evidence that the director met with consumer groups concerned with food safety. There are also allegations that donations to a national political party were requested of applicants for the CVM directorship, and that such a donation was ultimately paid by the regulated industry. Growing evidence indicates that corporate lobbyists "enjoy almost unlimited access" to CVM officials, and that the review process is characterized by illegal gratuities, favoritism, and rigging of assignments to "cooperative" staff members (13).

Q: Has the FDA undertaken unprecedented and inappropriate actions in support of an INADA for rBGH?
A: Yes. High-ranking CVM and other senior agency personnel have spoken out in support of rBGH. It is unprecedented for the FDA to publicly support or otherwise advertise an approved or unapproved animal drug.

Q: Is there a precedent in the CVM for the review of products exclusively in a single Division, without appropriate input from other Divisions and qualified CVM experts?
A: No. The Production Drugs Division (PDD) sequestered the BGH data and excluded any role for the Division of Toxicology and for the Biometrics Branch of the Division of Biometrics and Information. Additionally, the PDD denied

experienced and board-certified CVM personnel, particularly veterinary pathologists and toxicologists, free access to BGH data.

Q: Are CVM statisticians inappropriately performing data entry and statistical reviews for industry?
A: Yes. The PDD has utilized two statisticians almost full-time for over three years to enter and analyze data for the regulated industry, apart from selecting animals for exclusion from the database without proper clinical input.

Q: Is the Biometrics Group being utilized in the standard manner for the analysis of BGH data?
A: No. Normal procedures have been abandoned. The chief of Biometrics no longer has final sign-off authority on the work of his reviewers, who instead regularly and improperly report to the director of the PDD.

Q: Are PDD personnel qualified for the review of the rBGH data?
A: No. PDD personnel have no previous experience with production drugs in dairy cattle. The PDD did not seek the counsel of qualified veterinary and animal science experts, and was thus inappropriately dependent on and influenced by the expertise of the regulated industry and its academic contractees.

Q: Did the CVM require the industry, in accordance with 21 CFR 514.1, to submit full reports by all reasonably applicable methods to show whether or not rBGH is safe and effective as suggested in the proposed labeling?
A: No. Based on past inspections and records, there is evidence that full reports have not been made; that data and procedures were improperly handled; that adequate testing in adequate numbers of animals was not conducted; that the data were confounded by inappropriate use of concurrent therapy with approved and unapproved products; that data entries were made by unqualified or inappropriately supervised individuals; and that a fully qualified "uncooperative" staff scientist was fired after raising critical questions on the veterinary hazards of rBGH (14). Furthermore, in spite of the reported INADA and other data on a wide range of adverse veterinary effects, the CVM has acquiesced in industry claims on the safety of rBGH.

Q: Did the CVM follow the published guidelines and regulations requiring public comment in the development of protocols for the investigation of efficacy and safety of rBGH?
A: No. Instead, the CVM developed a unique internal Technical Assistance Document with the admitted intent of avoiding the requirement for public comment.

Q: Did the CVM require that the Target Animal Safety tests on rBGH be conducted under appropriate laboratory conditions?

A: No. Testing under dose confirmation studies or field conditions of use was allowed, contrary to 21 CFR 514.l. This allowed the use of diagnostic and therapeutic procedures that could mask adverse veterinary effects.

Q: What other BGH-related animal drugs, besides rBGH intended for dairy cattle use, are now (as of 1990) under review in the FDA?
A: These include: rBGH for beef animals; rBGH growth hormone releasing factor; anti-somatotropin antibody; and insulin growth factors.

Q: Were qualified CVM personnel involved in the review process on human food safety?
A: No. Such review appears to have been cursory in the extreme and to have been conducted by unqualified PDD personnel. Illustratively, current human safety evaluation is being conducted by an ex-PDD staffer, with no background or qualifications in toxicology, veterinary medicine, or public health, acting as an FDA consultant and residing in Nova Scotia.

Q: How many rBGH trials have been undertaken, by each named industry, involving how many herds and how many cows; how much milk, meat, and dairy products from these trials have been sold to the public over the last six years; how many members of the public have consumed such foods; have any tests or studies been conducted on any such consumers; and are any tests, studies, or future surveillance planned for such consumers?
A: No information is available on any of these questions.

Q: Is the FDA review process on rBGH consistent with its track record for other animal drugs and feed additives?
A: Yes. It demonstrates reckless irresponsibility and regulatory abdication. This was fully recognized in a recent Congressional report which concluded that "FDA has consistently disregarded its responsibility . . . repeatedly put what it perceives are interests of veterinarians and the livestock industry ahead of its legal obligation to protect consumers . . . jeopardizing the health and safety of consumers of meat, milk and poultry" (15). Confirmation of such regulatory abdication is provided by the FDA's admission, in a November 1988 consumer report, that "illegal use of veterinary drugs can be an even greater threat to the public health than the illegal use of human drugs." These concerns are still further emphasized by the results of recent investigations demonstrating that up to 38 percent of milk sampled nationally is contaminated by illegal residues of antibiotics and animal drugs, posing grave potential public health hazards, including antibiotic resistance, carcinogenicity, and allergic reactions (13). In this connection, without public notification, the CVM has recently tripled the allowable residues in milk of new antibiotics used for treatment of bovine mastitis, a common complication in *srBGH-treated cows*.

ADDENDUM

Review of confidential INADA files submitted by Monsanto to the FDA has confirmed evidence on a wide range of adverse veterinary effects induced by rBGH, besides public health concerns, as previously reported by the author (1; see Chapter 10, Part A) but stridently denied by the FDA and industry and its academic consultants. These adverse effects include a major reduction in pregnancy rates; a high incidence of mastitis, necessitating extensive treatment with unapproved antibiotics and drugs; chronic toxic effects, evidenced by increased weight of body organs and disseminated pathological lesions; injection site reactions, sufficiently severe to cause carcass damage; and elevated milk and blood hormone levels. The suppression of such data has raised further serious public health concerns, and emphasized the need for independent review of all INADA files on rBGH and for a high-level investigation of industry and FDA misconduct.

Accordingly, on May 8, 1990, Congressman John Conyers (D-MI), chairman of the House Committee on Government Operations, requested Inspector General Richard Kusserow of the Department of Health and Human Services to immediately investigate the FDA for "abdication of regulatory responsibility" with regard to its review of rBGH used to artificially boost milk production. Congressman Conyers further charged that "Monsanto and the FDA have chosen to suppress and manipulate animal health test data . . . in efforts to approve commercial use of BGH." In a prompt reaction to these revelations, Senator Patrick Leahy (D-VT) pressured the FDA into accepting an independent review of industry data by the National Institutes of Health to evaluate consumer hazards from milk produced by rBGH-treated cows. European reactions and concerns are not lagging far behind, as illustrated by the following International Resolution on BGH, unanimously approved at an international convention in Bonn, Germany, on May 15, 1990.

International Resolution on Synthetic Bovine Growth Hormone

We, the undersigned, as U.S. and European farmers, consumer and citizen groups, and independent scientists on the International Day of Milk, 15 May, 90, recognize that Bovine Growth Hormone (bGH) is just the first of the new animal husbandry biotechnologies. In today's world, these technologies are more likely to serve the interests of rich and powerful industries rather than the needs of consumers for safe food; family farmers and rural communities for economic stability; and third world countries for agriculture self-sufficiency.

Biotechnology industries claim that bGH will increase production and reduce costs. However, bGH is more likely to increase costs to the farmer; to destroy the small traditional family farm; to seriously damage animal health and welfare; to contaminate dairy products and meat and pose major potential public health hazards.

- We demand an immediate international ban on the manufacture of bGH.
- We demand an immediate international ban on the manufacture of bGH-related products, such as bGH Growth Hormone Releasing Factors, anti-Somatotropin antibody, and Insulin Growth Factors.
- We demand an immediate ban on the international transshipment of bGH and bGH-related products.
- We demand an immediate ban on the sale of milk, other dairy products and meat from cows and from other meat animals treated with bGH and bGH-related products.
- We demand the immediate identification of herds of cattle and other meat animals treated with bGH and bGH-related products together with independent assurance that no milk, dairy products or meat will be sold to the public, and that all such products will be destroyed under independent supervision.
- There is more than adequate evidence that bGH induces a wide range of serious adverse health effects in cattle, and that consumption of contaminated milk from bGH-treated cows poses serious potential public health dangers.
- There is unarguable evidence from confidential files submitted by Monsanto, a major manufacturer of bGH, to the US Food and Drug Administration (FDA) confirming the evidence of these veterinary and public health hazards. For example, in flagrant contradiction to assurances of the industry and the FDA, milk from bGH-treated cows is contaminated with high levels of the synthetic bGH-hormone.
- We commend the EEC [European Economic Community] for its moratorium on the use of bGH.
- We commend Raymond McSharry, the EEC Agriculture Commissioner for recently proposing a ban on bGH on grounds of consumer concerns.
- We commend the European Parliament for its proposed ban on bGH.
- We commend the US Congress for their concerns with relation to bGH. In particular, we commend the actions by the House Committee on Government Operations, and the Senate Agriculture Committee in directing the General Accounting Office to investigate charges of misconduct by the FDA with regard to their review of bGH. We also commend Congressman Conyers, Chairman of the House Committee on Government Operations, for his more recent request to the US Inspector General for an independent investigation of Monsanto and the FDA for their willful suppression of critical information on the veterinary and public health hazards of bGH.
- We commend the states of Wisconsin and Minnesota for their recent moratoria on the sale of bGH dairy products in their states.
- We urge that immediate funding be made available to independent consumer-, farmers-, environmental-, animal rights and other concerned groups in order to ensure effective implementation of our recommendations.
- We urge an immediate investigation of Monsanto and other bGH manufacturing industries for possible violation of civil and criminal laws, both nationally and internationally, with respect to their deliberate misrepresentation and suppression of information on the hazards of bGH.

Based on our experience with bGH, quite apart from a wide range of other consumer products, drugs and industrial chemicals, it is clear, that the EEC and each individual nation world wide must fully and independently evaluate the detailed and raw industry data before accepting possibly misleading and self-serving assurances of safety.

• Finally, we reaffirm the rights of individual nations and states to set food and environmental safety policies without outside interference, and opposition to any General Agreement on Tariffs and Trade (GATT) proposal which would circumvent these rights, especially in the areas of new biotechnotogies and food safety.

Bonn, May 14, 1990. CAMPAIGN AGAINST BGH, representing 30 German organizations; EUROPEAN FARMERS COORDINATION, representing 10 European organisations; NATIONAL FAMILY FARM COALITION, representing 30 US Organizations; PROF: SAMUEL EPSTEIN MD, representing independent scientists and the Rachel Carson Council, Washington, D.C.

UNLABELED MILK FROM COWS TREATED WITH BIOSYNTHETIC GROWTH HORMONES: A CASE OF REGULATORY ABDICATION

In 1985, the Food and Drug Administration (FDA) approved the commercial sale of unlabeled milk and meat from large-scale veterinary trials on cows treated with the synthetic bovine growth hormones (rBGH); these hormones are manufactured using recombinant DNA biotechnology by Monsanto, American Cyanamid, Dow Chemical, Upjohn, and Eli Lilly companies. FDA and industry claimed that rBGH had no adverse veterinary effects and that rBGH milk was indistinguishable from natural milk and safe for human consumption.

By 1990, evidence from published and unpublished industry sources had raised a wide range of concerns about the safety of rBGH milk (1–3) (see Chapter 10, Part A). These included: contamination of rBGH milk with pus from mastitis and with antibiotics used in its treatment; contamination of milk with rBGH that FDA admitted differed significantly in its molecular structure from the natural growth hormone; and contamination of milk with excess levels of insulin-like growth factor 1 (IGF-1). In spite of these unresolved veterinary and public health concerns, in November 1993 FDA approved large-scale commercial use and sale of rBGH milk, and shortly after issued regulatory guidelines effectively banning the labeling of such milk (4, 5). This chapter presents an analysis of available information on potential risks of breast and gastrointestinal cancers from IGF-1 in rBGH milk.

Insulin-like growth factor 1 is a potent low molecular weight polypeptide growth factor that mediates the action of the pituitary growth hormone on somatic growth. IGF-1 induces profound metabolic effects through endocrine, paracrine, or autocrine mechanisms (6–10), including regulation of transport processes, macromolecular synthesis, cell growth, replication and differentiation, and milk production. Although the gene encoding IGF-1 is expressed in many tissues, most circulating IGF-1 is produced by liver cells where transcription is regulated

Published in *International Journal of Health Services*, Volume 26, Number 1, 1996.

by a complex hypothalamic-pituitary-hepatic axis (6, 7). IGF-1 is also synthesized at the local level by both normal and malignant cells (7, 8). It should be further noted that the amino acid sequences of human and bovine IGF-1 are identical (9, 10).

ELEVATED IGF-1 LEVELS IN rBGH MILK

In an early report relating IGF-1 milk levels to natural BGH isolated from bovine pituitaries, administration of the hormone increased IGF-1 levels in goat's milk from a mean pretreatment level of 16 ng/ml to 25 ng/ml within four days (11). Normal cow's milk collected just after parturition contained high IGF-1 levels, about 150 ng/ml, which rapidly fell to about 25 ng/ml within one week and then declined to only 1 to 5 ng/ml by 200 days, when levels of IGF-1 induced by rBGH ranged from 6 to 20 ng/ml, up to a 20-fold increase (12). In a subsequent short-term study on 35 to 47 weeks post-partum cows, a sixfold increase in IGF-1 milk levels was reported as early as 7 days following rBGH treatment (13). Of particular interest was the finding that "a significant proportion [19 percent] of the total IGF-1 was present in the [protein] free unbound form" (13), and was thus probably more bioactive or potent than the protein-bound form (14). Furthermore, pasteurization increases milk IGF-1 levels by some 70 percent, presumably by disrupting protein binding (15). The significance of these findings is emphasized by recent evidence that free IGF-1 levels in human serum are as low as 0.38 percent (16). No data are available, however, on the ratios of free to unbound IGF-1 in the sera and milk of cows treated or untreated with rBGH, and in the sera of humans drinking milk from cows treated or untreated with rBGH.

In some six unpublished, confidential industry studies, disclosed by FDA in a highly abbreviated summary form, IGF-1 levels in rBGH milk were consistently increased (15); these increases were statistically significant, ranging from 25 to 70 percent (17). Illustratively, in a 1989 Monsanto trial, milk IGF-1 levels in cows increased from control levels of 3.5 ng/ml to 5.9 ng/ml and 6.1 ng/ml following intramuscular or subcutaneous rBGH injections, respectively; higher levels still, up to 25 ng/ml, were subsequently reported by Monsanto (18). More recently, Lilly Industries, in its application for marketing authorization to the European Community Committee for Veterinary Medicinal Products, has admitted that rBGH milk may contain more than a 10-fold increase in IGF-1 concentrations (19).

A summary report of the 1990 National Institutes of Health Technology Conference noted that IGF-1 levels in unspecified samples of rBGH milk were 3.5 to 13 ng/ml, approximately three to four times the levels in human milk, in contrast to 1.5 to 8 ng/ml in untreated cows (20). This report also noted that IGF-1 levels in meat of rBGH animals were approximately twice as high as in untreated controls.

The results of virtually all these studies are, however, based on flawed analytic techniques that underestimated IGF-1 levels, as recognized by the technique developers and others (17, 21, 22). Problems with these techniques included their inability to separate the IGF-1 molecule from a complex of associated large carrier proteins to which IGF-1 is usually bound. These problems were further extended by the finding that standard IGF-1 analytic techniques underestimate, by a factor of four, levels of a truncated form of IGF-1 (–3N:IGF-1) which is approximately 10 times more potent in stimulating protein and DNA synthesis than normal IGF-1, resulting in a potential 40-fold underestimate of levels in rBGH milk (14, 23). The significance of these considerations was further emphasized: "The presence in colostrum of –3N:IGF-1 and of large amounts of free IGF-1 may be pointers to likely changes occurring in milk in response to bST [rBGH] treatment, since a strong parallel has been suggested between the increased milk secretion which occurs post partum and that following bST treatment" (14).

ABSORPTION OF IGF-1 FROM THE GASTROINTESTINAL TRACT

There is unequivocal evidence that a wide range of intact proteins are absorbed across the gut wall in a wide range of species including humans (15, 24). In humans, this evidence is largely based on the detection of serum antibodies to food proteins (25). The infant gut is more permeable to protein than the adult gut, particularly pre-term and prior to "closure" at about 3 months of age (26–28). Infants and young children have higher serum levels of cow's milk protein antibodies than adults (24, 29). These varying lines of evidence on absorption of intact proteins further confirm that smaller molecular weight polypeptides, such as IGF-1, can also be absorbed from the gut. Even more compelling is evidence of marked systemic effects following short-term IGF-1 feeding tests in rats (15).

FDA recently responded to this evidence with a wide range of tenuous and inconsistent claims (30). These include: "There is no evidence that IGF-1 survives digestion in humans," in contrast to FDA's prior publication of Monsanto/Hazleton data on systemic effects of IGF-1 following short-term oral administration (15). And "the IGF-1 content of milk is not altered by BST supplementation" on the basis of "more comprehensive [industry] studies" (31), although these studies in fact conclude that "mean IGF-1 levels in the [rBGH] treated animals are always higher than those found in the controls." Excess IGF-1 milk levels were trivialized in comparison with endogenous levels in human saliva and blood by FDA's use of highly speculative and misleading calculations (30).

More appropriate calculations should be based on the following considerations and data. Adult humans produce daily about 1.2 liters of saliva containing an IGF-1 level of about 3 ng/ml, equivalent to a daily recycling of some 3 μg of

IGF-1 (32); corresponding intake levels in infants are substantially lower. This should be contrasted with an infant's daily consumption of 1 liter of rBGH cow's milk containing the maximum 25 μg level of IGF-1 admitted by Monsanto (18), well over an order of magnitude excess exogenous exposure. While exaggerating endogenous in relation to exogenous exposures from rBGH milk in infants, neither FDA nor industry has presented any data on salivary and blood levels of IGF-1 in infants. A 1990 letter from Monsanto to NIH claimed that plans to obtain the salivary data "will be forthcoming" (33); however, no such data are yet (as of late 1995) available. FDA's quantitative comparison between IGF-1 levels in bovine milk and human blood is equally misleading (30). Assuming an adult blood volume of 3.5 liters and adult IGF-1 levels of 100 ng/ml, adults have a total circulatory level of 350 μg of IGF-1, rather than the 600 μg calculated by FDA (30). Thus, assuming a neonate blood volume of 0.25 liters, based on a body weight of 3 kg and a volume of 80 ml/kg, this would correspond to a circulatory level of about 25 μg. This should be contrasted with a daily intake of up to 25 μg/l of IGF-1 in rBGH milk, which may be up to 40 times more potent or bioactive than blood IGF-1 (14), constituting a daily intake of 1000 μg blood equivalents.

Such calculations not only are based on a wide range of assumptions, but also reflect very substantial data gaps despite over a decade of industry experience with rBGH. What is clear, however, is that simplistic quantitative comparisons by FDA and industry that trivialize milk versus endogenous IGF-1 levels are not meaningful. Alternative calculations raise serious concerns on the potential hazards, particularly to infants, of excess IGF-1 levels in rBGH milk.

ORAL ACTIVITY OF IGF-1

There are no published studies, in the scientific literature or in FDA or industry reports, on the oral activity of IGF-1. FDA, however, in 1990 released a highly condensed summary of 1989 toxicity tests by the two major rBGH industries, Eli Lilly & Co. (Elanco) and Monsanto Agricultural Co. (15). The Elanco test was conducted at the company. The Monsanto test was contracted out to Hazleton Laboratories. Apart from a wide range of other flaws, the relevance of both these studies is questionable as they were short rather than long term, were conducted on adult rather than infant rats, and were conducted on rIGF-1 rather than on IGF-1–containing rBGH milk or IGF-1 isolated from rBGH milk.

The FDA report on the Elanco oral toxicity test was cryptic, even more so than that on the Monsanto/Hazleton study (15). The Elanco test used groups of 10 male and female hypophysectomized adult rats, given oral doses of rIGF-1 for two weeks at 0.01, 0.1, or 1.0 mg/kg/day, with a subcutaneous infusion positive control at 1.0 mg/kg. Gross organ weights were increased in positive control rats but not test rats. No data were presented on epiphyseal width and tibia length. On the basis of these minimal parameters, rIGF-1 was alleged to be devoid of oral toxicity.

In the Monsanto/Hazleton test, groups of 20 male and female 36-day-old rats were dosed orally for two weeks with rIGF-1 at concentrations of 0.02, 0.2, or 2.0 mg/kg/day (15). Two groups of rats served as positive controls. The first was infused subcutaneously with rIGF-1 doses of 0.05 or 0.2 mg/rat/day corresponding to about 1 to 4 mg/kg/day, and the second with porcine growth hormone (pGH) at doses of 4.0 mg/rat/day corresponding to about 80 mg/kg/day, assuming a 36-day-old rat weighs approximately 50 g. Statistically significant increases in body weight were seen with male test rats at 2.0 mg/kg, with a positive linear trend at all dose levels in test females. In addition, statistically significant increases in liver weight and tibia length and decreases in epiphyseal width were seen in test males at doses of 2.0 mg/kg, significant increases in tibia length of test males at 0.02 mg/kg, and significant decreases in epiphyseal width of test females at 2.0 mg/kg. The statistically significant lowest observed effect level (LOEL) of 0.02 mg/kg/day is thus approximately 1/4000 of the positive infusion control pGH dose and approximately 1/50 of the positive infusion control rIGF-1 LOEL.

In spite of the tabulated Monsanto data on the statistically significant sensitivity of rats to oral administration of rIGF-1, FDA asserted "that rIGF-1 is orally inactive at doses up to 2 mg/kg per day" (15). This conclusion conflicts with the cited data and was based on a series of tenuous claims that have been subject to detailed criticism (14, 34). FDA claimed that there were no significant increases in body weight of orally dosed females in contrast to males, even though a similar difference in sensitivity was noted in female rIGF-1 controls injected at 0.05 mg/rat/day. FDA also claimed (a) that the increase in body weight of test males should be discounted as it only occurred in one "block" of half the control rIGF-1 rats, raising questions about the validity of the experimental design of the test on which FDA based its conclusion; (b) that there were no increases in serum IGF-1 of test rats, although no supportive data were cited; and (c) that decreases in epiphyseal width and increases in tibia lengths in test animals should be disregarded as "contradictory [and] sporadic," even though such effects in rIGF-1 control groups were also inconsistent and not even cited at the 0.05 mg/rat dose.

FDA's flawed analysis of their cited test data is compounded by a misleading presentation of the data. Notably, in Tables 4 and 5 of the Monsanto/Hazleton report, the dosages of test rats are presented in mg/kg, while those for the positive infused controls are presented in mg/rat, thus using incomparable dose units for test and control animals (15). This resulted in a misleading reduction of oral dose levels in test rats compared with control rats by a factor of some 20, thus substantially underestimating their sensitivity to oral IGF-1 (34). Such data manipulation is consistent with the documented track record of Hazleton Laboratories (35). Under the circumstances, it is not surprising that FDA and Monsanto refused to comply with a May 1994 Congressional request for an unabridged copy of the 1988 Hazleton report on which FDA bases its near exclusive reliance for the alleged nontoxicity of IGF-1 in rBGH milk (36).

The unpublished Monsanto/Hazleton oral toxicity test was conducted on rIGF-1, rather than more relevantly on IGF-1 in rBGH milk, which may differ from rIGF-1 (14). This study is also seriously flawed as it violated standard protocols on routine lifetime chronic toxicity and carcinogenicity tests based on two species. This study was only two weeks long and included groups of only 20 male and female adult rats. Maximally tolerated doses (MTD) were not determined and test doses were not extended up to this range, nor was testing extended below 0.02 mg/kg in order to determine the no observable effect level (NOEL). No autopsy data were provided, except body and organ weight and epiphyseal width; and no histological data were reported. Moreover, no three-generation and transplacental tests were conducted, nor any tests involving neo-natal rodents or neonatal and adult subhuman primates. Finally, no investigations were undertaken on sensitive subcellular effects, including IGF-1 binding and receptor levels in tests and controls.

Of further interest, a recent industry report noted a statistically significant increase in the body weight at weaning of calves from rBGH-treated cows compared with calves from untreated cows (37). While this result suggests that increased IGF-1 milk levels induce growth factor effects, in the absence of paired feeding data it is not possible to exclude the effect of increased avail-ability of milk.

ABSENCE OF SAFETY MARGINS FOR IGF-1 FOLLOWING CONSUMPTION OF rBGH MILK

As recently emphasized (14), consumption of rBGH milk would expose infants and young children to IGF-1 levels substantially in excess of the safety margin based on the 0.02 mg/kg (20 μg/kg) LOEL identified in the Monsanto/Hazleton oral toxicity test (15). Assuming a 10 kg child consumes 1 liter daily of rBGH milk with an IGF-1 concentration of 25 ng/ml (25 μg/l), this would then result in an intake of 2.5 μg/kg, one-eighth of the 20 μg/kg LOEL (14). Safety margins for noncarcinogenic toxic effects are conventionally set on the basis of 1/100 of NOELs and 1/1000 of LOELs, which for IGF-1 would thus be 0.02 μg/kg. Thus, an intake of 2.5 μg/kg would actually be 125-fold in excess of the standard safety margin.

Such estimates are conservative for a range of reasons discussed above: pasteurization of rBGH milk increases IGF-1 levels by approximately 70 percent (15); IGF-1 in rBGH milk is more bioactive than IGF-1 in untreated milk; standard analytic techniques underestimate IGF-1 levels by a factor of 4; and IGF-1 in rBGH milk may well be present, at least in part, in a truncated form that is some 10 times more potent than IGF-1 in untreated milk (14).

IGF-1 IN rBGH MILK AS A POTENTIAL RISK
FACTOR FOR BREAST CANCER

FDA made its decision on the safety of rBGH milk in 1985 in the absence of data on a wide range of public health concerns, including information about excess IGF-1 levels in rBGH milk, and without consideration of the cellular proliferative effect of IGF-1. Over recent years, several converging lines of evidence have implicated IGF-1 in the initiation or promotion of breast cancer. This evidence raises serious concerns about the potential carcinogenic effects, particularly for female infants, of increased IGF-1 levels in rBGH milk and dairy products.

In the normal lactating bovine mammary gland, IGF-1 is almost exclusively located in intralobular stromal or connective tissue cells with minimal epithelial reactivity (38). In contrast, there is a markedly prominent epithelial uptake of IGF-1 following increased serum levels induced by rBGH (38). Furthermore, IGF-1 binds to specific surface receptors identified in cultured mammary epithelial cells of a wide range of species including pigs, cattle, and humans (39–41). These receptors are proteins in the tyrosine kinase family, to which retrovirus oncogenes also belong (42). IGF-1 receptors have also been identified in normal and malignant human breast tissue (43, 44); levels in malignant tissue are some 10-fold elevated. Related growth factors, such as epidermal growth factor (EGF) and fibroblastic growth factor (FGF), also bind to receptors of breast cancer cells (43). Of further interest, estradiol and progesterone regulate IGF-1 receptors in cultured normal and neoplastic human uterine endometrial cells (45).

More direct evidence on the role of elevated levels of IGF-1 in rBGH milk as a potential risk factor for breast cancer is based on the following considerations. IGF-1 induces highly potent mitogenic effects in a variety of cell types (46), including normal human breast cells maintained in long-term tissue culture (39). IGF-1 is also a potent regulator of cultured human breast cancer cells (47, 48) and is more mitogenic than the potent estradiol (49). While distinct from carcinogenesis, mitogenesis is likely to promote malignant transformation induced by estradiol in breast epithelium (43). Furthermore, estrogens induce IGF-1 synthesis in both normal and malignant breast epithelia (50, 51). Accordingly, it is now recognized that growth factors such as IGF-1 "are responsible at least in part for the evolution of normal breast epithelia to breast cancer" (52). IGF-1 and related growth factors are critically involved in the aberrant growth of human breast cancer cells, and maintain their invasive or metastatic phenotype (43, 53). Of further interest is the fact that IGF-1 plasma concentrations are higher in breast cancer patients than healthy controls: "even if there is no direct evidence that elevated plasma levels of IGF-1 reflect elevated levels of the growth factor at the tumor level, the possibility exists that increased levels of circulating IGF-1 may contribute to breast tumor growth" (44). Relevant in this connection is the suggestion that tamoxifen used in the chemotherapy of breast cancer acts by reducing blood IGF-1 levels (49).

These unresolved concerns about the potential carcinogenicity of IGF-1 in rBGH milk are heightened by evidence that the undifferentiated prenatal and infant breasts are particularly susceptible to "imprinting" by hormonal influences (54). This may implicate IGF-1 itself as a direct breast cancer risk factor. It may also act indirectly by sensitizing the breast to subsequent unrelated risk factors, such as carcinogenic and estrogenic pesticide contaminants in food, and radiation, particularly mammography in premenopausal women (55, 56) (see Chapter 18).

IGF-1 IN rBGH MILK AS A POTENTIAL RISK FACTOR FOR GASTROINTESTINAL CANCER

IGF-1 stimulates proliferation of intestinal epithelial cells in culture (57). Such mitogenic effects are induced at concentrations equivalent to those occurring in mature bovine milk. Furthermore, a related growth factor with similar biological effects on the human gut, epidermal growth factor, passes undigested through the stomach to the small intestine from where it is rapidly absorbed into the blood stream, suggesting the likelihood that IGF-1 is similarly absorbed (57). Subsequent studies have demonstrated that EGF-1 is protected from digestion by casein, a protein in milk (58). Reflecting these considerations, the 1990 NIH Technology Conference concluded: "Whether the additional amounts of IGF-1 in milk from [rBGH-treated] cows has a local effect in the esophagus, stomach or intestines is unknown." It was accordingly recommended: "Determine the acute and chronic action of IGF-1 if any, in the upper gastrointestinal tract" (20). However, no information is yet available on the local effects of IGF-1, particularly increased levels of the probably more bioactive IGF-1 in rBGH milk, on the gastrointestinal tract of infants and adults.

More recent studies have demonstrated that following consumption of rBGH milk, IGF-1 in the gastrointestinal lumen, unlike serum IGF-1, is not protein bound and thus more likely to "exert biological activity" (59). Intraluminal infusion of IGF-1 in rats at concentrations equivalent to those in bovine milk has been found to increase the cellularity of the intestinal mucosa (60). In one study, rIGF-1 at concentrations of 100 ng/ml induced statistically highly significant mitogenic effects in crypt epithelial cells of cultured human duodenal explants (61). The authors concluded: "The combination of IGF-1 in BST-milk and IGF-1 normally secreted into the human gastrointestinal lumen would augment intraluminal concentrations of this hormone, increasing the possibility of local mitogenic effects on gut tissues" (61), and expressed concerns about local carcinogenic effects (62). Research has also shown that human colorectal cancer cell lines are responsive to IGF-1 (63), and that IGF-1 is mitogenic to five of eight carcinoma cell lines and synergizes the effects of another growth factor, transforming growth factor (TGF). The authors concluded that their results illustrated the importance of IGF-1 as "stimulators of growth of colorectal carcinoma." There is also evidence that human gastric cancer cells have IGF-1 receptors (64).

These results raise questions about IGF-1 residues in rBGH milk posing potential risks for the initiation or promotion of gastrointestinal cancer. An extensive recent review of rBGH milk further emphasized these concerns (65): "It could be considered an oversight for [the FDA] to suggest that ingested IGF-1 is inactive. . . . Many more potential effects of ingested IGF-1 on the gastrointestinal tract and the local immune system of the gut need to be explored."

DISCUSSION

Critical information on a wide range of potentially adverse health effects of IGF-1 is still unavailable (e.g., 14, 17, 19, 63, 65, 66). This is particularly disturbing because FDA made its decision on the safety of rBGH milk in 1985, when there had been no consideration of the effect of IGF-1 on cell proliferation. Needed studies include (a) determination of free versus protein-bound IGF-1 in sera of cows treated with rBGH and of untreated cows; (b) study of the lifelong, three-generation, and subcellular effects in rodents and subhuman primates of rBGH milk and derived IGF-1; (c) chemical characterization of IGF-1 in rBGH milk; (d) radioactive label studies on gastrointestinal absorption of IGF-1 in rBGH milk; (e) pharmacological studies on binding to receptor sites; and (f) even more critically, extensive studies on humans who drink rBGH milk, with particular reference to absorption and characterization of serum IGF-1, determination of free versus bound forms, and subcellular binding. The significance of such data gaps is compounded by converging lines of evidence implicating IGF-1 in rBGH milk as a potential risk factor for breast and gastrointestinal cancers. Nevertheless, FDA has dismissed these concerns without investigation and on the basis of unpublished "confidential" short-term toxicity data, primarily from an industry consulting firm with a tainted track record. Furthermore, contrary to FDA and industry claims and in spite of misleading data, the results of this test revealed statistically significant growth-promoting effects.

In spite of these serious and still unresolved public health concerns, in November 1993 FDA approved commercial sale of rBGH milk, some eight years after the agency approved the sale of unlabeled rBGH milk from large-scale veterinary trials. This was soon followed by regulatory guidelines effectively banning the labeling of such milk (4, 5). The rationale for this continued denial of consumers' right to know was developed by Michael Taylor, then Deputy FDA Commissioner and formerly chief counsel for the International Food Biotechnology Council and Monsanto (5). This ban has since been challenged by nationwide grassroots consumer groups and by two milk suppliers, both of whom have been sued by Monsanto.

In short, with the active complicity of the FDA, the entire nation is currently being subjected to an experiment involving large-scale adulteration of an age-old dietary staple by a poorly characterized and unlabeled biotechnology product. Disturbingly, this experiment benefits only a very small segment of the agrichemical industry while providing no matching benefits to consumers. Even more disturbingly, it poses major potential public health risks for the entire U.S. population.

POSTSCRIPT

The potential carcinogenicity of incremental IGF-1 in rBGH milk is confirmed by studies on acromegaly, in which levels of total and free serum IGF-1 are significantly elevated (67). A recent review has reported increased rates of pre-malignant polyps and colon cancer, and also of overall cancers, in acromegalics (68).

Chapter 13

THE CHEMICAL JUNGLE:
TODAY'S BEEF INDUSTRY

The United States is isolated among meat-exporting countries, such as Argentina and Australia, in having threatened retaliatory sanctions against the European Economic Community (EEC) and accusing it of unfair trade practices because of its January 1, 1989, ban on hormone-treated U.S. meat. The accusations ignore serious questions about the carcinogenic and other risks of hormonally contaminated meat that are of major concern to European consumers who, in the late 1980s, pressured the EEC into banning the use of all hormone additives.

Growth-promoting hormone additives, fed, implanted, or injected in more than 95 percent of U.S. cattle, are mostly synthetic nonsteroids such as Zeranol, natural sex steroids such as estrogens, or synthetic pituitary hormones such as bovine growth hormone (1; see Chapter 10, Part A). Although the carcinogenicity of the synthetic diethylstilbestrol (DES) in test animals was known as early as 1938, its use as a feed additive was approved by the U.S. Department of Agriculture (USDA) and the Food and Drug Administration (FDA) in 1947. After repeated hearings on the hazards of DES in 1958, Congress passed the Delaney Amendment to the Federal Food, Drug, and Cosmetic Act, banning the deliberate addition of any level of carcinogens into food. This law reflected the overwhelming scientific consensus, which still prevails, that there is no way of setting safe levels or tolerances for carcinogens. Nevertheless, the USDA and the FDA allowed continued use of DES on the alleged grounds that this did not result in detectable and illegal residues in meat products and that the Delaney Amendment could not be applied retroactively. By 1971, DES was being used in 75 percent of U.S. cattle. In spite of infrequent federal sampling and insensitive monitoring, DES residues were found in cattle and sheep at levels in excess of those inducing cancer experimentally. At about the same time, vaginal cancers were reported in the daughters of women treated with DES during pregnancy. Based on these findings, DES-treated meat was subsequently banned in more than 20 foreign countries, mostly European. However, misleading assurances of safety

Published in *International Journal of Health Services,* Volume 20, Number 2, 1990.

and stonewalling by the FDA and USDA, including the deliberate suppression of residue data, managed to delay a U.S. ban on DES until 1979.

The meat industry then promptly switched to other carcinogenic additives, particularly natural sex hormones, which are implanted in the ears of commercially raised feedlot cattle. Unlike the synthetic DES, whose residues can be monitored and whose use was conditional on a seven-day preslaughter withdrawal period, residues of natural hormones are not routinely detectable because they cannot be differentiated from the same hormones produced by the body. Since 1983, the FDA has allowed virtually unregulated use of these natural additives right up to the time of slaughter, subject only to the nonenforceable requirement that residue levels in meat must be less than 1 percent of the daily hormonal production in children.

A dramatic warning of the dangers of growth-promoting additives was triggered by an epidemic of premature sexual development and ovarian cysts involving about 3,000 Puerto Rican infants and children from 1979 to 1981. These toxic effects were traced to hormonal contamination of fresh meat products and were usually reversed by simple dietary changes. Using highly specialized research techniques, independent testing found that samples of the meat products were contaminated with estrogen residues more than tenfold in excess of normal ranges. Additionally, elevated levels of estrogen and the synthetic Zeranol were found in the blood of afflicted children. Increased rates of uterine and ovarian cancers in adult women were also associated with this epidemic.

More than a decade ago, Roy Hertz (2), then director of endocrinology of the National Cancer Institute and a world authority on hormonal cancer, warned of the carcinogenic risks of estrogenic feed additives, particularly for hormonally sensitive tissues such as breast tissue, because they could increase normal body hormonal levels and disturb delicately poised hormonal balances. Hertz pointed to evidence from innumerable animal tests and human clinical experience that such imbalance can be carcinogenic. Hertz also warned of the essentially uncontrolled and unregulated use of these extremely potent biological agents, no dietary levels of which can be regarded as safe. Even a dime-sized piece of meat contains billions of trillions of molecules of these carcinogens.

Virtually the entire U.S. population consumes, without any warning, labeling, or information, unknown and unpredictable amounts of hormonal residues in meat products over a lifetime. In 1986, as many as half of all cattle sampled in feedlots as large as 600 animals were found to have hormones illegally implanted in muscle rather than the ear skin, to induce further increased growth. This practice results in very high residues in meat, which even the FDA has admitted could produce "adverse effects." Left unanswered is whether such chronic and uncontrolled estrogen dosages are involved in increasing cancer rates (now striking one in three Americans), particularly the alarming 50 percent increase in the incidence of breast cancer since 1965. These questions are of further concern in the light of recent evidence confirming the association between breast cancer and oral contraceptives, whose estrogen dosage over a fraction of a lifetime is known and controlled, in contrast with that from residues of growth hormones in meat products.

Hormonal feed contamination in the United States is only part of a much larger problem caused by the use of thousands of feed additives. These include antibiotics, tranquilizers, pesticides, animal drugs, artificial flavors, and industrial wastes, many of which are carcinogenic in addition to their other harmful effects. The runaway technologies of the meat-product and pharmaceutical industries are supported by an eager cadre of academic consultants, contractees and apologists, tremendous lobbying pressures, and a revolving door between senior personnel in industry and regulatory agencies. This was personified by Reagan administration agriculture secretaries John Block, a former Illinois hog farmer, and Richard Lyng, a former head of the American Meat Institute.

As clearly evidenced in a series of General Accounting Office investigations and Congressional hearings, USDA inspection and FDA registration and residue-tolerance programs are in near total disarray, aggravated by brazen denials and cover-ups by these agencies. A January 1986 report, "Human Food Safety and the Regulation of Animal Drugs," unanimously approved by the House Committee on Government Operations, concluded that the "FDA has consistently disregarded its responsibility—has repeatedly put what it perceives are interests of veterinarians and the livestock industry ahead of its legal obligation to protect consumers-jeopardizing the health and safety of consumers of meat, milk, and poultry" (3). The great majority of feed additives are used in the absence of evidence of efficacy, practical and sensitive monitoring methods, and minimal if any safety test data, apart from the widespread use of illegal and unapproved drugs. The hazards of U.S. meat have retrogressed from the random fecal and bacterial contamination of Upton Sinclair's *The Jungle* to the brave new world of deliberate chemicalization.

Any possible trade basis for the EEC embargo, as alleged by the U.S. administration, is extremely unlikely, particularly in view of tough regulations and criminal sanctions against use of hormonal additives in European beef. Contrary to repeated assertions by the U.S. meat industry, the EEC's 1985 Scientific Risk Assessment Committee did not exculpate the use of hormonal additives, but recommended against the use of synthetics and emphasized the need to further evaluate the safety of natural hormones. Rather than finger-pointing at Europe, the embargo should prompt a highlevel, independent investigation and drastic reform of meat industry practices and federal regulation to include the use of hormones in particular and feed additives in general. Immediate action, not further study, is well overdue. The U.S. position also reflects a disturbing double standard, since the administration banned imports of Australian beef in 1987 on the grounds of excess residues of the carcinogenic pesticide heptachlor.

All hormonal and other carcinogenic feed additives should be banned immediately, as should all other animal additives in the absence of conclusive evidence of their efficacy and safety. Any additive use should be subject to explicit labeling requirements of use and of residue levels in all meat products, including milk and eggs.

Until then, initiatives at the state level, such as State Agriculture Commissioner Jim Hightower's "Texas Plan" (proposed in February 1989 and implemented two months later) to establish a hormone-free certification program for shipments to Europe, should be applauded and vigorously extended to the domestic market. Meanwhile, consumers should avoid chemicalized meat products in favor of organic ones. Consumers should also insist on their absolute right to know which additives have been used in their meat products, their residue levels, and their known adverse effects. Finally, they should demand independent certification and verification for hormones and other feed additives, such as the California Nutri-Clean program for testing pesticide residues on fruits and vegetables that is now available in about 600 supermarkets nationwide.

Note — This chapter is based in part on an editorial in the *Los Angeles Times*, January 30, 1989.

Chapter 14

PREVENTING PATHOGENIC FOOD POISONING: SANITATION, NOT IRRADIATION

The food and nuclear industries, with strong government support, have capitalized on recent outbreaks of pathogenic *E. coli* 0157 meat poisoning to mobilize public acceptance of large-scale food irradiation. Already, the Food and Drug Administration (FDA) is allowing the use of high-level radiation to "treat" beef, pork, poultry, eggs, vegetables, fruit, flour, and spices, while the U.S. Department of Agriculture (USDA) proposes the imminent irradiation of imported fruit and vegetables.

Caving in to powerful corporate industry interests, both House and Senate Appropriations Committees have recently (as of late 2000) proposed to sanitize the FDA's weak labeling requirements for irradiated food by eliminating the word "irradiated" in favor of "electronic pasteurization" (1); this term was proposed by the San Diego–based Titan corporation, an erstwhile major defense contractor using highly costly linear accelerator "E-beam" technology, originally designed for President Reagan's "Star Wars" program, to shoot food with a stream of electrons traveling at the speed of light. However, the proposed "electronic pasteurization" label is a euphemistic absurdity, especially since the FDA's approved meat irradiation dosage of 450,000 rads is approximately 150 million times greater than that of a chest X-ray, besides circumventing consumers' fundamental night to know.

Furthermore, the new labeling initiative is reckless. Irradiated meat is a very different product from cooked meat. Whether the meat is irradiated by linear accelerators or by pelletized radioactive isotopes, the resulting ionizing radiation produces highly reactive free radicals and peroxides from unsaturated fats. U.S. Army analyses in 1977 revealed major differences between the volatile chemicals formed during irradiation and during the cooking of meat (2). Levels of the carcinogen benzene in irradiated beef were found to be some tenfold higher than in cooked beef. Additionally, high concentrations of six poorly characterized

Coauthored with Wenonah Hauter; published in *International Journal of Health Services*, Volume 31, Number 1, 2001.

"unique radiolytic chemical products," admittedly "implicated as carcinogens or carcinogenic under certain conditions," were also identified (2).

Based on these striking changes in the chemistry of irradiated meat, the FDA's 1980 Irradiated Food Committee explicitly warned that safety testing should be based on concentrated extracts of irradiated foods, rather than on whole foods, to maximize the concentration of radiolytic products (3). This would allow development of sufficient sensitivity for routine safety testing. In 1984, Epstein and Gofman more specifically urged that "stable radiolytic products could be extracted from irradiated foods by various solvents which could then be concentrated and subsequently tested. Until such fundamental studies are undertaken, there is little scientific basis for accepting industry's assurances of safety" (4). In an accompanying comment, the FDA was quoted as admitting that "it is nearly impossible to detect [and test radiolytic products] with current techniques" on the basis of which the agency's claims of safety persist (5).

While refusing to require standard toxicological and carcinogenicity testing of concentrated extracts of radiolytic products from irradiated meat and other foods, the FDA instead has relied on some five studies selected from 441 published prior to the early 1980s, on which its claims of safety are still based. However, the chairperson of the FDA's Irradiated Food Task Committee, which reviewed these studies, insisted that none were adequate by 1982 standards (6), and even less so by 1990s standards (7). Furthermore, a detailed analysis of these studies revealed that all were grossly flawed and non-exculpatory (8).

These results are hardly surprising given that a wide range of independent studies before 1986 clearly identified mutagenic and carcinogenic radiolytic products in irradiated food and confirmed evidence of genetic toxicity in tests on irradiated food (9). Studies in the 1970s by India's National Institute of Nutrition reported that feeding freshly irradiated wheat to monkeys, rats, and mice and to a small group of malnourished children induced gross chromosomal abnormalities in blood or bone marrow cells, and mutational damage in the rodents (10).

Food irradiation results in major micronutrient losses, particularly in vitamins A, C, and E and the B complex (11). As admitted by the USDA Agricultural Research Service, these losses are synergistically increased by cooking, resulting in "empty calorie" food (12); this is a concern of major importance for malnourished populations. Radiation has also been used to clean up food unfit for human consumption, such as spoiled fish, by killing odorous contaminating bacteria.

While the USDA is strongly promoting meat and poultry irradiation, it has been moving to deregulate and privatize the industry by promoting a self-policing Hazard Analysis and Critical Control Point control program (13); in late 2000, the agency will start a rule-making process to privatize meat inspection. Moreover, the Department of Energy continues its decades-long aggressive promotion of food irradiation as a way of reducing disposal costs of spent military and civilian nuclear fuel by providing a commercial market for cesium nuclear wastes.

Irradiation facilities using pelletized isotopes pose risks of nuclear accidents to communities nationwide from the hundreds of facilities envisaged for the potentially enormous irradiation market; in contrast to nuclear power stations, these facilities are small, minimally regulated, and unlikely to be secure and they require regular replenishment of cobalt (Co-60) or cesium (Cs-137) isotopes, entailing nationwide transportation hazards. Furthermore, linear accelerators besides plants using radioactive isotopes, pose grave hazards to workers and are subject to virtually no regulation (9, 14).

The track record of the irradiation industry is, at best, unimpressive. Robert Alvarez, former senior policy advisor in the Department of Energy, recently warned that the Nuclear Regulatory Commission files are bulging with unreported documents on radioactive spills, worker overexposure, and off-site radiation leakage (15). Strangely, the Environmental Protection Agency has still failed to require an Environmental Impact Statement before the siting of food irradiation facilities.

The focus of the irradiation and agribusiness industries is directed to the highly lucrative cleanup of contaminated food rather than to preventing contamination at its source (16). However, *E. coli* 0157 food poisoning can be largely prevented by long overdue improved sanitation. Feedlot pen sanitation, including reduced overcrowding, drinking water disinfection, and fly control, would drastically lower cattle infection rates. Moreover, *E. coli* 0157 infection rates could be virtually eliminated by feeding hay, rather than the standard unhealthy starchy grain, for seven days prior to slaughter (17). Sanitation would also prevent water contamination from feedlot runoff, incriminated in the recent outbreak of *E. coli* 0157 poisoning in Walkerton, Ontario (18); runoff will remain a continuing threat even if all meat is irradiated.

Pre-slaughter, post-knocking, and post-evisceration sanitation at meat packing plants is highly effective for reducing carcass contamination rates (16). Testing pooled carcasses for *E. coli* 0157 and *Salmonella* contamination is economical, practical, and rapid. The expense of producing sanitary meat would be trivial compared with the high costs of irradiation, including possible nuclear accidents, which would be passed on to consumers. Additional high costs are likely to result from an expected international ban on the imports of irradiated U.S. food, and also from losses of tourist revenues.

We charge that support of the "electronic pasteurization" label by the food and irradiation industries, governmental agencies, and Congress is a camouflaged denial of citizen's fundamental right to know. Rather than sanitizing the label in response to special interests, Congress should focus on sanitation, not irradiation of the nation's food supply.

Note — This chapter was adapted from a June 6, 2000, P.R. Newswire press release by the Cancer Prevention Coalition and Public Citizen. The statement was endorsed by 45 public health and other professionals (see Appendix, pp. 304–305).

PART III

Pro-Industry Bias, Corporate Crime, and Poorly Recognized Industrial Risks of Cancer

Chapter 15

PRO-INDUSTRY BIAS IN *SCIENCE*

Science is the most highly respected scientific journal in the United States, and as such is read worldwide not only by scientists but also by industrialists, policy-makers, trade unionists, and public health and other professionals who rely upon it as a source of objective and accurate information. It is therefore a matter of grave concern to find unarguable evidence of increasing political bias in the journal's editorials, a bias that leans heavily in favor of industry and against environ-mentalists, consumers, workers, and public health professionals (see also Chapter 10B). Such bias has been reflected in *Science* editorials over the last two decades. The track record establishes that *Science* has used its editorial columns as a bully pulpit to trivialize concerns on environmental pollution and occupational hazards, which are revealingly dismissed as "chemophobia."

I first raised concern over such editorial bias in *Science* in 1987 after the journal carried an editorial (1) enthusiastically endorsing a lengthy article by Dr. Bruce Ames, which effectively trivialized the significance of environmental contamination by synthetic and other industrial carcinogens as chemophobic, and concluded that such contamination did not warrant "the high costs of regulation" (2). Ames's current position (as of 1990) is in complete contradiction to views he advocated only a few years ago. The article received wide publicity in the U.S. press and has since been extensively circulated by various industry lobbying groups as part of a national strategy to oppose stricter controls at the federal and state levels. Together with a group of some 15 nationally recognized authorities on public health, environmental carcinogenesis, and epidemiology, I wrote a detailed scientific rebuttal to Ames's article, but it was initially rejected by *Science*. After a lengthy correspondence and repeated vigorous protests to *Science* editor Dr. Daniel Koshland, who used a variety of inconsistent reasons to stonewall for nearly a year, a severely shortened version was eventually published, and then only in drastically abbreviated form (3).

A more recent illustration of grave bias is an editorial (1988) by Dr. Philip Abelson, *Science's* deputy director (4). Dr. Abelson charged that product liability suits (that is, lawsuits brought by individuals against companies and professionals

Published in *International Journal of Health Services,* Volume 20, Number 2, 1990.

for damages incurred as a result of faulty products or malpractice) are rendering U.S. industry less competitive, have negatively affected medical practice, and constitute "a form of legalized extortion." Together with Mr. Ronald Simon, a leading labor lawyer in Washington, D.C., I submitted a detailed response to *Science,* documenting Dr. Abelson's errors of omission and commission. This reply, subsequently endorsed by the American Association of Trial Lawyers and the United Automobile, Aerospace and Agricultural Implements Workers of America, was initially rejected on the grounds of length. Following our protests, *Science* offered to consider the reply as a short letter. We then reduced the original to 200 words, the stipulated length, although letters of 400 words or more are regularly published in *Science.* This letter was also rejected, this time on the alleged new grounds that it "might prove actionable." In order that Abelson's views should not go unchallenged, I reproduce below our abbreviated response to his editorial:

> Abelson's editorial of 17 June 1988 excoriates the "product liability crisis" in the United States. However, available evidence demonstrates that his assertions and opinions are uninformed and biased.
> Abelson relies heavily on a 1988 Conference Board report, which characterizes product liability litigation as "pure and simple blackmail." Yet, Abelson fails to indicate that this report is based on a questionnaire survey of Chief Executive Officers of major corporations, and merely summarizes their opinions and anecdotal comments.
> Contrary to Abelson, extensive studies have proven that there is no explosion of tort litigation. The National Center for State Courts concluded that there was "no evidence to support the often cited evidence of a national 'litigation explosion' in the state trial courts during the 1981–1984 time period" [5]. The Rand Institute of Civil Justice reported that tort filings have increased by only 3 percent above population growth since 1981 and, contrary to Abelson's fantasies about the large tort verdicts, that "the median jury award has not increased more than the rate of inflation," and also that median tort awards have been stable from 1960 to 1985 [6]. In a subsequent study, Rand confirmed that ". . . the amount of tort litigation nationwide is growing relatively slowly" [7].
> In the absence of any supportive evidence, Abelson claims that, due to product liability litigation, "the competitiveness of the U.S. has been lessened . . . (and that) the product liability system imposes a heavy burden on the firms that make long-lasting high quality products." Similarly, he asserts that such litigation has a "negative impact on medicine," without reference to the consequences of medical negligence and incompetence, and the failure of the medical community to remedy these problems. Another undocumented assertion is that "some of the huge punitive awards that are made seem to be motivated by a desire to injure the rich or powerful rather than to render justice." Abelson's understanding of "justice" excludes countless American workers and consumers who have been injured or killed by dangerous products.

The bulk of product liability litigation relates to a relatively few highly hazardous products, such as asbestos and the Dalkon Shield. In litigation on these products, it has been proven that their hazards were fully known and wilfully concealed by the companies that sold them. A principal reason why product and toxic tort litigation can be expensive is because corporations, their insurance carriers and lawyers, go to extraordinary lengths to block the plaintiffs and the public from discovering how much and for how long they [the corporations] have known about the hazards of their products, and how little, if any, they have done to correct or warn about such defects. Defendants spend lavishly in litigation, not only to make it prohibitively expensive to sue them, but also precisely because they fear punitive damages should such information become known to the courts. The high cost of litigation is thus largely created by the practiced strategy of corporate defendants who refuse to surrender product information as required by law, and who practice delay and stonewalling, necessitating extensive depositions and subpoenas, and repeated motions to the court to enforce the law.

Abelson ignores recent anti-trust litigation, filed by the attorneys general of some twenty states, which demonstrates that the so-called "liability crisis" is no more than a blatant public relations campaign mounted by the insurance industry to justify massive rate increases to cover losses from past bad investment decisions. The insurance industry is charged with manufacturing the "liability crisis" by conspiring to deny insurance in order to raise rates and coerce the public to accept unconscionable limitations in their coverage.

Abelson's unfounded assertions on the "product liability crisis" are consistent with a series of other biased positions he has previously expressed in *Science* editorials. Whether the editorial columns of *Science* are appropriate forums for the continuing advocacy of such undocumented and prejudiced opinions is a matter of critical concern to the membership of the AAAS [American Association for the Advancement of Science].

With worldwide campaigning by public health professionals and consumer associations for stricter laws to protect individuals from defective products and from professional malpractice, product liability is an important issue. *Science's* willingness to publish factually incorrect and biased information on the subject— and its intransigent refusal to publish a response correcting those errors—must bring into question its integrity, particularly on issues relating to environmental and consumer affairs.

At July 1989 Congressional hearings, Koshland testified that scientific fraud and fakery is extremely rare and "that 99.9999 percent of reports are accurate and truthful" (8). Regrettably, it is now apparent that the accuracy and truthfulness of *Science* have been gravely jeopardized by its editorial policies.

Dr. Richard Atkinson, President of the AAAS Board of Directors, has so far failed to recognize the gravity of these problems. In a letter to the author of October 2, 1989, he rejected the substantive evidence of bias and prejudice and expressed strong support for editorial policy. Finally, it would seem appropriate that those Congressional Committees recently involved in the investigation of individual cases of scientific fraud should now turn their attention to systemic problems in *Science,* which are of much graver significance with relation to national decision-making policies.

Note — This chapter is based in part on Epstein's editorial in *The Ecologist* 19: 128–129, 1989.

Chapter 16

CORPORATE CRIME:
WHY WE CANNOT TRUST
INDUSTRY-DERIVED SAFETY STUDIES

It is generally assumed that the industry-generated database on toxic chemicals provides a reliable basis for the scientific evaluation of their public health hazards and for governmental regulation. In fact, as has been documented in detail, this is generally not the case (1–3). A critical, but not atypical, illustration is provided by an evaluation of the track record of Velsicol Chemical Company, the sole manufacturer of the ultrahazardous, carcinogenic, and highly persistent hydrocarbon pesticides chlordane and heptachlor. These chemicals were widely used for agricultural purposes in the United States until 1974, when the Environmental Protection Agency (EPA), on the basis of prolonged cancellation and suspension hearings, determined that their continued use posed an "imminent hazard" to public health due to their carcinogenicity.

The use of chlordane and heptachlor for treating termites in homes—a major use in the United States and elsewhere—was, however, exempted from regulation, as the agency accepted the industry's misleading assurances that subterranean application of the chemicals did not result in human exposure. The pesticides have thus been used extensively for termite treatment in tens of millions of homes in the United States, with a resulting high incidence of contamination, posing major carcinogenic, besides other, hazards. They were finally withdrawn from commerce in the United States in April 1988 following a secret "Memorandum of Understanding" between the EPA and Velsicol. However, these pesticides are still extensively used for agricultural and other purposes in many countries (such as for the control of Argentine ants in Western Australia), particularly in the Third World, in the virtual absence of available information on their ultrahazardous and carcinogenic properties (Table 1).

Published in *International Journal of Health Services,* Volume 20, Number 3, 1990.

Table 1

Velsicol's pesticide exports, 1987–1989

Importing nation and port of loading	Exports, pounds		
	Chlordane[a]	Heptachlor[a]	"Other pesticides," 1987 only[b]
Argentina			
New Orleans, LA	3,536	328,991	
	3,356 (T)	229,484 (T)	9,459 (OC)
Australia			
New Orleans, LA	21,216 (T)	489,656	
		128,818 (T)	
Long Beach, CA			122,850 (OC)
Belgium			
New Orleans, LA		37,022	
Brazil			
Jacksonville, FL		123,600	
		56,856 (T)	
Colombia			
Jacksonville, FL	23,868		
Costa Rica			1,206
New Orleans, LA		41,200 (T)	
Dominican Republic			
New Orleans, LA	4,248	1,596	10,384 (OC)
Miami, FL	10,870		
Finland			
New Orleans, LA	40,788 (T)		
	40,788		
French West Indies			
Miami, FL			1,266
Guatemala			
New Orleans, LA	22,652		
	33,990 (T)		

Table 1

(Cont'd.)

Importing nation and port of loading	Exports, pounds		
	Chlordane[a]	Heptachlor[a]	"Other pesticides," 1987 only[b]
India			
New Orleans, LA	8,398	112,797	9,526
			16,671 (OC)
Houston, TX	1,326 (T)	4,339	
Indonesia			
Tacoma, TA	13,620		
Israel			
Norfolk, VA			18,128
Charleston, SC			19,052 (OC)
Galveston, TX		6,798 (T)	
New Orleans, LA		16,671	
Ivory Coast			
New Orleans, LA		38,537	
Jamaica			
New Orleans, LA	4,248		
Korea, Republic of			
Seattle, WA	42,432 (T)		
Tacoma, WA	42,432 (T)		
Malaysia			
Tacoma, WA		29,600	61,800 (OC)
Netherlands			
New Orleans, LA	127,296	254,334	
	169,728 (T)	323,833 (T)	
Pakistan			
New Orleans, LA		31,826 (T)	
		81,188	
Peru			
New Orleans, LA		20,600	

Table 1

(Cont'd.)

Importing nation and port of loading	Exports, pounds		
	Chlordane[a]	Heptachlor[a]	"Other pesticides," 1987 only[b]
Philippines			
Tacoma, WA	127,440	11,691	
		11,691 (T)	24,669 (OC)
Singapore			
Tacoma, WA	678,913	164,800	252,128 (OC)
Los Angeles, CA	43,420		
South Africa			
New York, NY			23,868 (OC)
Thailand			
Tacoma, WA	21,658	115,841	43,400 (OC)
	42,145 (T)		
Trinidad			
Tacoma, WA	2,568		2,568 (OC)
New Orleans	7,888		
Grand Total	1,358,641	1,842,132	616,875

Total pounds technical chlordane	=	280,490
Total pounds technical heptachlor	=	947,429
Total chlordane, heptachlor, unspecified, and organochlorines	=	4,817,648
Total number of importing countries	=	25

Sources: The Journal of Commerce Port Import/Export Reporting Services (PIERS) database, January 1987–June 1989; see also *Exporting Banned Pesticides: A Case Study of Velsicol Chemical Corporation's Export of Chlordane and Heptachlor.* A Greenpeace Report, August 1989.

Note: The list includes only the original point of destination for Velsicol's products. Because of trans-shipments, the ultimate number of importing countries is reportedly almost double the number listed. Also, since Velsicol or its shipper does not always list the name or the grade of the product it is exporting on forms on which the source depends, the figures may actually be much larger.

[a](T): designated as "technical grade" (unformulated).

[b](OC): designated as "organochlorine pesticide."

FAILURE TO TEST

Velsicol has conducted its chronic toxicity, carcinogenicity, and reproductive toxicity tests on chlordane and heptachlor exclusively by oral administration. This route precludes determination of the incremental effects of the high concentration in technical-grade (unformulated) chlordane/heptachlor of a wide range of volatile ingredients, besides additives and contaminants. The continuing failure of Velsicol to undertake chronic inhalation tests is consistent with its failure to publish information on the composition of technical chlordane/heptachlor, and to warn and label with regard to volatile ingredients. Even in the absence of such information, the National Academy of Sciences strongly recommended the need for "long-term animal inhalation studies [as] the primary route of human exposure is inhalation. Biologic endpoints to investigate in these studies include neurotoxicity, carcinogenicity, effects on blood-forming tissues, and teratogenic and reproductive effects" (4).

Velsicol has also failed to undertake or sponsor epidemiological studies on population groups known to have been exposed to chlordane/heptachlor in contaminated homes over long periods. As early as 1965, concerned by claims for contamination of treated homes, one of the largest pest control industries, Orkin, recognized that "slab treatment is at best a hazardous operation" (5); nevertheless, Orkin continued with such treatment until 1979 (6). In 1974, Velsicol was informed by the U.S. Air Force of contamination in some 800 homes at the Wright Patterson Base which had been treated with chlordane/ heptachlor in about 1972 (7). This information was followed by a series of U.S. Air Force investigations and reports confirming such contamination in other bases and also its persistence and resistance to the most rigorous decontamination procedures (e.g., 8, 9). Accordingly, the National Academy of Sciences in 1979 recommended that "epidemiologic data be collected on inhabitants of the Air Force housing units from the 1970, 1974, and 1978 episodes of chlordane exposure, focusing on both acute and chronic health effects" (10). This recommendation was subsequently endorsed by the General Accounting Office in 1980 (11), the National Academy of Sciences in 1982 (4), and, belatedly, Velsicol in 1982 (12). Yet Velsicol has still failed to act on these recommendations, and, with a catch-22 strategy, matches such failure by denigrating the human relevance of chronic toxicity and carcinogenicity test data while alleging the lack of affirmative epidemiological evidence.

FAILURE TO PUBLISH TEST DATA

Over the last 40 years (as of 1990), Velsicol has a near-consistent record of failure to publish in-house research and contracted research by commercial laboratories on the toxic and carcinogenic effects of chlordane/heptachlor. Suppression of such information has prevented the issuance of appropriate warnings to householders and pest control operators, and has also prevented independent review of the validity of the test data, methodology, and conclusions. Furthermore, the extreme difficulty in obtaining such unpublished reports, except in response to persistent subpoenas and protective orders, has created major and inequitable restrictions on the rights of plaintiffs in chlordane/heptachlor-related law suits.

Unpublished in-house research includes reports on product composition, ingredient identity, additives, and contaminants (13); on household contamination following termiticidal treatment with chlordane/heptachlor, even by trained applicators in accordance with label directions (14); and on the experimental reduction of such contamination by the addition of surfactants to technical chlordane/heptachlor (15). Velsicol's failure to publish the latter data is compounded by the company's failure to use additives to reduce contaminant levels following application of chlordane/heptachlor.

Unpublished contract research includes a study on household contamination following chlordane/heptachlor treatment by trained applicators (16); a subacute inhalation test on chlordane, in which statistically significant leucopenia and thrombocytopenia were induced in monkeys (17); seven carcinogenicity tests in mice and rats completed between 1955 and 1983 (18–23); and 11 reproductive and teratogenicity tests completed between 1959 and 1972 (24–28). Of interest in this connection is a 1972 meeting of a Canadian Pesticide Advisory Committee in which Michael Gilbertson of Environment Canada called for a ban on chlordane/heptachlor, because "nothing was known about the reproductive potentials in various species." He was "soundly criticized . . . for making disparaging remarks [and] informed by a Velsicol participant of the elaborate studies available to him," in the form of petitions to the Canadian Government (29).

Problems of biased interpretation apart, the validity of such unpublished data, on the basis of which false promotional and other claims of product safety were made by Velsicol, is commonly negated by incompetent and misleading test procedures. For example, in 1955 and again in 1959, a series of rat carcinogenicity tests were carried out in which ethanolic solutions of heptachlor or heptachlor epoxide were sprayed on pelleted feed rather than being incorporated within the feed as is the standard technique. The high autolysis rate and low percentage of mice examined histopathologically in a series of 1973 tests, and the surgical removal of an unspecified number of undiagnosed subcutaneous tumors from rats during the course of a 1965 rat carcinogenicity test (30), are also illustrative of gross incompetence on the part of the company. The latter procedure, "discovered [by the EPA] only as a consequence of going into one of the very intensive administrative proceedings," was characterized at a congressional hearing as "unorthodox and misleading" (31). Further, examples of highly misleading test procedures are the small sample size, restrictions to only one test dose, and the limited duration of dosing in various contracted reproductive tests.

MISREPRESENTATION OF TEST DATA

The misinterpretation and misrepresentation of unpublished test data by Velsicol's contractees is commonplace. Evidence for this has been developed by independent reanalysis of such data as and when they become available, sometimes not until decades later.

From 1959 to 1972, five contract laboratories submitted reports to Velsicol on some 11 reproductive and teratogenicity tests in chickens, rats, rabbits, and dogs (24–28). These unpublished reports, which by December 1986 had apparently not been submitted to the EPA (in violation of the Federal Insecticide, Fungicide, and Rodenticide Act) (8, 9), only belatedly became available under a protective order in response to a 1987 Velsicol subpoena (32). The various reports alleged that chlordane/heptachlor and related compounds induce no adverse reproductive effects or that, where induced, any such effects are insignificant and can be discounted. However, contrary to these claims, subsequent independent reanalysis of the raw data demonstrates—methodological flaws apart—a wide range of compound-related and statistically significant reproductive toxicity in most tests (33). In general, fetotoxicity, miscarriages, and teratogenicity were induced in rabbits, and excess postnatal mortality in rats and dogs.

From 1955 to 1973, two commercial testing laboratories submitted reports to Velsicol on five carcinogenicity tests in mice and rats (18–22). All these unpublished reports alleged that chlordane and heptachlor were noncarcinogenic, although a dose-related incidence of "liver nodules" was noted in some tests in mice and rats, but discounted. These conclusions remained unchallenged until November 1974, when the EPA announced its intent to cancel all agricultural and domestic uses of chlordane/heptachlor, excluding subterranean termite control; this exclusion was based on the mistaken belief that such treatment would not result in contamination of the home, although Velsicol clearly had contrary information. In the course of the cancellation proceedings, the EPA decided to subject the industry data to independent review by a team of five consulting pathologists. Where the Velsicol contractees reported either no abnormality or nonmalignant nodular liver lesions in test mice and rats, the EPA team found a high incidence of unequivocal liver cancers, which in most cases were statistically highly significant (30). These substantial discrepancies cannot be explained away by an honest difference of opinion between the industry and independent experts, since there were no diagnostic differences among untreated controls or among positive control animals treated with a known potent carcinogen.

Velsicol was actively involved in these misrepresentations, on the basis of which it insisted that chlordane and heptachlor were noncarcinogenic. A 1971 internal memorandum expressed concerns about a "warning signal [of] some suspicions of carcinogenicity," demonstrated in a 1959 rat carcinogenicity test (34). A subsequent memorandum referred to "an unusually high incidence of liver cancers" in mouse tests (35). A transcript of a telephone conversation between two senior Velsicol executives reveals the following exchange relating to the mouse carcinogenicity tests (36):

H. GOLD: Well, not having seen the data, I really can't make any more comment. It's looking very bleak from what I've heard.

K. L. SCHULZ: Well, I'll give you a little rundown because they gave us the updated sheets; I've got them right here. For chlordane, the negative control after 43 weeks, no tumors. The positive control after 43 weeks, no tumors. Five ppm [parts per million] chlordane, no tumors. Twenty-five ppm, one tumor at week 43. Now that's of the animals that have died. You know, we don't know what's in the ones that are still alive. At 50 ppm, 12 tumors. The first one showed up at week 28, so you see it's showing earlier than in the heptachlor study. With the heptachlor on negative control after 63 weeks, no tumors. Positive control, six. Heptachlor/heptachlor epoxide mixture at one ppm total, two tumors. At five ppm, two. At 10 ppm, 24. You know it's clear cut.

H. GOLD: Are these CFI mice?

K. L. SCHULZ: No, these are CDF1 Charles River. The natural incidence of tumors based on 1000 animals is three tumors just under normal circumstances, so it's a very nonsusceptible animals. And Dr. Geil had the statistics on this. He's the pathologist.

H. GOLD: It doesn't look good, Ken.

K. L. SCHULZ: No, it doesn't. . . .

K. L. SCHULZ: Well, the thing that worries me so much, Harvey, if we submit this information, I think Ruckelshaus [then Administrator of the EPA] has no choice but to suspend registration of the agricultural uses for chlordane and heptachlor.

H. GOLD: I agree, I agree, and f think it will happen . . .

H. L. SCHULZ: With great rapidity.

H. GOLD: That's right. And you know, if it does happen . . .

K. L. SCHULZ: Heptachlor, I would say, wouldn't be a great impact because they're only projecting something like a million pounds total for all of next year, worldwide. Chlordane's a different matter, a far different matter.

H. GOLD: Well, I think that if it ever gets to a public hearing on the basis of what you've already told me, and Charlie has told me, I agree we·wouldn't have a chance in hell, Ken. It would be a clear-cut issue and we wouldn't have to discuss the ADI ["acceptable" daily intake] or anything else. It would mean it is carcinogenic, and that's it; that's the ball game.

K. L. SCHULZ: Well, its tumorigenic, and that's enough.

H. GOLD: Yeah, right. So . . .

K. L. SCHULZ: You know with a new chemical if you came up with these results, you'd just stop right there. You wouldn't have a ghost of a chance.

In December 1972, Velsicol submitted liver sections from the mouse tests to two consultants, who subsequently warned that these clearly showed carcinogenic effects (37, 38). Velsicol was alarmed by these findings. "Drs. Rust and

Newberne's reports on their evaluations of liver sections have been received. Both men generally agree in their appraisal that the findings are serious and reflect a definite carcinogenic potential" (39). However, Velsicol's subsequent failure to submit this information to the EPA resulted in the company's criminal indictment before the Federal Court of Chicago on April 4, 1977 (40). In December 1977, a grand jury handed down an 11-count felony indictment, naming six present or former company executives, charging (41–43): "From August 1972 to July 1975 the defendants . . . conspired to defraud the United States and conceal material facts from the United States Environmental Protection Agency by failing to submit data which tended to show that heptachlor and chlordane induced tumors in laboratory animals and thus might pose a risk of cancer to humans." Without reaching the merits of the original issue of conspiracy raised by the indictment, the case was, however, subsequently dismissed on procedural grounds.

Just as disturbing as Velsicol's misrepresentation of the unpublished reproductive and carcinogenicity test data is the misrepresentation by an academic contractee of the epidemiological data on chlordane manufacturing workers at a Velsicol plant (44). It was alleged that there was no significant excess morbidity or mortality. Apart from major methodological flaws, such as the failure to provide any data on duration of exposure, analysis of the unpublished report by the National Academy of Sciences clearly demonstrated a statistically significant positive trend in standard mortality ratios for cancer deaths, with increasing duration of employment (4). An updated industry epidemiological study, again claiming no significant excess cancer mortality in chlordane manufacturing workers (45), has been effectively rebutted by government scientists who demonstrated contrary conclusions (46).

IGNORING EXPERT WARNINGS

Velsicol has employed an extensive battery of consultants, principally from academic backgrounds, in aggressive attempts to support its position on the safety of chlordane/heptachlor, and to defend itself in toxic tort litigation. However, contrary advice and warnings from its consultants, and also from its outside attorneys, have been ignored or discounted.

Such advice includes the explicit warnings by Velsicol's clinical consultant on the causal association between exposure to chlordane/heptachlor and blood dyscrasias (47); the warnings by two consulting pathologists that, contrary to the claims of a contract testing laboratory, heptachlor induced carcinogenic effects in mice (18–22); warnings by three Velsicol consultants, Drs. Golberg, Shubik, and Becker, transmitted through an outside Velsicol attorney, on the carcinogenicity of chlordane/heptachlor, together with suggested defensive strategies (48); and a warning by another consultant pathologist, that "in the absence of new data, the view that both heptachlor and chlordane are carcinogenic would be upheld," accompanied by a request for more research funds to develop such new data (49). The following revealing warning from an outside attorney had no apparent impact on Velsicol's policy on the use of chlordane/heptachlor termiticides (50):

> On cancer risk, we are in a very poor, almost no-win posture. While Stemmer and Geil will present a no-cancer evaluation of the slides, we know that Reuber, Stewart, and Davis will find either malignancy or at least tumors. Saffiotti will support the aldrin/dieldrin principle of equating tumors with carcinogenic risk. The judge can be expected to follow this group. Further, they will contend that because of wide variance in response, a threshold level cannot be established for an entire population.
>
> A finding of cancer risk to humans will result in cancellation of all uses in issue and may trigger an attack by EDF [Environmental Defense Fund] on even termite use.
>
> You must also consider the company's position after a finding of a carcinogenic risk. Those permitted uses—termites—may well expose the company to product liability claims which, though remote at causation, could create the need for another major defensive effort. Avoiding a determination of a cancer risk to humans should be explored carefully and in depth.
>
> We certainly dislike a prediction of defeat, but we also cannot ignore reality. Thus, serious thought must be given to relinquishing all household and garden uses. They cannot be defended if a cancer risk finding is entered. In fact, we should realistically look at those uses for which we can argue a lack of human exposure other than to trained, professional applicators.

FALSE AND MISLEADING STATEMENTS

There is substantial evidence of self-serving statements by Velsicol executives which are clearly inconsistent with their own knowledge of the facts, and which cannot be explained away by possible ambiguities or misunderstandings. Illustrative of these are statements by Velsicol on the composition of technical chlordane/heptachlor, and denials of any association between exposure to chlordane/heptachlor and blood dyscrasias, such as aplastic anemia and leukemia.

The official Velsicol 1971 standard for technical chlordane specifies a concentration of 43 percent for the alpha and gamma chlordane isomers and less than 4 percent for the volatile constituents (13). Velsicol Material Safety Data Sheets specify a 60 percent concentration for the chlordane isomers and 40 percent for "related compounds." These alleged compositions are at striking variance with testimony of Velsicol scientists and expert witnesses.

At the 1975 EPA cancellation hearings on chlordane/heptachlor, a Velsicol expert witness admitted that (51): "The real composition of technical chlordane is very different from that specified in the standard, including only 13–15 percent of each of the two chlordane isomers and only 5–8 percent of heptachlor. Thus, the standard method of analysis substantially over-weights the contribution of the major constituents of the mixture, and under-weights that of the minor constituents."

This admission was subsequently confirmed by another Velsicol expert witness, who stated that technical chlordane contains "more than three dozen different singular chemicals. Of these chemicals, alpha and gamma chlordane are probably the two most important ingredients. Together they comprise slightly less than 30 percent wet weight of the product" (52). Most recent estimates confirm the unpublished position of Velsicol scientists, and support approximate concentrations of 25 percent for the chlordane isomers and 17 percent for the volatile components (53). It is thus clear that, contrary to its own scientific data, Velsicol has grossly exaggerated the concentration of the chlordane isomers in technical chlordane/heptachlor at the expense of the undisclosed toxic and carcinogenic volatile components, which are thus deliberately underestimated. This deception, arguably perjurious, has been further perpetrated by two leading Velsicol attorneys, although both were fully aware of the contrary scientific data (54, 55).[1] Apart from major discrepancies between the real composition of technical chlordane and that misleadingly specified in the standard, as well recognized by Velsicol, there are striking batch-to-batch variations in composition (56):

> It seems somewhat inconceivable, but apparently, even after some 20 years of experience, we still do not produce a consistent quality chlordane.
>
> Unfortunately, chlordane is not, and apparently cannot be, covered with the normal chemical component-type specification. However, we do have very specific manufacturing specifications, an original "profile" or "fingerprint," a biological assay, an LD_{50} [median lethal dose] specification, and a color specification.
>
> I understand the cause of "black" chlordane is well known, and yet I am told that every summer we produce such material, and now have 581,000 pounds of off-color material in inventory. Of even more importance, there have been variances in the "fingerprint," the biological assay, and the LD_{50} specification and color specification.
>
> The above problem must be given top priority, as I am sure you know that chlordane patents have expired, and it is quite possible one or more competitors will enter the market. Certainly if I were a potential competitor, I think my major selling point would be the offering of a consistent quality product. And certainly I could point to many inconsistencies of quality in the chlordane produced by Velsicol.

With reference to blood dyscrasias, Velsicol was informed in 1969 by Kasik (47), its clinical consultant, of published information on the association between

---

[1] Note that Richmond (54) was in possession of contrary data from Polen's (51) and Whitacre's (52) testimony, and that Hollingsworth (55) was in possession of contrary data from Polen's and Whitacre's testimony and from the June 10, 1987, deposition of I. Nisbet.

12 cases of aplastic anemia and exposures to chlordane/heptachlor, in four of which chlordane "was the sole agent responsible." Kasik clearly warned of the significance of this report. "In my opinion, it would carry a great deal of weight, both legally and medically." Nevertheless, just one year later, a senior Velsicol executive, referring, to a recent death from aplastic anemia following chlordane/heptachlor exposure, stated that "I intend to let [the U.S. Department of Agriculture] know that there is no evidence linking chlordane with his death" (57). Equally striking is a 1976 letter from a Velsicol vice-president to the Australian government in response to an inquiry as to whether heptachlor could cause aplastic anemia. The reply stated that, based on a thorough literature search, including consultation with Kasik, "Our review has yielded no reference which would implicate heptachlor as a responsible agent in causing aplastic anemia" (58).

FAILURE TO WARN

Velsicol has continually failed to warn of a wide range of information on hazards following exposure to chlordane/heptachlor. Such failure extends to homeowners (as illustrated by the gross deficiencies of the product label); to pest control applicators, industries, and trade associations (as illustrated by gross deficiencies and misleading information in promotional literature, technical bulletins, manuals, and Manufacturing Safety Data Sheets); and also the EPA (as illustrated by their extensive 1986 "data call in," some four decades after chlordane and heptachlor were first introduced into commerce).

In an early publication on two cases of fatal aplastic anemia following chlordane exposure, B. E. Conley stated, "chlordane is one of the most hazardous hydrocarbon insecticides. Perhaps of the greatest significance is the fact that the technical preparation is still an uncharacterized mixture of chlorinated hydrocarbons whose toxic properties and metabolic fates are poorly understood" (59). This statement is as appropriate today as when it was made more than 30 years ago. In spite of detailed knowledge of the product composition of technical chlordane/heptachlor, Velsicol's labels still fail to disclose the presence of a variety of toxic and carcinogenic ingredients, additives, and contaminants, attention to which is diverted by exaggerating the concentration of the chlordane isomers (13, 51, 52).

The ultrahazardous nature of chlordane/heptachlor is in no way indicated in the uninformative and misleading label issued with the product. Chlordane has very high acute toxicity and, according to a Velsicol consultant and expert witness, the estimated human LD_{50} is 30 mg/kg, and the toxic human dose is 3 mg/kg (60), equivalent to about two teaspoons of diluted formulation. The label makes no mention of chronic effects on organs, such as hepatic or neurotoxic damage. The omission of reference to neurotoxicity is of particular interest, in view not only of the substantive published literature on these effects in experimental animals and humans (e.g., 4, 61, 62), but also of Velsicol's own admission in a technical bulletin of such effects (63), and its admission, in response to legal inquiries, of numerous complaints from 1953 onward.

The label omits reference to reproductive toxicity and teratogenicity, in spite of the published literature in experimental animals and humans (e.g., 64–67), and Velsicol's own unpublished studies (24–28), some clearly showing adverse effects, although these are substantially understated (33). Furthermore, such effects are induced at dose levels within an order of magnitude of exposures commonly encountered in contaminated homes (33).

Since 1978, Velsicol's own labels have belatedly referred to the carcinogenicity of chlordane/heptachlor in mice, but with the trivializing qualification that there is no supportive human evidence. However, the label makes no reference to the additional carcinogenicity data in rats, including unpublished studies contracted by Velsicol between 1955 and 1973 that demonstrated the induction of liver tumors (18–22) and more recent studies confirming these findings, besides reporting tumors at other sites (23). Nor does the label make reference to several published epidemiological studies in which carcinogenic effects were noted and which, minimally, are supportive of the test data. These include contracted studies demonstrating a statistically significant excess of lung cancers, as well as excess cancers at other sites, in pest control applicators and in chlordane/heptachlor manufacturing workers, among whom a statistically significant excess mortality from cerebrovascular disease was also reported (68, 69). It may be noted that these studies, which were submitted to Velsicol for clearance prior to publication, evoked a cautionary letter on potential conflicts of interest from the dean of the contractee's university (70). More recently, a 1983 National Cancer Institute epidemiological study confirmed the statistically significant excess of lung cancers, as well as excess cancers at other sites, in pest control applicators (71). In recent litigation involving neurotoxicity and cancer risk following exposure to chlordane/heptachlor in a contaminated home, Velsicol and its attorneys attempted to deceive the court as to the relevance of the National Cancer Institute's epidemiological study by claiming that such exposure predated their knowledge of this study, when in fact they were in possession of a draft of this study during the exposure time in question, and some three months prior to its publication (72). The significance of this deception is further emphasized by the strong endorsement by a Velsicol consultant of the conclusions of this study: "The association with carcinoma of the lung is striking and deserves attention. The methodology of this study is beyond reproach" (73). Furthermore, the label makes no reference to the association between chlordane/heptachlor exposure and fatal blood dyscrasias, including aplastic anemia and leukemia, in spite of some 34 case reports in the published literature and some 25 available complaints and litigations for these diseases (74).

Apart from such a panoply of acute and delayed toxic effects, the label makes no reference to the high frequency of contamination of homes following treatment by licensed applicators (14–16), much less following misapplication; no reference to the knowledge as early as 1965 that treatment of slab homes is a hazardous procedure because of the risks of contamination and ensuing litigation (5); no reference to the numerous complaints received annually from homeowners and pest control operators for problems including misapplication and adverse health effects (75); no reference to the prolonged persistence of such contamination and to the extreme difficulty (if not impossibility) of decontamination (8, 9); and no reference to the availability of less persistent, less hazardous, and more easily decontaminated alternative termiticides, such as Dursban.

The failure of the label to warn homeowners of the wide range of adverse health effects and contamination problems is, in general, matched by a similar failure to warn pest control applicators, in spite of their much higher levels of exposure. Velsicol training manuals, until recently, have shown applicators working in crawl spaces and cleaning up spills without respiratory protection (76, 77). Velsicol manuals, promotional literature, and advertisements are replete with false and misleading statements such as the following (78–82):

- Chlordane has an "unmatched safety and performance record."
- Chlordane is "the safest [termiticide] to use."
- "Chlordane is not hazardous when used properly."
- "Significant air residues after a proper termiticide treatment are extremely rare."
- "The sum of toxicological and epidemiological data supports the conclusion that the uses of chlordane and heptachlor pose no identifiable health hazard."
- Based on occupational health studies, "there is no evidence of any long-term latent effect on health."

More disturbing than Velsicol's failure to warn the domestic market of the ultrahazardous properties of chlordane/heptachlor, even when applied subterraneanly by licensed applicators, is its continuing failure to warn the export market of the much greater hazards of routine indoor spraying, apart from the hazards of agricultural use. A telex from Indonesia inquiring whether the indoor spraying of chlordane/heptachlor every six weeks for the past six years was safe and devoid of possible long-term toxic effects, evoked the reassuring response that it had been "used for many years inside homes with only rare illnesses" (83).

Apart from its failure to warn homeowners and pest control applicators, Velsicol has failed to submit critical unpublished data to the EPA. Such data include the results of reproductive and teratogenicity tests (24–28) and a wide range of other information, such as data on ingredient composition and identity (13, 51, 52) and applicator exposure studies (16). Velsicol has apparently also failed to submit information to the EPA on some 1200 complaints received annually from homeowners and from pest control operators (75), and on adverse health effects, such as blood dyscrasias, obtained from depositions by expert witnesses in recent law suits. Such omissions appear to be in violation of the Federal Insecticide, Fungicide, and Rodenticide Act 6(a)(2).

WHITE-COLLAR CRIME

Pesticide use in most nations is controlled by statutory and regulatory law. Ideally, the pesticide must be tested thoroughly and registered before it can be introduced into commerce. Labels, directions, and methods of use or application must be approved. All active ingredients and components must be disclosed. Governments usually require the company that wants to register the product to conduct any studies or investigations deemed necessary. This continuing process of governmental monitoring and surveillance requires the company to report all adverse effects of the product of which it becomes aware. This includes studies done by others, studies done by the company, and all reports the company receives regarding adverse health effects.

Such a regulatory system can only be effective if the company conducting and reporting the studies makes honest and complete disclosures, and if the underlying database is reliable. The regulatory system is potentially only as valid as the information generated is reliable. When the ingredients are not identified, when the proper studies are not conducted, when the results of studies are not published for review, and when the results of studies state conclusions contrary to the actual data, effective regulation becomes virtually impossible. The ineffectiveness of the regulatory system is exacerbated by the fact that private citizens and public interest groups have no right to bring a legal action to enforce the statute. When faced with misrepresentation by the manufacturers of pesticides, the judicial system (and through it the possibility of punitive damages) still provides the only effective avenue not only for redress, but also for deterrence. In addition, there is a growing congressional interest in the United States in the legislative development of criminal sanctions against industries, and their executives and scientists (84), who knowingly suppress or manipulate scientific information with resulting adverse public health and ecological consequences, offenses that are now, belatedly, recognized as "white-collar crime." Legislation on the continuing export of hazardous products banned or rigorously restricted in the United States is also overdue.

An overwhelming record confirms the premise that scientific information generated and interpreted by institutions and individuals with direct or indirect economic interests in its outcome must be regarded as suspect until proven otherwise by independent validation. There is a critical need to change standard practices in the generation and interpretation of health and safety data on industry products and processes, and to interpose a buffer or barrier between those who sell and those who test. The theoretical basis of such safeguards has been developed (1), and their implementation is overdue.

Chapter 17

INDUSTRIAL RISKS OF
COLORECTAL CANCER

INTRODUCTION

After lung cancer, colorectal cancer is the second most common malignancy in the United States, with more than 120,000 annual incident cases (as of 1990); colorectal cancer accounts for 15 percent of all newly diagnosed cancers in women and 14 percent in men (1–6). The distinction between colon and rectal cancers is anatomic, rectal cancer being defined as malignant disease within 11 cm of the anus; about 10 percent of these cancers are located in an area of diagnostic uncertainty between the colon and rectum (7). Even though colon and rectal cancers are identical in pathology, most being adenocarcinomas, their trends in incidence and mortality rates, risk factors, and natural history are sufficiently different to warrant separate consideration. The United States is a relatively high-risk country for colon cancer, with four times the incidence of a low-risk country such as Japan, while the incidence rates for rectal cancer in both countries are approximately equal (1, 8). It is estimated that 22 percent of colorectal cancers in the United States are rectal, and that the remaining 78 percent are distributed proximally throughout the colon: 35 percent sigmoid, 6 percent descending, 13 percent transverse, 8 percent ascending, 15 percent cecum, and 1 percent appendix (1). Incidence rates in the United States increase exponentially with increasing age in men and women (5).

Trends in Incidence and Mortality

Incidence rates for colon cancer are rising, particularly sharply in males (Table 1); from 1947 to 1984, rates in white males and females have risen by 67 percent and 10 percent, respectively, largely in age groups over 65. Mortality rates for colon cancer are also increasing substantially in white and black men and in black

Coauthored with Bret A. Lashner; published in *International Journal of Health Services,* Volume 20, Number 3, 1990.

Table 1

Incidence and mortality rates of colon and rectal cancers in white males and females,
United States, 1947–1984

| | Colon cancer[a] | | | | Rectal cancer[a] | | | |
| | Incidence | | Mortality | | Incidence | | Mortality | |
Years	M	F	M	F	M	F	M	F
1947–50	26.6	30.3	18.6	19.9	20.8	14.1	10.9	6.7
1969–71	35.6	31.0	19.4	17.7	19.8	12.0	7.9	4.6
1975–76	38.9	32.7	20.6	16.8	20.8	12.9	6.6	3.7
1977–78	41.4	33.6	21.7	16.5	21.9	12.6	5.8	3.4
1979–80	41.7	33.6	22.4	16.8	21.1	12.8	5.3	2.9
1981–82	43.3	33.7	22.0	16.6	20.3	12.7	5.0	2.9
1983–84	44.4	33.3	21.1	15.4	19.9	12.4	4.4	2.4
Percentage change, 1947–84	+67%	+10%	+13%	–23%	–4%	–12%	–60%	–64%

Source: Devesa et al. (5).
[a]Expressed as age-adjusted rates per 100,000 population in five U.S. geographic area databases. Mortality rates were read from curves on a log-linear plot.

women, particularly in older ages, and are decreasing in white women, particularly in younger ages (1, 5, 6, 9).

Although incidence rates for rectal cancer in males and females have remained largely unchanged or have declined slightly for over three decades, mortality rates are decreasing sharply (Table 1). Declining mortality from rectal cancer is evident in all age groups (5). The divergences between incidence and mortality rates for both colon and rectal cancer are increasing, reflecting improved survival which could be due to both increases in routine screening facilitating earlier diagnosis and, more importantly, improved surgical techniques. However, the increased incidence of colon cancer, particularly in males, more than negates diagnostic and surgical advances (10–12). Since the proportion of cancers discovered at all pathologic stages has remained relatively constant over the years, the rising incidence of colorectal cancer is not apparently due to earlier diagnosis, but, more likely, is due to incremental increases in risk factors.

The incidence of colorectal cancer is high in developed, industrialized countries of North America and northwest Europe, while rates are low in Africa, South America, Japan, and India (1, 8). Japanese, Scandinavian, and African migrants to the United States assume the risk of the host country by the second generation, strongly suggesting an etiologic role for environmental factors (8, 13, 14). There are also regional differences within countries. In the United States, colon and rectal cancer risks in males and females are highest in northeastern states, especially New York, New Jersey, Connecticut, Rhode Island, Massachusetts, and in the Great Lakes industrial areas (7, 15), and are increasing rapidly in hitherto lower risk southern states (16). Residence in certain New Jersey counties appears to be a risk factor (9). Higher urbanization and industrialization, male sex, and residence in proximity to chemical industries and toxic waste disposal sites are associated with excess colon and rectal cancers (9); rectal cancer is also associated with the proportion of the population employed in the chemical industry (9). In low-risk countries, higher socioeconomic status is associated with approximately fourfold higher colon, but not rectal, cancer risks (17).

Genetic and Environmental Studies

Recently, a likelihood analysis of 34 kindreds with at least one member with colonic neoplasia suggested that a dominant genetic trait with a 19 percent gene frequency (95 percent confidence interval, 14–28 percent) could account for at least half (95 percent confidence interval, 53–100 percent) of colonic neoplasms (18); this genetic susceptibility possibly requires an environmental risk factor to promote neoplastic transformation. Genetic syndromes such as familial polyposis, Gardner's syndrome, and the cancer family syndrome are strong risk factors (1, 19). A wide range of iatrogenic and environmental factors has also been associated with excess colorectal cancer risk. Predisposing pathology includes benign adenomas and inflammatory bowel disease (1). The association of the iatrogenic factor of cholecystectomy with right-sided colon cancer has been demonstrated in females in an historical cohort study (relative risk 1.7; 95 percent confidence interval, 1.1–3.6) (20), and in a case-control study (odds ratio 1.86; not significant) (21). However, other studies indicate that this association is weak and without a "duration of exposure" effect (22). Lifestyle factors have been extensively studied, with weak, inconsistent, or inconclusive results. Prominent among these studies have been dietary factors, particularly fiber, fat, cholesterol, calcium, vitamin A, vitamin E, and selenium (13, 23). The National Academy of Sciences has concluded that, although the data are inconsistent, high dietary total and saturated fat may be possible risk factors for colorectal cancer, but that there is less, if any, evidence implicating low-fiber diet (13). There is no evidence of any association between tobacco smoking and colorectal cancer (24).

Epidemiologic Studies

Mormons and Seventh Day Adventists, both alcohol abstainees, have approximately two-thirds of the general U.S. population's risk for rectal cancer (1, 7). An ecologic analysis on whites in 47 states has demonstrated significant correlations, as high as 0.81, between beer drinking (but not other forms of alcohol consumption) and colorectal, particularly rectal, cancer (25). Furthermore, changes in statewide beer consumption are significantly correlated with colon and rectal cancer incidence rates (25), as are international differences in beer consumption (26). However, these indirect ecologic data are of limited value because of the impossibility of controlling for all confounding variables. The weight of the epidemiologic literature concerning the general population does not demonstrate any association between beer consumption and rectal cancer (13). Occupational studies have demonstrated that Irish (27), but not Danish (28, 29), brewery workers have a significantly increased rectal cancer risk. Possibly relevant to this association is a study demonstrating the co-carcinogenic effect in rats of chronic alcohol ingestion on the incidence of rectal cancer induced by parenteral administration of dimethylhydrazine (30); this effect is associated with the induction of alcohol dehydrogenase in rectal mucosa.

Job activity per se appears related to colon cancer risk. In a study of 2,950 cases of colorectal cancers, sedentary workers had 60 percent higher rates for colon, but not for rectal, cancer than highly active workers (95 percent confidence interval, 30–80 percent) (31). While these relationships have been confirmed (32), job activity may well be confounded by industrial exposures and other variables.

Industrial Risk Factors

The sharply increasing incidence of colon cancer, particularly in males, and the high incidence rates in industrialized areas within the United States suggest a causal role for industrial risk factors. However, industrial risk factors, both occupational and environmental, are largely ignored in the clinical literature (1, 3, 5, 6, 33, 34). This reflects the prevailing tendency among the National Cancer Institute, the American Cancer Society, and clinicians to "blame-the-victim" by attributing most causes of cancer, including colorectal, to faulty lifestyle, rather than to investigate and recognize the role of preventable industrial exposures (11, 12).

Definition of Epidemiologic Terms

The measures of association presented in this chapter are generally dependent on the study design and standardization technique. Relative risk (RR), a measure of exposure-disease association in a cohort study, is calculated by dividing the measured disease incidence rate in the exposed population by the incidence rate in the unexposed population. The odds ratio (OR) is a measure of exposure-disease association, most commonly derived from a case-control study. For rare diseases, the OR approximates the RR. The proportional mortality ratio (PMR) and standardized mortality ratio (SMR) are indirectly standardized measures commonly used in occupational epidemiology (35). The SMR is a ratio of the number of observed deaths from a disease to the number of expected deaths in a population, multiplied by 100; numbers of expected deaths are usually derived from published age- and sex-specific rates in a defined area or an entire country. When industry- or occupation-specific mortality rates are used to calculate the expected number of cases, the PMR is the ratio of observed to expected, times 100. It should be noted that employed populations usually have SMR values less than 100. This is attributed to the "healthy worker effect," since employed persons have a lower prevalence of chronic diseases than the general population (36). An SMR, therefore, represents an underestimate of the true risk. All statistically significant associations ($P < 0.05$) are stated or implied when the 95 percent confidence interval of RR and OR excludes unity, or excludes 100 for SMR and PMR. While these different measures of association are not directly comparable, for the purposes of this chapter they are summarized to approximate the magnitude of the risk. Dose and duration of exposures are stated when known.

Attributable risk (AR) is calculated by the formula: $AR = Pe(RR - 1)/[1 + Pe(RR - 1)]$, where AR is the population attributable risk and Pe is the proportion in a population exposed (37). AR is a measure of the burden of an exposure for disease in a population. If the exposure is removed from the population, it is assumed that the incidence of disease will be reduced by the AR. For example, for exposures with an RR of 2 in a population where 100 percent are exposed, the AR is 50 percent which means that half of the colorectal cancer observed in this population can be attributed to the exposure. Therefore, even relatively low-risk exposures, particularly when large population groups are exposed, can be associated with a high attributable risk.

In this chapter we analyze the epidemiologic literature on the role of industrial exposures as risk factors for colorectal cancer (Table 2); the relevant experimental literature is also briefly summarized. The chapter concludes with recommendations for the prevention of colorectal cancer and for the screening of populations at possible excess risk.

OCCUPATIONAL EXPOSURES

Asbestos Workers

After lung cancer and mesotheliomas, colorectal cancer is the third most common malignancy in asbestos workers, accounting for up to one-third of their excess cancer mortality (12, 38). Primary occupational exposures, including mining, cement pipe manufacture, insulation, textile, paint, friction products, and paper manufacture, and secondary exposures, including automotive, boilermaking, carpentry, construction, electrical, welding, machinery, masonry, painting, and shipyard industries, are both associated with high colorectal cancer risks. The importance of such risk factors is emphasized by the fact that some 80,000 full-time and 1,200,000 part-time workers are currently employed in asbestos-related industries (39).

Epidemiologic studies have reported an increased RR for colon cancer in the range of 1.4 to 3.0 (Table 2), compared with an approximate RR of 7 for lung cancer (12, 34, 38–42). Investigations on four industrial cohorts comprising insulators, asbestos factory workers, and miners have demonstrated SMR values from 145 to 277, associated with a 20- to 40-year latency after initial exposure (39). There is no evidence for synergism between asbestos exposure and cigarette smoking for colon cancer, as is the case for lung cancer (38). The high risk of asbestos workers for colon cancer probably reflects exposure of colonic mucosa to swallowed asbestos-contaminated sputum (38).

The relationship between asbestos exposure and gastrointestinal cancer satisfies the major epidemiologic criteria of causality (37, 40). There is no evidence of a confounding variable effect; the association is consistent from study to study; there is a clear temporal relationship, with exposure preceding malignancy by at least 20 years; there is evidence of a dose-response relationship, although relatively weak; and, the cause-effect relationship is biologically plausible in that it is further supported by experimental data (Table 3). Rats fed 10 percent chrysotile asbestos develop a twofold, though not statistically significant, excess of colon cancers (43). Furthermore, asbestos ingestion alters colonic metabolism. Rats fed a single dose of chrysotile (5 or 100 mg/kg) increase their rates of colonic cell turnover and epithelial DNA synthesis (44). Large particles of asbestos, up to 120 μm long, are known to penetrate between single cell layers of colonic enterocytes by persorption and to become hematogenously disseminated (38, 44, 45). Asbestos bodies have been identified among colonic cancer cells, but not in surrounding nonneoplastic tissues, in an asbestos worker (46). Consistent and strong epidemiologic evidence, with supportive experimental evidence, thus makes occupational asbestos exposure a major colorectal cancer risk factor.

Acrylonitrile Workers

Acrylonitrile, a gaseous monomer, is widely used for the synthesis of plastic and synthetic rubber and fiber polymers, with annual exposures of over 25,000 full-time and 350,000 part-time workers (36, 47, 48). The use of acrylonitrile polymers in plastic beverage containers has been banned since 1977 owing to the leaching of unreacted acrylonitrile into beverages and its carcinogenicity in rats (12, 49-51) (Table 3). In an unpublished industry study involving over 200 rats exposed to 35, 100, and 300 parts per million (ppm) acrylonitrile in drinking water for two years, a significant excess of brain, breast, and gastrointestinal malignancies, primarily stomach and small intestine and including four colorectal cancers, were induced (49). This experimental evidence is also confirmed epidemiologically (Table 2). In an historical cohort study of 1,345 acrylonitrile

Table 2

Occupational and environmental exposures associated with
colon, rectal, and colorectal cancers

Exposure	Observed/expected[a]			Reference(s)
	Colon	Rectal	Colorectal	
Occupational				
Asbestos	1.4–3.0			(12, 34, 38–42)
Acrylonitrile	1.8		1.4	(47, 52)
Ethylacrylate and				
methyl methylacrylate	2.2	1.8	2.1	(55)
Synthetic fabric	2.3–11.4			(57–60)
Dibromochloropropane		2.3–4.2		(64, 67, 68)
Dibromopropylphosphate	1.9			(67)
Polybrominated biphenyls	1.5			(67)
Chlordane	1.8			(68)
Heptachlor, endrin	1.8			(68)
Printing	1.4			(69)
Pattern and modelmaking	1.7	1.4	1.2–4.9	(71–73)
Synthetic rubber	1.2–1.9		1.2–1.8	(75–77)
Brewery	1.1–1.3	1.0–1.6		(75–77)
Paint and professional artists	1.2–1.5	1.0–3.8		(79, 80)
Radium dial painters	2.0–2.9			(81)
Grinding wheel dust, cutting oil,				
dye, solvents, fuel oil, abrasives	1.3	1.3	1.2–2.9	(82, 85, 86)
Metal and transportation	2.1		1.2–3.4	(35, 96)
Spinners/weavers/fabric	1.4		1.1–1.6	(35, 96)
Leather			1.6–1.7	(83)
Linemen			1.3–1.4	(35)
Firemen			1.7–2.8	(35)
Plumbers/pipefitting	1.1	1.1		(94)
Copper smelting	5.0			(93)
Paper industry		2.3	1.7–2.5	(89, 96)
Laundry/dry cleaning			1.5	(90)
Oil refinery	1.0–2.0			(34, 97–99)
Embalmers	1.4			(100)
Vinyl chloride	3.3			(102)
Environmental				
Trihalomethanes	1.1–1.6	1.3–2.1	2.2	(113–116)
Ionizing radiation	1.3–1.7	1.6–2.8	1.2–8.3	(119, 122–124)

[a]Observed/expected refers to the SMR/100 and the PMR/100. Odds ratios from case-control studies are included in the table to demonstrate the magnitude of the excess risk, even though observed/expected ratios are not used to calculate odds ratios. No epidemiologic effect of the exposure on the risk of disease has an observed/expected of 1.0.

Table 3

Colorectal carcinogens[a,b]

Carcinogen	Evidence for induction of colorectal cancer		Evidence for induction of cancer at other sites	
	Epidemiol.	Expt.	Epidemiol.	Expt.
Asbestos	+	+ (43, 132)	+ (50, 132)	+ (43, 132)
Acrylonitrile	±	+ (49–51)	+ (50, 132)	+ (12, 49–51)
Ethylacrylate and	+			
methyl methacrylate	±	– (48)	ND	+ (48, 54)
Dibromochloropropane	±	– (50, 132)	+ (50, 62, 63)	+ (50, 132)
Polybrominated biphenyls	±	– (50, 132)	ND (132)	+ (50, 132)
Polychlorinated biphenyls	ND	+ (50, 132)	+ (132)	+ (50, 132)
Bromodichloromethane	+	+ (91, 103)	+ (108–112)	+ (91, 103)
Chloroform	+	+ (91, 92)	+ (108–112)	+ (91)
Perchlorethylene and				
trichloroethylene	±	– (91, 92)	+ (90)	+ (92)
Azoxy compounds	ND	+ (50, 133)	ND	+ (50, 133)
Aliphatic amines	ND	+ (50, 87)	ND	+ (50, 87)
Nitrosamines	ND	+ (87, 88)	ND	+ (87, 88)
Nitrosoethanolamines	ND	+ (87, 88)	ND	+ (87, 88)
Aflatoxin	ND	+ (133, 135)	+ (50, 132)	+ (50, 133)
Metronidazole	–	+ (136)	+ (138, 139)	+ (137)
Proflavine	ND	+ (134)	ND	+ (134)
Thiodianiline	ND	+ (87, 134)	ND	+ (87, 134)
Aminoethylcarbazone	ND	+ (87 134)	ND	+ (87, 134)
Phenazopyridine	ND	+ (134)	ND	+ (134)

[a]Epidemiol., epidemiological evidence; Expt., experimental evidence in laboratory animals; ND, no data available; +, carcinogenic effect statistically significance; ±, carcinogenic effect not statistically significant; –, no carcinogenic effect.

[b]References given in parentheses. References on the epidemiologic evidence for induction of colorectal cancer are given in Table 2 and throughout the text.

workers exposed between 1956 and 1979 at a single DuPont plant in South Carolina, the PMR was 122 (25 observed, 20.5 expected) for all cancers combined, and 139 (3 observed, 2.2 expected) for colorectal cancer (47); all colorectal cancers occurred in workers with more than six months' exposure and with long latent periods. In another historical cohort study of 1,111 acrylic fabric factory workers, 21 cancer deaths were discovered after a 10- to 30-year latency (52). The SMR for colon cancer was 180 (2 observed, 1.1 expected) with no age effect; excess cancer rates were also noted for lung, stomach, and brain. Thus, though statistical significance is not attained, the consistent epidemiologic effect, supported by experimental data, incriminates acrylonitrile as a colorectal cancer risk factor.

Ethylacrylate and Methyl Methacrylate Workers

Ethylacrylate and methyl methacrylate are monomers that can be converted into versatile transparent polymers. They were widely used during World War II, mostly in the manufacture of airplanes. Currently, the polymers have a wider range of uses, including latex paints, textiles, paper coatings, fabric finishes, and specialty plastics (48, 53). Both monomers are skin and respiratory tract irritants, and in rodents induce forestomach adenocarcinomas following gavage (54). An historical cohort study of mortality among workers employed between 1933 and 1946 at a single Bristol, Pennsylvania, plant manufacturing monomers and polymers found a statistically significant excess of colorectal cancer (SMR 210, 43 observed, 20.5 expected) (55) (Table 2). Colon cancer (SMR 222, 33 observed, 14.9 expected) had a higher risk than rectal cancer (SMR 177, 10 observed, 5.7 expected); there was at least a ten-year latency, the risk peaking between 45 to 54 years old. While a further case-control study failed to identify the specific causative agent (56), ethylacrylate and methyl methacrylate were not investigated specifically, nor was the study of sufficient power to be accepted as truly negative.

Synthetic Fiber Manufacturers

In 1975, five workers in a Canadian plant involved in the manufacture of synthetic fiber textiles developed undifferentiated colon cancer over 18 months (57). All were relatively young, from 31 to 58 years old, and had been employed for 10 to 32 years. Comparing the observed number of colon cancers with that expected in matched plant workers, the adjusted PMR was 1,030; comparing the observed number with that expected in matched community controls, the SMR was 1,140 (Table 2). In a case-control study, in which 207 colon cancer cases were age-matched to community controls, a statistically significant OR of 2.3 was found for all mates who worked in the plant and 3.0 for males less than 75 years old (58). This association was more pronounced for colon than rectal cancer, and persisted after controlling for past medical and family history and smoking. An attempt to identify the causative agent from a second case-control study demonstrated highest risks in the extrusion process of converting liquid polypropylene to microfilaments (59). It was concluded that unidentified chemicals involved in synthetic fiber manufacture were probably causative, and that continued uncontrolled exposure would be associated with high mortality from colon cancer. To verify this association, a case-control study of colon cancer deaths in the textile industry, where exposures to dyes, solvents, spinning oils, dusts, pigments, finishers, and binders are common, demonstrated an increased risk of colon cancer in black men (OR 2.0 for age below 65 years, 4.0 for age 65 or above), but not in white men (60). Despite the high OR in blacks, the results were not statistically significant since the power of this study was low, being based on only 11 colon cancer deaths.

Dibromochloropropane and Other Halogenated Organics Workers

Since 1955, dibromochloropropane (DBCP) has been widely used agriculturally as a nematocide (61, 62). However, its use was banned in 1977, following the finding of a high incidence of sterility in exposed male workers (63–65).

DBCP is a potent carcinogen, including a wide range of tumors in mice and rats in sites including stomach, nasal cavity, pharynx, breast, kidney, and liver, following oral or inhalation administration (50) (Table 3). Additionally, subacute inhalation exposure of rats to 20 ppm of DBCP induces gross mucosal lesions throughout the gastrointestinal tract (61). High-level irreversible binding of labeled DBCP to protein, DNA, and RNA of large bowel is also found within four hours after intraperitoneal administration (66).

DBCP and related halogenated organics have been causally associated with rectal (Table 2) and other cancers. The National Institute for Occupational Safety and Health (NIOSH) DBCP Registry, based on 215 deaths in 63 companies employing some 3,000 workers distributing, formulating, and manufacturing DBCP, identified a statistically significant excess mortality for liver and bile duct cancers, and excess mortality for esophageal, kidney, central nervous system, lymphatic, and rectal cancers; the PMR for rectal cancer was 229 (3 observed, 1.31 expected) (64). However, the NIOSH study was small and insensitive as it was based on mortality, not incidence, ascertained over a relatively brief duration of follow-up and on relatively few cancer deaths prior to January 1981 among workers in 14 plants, generally with low and relatively brief exposure from formulating and packaging rather than from manufacturing. Recognizing these limitations, NIOSH recommended that this registry should be expanded and updated. Of interest in this connection, as learned by one of the authors (SSE), is the finding of colorectal cancer in two of four full-time laboratory technicians in a Lathrop, California, plant manufacturing and formulating DBCP. Dow Chemical, the major manufacturer of DBCP employing some 300 workers with higher exposure levels for up to 25 years, refused to participate in the NIOSH study. In a subsequent, admittedly small and insensitive cohort study of 550 Dow workers involved in the production and formulation of DBCP from 1957 to 1976, the overall cancer rate was significantly increased (SMR 156, 12 observed, 7.7 expected), largely due to excess lung cancer (62); no digestive tract cancers were reported.

In an historical cohort study of 3,579 white males intermittently exposed in four plants to halogenated organics from 1935 to 1976, excess mortality from lung, bladder, testis, and colorectal cancer, including six colon and two rectal cancers, was noted (67). For workers exposed to DBCP alone, the SMR for rectal cancer was 419 (2 observed, 0.48 expected); for workers exposed to the structurally related flame retardant TRIS (dibromopropyl phosphate) and PBBs (polybrominated biphenyls) alone, the SMR for colon cancer was 186 and 152, respectively. In another historical cohort study, increased rectal cancer risk was noted in a plant producing DBCP, besides aldrin, dieldrin, endrin, and unspecified organophosphates (SMR 242, 3 rectal cancers observed, 1.24 expected) (68); increased colon cancer risk was also noted in a chlordane plant (SMR 178), and in a heptachlor and endrin plant (SMR 175). In this study, the overall cancer rate was lower than expected owing to the "healthy worker effect," suggesting that the observed SMRs for colon and rectal cancer underestimate true risk. Thus, occupational exposures to DBCP and related halogenated organics are risk factors for colorectal cancer.

Printers

In an historical cohort study on printing workers, the SMR for colon cancer was 136 (42 observed, 30.9 expected; 95 percent confidence interval, 110–180) (69); no excess risk was found for rectal cancer (Table 2). Similar relative risks for colon cancer mortality were found among compositors (SMR 131), binders (SMR 124), pressmen (SMR 158), and other workers (SMR 123) (69). Additionally, a statistically significant excess of rectal cancers has been reported in a study based on 2,604 commercial pressmen over 65 years old (70). Thus, the measured colon cancer association appears real, though relatively small.

Automobile Model and Pattern Makers

In 1979, a cluster of cancers at a wide range of sites was noted among automotive workers making wooden models and patterns (71). Using a database linkage between a cancer registry and corporate records, statistically significant SMRs were found for colorectal cancer, ranging between 286 and 487 (71, 72) (Table 2). This association was greatest in workers aged 45 to 59, and was unrelated to duration of employment. A union-sponsored study, using NIOSH age-adjusted rates, found a PMR of 167 and 135 for colon and rectal cancers, respectively (73). Rates were highest in woodshop locals where there was routine exposure to cutting oils, metal fumes, metal dusts, and solvents. Subsequent sigmoidoscopy of 902 asymptomatic workers with high-risk exposures identified 150 with adenomatous colonic polyps and four with colonic adenocarcinomas (74). Using separate registries for comparisons, the age-adjusted ORs for colorectal cancer ranged between 1.2 and 2.7 and were statistically significant. However, rightsided lesions were missed from sigmoidoscopic screening, possibly underestimating true risks. Thus, epidemiologic evidence has clearly identified automotive model and patternmaking as high-risk occupations for colorectal cancer.

Synthetic Rubber Workers

An historical cohort study of 2,666 synthetic rubber workers demonstrated excess colorectal cancer mortality, as well as leukemia and gastric and biliary tract cancers (75). The SMR for colorectal cancer was 136 (31 observed, 22.8 expected; 95 confidence interval, 93–193) (Table 2). The largest colorectal cancer excess was seen in workers performing front processing (SMR 180), involving compounding, mixing, and milling of rubber with accelerators, antioxidants, oils, fillers, and pigments, rather than in workers performing back processing (SMR 120), involving extrusion, cement mixing, and rubberized fabric operations; excess risks were poorly correlated with employment duration. This occupational association was confirmed in another historical cohort study based on 1,783 deaths, in which the SMR for colon cancer was 121 (10 observed, 8.26 expected) (76). A Swedish historical cohort study of 2,345 rubber industry workers demonstrated highest risks for esophageal (SMR 1,008), laryngeal (SMR 384), and colon cancers (SMR 187, 9 observed, 4.8 expected; 95 percent confidence interval, 85–355) (77). A British study, however, failed to confirm this association, although increased risks for lung cancer (SMR 123) and gastric cancer (SMR 129) were noted (78). While American, Swedish, and British studies appear valid with sufficient power and sensitivity, their inconsistencies relating to colorectal cancer may reflect differing work practices.

Brewery Workers

Irish brewery workers, given a free daily ration of two pints of stout, had SMRs for rectal cancer of 162 (32 observed, 19.7 expected; $P < 0.01$), and 133 for colon cancer (32 observed, 24.1 expected; not significant) (27). These effects were based on 1,628 deaths over 20 years and persisted after adjustment for confounding variables. It must be stressed that SMRs were not elevated for cancers where alcohol is known to be a risk factor. Discrepantly, a study on 14,313 Danish workers, given a free daily ration of six bottles of beer, reported no significant excess of colon cancer (SMR 107; 95 percent confidence interval, 77–136) or rectal cancer (SMR 102; 95 percent confidence interval, 81–126) (28, 29) (Table 2). However, SMRs were high for known alcohol-associated cancers, such as pharyngeal and esophageal (SMR 209 for each), laryngeal (SMR 198), and hepatocellular (SMR 151). While the discrepant Irish and Danish studies may reflect differences between stout and beer, they also reflect inherent problems in studying weak effects.

Paint Industry Workers and Professional Artists

An historical cohort study of 16,243 paint and varnish workers employed for at least one year since 1946 demonstrated statistically significant SMRs of 138 for colon cancer and 139 for rectal cancer (79) (Table 2); colon and rectal cancers had the highest risks of any neoplasm studied. Stratifying by exposure, pigment workers (SMR for colon cancer 144, SMR for rectal cancer 104), solvent workers (SMR for colon cancer 124, SMR for rectal cancer 196) and vehicle manufacturing workers (SMR for colon cancer 145, SMR for rectal cancer 138) had the highest risks; lacquer manufacture was not associated with any reported excess risks. In a study of 1,598 deaths among professional artists, males had a statistically significant increase in colon cancer (PMR 173, 34 observed, 19.6 expected) and rectal cancer (PMR 168, 17 observed, 10.1 expected) (80). Excess rectal cancers were also observed in females (PMR 380, 7 observed, 1.8 expected). These results suggest a real risk for colorectal cancer among painters and professional artists, although the specific carcinogenic agents have not been identified.

Radium Dial Painters

In a study of 634 women working in a watch dial-painting factory early this century, an excess of overall cancers (SMR 127), especially colon cancer, osteogenic sarcoma, and leukemia, was noted (81). The SMR for colon cancer was 202 (10 observed, 4.96 expected). An increased risk also was observed in women with short duration of employment, for whom the SMR was 291 (5 observed, 1.72 expected) (Table 2). There was no demonstrable association with year or age at first exposure or duration of exposure.

Miscellaneous Industrial Workers

Associations between a wide range of occupational exposures and colorectal cancer risks have been investigated using three different data bases; the Third National Cancer Survey, based on all incident cancer cases from 1969 to 1971 in seven metropolitan areas and two states covering 10.3 percent of the entire U.S. population; the National Occupational Hazard Study, based on occupational exposure data; and the National Health and Nutrition Examination Survey, based on nutritional variables (82). Using these data, a case-control study was performed on a sample of 378 colon and 175 rectal cancer patients; matched controls were patients with malignancies not believed to be "industrially related," such as tumors of soft tissues, brain, endocrine organs, breast, and prostate (82). A logistic regression analysis demonstrated that many occupational exposures were positively associated with excess colorectal cancers, particularly in males, and that the associations were similar for colorectal and colon cancers (Table 2). ORs for asbestos, grinding wheel dust, cutting oil, and dye work were between 1.2 and 1.3. Statistically significant effects and trends were noted for workers exposed to solvents (OR 1.60), fuel oil (OR 1.53), and abrasives (OR 1.40). Moreover, there is little basis for excluding the possible causal role of occupational exposures in the nongastrointestinal malignancies of controls, with a resulting misclassification bias toward the null and underestimation of true risks.

Census and death certificate data have been used to measure the colorectal cancer risk of occupational exposures in the United States and the United Kingdom (35). Of 87 job categories, 45 had an SMR of more than 115, of which 18 had a nonelevated PMR, suggesting overreporting of cancer in an entire category. Thirteen of the 45 job categories with an elevated SMR were professional categories with no obvious industrial exposures; accountants (SMR 140, PMR 139), lawyers (SMR 148, PMR 166), and musicians (SMR 222, PMR 130) had the highest risk. Of the 14 job categories with a high SMR and PMR that had industrial exposures, several categories were recognized (Table 2). These include metal workers, such as millwrights (SMR 182, PMR 183), machinists and jobsetters (SMR 167, PMR 127), and toolmakers, diemakers, and setters (SMR 115, PMR 135), all of whom are routinely exposed to cutting oils, lubricating oils, and metal-cleaning solvents; transportation equipment workers (SMR 340, PMR 117), whose exposures overlap with metal workers; spinners and weavers (SMR 162, PMR 164); fabric workers (SMR 130, PMR 112); shoemakers (SMR 175, PMR 124); leather workers (SMR 160, PMR 174), exposed to dyes, metallic compounds, and solvents (83); linemen (SMR 139, PMR 131), exposed to chlorodiphenyls, chloronaphthalenes, dyes, resins, and solvents; and firemen (SMR 279, PMR 172), exposed to smoke and carbon tetrachloride of fire extinguishers. It was claimed that cancer mortality rates among firemen were rising, from 15.4 percent in 1949 to 38.4 percent in 1970 (84). The magnitude of the colorectal cancer risk association with these varied occupational exposures is nearly twice the expected rate (35).

In an historical cohort study of 2,485 metal workers exposed to cutting oils, 1,137 of whom had heavy exposures and more than five years of employment, the SMRs for colon and rectal cancers were 130 and 125, respectively (85). Workers in the optical manufacturing industry are frequently exposed to abrasives and cutting oil mists. A study of 519 deaths in this industry demonstrated excess colorectal cancers (SMR 290, 20 observed, 6.9 expected; $P < 0.05$) associated with both medium-term (less than 20 years) and long-term employment (86). These effects are consistent with previously noted associations (36, 82). Nitrosamines, derived from the nitrosation of ethanolamine wetting agents in cutting oil, have been incriminated as possible causative agents for colorectal cancer (82). This is consistent with experimental evidence on the carcinogenicity of nitrosamines (Table 3), including the induction of colon cancer in rodents by oral, intraperitoneal, and rectal administration (50, 87, 88).

In a case-control study, 13,000 cancer patients were compared with an equal number of cancer-free patients (89). Using clerical jobs as a baseline, the OR for colorectal cancer was 1.17 for all industrially related occupations and 1.67 for workers in the paper industry; the colorectal cancer OR was 2.49 for paper industry workers with over five years' employment.

More than 225,000 people are employed in the dry cleaning industry. Dry cleaning and laundry workers have been generally exposed to carcinogenic chlorinated hydrocarbon solvents (Table 2) such as carbon tetrachloride and trichloroethylene and, more recently, to perchloroethylene (90–92). An historical cohort study of 330 deaths among these workers reported a PMR for colorectal cancer of 152 (9 observed, 5.9 expected) (90), which was unrelated to duration of employment.

A total of 190 malignancies was found among 2,675 male copper smelters at a Japanese metal refinery plant from 1949 to 1971 (93). The SMR of 1,189 (29 observed, 2.44 expected) for lung cancer varied with the level of exposure and length of employment. The SMR for colon cancer among copper smelters was 508 (3 observed, 0.59 expected; $P < 0.05$). However, no colon or rectal cancers were found in nickel and lead workers. Even though the SMR was high, colon cancer is a rare malignancy in the Japanese, making estimates of SMRs imprecise.

Plumbers and pipefitters can be exposed to carcinogens including asbestos, heavy metals, acrylonitrile, vinyl chloride, and chlorinated solvents (94, 95). An historical cohort study of these workers, which failed to evaluate specifics of the exposures, found the PMR to be 113 for colon cancer and 106 for rectal cancer (94). However, it should be noted that California plumbers and pipefitters have increasing cancer rates with duration of exposure (95); site-specific rate data are not available.

An unpublished study evaluated mortality patterns among major occupational groups for all deaths in New Hampshire residents aged over 20 between 1975 and 1985 (96). Significantly elevated risks for colon cancer were noted in fabric (PMR 139), metal machinery (PMR 209), and electric machinery industries (PMR 211). A significant excess of rectal cancers was noted in the paper industry (PMR 230). Nonsignificant increases in risk for both colon and rectal cancer also were noted in a wide range of other occupations.

Many other industries have demonstrated associations with excess colorectal cancer mortality. Studies of oil refinery workers have been inconclusive with regard to colorectal cancer risks (34, 97). Despite a single refinery study demonstrating an approximate twofold excess of colon cancers (98), other studies were not confirmatory (34, 97, 99); oil refinery workers, however, appear to have increased cancer risks at other sites such as brain, stomach, and pancreas, and for melanoma of the skin. Embalmers, exposed to formaldehyde and related chemicals, have a significantly increased mortality from skin cancer, and colon cancer (PMR 143, 29 observed, 20.3 expected); this study was based on 1,263 deaths in licensed embalmers between 1902 and 1980 (100). A smaller study, though, failed to confirm these carcinogenic effects (101). In a study of 454 Norwegian vinyl chloride and polyvinylchloride workers, an increased incidence of hepatic angiosarcoma, lung cancer, malignant melanoma, and colon cancer (SMR 333, 3 observed, 0.9 expected) was noted, but the results were not significant (102).

As noted in Table 2, many large industries such as asbestos, synthetic fabric, automotive, and synthetic rubber, are associated with excess colorectal cancer risks. Although these individual risks may appear small, their effect on large populations of workers can account for a substantial number of preventable malignancies.

ENVIRONMENTAL EXPOSURES

Trihalomethanes in Drinking Water

Chlorine was first used as a disinfectant in drinking water in 1908 to help prevent typhoid fever (103). Not until the 1970s did evidence implicate chlorination as a potential hazard. This results from the reaction in water between chlorine and natural and synthetic organic chemicals, particularly industrial pollutants, to produce a family of related chemicals known as trihalomethanes (THMs), the principal members of which are trichloromethane (chloroform), bromodichloromethane, and dibromochloromethane. In general, concentrations of THMs in drinking water are directly related to concentrations of synthetic organic pollutants from industrial effluents. In 1979, the Environmental Protection Agency promulgated a THM drinking water standard of 100 parts per billion (ppb) based on carcinogenicity (103). However, 3,000 municipal systems do not comply with this standard, and more than 40 million people drink water with higher THM levels (103); even groundwater is contaminated with unacceptable levels of THMs in at least 40 states (104, 105). The median consumption of THMs in the United States is estimated to be 18 ppb (106).

Ecologic studies have demonstrated that excess cancers of the colon, rectum, stomach, and bladder are associated with drinking water derived from chlorinated surface sources, rather than from groundwater (107–110). An ecologic study compared THM levels among 4,255 cases of gastrointestinal and urinary tract cancers in a tumor registry with age-matched controls (111); the mean THM level was 46 ppb (range 0 to 71). Non-statistically significant positive correlations between THM levels and the incidence of cancers of the colon, rectum, bladder, pancreas, stomach, and esophagus were noted. These results, however, suffer from an exposure misclassification bias toward the null.

Case-control studies have demonstrated associations between chlorinated surface drinking water and cancers of the colon, rectum, and bladder (108, 110, 112) (Table 2). Comparing high to low THM exposures, the ORs are statistically significant, ranging from 1.26 to 1.93 for rectal cancer, and 1.08 to 1.61 for colon cancer (113). A case-control study of 200 incident cases of colorectal cancer in North Carolina examined the relationship with chlorination in the principal water source (114). After adjusting for age, high ORs were related to chlorinated drinking water. The predicted colorectal OR for a 70-year-old drinking chlorinated drinking water for 15 years compared to a 70-year-old drinking nonchlorinated water was 2.15 (95 percent confidence interval, 1.70–2.69). Another case-control study compared 8,029 cancer deaths at all sites to matched controls, and demonstrated an increased risk of colon cancer (OR 1.51; 95 percent confidence interval, 1.02–2.14) and of rectal cancer (OR 1.39; 95 percent confidence interval, 0.67–2.86) (115); these associations persisted after controlling for occupation, urbanization, and marital status.

In a study of 20 Louisiana parishes (counties) with chlorinated surface drinking water derived from the Mississippi River, 4,723 colorectal cancer deaths between 1960 and 1975 were sampled and compared with randomly selected controls matched for age, race, sex, year of death, and parish (115, 116); controls were matched for industrial or urban characteristics, except for their principal potable water source. Comparing groups drinking most of their water from surface sources with those drinking the least proportion of water from surface sources, the OR was 2.07 for rectal cancer (95 percent confidence interval, 1.49–2.88) with a positive dose-response effect, and 0.96 for colon cancer (95 percent confidence interval, 0.75–1.24). Two parishes downriver along the Mississippi, Orleans and Jefferson, had unusually high cancer risks, with ORs for colon cancer approximating 3.0. However, this study suffers from possible confounding effects, in view of the many uncharacterized exposures in both case and control groups. Other studies have reported that colon and rectal cancer rates are highest in the southern part of Louisiana, associated with high levels of pollutants in the Mississippi River and related surface sources (117).

A case-control study of 395 cancer deaths among New York State teachers compared cases with an equal number of occupation- and age-matched controls who died of nonmalignant causes (118). A multiplicative statistical model measured cumulative THM exposure from drinking water supply based on 20-year home and work addresses. A logistic model, adjusting for a few confounding variables, provided an OR for colon cancer of 1.07 (90 percent confidence interval, 0.79–1.43). However, misclassified exposures may have biased the results toward unity.

Even at levels below the 100 ppb standard, EPA estimates that lifelong THM exposure will result in at least 200 excess U.S. cancer deaths per year from all sites, including colon and rectum (103). In 1980, the Council on Environmental Quality estimated that THMs above the 100 ppb standard pose a 53 percent increased risk for colon cancer and a 13 to 93 percent increased risk for rectal cancer, compared with populations supplied with untreated water (103). In view of the large populations exposed to THM-contaminated waters, even relatively small increased risks can be responsible for a large national excess of colorectal cancers.

Experimental evidence directly supports the epidemiologic associations between THMs and colorectal cancer (Table 3). Rats gavaged with bromodichloromethane dosages of 50 to 100 mg/kg/day for two years developed statistically significant and dose-related increases of colonic adenomas and carcinomas, with a zero incidence in controls (50). Chloroform is carcinogenic in mice and rats at sites including liver, kidney, and thyroid, but not colon or rectum (92).

Ionizing Radiation

Radioactivity is ubiquitous in the earth's crust, air, and water (110). Incremental sources include nuclear power stations, nuclear weapons testing, and medical isotopes, diagnostics, and therapeutics. Among 82,000 Japanese atomic bomb survivors exposed to "low-dose" radiation, there was an increased incidence of colon cancer, with an RR of nearly 3, but not of rectal cancer (6, 119–121). Associations were found between ionizing radiation and colon and rectal cancers in case reports of 49 patients exposed to therapeutic ionizing radiation for non-colonic malignancy (119), and also in cohorts exposed to therapeutic radiation for benign diseases (Table 2). In a cohort study of 923 women treated with radium for cervical cancer, the SMR for colon cancer was 131 (13 observed, 9.94 expected) and for rectal cancer was 276 (12 observed, 4.35 expected) (122). In another cohort study, approximately 14,000 patients radiated for ankylosing spondylitis were found to have a significantly high rate of colon cancer (SMR 162, 28 observed, 17.3 expected) (123). This disease, however, is associated with ulcerative colitis which, in turn, may predispose to colon cancer. In a cohort of 2,068 women followed for 19 years subsequent to pelvic irradiation for benign conditions, such as uterine fibroids, excess colon (SMR 173) and rectal (SMR 160) cancers were noted (124).

Based on linear modeling of a wide range of dose-response studies on pelvic irradiation, 0.1 to 1.7 excess cases of colorectal cancer were estimated to occur per year per million exposed to one rad to the colon (125); the lower figure is derived from atom bomb survivors and the higher figure from ankylosing spondylitis studies. From this regression, the relative risk for colorectal cancer from an average therapeutic dose of 3,000 rads for cervical cancer is estimated to be between 2.0 and 3.6 (119); the risk is highest after 10 years of exposure, with the range of RRs from 1.2 to 8.3. Experimental data are also supportive. X-irradiation with over 3,500 rads to the colon of rats induced a 50 percent incidence of adenocarcinoma, compared with 0 percent in nonirradiated controls ($P < 0.05$) (126). Thus, ionizing radiation, even in low doses of environmental exposures, poses a risk for colon and rectal cancers.

Asbestos in Drinking Water

After World War II, 200,000 miles of asbestos-cement drinking water pipes were installed in the United States (103). Acid erosion has resulted in leaching of asbestos, as a result of which, approximately 5 percent of the North American population now drinks water with over 10 million fibers per liter (110). In

San Francisco, naturally occurring high chrysotile fiber counts were associated with excess colon malignancies, particularly in males (127). However, studies in populations exposed to asbestos in drinking water have generally failed to identify excess colon cancer risks. Illustratively, in Duluth, Minnesota, with amphibole fiber concentrations of 30 million per liter, and in Everett, Washington, with chrysotile fiber counts of 200 million per liter, excess risks were noted with cancers of the esophagus, stomach, pancreas, and prostate, but not with colon cancer (128–130). Control groups in these studies were residents of nearby cities whose drinking water was contaminated with low levels of asbestos, which biased the results toward the null. Asbestos exposure in drinking water, to date, has not been associated with colorectal cancer, but unbiased studies with sufficient statistical power are not available.

DISCUSSION

Industrial exposures are important but neglected risk factors for colon and rectal cancers. Recent sharp increases in the incidence rates of colon cancer in males (Table 1) coupled with high incidence rates in industrialized areas within the United States suggest a causal role for industrially related exposures, particularly occupational. A wide range of carcinogenic occupational and environmental industrial exposures is associated with excess colorectal cancer risk (Table 2). While these excess risks are generally small, with exposed groups usually having approximately twice the risk of unexposed groups, large numbers of occupations and workers are involved. Additionally, occupationally related colorectal cancers may occur in young age groups, as observed in synthetic fiber plants (57). Environmental exposures to THMs in chlorinated drinking water increase the risks of colon and rectal cancers by 1.5 to 2 times unexposed rates, and are thus major potential causal factors, particularly in view of the very large populations at risk. Table 4 lists the calculated AR and the expected number of colorectal cancers per year attributable to environmental and occupational exposures with RR of 1.5 or 2.0 and the proportion exposed in the population ranging from 5 to 25 percent. These derived risks are based on estimates that at least 5 percent of the U.S. population are occupationally exposed to colorectal carcinogens, particularly in the asbestos, acrylonitrile, and synthetic rubber industries, and at least 15 percent are exposed to environmental colorectal carcinogens, particularly THMs. Based on these conservative assumptions, colorectal carcinogens of industrial origin are likely to account for up to 20 percent of all incident colorectal cancers.

Experimental Colorectal Carcinogens

The epidemiologic evidence for the causal role of industrial risk factors is directly supported by experimental evidence (Table 3) for the induction of the

Table 4

Attributable risk of populations hypothetically exposed to colorectal
carcinogens, United States

Proportion of the population exposed	Relative risk	Attributable risk	No. of incident colorectal cancers per year[a]
0.05	1.5	0.0244	2,927
0.05	2.0	0.0476	5,714
0.10	1.5	0.0476	5,714
0.10	2.0	0.0909	10,909
0.15	1.5	0.0698	8,372
0.15	2.0	0.1304	15,652
0.20	1.5	0.0909	10,909
0.20	2.0	0.1667	20,000
0.25	1.5	0.1111	13,333
0.25	2.0	0.2000	24,000

[a]Figures are based on 120,000 incident cases of colorectal cancer in the entire U.S. population per year.

otherwise rare colorectal cancer in rodents by asbestos (43), acrylonitrile (49, 50), bromodichloromethane (91), and nitrosoethanolamines (50, 87, 88). However, as there is no necessary correspondence between the site of induction of neoplasms by carcinogens from species to species, including humans (131), a carcinogen inducing neoplasms in sites other than the colon and rectum in experimental animals may well induce colorectal cancer in humans. Thus, the suggestive epidemiologic evidence for DBCP as a colorectal human cancer risk factor, based on clearly insensitive epidemiologic studies, is supported by its carcinogenicity at other sites in mice and rats following oral and inhalation exposures (50); further evidence is afforded by the specific organotropic effects of DBCP in the large intestine of rodents (61, 66). It should also be emphasized that experimental evidence of carcinogenicity cannot be negated by apparently negative or weak epidemiologic evidence, unless such evidence satisfies rigorous criteria of validity, adequacy, power, sensitivity, and prolonged post-exposure evaluation (131). Thus, an industrial chemical inducing experimental carcinogenic effects at sites other than the colon and rectum may be a major risk factor for human colorectal cancer.

Many experimental colorectal carcinogens have not been studied epidemiologically (50, 132) (Table 3). These include azoxy compounds, such as cycasin and methylazoxymethanol, which induce cancers in the colon, kidney, and liver following oral administration (133); aliphatic amines, such as dimethylhydrazine, which induce colorectal cancer at such a predictable rate that they are used as models in laboratory animals (87, 134); and N-nitroso compounds, such as nitrosomethylurea and methylnitrosoguanidine, which induce tumors in the colon, stomach, and small bowel when administered orally (87, 88). Experimental colorectal carcinogens inducing cancers at sites other than the colon and rectum in humans include aflatoxin, which induces carcinomas of the colon, liver, and kidney in experimental animals (133, 135) and liver cancer in humans, and metronidazole, which induces carcinoma of the colon and lung in experimental animals, especially in combination with a low fiber diet (136, 137), and which has been associated with an excess of cervical and lung cancer in humans (132, 138,139).

Reducing Colorectal Cancer Mortality

The two basic approaches for reducing the incidence and mortality from industrially related cancers, in general, and colorectal cancers, in particular, are to reduce exposure to the causal agent(s) and to institute surveillance of exposed population groups to allow early diagnosis and treatment. Reducing exposure levels is the primary responsibility of industry and the Occupational Safety and Health Administration, with a scientific data base largely drawn from NIOSH. The clinical surveillance of industrially exposed population groups at high risk of colorectal cancer depends on available, inexpensive, and effective screening tests. Two large ongoing randomized clinical trials in Minnesota and New York have demonstrated that, in asymptomatic persons over the age of 50, routine screening for colorectal cancer with fecal occult blood testing facilitates early diagnosis and treatment and thus reduces mortality (1, 140, 141). However, fecal occult blood testing is an imperfect screening test since its specificity is only 95 percent, and its sensitivity for cancer is approximately 70 percent and for polyps approximately 20 percent (142).

The cost effectiveness of colorectal cancer screening among asbestos workers has been demonstrated by decision analysis (41). This study made the following assumptions: the RR for colorectal cancer was assumed to be between 1.56 and 3.0; the elevated RR was assumed to be present ten years after exposure; fecal occult blood testing was assumed to advance cancer diagnosis to a more favorable pathologic stage by 1.3 years; and colon cancer was assumed to take 2.5 years to develop from an early to an advanced stage (41). Cost estimates for fecal occult blood testing were $2 per test, $35 for sigmoidoscopy, and $500 to $6,000 for the evaluation of positive tests and subsequent treatment; estimates were discounted 6 percent per year and averted lost wages were calculated individually. It was then estimated that for asbestos workers exposed at the age of 25 and with an RR of 1.56 or 3.0, it would cost $361 or $117 per year of life saved, respectively, for annual fecal occult blood testing and sigmoidoscopy every five years when screening begins at age 35. For screening commencing at age 50, the cost per year of life saved would be $164 or less than $0 for a relative risk of 1.56 or 3.0, respectively; values less than $0 are obtained from discounting and from averting lost wages. Values are lower for higher relative risks due to the larger number of lives saved in the denominator of the cost effectiveness measure. Screening for colorectal cancer, even for those at moderately increased risk, is thus highly cost effective. However, since more than 30 percent of neoplasms are beyond the reach of a flexible sigmoidoscope and more than 70 percent are beyond the reach of a rigid sigmoidoscope (143), only colonoscopy, a more expensive and thorough test, would effectively screen for malignancy. Introducing colonoscopy into the decision analysis would increase the cost and effectiveness of screening and would make changes in cost effectiveness uncertain.

Conclusions

The recent and continuing increases in colorectal cancer incidence merit serious research attention. If even 10 percent of such cancers are linked to preventable occupational and environmental exposures, then at least 12,000 colorectal cancers per year are avoidable in the United States alone. While dietary and genetic factors may be important, they are much less amenable to control and manipulation and are likely to reflect the influence of controllable environmental exposures. Primary prevention strategies need to be developed to reduce the burden of this disease, secondary prevention strategies should be strengthened to enhance screening of populations at risk, and more research should be conducted to identify other environmental risk factors.

Clearly, for all populations with known or suspected exposure to industrial colorectal cancer risk factors, measures should be taken to reduce such exposures and to implement surveillance programs. Preventing cancer mortality from industrial exposures is likely to improve public health in a manner similar to that achieved by improved sanitation and working and housing conditions in the 19th century (36). The clinical and gastroenterological professions, as well as occupational and general population groups at risk, should be more aware of the importance of industrial causes of cancer in general, and of colorectal cancer in particular.

Chapter 18

INDUSTRIAL RISKS OF
BREAST CANCER

Breast cancer is a complex and heterogeneous group of malignancies that encompass distinct clinical entities, pathologies, and etiologies. Nevertheless, three major classes of overall risk factors for breast cancers have been and still are conventionally recognized. The first is a familial history of breast cancer, particularly early age at onset. The second is reproductive or "estrogen-window" factors: early menarche; nulliparity; late menopause; and exogenous hormones including prolonged use of oral contraceptives from an early age, injectable Depo-provera contraceptives, long-term postmenopausal estrogen replacement therapy, especially when combined with progestogens, and diethylstilbestrol (1–4). The third is a high-fat diet. However, as confirmed by a series of recent case control and cohort studies, evidence for the role of dietary fat per se is at best inconsistent and tenuous (2). The role of these risk factors in the aggregate has been incriminated in only 20 to 30 percent of all breast cancers (5, 6). Furthermore, they cannot account for the escalating incidence of breast cancer, particularly in postmenopausal women, in the United States and other major industrialized nations; incidence rates in white women in the United States from 1950 to 1989 increased by 53 percent, or by over 1 percent annually (7). These trends are real and, in large measure, cannot be explained away by the relatively recent large-scale use of mammography screening (8, 9). However, these trends are not unique as they are paralleled or even sharply exceeded by those for a wide range of other cancers (7, 8, 10).

Not one of the heavily funded U.S. and other nutritional studies on the relation between dietary fat and breast cancer has investigated, let alone even considered, the role of carcinogenic dietary contaminants (10) (see Chapter 4). However, it has been known since the late 1960s that carcinogenic organochlorine pesticides that concentrate in animal and human fat, such as aldrin, dieldrin, chlordane, and heptachlor, induce breast cancer in rodents (11–14). This creates the strong

Published in *International Journal of Health Services,* Volume 24, Number 1, 1994.

presumption for a causal role of such contaminants in human breast cancer, as the sites of cancer induced by carcinogens in experimental animals and humans are generally similar (15). Furthermore, DDT promotes breast cancer induced in male rodents by the unrelated carcinogen acetamidophenanthrene (16). The authors of the latter study concluded that: "Because of their fat-solubility and tendency toward long-term deposition in body fat, particularly in the female breast, and the apparent ability of DDT to promote tumors in the mammary gland of the male rat, such agents might be considered possible contributors to the high incidence of breast cancer among women."

Further evidence for the role of organochlorine carcinogens is provided by findings that DDT and polychlorinated biphenyls (PCBs) concentrate in human breast cancer itself in contrast to adjacent non-neoplastic tissue (17). These organochlorines also concentrate in breasts with cancer in contrast to those with fibrocystic disease (18). Additionally, the pesticide hexachlorocyclohexane concentrates in breasts with cancer in contrast to normal breasts (19). Other and unique supportive evidence comes from reports that, in spite of increasing fat consumption and decreasing parity, breast cancer mortality in premenopausal Israeli women declined by 30 percent following strong representations by this author (20) and subsequent regulations, opposed by the Israeli cancer establishment, reducing the high levels of hexachlorocyclohexane and DDT in dairy products (21). The mechanism of action of organochlorine carcinogens in relation to breast cancer probably involves their estrogenic properties, well known for decades, reflecting their potent induction of cytochrome P-450 mixed-function oxidases, stimulation of estrogen metabolism, and binding to human estrogen receptors (21); such properties reflect the recent belated recognition of these organochlorines as xeno-estrogens (22).

Atrazine, a carcinogenic chlorinated triazine, has been and still is one of the most heavily used herbicides in the world (23). In view of its mobility in soil and its aquatic stability, it is one of the commonest carcinogenic pollutants in European and U.S. surface waters, often exceeding the U.S. Health Advisory Level of 3 parts per billion. Atrazine exerts hormonal effects on the hypothalamic-pituitary-gonadal axis, with marked inhibition of 5-alpha steroid reductase, and induces breast and other reproductive tumors in rats (23). It has also been incriminated in human ovarian cancer and lymphohematopoietic malignancies (24). Nevertheless, the role of atrazine in human breast cancer has still not been investigated. Still also ignored is the role of other carcinogenic and estrogenic chlorinated pesticides such as endosulfan and the DDT-contaminated Dicofol.

Estrogens are another important class of dietary contaminants, resulting from their virtually unregulated use as growth-promoting feed additives for cattle, hogs, and poultry (25) (see Chapter 13). In view of the known carcinogenicity of exogenous estrogens, lifelong exposure to these contaminants is clearly a risk factor for breast cancer, as emphasized by Roy Hertz, the National Cancer

Institute's former leading authority on endocrine cancer (26). Furthermore, estrogens are known to synergize the carcinogenic effects of radiation of the breast (27, 28), thus possibly further increasing risks of mammography (10). Estrogens also synergize the carcinogenic effects in the breast of polynuclear hydrocarbon carcinogens (29). More recent concerns on estrogenic dietary contaminants are provided by findings of increased breast cancer risk among women with prenatal exposure to elevated estrogen levels (30). This also raises the possibility of similar effects of prenatal exposure to maternal residues of organochlorine carcinogens.

Proximity of residence to hazardous waste sites has been associated with major increased risks of breast and other cancers (31). Most recently, the high increase in breast cancer incidence and mortality in Connecticut and suburban New York counties, especially Nassau and Suffolk, has been associated with consumption of milk and water contaminated over the last two decades with nuclear fission products, the short-lived radioactive iodine and the long-lived bone-seeking strontium-90, from the Millstone and Indian Point civilian nuclear reactors (32). An additional environmental risk factor in Nassau and Suffolk Counties may reflect past exposure from extensive agricultural use of carcinogenic soil fumigant pesticides, the organochlorine dichloropropane and the highly potent organohalogens ethylene dibromide and dibromochloropropane, all of which induce breast cancer in rodents (33–37).

A variety of occupational exposures has been incriminated as risk factors for breast cancer. Excess incidence and mortality have been reported among women exposed to dioxin, the most potent known inducer of P-450 enzymes, in a German pesticide plant (38), among women exposed to petroleum products including chlorinated organic solvents (39), among professional chemists (40), and among hairdressers, as well as users of hair dyes (41).

Not surprising is the recent conclusion "that there has been no progress in preventing the disease," despite U.S. expenditure of over $1 billion on breast cancer over the last two decades (5). More surprising, however, is the persisting failure of the U.S. cancer establishment, the National Cancer Institute, and the American Cancer Society, to have recognized and investigated longstanding evidence on the role of a wide range of avoidable environmental and occupational risk factors for breast cancer besides for a wide range of other cancers (10) (see Chapter 4). Their recognition should result in the belated development of public health policies directed to primary prevention of breast and other cancers, and should also further reinforce recommendations for major reforms in the priorities and leadership of the cancer establishment (10).

PART IV

Epilogue

Why We Are Still Losing the
Winnable Cancer War

We have been losing the war on cancer for more than 30 years because we have been fighting with the wrong "generals" and wrong strategies.

The war has been, and still is, waged with the primary goal of "damage control"—screening, diagnosis, treatment, and related research. Cancer prevention, by reducing avoidable exposures to carcinogens in the totality of the environment, has been and remains a minimal priority.

Ever since President Nixon declared the 1971 "War on Cancer," its generals—at the federal National Cancer Institute (NCI), and at the world's wealthiest non-profit, the American Cancer Society (ACS)—have misled the nation. At first, they promised a cure in time for the nation's 1976 bicentennial. Then in 1984, and again in 1986, the NCI declared that cancer mortality would be halved by 2000. In 1998, the NCI and ACS trumpeted that the nation had "turned the corner" in the war. Then again in 2003, NCI's director made the incredible pledge to "eliminate the suffering and death from cancer by 2015" (has he been talking with God?). This pledge was shortly followed by a joint NCI and ACS claim that "considerable progress has been made in reducing the burden of cancer."

On June 3 last year, a joint NCI and ACS "Annual Report to the Nation on the Status of Cancer, 1975–2001" stated that "cancer incidence and death rates are on the decline from 1991–2001, due to progress in prevention, early detection, and treatment."

This report prompted a flurry of assuring headlines in national newspapers, such as "Cancer cases, death rates declining," by 7–8 percent from 1991–2001. However, these decreases are largely due to the reduction of lung cancer cases and deaths following decreased smoking by men and, to a lesser extent, women. Also, with few exceptions, the incidence rates of a wide range of non-smoking related cancers have continued to increase from 1991 to 2001, disturbingly the

Reprinted, with permission, from *The Humanist,* December 2004/January 2005.

285

latest available NCI data. (These rates are based on statistics which are adjusted for the aging population, see Table 1).

Confidence in the NCI and ACS latest claim of declining death rates was further shaken by NCI's admission, in a "Questions and Answers" release, of "statistical uncertainties related to changes in data collection." These included discrepancies between the claim that death rates "are on the decline from 1991–2001," in contrast to their previous annual report that "death rates were stabilizing." Even more to the point is the alarming fact that death rates have remained virtually unchanged since 1975.

Today, cancer strikes about 1.3 million annually; nearly one in two men and more than one in three women develop cancer in their lifetimes. This translates into approximately 56 percent more cancer in men, and 22 percent more cancer in women over the course of just one generation. Cancer has become a "disease of mass destruction."

These trends have developed over the last three decades during which NCI's annual budget has skyrocketed by about thirty-fold, from $220 million in 1972 to $4.6 billion in 2004, with over $6 billion requested for 2005. By one recent estimate, total public and private spending on cancer will amount to over $14 billion this year.

Paradoxically, it seems that the more money we spend fighting cancer, the more cancer we get. Certainly, major funding is essential for early detection, treatment, and related research. But much less money would be needed if more cancer was prevented, with less to treat.

Table 1

Incidence rates of non-smoking cancers

Cancer*	% change, 1975–2001	% change, 1991–2001
Melanoma	+137	+28
Liver	+100	+21
Kidney	+69	+13
Thyroid	+67	+48
Non-Hodgkin's lymphoma (female)	+63	+8
Brain (childhood)	+61	+6
Testes	+46	+6
Breast (post-menopausal)	+37	+4
Acute myeloid leukemia	+15	+18
Multiple myeloma	+8	−12
Colorectal	−13	−13

*Prostate cancer omitted because of diagnostic uncertainties relating to the PSA test.

John Conyers, the Michigan Democrat, and ranking minority member of the House Judiciary Committee, recently warned that "so much carnage is preventable. Preventable that is, if the NCI gets off the dime and does its job."

THE CANCER ESTABLISHMENT

The NCI is a federal agency funded by taxpayers, while the ACS is a private nonprofit "charity." In spite of their institutional independence, the NCI and ACS are locked at the hip. They are well dubbed the "cancer establishment" [see Chapter 1].

The ACS powerfully, and seemingly independently, reinforces NCI's strategies by well-orchestrated and aggressive PR directed to the public, media, and Congress. This PR is underwritten by the multi-billion dollar cancer drug industry ("Big Pharma"), and other industries that are major ACS donors, and public donations. In spite of its smaller size and budget, the ACS is the dominant partner in the cancer establishment—"the tail that wags the NCI dog."

The institutional relationship between the NCI and ACS is reinforced nationally at the rank and file level. About half of ACS board members are surgeons, radiologists, oncologists, and basic scientists. Most are interlocked with the NCI, particularly with regard to funding for treatment and related research. With the February 2002 appointment of ACS President-elect Andrew von Eschenbach as NCI Director, the relationship between ACS and the NCI has become further consolidated.

The Wrong Strategies

The cancer establishment's strategies are overwhelmingly imbalanced. They are fixated on damage control—screening, diagnosis, and treatment—and related research, to the virtual exclusion of prevention.

These strategies reflect professional mindsets in the cancer establishment's leadership, predominantly oncologists, surgeons, radiotherapists, and research scientists. Such biases are exacerbated by strong and pervasive conflicts of interest.

At the April 2004 annual meeting of the American Association of Cancer Research, Leland Hartwell, President of the Fred Hutchinson Cancer Research Center and 2001 Nobel Laureate, admitted that the emperor has no clothes. "Congress and the public are not paying [NCI] $4.7 billion a year just to learn about cancer [through basic research]. They are paying to cure the disease." Hartwell further stressed that most resources for cancer research are spent on "promoting ineffective drugs" for terminal disease.

Hartwell was not the first establishment figure to admit these facts. As reported by the AP on July 27, 2003, leading oncologists questioned whether cancer "will ever be reliably and predictably cured." They also admitted that the biotech industry's new magic bullet "targeted" drugs have turned out to be "as powerless as old-line chemotherapy," increasing survival by a few months, at best. In this connection, Memorial Sloan-Kettering's Leonard Saltz estimated that the price for new biotech drugs "has increased 500-fold in the last decade." Unchecked, these runaway costs could implode the entire health care system.

Hartwell also agreed with Clifton Leaf's *Fortune* (March 22, 2004) article, "Why We're Losing the War on Cancer," that cancer mortality rates have remained almost stable over the past five decades, during which there have been major reductions in mortality from heart disease and stroke.

Taken aback, NCI Director von Eschenbach responded with an irrelevant stump speech. "You are transforming the world. You are saving lives. God bless you for it, and God continue to bless you in your work."

In this connection, it should be stressed that the standard criterion for the success of drug treatment is based on the shrinkage of tumor size by over 50 percent within six months, regardless of whether the patient's life is prolonged. In fact, some "successful" treatments actually shorten survival due to drug toxicity, while successes, particularly with the recent targeted drugs are questionably based on brief increased survival in small trials.

When it comes to prevention, NCI and ACS strategies are fixated on faulty lifestyle, particularly smoking, to the virtual exclusion of a wide range of other avoidable causes of cancer. These include: pervasive environmental contamination of air, water, hazardous waste sites, and the workplace with carcinogenic industrial chemicals; contamination of food with carcinogenic pesticides; carcinogenic ingredients in cosmetics and toiletries, and household products; and carcinogenic prescription drugs, and high dose diagnostic radiation.

Arthur Andersen's silence regarding Enron's misconduct pales in comparison to the cancer establishment's silence regarding reckless misconduct by the petrochemical and other industries. The former has caused a financial meltdown, while the latter has resulted in the cancer epidemic.

In sharp contrast to inflationary expenditures on treatment, NCI's prevention budget has been and remains parsimonious. For instance, an unchallenged published analysis of its $2 billion 1992 budget revealed that less than 2.5 percent—not the 20 percent NCI had claimed—was earmarked for research on avoidable causes of cancer [see Chapter 4]. Furthermore, no funds were allocated to making any such information available to the public.

In 1998, the Wisconsin Democrat Congressman David Obey asked then-NCI Director Richard Klausner to back up his claim that 20 percent of NCI's $2.5 billion budget was allocated to research on environmental causes of cancer. Klausner simply increased his 20 percent figure to 40 percent without providing any supportive evidence.

NCI's frank misrepresentation of its prevention policies is further revealed in the "Highlights" of its 2001 *Cancer Facts*. The opening sentence states

"Cancer prevention is a major component and current priority—to reduce suffering and death from cancer."

Sometimes NCI's false claims and indifference to avoidable causes of cancer extend to outright denial. For example, it holds that the causes of childhood cancer are largely unknown, in spite of substantial contrary evidence. The ACS takes a similar position. In the childhood cancer section of its 2003 *Cancer Facts & Figures,* no mention is made of any avoidable causes (see Table 2).

Indifference and denial can extend even to the outright suppression of information. At a 1996 San Francisco "Town Hall Meeting" on breast cancer, chaired by Congresswoman Nancy Pelosi (a California Democrat, now the house minority leader), Klausner insisted that "low-level diagnostic radiation does not demonstrate an increased risk." Actually, NCI's long-term studies on patients with spinal curvature (scoliosis) showed that such radiation was responsible for 70 percent excess breast cancer mortality.

Table 2

Avoidable causes of childhood cancer

Environmental

- Proximity of residence to nuclear energy plants.
- Proximity of residence to petrochemical industries.
- Exposure to carcinogenic pesticides from agricultural and urban spraying, and uses in schools, including wood playground sets treated with chromated copper arsenate.
- Maternal or paternal exposures (pre-conception, conception, and post-conception) to occupational carcinogens.

Domestic

- Drinking and cooking water contaminated with carcinogenic pesticides or other industrial pollutants.
- Exposure to carcinogenic pesticides from uses in the home and garden, and pet flea collars.
- Contamination of infant and childhood food with carcinogenic pesticides.
- Nitrite preservatives in hot dogs (interacting with naturally occurring amines to form carcinogenic nitrosamines).
- Maternal or paternal carry home of occupational carcinogens.

Medical

- Maternal X-radiation during late pregnancy.
- Ionizing radiation for treatment of scalp ringworm or enlarged tonsils.
- High-dose diagnostic X-radiation, particularly computerized tomography scans.
- Prescription drugs during pregnancy, such as DES and Dilantin.
- Pediatric prescription drugs, such as Lindane shampoos and Ritalin.

Perhaps the most egregious violation of the public's right-to-know concerns the belated release in 1997 of decade-old data predicting up to 210,000 thyroid cancers from exposure to radioactive fallout, following atom bomb tests in Nevada in the 1950s. Had the public been warned in time, these cancers, whose incidence almost doubled since 1973, could have been readily prevented with thyroid medication. In a 1999 hearing, the Senate Committee on Governmental Affairs charged that the NCI investigation was "plagued by lack of public participation and openness," and that failure to "release this information (to the public) was a travesty."

As long as the NCI shirks its job of providing Congress and regulatory agencies with scientific evidence on avoidable causes of cancer, corrective legislative and regulatory action remains discouraged. Meanwhile, this silence also encourages petrochemical and other industries to continue manufacturing carcinogenic products, and corporate polluters to continue polluting unchallenged.

Responding to growing criticism of its policies, NCI now claims to allocate 12 percent of its budget to "prevention and control," and requires its nationwide Comprehensive Cancer Centers to have a "prevention component." However, prevention continues to be narrowly defined in exclusionary terms of faulty lifestyle, and screening, with no reference to environmental causes due to exposures to a wide range of industrial carcinogens.

NCI goes even further by defining environmental causes of cancer as those other than genetic in origin. Commenting on NCI's June 17, 2004, news release, "The Majority of Cancers are Linked to Environment," Dr. Aaron Blair, NCI's leading epidemiologist, explained that the term environment includes all causes of cancer, other than genetic. Blair thus claimed that environmental causes are predominantly smoking, diet, alcohol, and obesity, and that industrial pollutants of air, water, and the workplace account for 5 percent or less of all causes of cancer.

The ACS indifference to prevention extends to hostility, as reflected in a decades-long history of pro-industry bias, and even frank collusion [see Chapter 5]. Examples are legion. In 1978, the ACS protected auto industry interests by refusing to support the Clean Air Act. In 1992, the ACS supported the Chlorine Institute in defending the continued use of chlorinated pesticides, despite clear evidence of their carcinogenicity, persistence, and pervasive environmental contamination. In 1993, just before PBS aired a *Frontline* program warning of contamination of infant and children's food with carcinogenic pesticides, the ACS blanketed its 48 regional divisions and 3,000 local offices with false reassurances of safety crafted by the agribusiness industry.

In its 2003 *Cancer Facts & Figures,* the ACS reassured that carcinogenic exposures from dietary pesticides, "toxic wastes in dump sites," and radiation from "closely controlled" nuclear energy plants are all "at such low levels that risks are negligible."

The ACS pro-industry agenda is further exemplified by research on prevention. In spite of bloated contrary claims, less than 0.1 percent of its approximately $800 million budget has been assigned to "Environmental Carcinogenesis."

Conflicts of Interest

The cancer establishment generals are riddled with longstanding conflicts of interest [see Chapter 4]. A current case in point is the highly touted "anti-cancer" nutritional supplement, PC-SPES.

PC-SPES (PC for prostate cancer, and SPES, Latin for hope) has been widely sold by International Medical Research (IMR) to prostate cancer patients, and also to healthy men, to maintain "good prostrate health without any adverse reaction." However, PC-SPES is illegally laced with prescription drugs, including the potent carcinogen DES (diethylstilbestrol, a synthetic estrogen). Aside from the lack of any evidence of benefits, symptoms and prostate-specific antigen (PSA) levels in cancer patients are likely to have been dangerously masked by DES in the supplement.

In February 2004, more than 20 personal injury suits, filed in Los Angeles County Superior Court, alleged that IMR Directors, Richard Klausner, and Michael Milken, securities felon-turned philanthropist and founder and chairman of the Prostate Cancer Foundation, systematically promoted PC-SPES. Other IMR directors include leading oncologists, and scientists in NCI's some 20 nationwide Comprehensive Cancer Centers.

Conflicts of interest of the PC-SPES type are not just matters of personal wrongdoing. The conflicts are deeply rooted in NCI's institutional structure. Founded in 1937, and incorporated into the National Institutes of Health (NIH) in 1941, the NCI was divorced from the NIH by the 1971 National Cancer Act. Far beyond a mere shuffling of bureaucratic boxes, this action in effect politicized the NCI, and effectively insulated it from the scientific and public health communities. The NCI director reports to the President through the Office of Management and Budget, bypassing the NIH, and the Department of Health and Human Services.

President Nixon created a three-member NCI executive President's Cancer Panel, naming as its first chairman Benno C. Schmidt, an investment banker, and senior drug-company executive with close ties to the oil, steel, and chemical industries. Schmidt's successor in the 1980s was Armand Hammer, the late chairman of Occidental Petroleum, one of the nation's largest manufacturers of industrial chemicals, involved in the Love Canal disaster. Not surprisingly, Schmidt and Hammer showed no interest in cancer prevention. Instead, they focused on the highly profitable development and marketing of cancer drugs.

The NCI's prototype Comprehensive Cancer Center, Memorial Sloan-Kettering, jointly funded by the ACS, represents another example of entrenched conflicts of interest. An analysis of the Center's Board revealed the predominant representation of cancer drug industries, and close affiliations with oil and petro-chemical industries [see Chapter 4, Table 3].

Dr. Samuel Broder, NCI director from 1989 to 1995, admitted the obvious in a 1988 *Washington Post* interview: "The NCI has become what amounts to a government pharmaceutical company." Broder left NCI to take executive posts at IVAX and Celera Genomics, two major manufacturers of cancer drugs.

This revolving door between NCI and industry, particularly industries indifferent or hostile to cancer prevention, has been and remains commonplace. The late Dr. Frank Rauscher, appointed NCI Director by President Nixon to spearhead his cancer war, resigned in 1976 to become ACS Senior Vice President for research. He then moved to become Executive Director of the Thermal Insulation Manufacturers Association, which promoted the unregulated use of carcinogenic fiberglass.

Dr. Richard Adamson, NCI's former director of Research and Policy on Cancer Causation, left NCI in 1994 to head the National Soft Drinks Association, which vigorously promoted the use of artificial sweeteners, particularly the carcinogenic saccharin.

In a CNBC program (June 30, 2003), "Titans of Cancer" hosted by Maria Bartiromo, four cancer "titans" enthused about alleged breakthroughs in treatment with targeted biotech drugs, while ignoring cancer prevention. Included on the program was Dr. Harold Varmus, President of Memorial Sloan-Kettering Cancer Center, and past recipient of major NCI research grants. In 1995, Varmus, then NIH Director, struck the "reasonable pricing clause," protecting against gross industry profiteering from cancer and other drugs developed with taxpayer dollars. Varmus's action also gave senior NCI and NIH staff free license to consult with the drug industry. Another "titan" was Dr. John Mendelsohn, President of NCI's University of Texas M.D. Anderson Comprehensive Cancer Center, embroiled in conflicts of interest over ImClone's targeted drug Erbitux.

Following the *Los Angeles Times* series of revelations on extensive private consulting by senior NCI scientists, some of whom have earned as much as $300,000 or more since 1995, the House Energy and Commerce Committee, and the Senate Appropriations Subcommittee convened hearings last December and January. An illustrative case was that of Dr. Jeffrey Schlom, head of NCI's Laboratory of Tumor Immunology and Biology since 1982. Schlom built himself another substantial career as consultant on Taxol to Cytoclonal Pharmaceutics, and on colorectal and prostate cancer vaccines to Jenner Biotherapie.

Meanwhile, further conflicts of interest hearings, and a General Accounting Office investigation are pending. Former NCI director Dr. Klausner, now Director of Global Health Programs of the Bill and Melinda Gates Foundation, remains under Congressional investigation for violating ethics rules. Allegedly, he accepted "Lecture Awards" from NCI's Comprehensive Cancer Centers while serving as NCI director more than two years ago. Congress is also investigating Klausner's questionable travel arrangements and business connections.

For all that, the NCI's conflicts of interest are dwarfed by those of the ACS. ACS openly trumpets its financial ties to Big Pharma, and polluting industries. So-called "Excalibur" donors, each contribute more than $100,000 annually. These include drug and biotech companies, such as Bristol-Myers Squibb, Pfizer, AstraZeneca, Eli Lilly, Amgen, Genentech, and Johnson & Johnson. Among polluting industries are more than 10 major petrochemical and oil companies, such as DuPont, Akzo Nobel, Pennzoil, British Petroleum, and Concho Oil.

A total of some 300 other industries and companies make similar contributions to the annual ACS budget of about $800 million, not counting government grants, or income from about $1 billion reserves. ACS returns these favors with more than a wink and a nod. Rarely does a non-profit organization flack for private industry. That the American Heart Association would ever advocate low tar cigarettes is unthinkable. But the ACS is doing something approaching that while escaping public notice. Not surprisingly, a report (January 28, 1992) in *The Chronicle of Philanthropy,* the nation's leading charity watchdog, has charged that "The ACS is more interested in accumulating wealth than saving lives."

Privatizing the War

The most disturbing development in the cancer war has been its privatization by ACS and NCI generals. In 1998, the ACS created and funded the National Dialogue on Cancer (NDC), co-chaired by former President George Bush and Barbara Bush [see Chapter 7]. Members included cancer survivor groups, some 100 representatives of the cancer drug industry, and Shandwick International PR. Dr. John Durant, executive president of the American Cancer Society for Clinical Oncology, charged that the hidden purpose of ACS was "protecting their own fund raising capacity . . . from competition from survivor groups. It has always seemed to me that this was an issue of control by the ACS over the cancer agenda."

Without informing the NDC, the ACS then spun off a small legislative committee. Its explicit aim was to increase NCI's autonomy and budget, and shift major control of cancer policy to the ACS—from the public purse to private hands. Shandwick International played a key role in managing the NDC, and drafting the proposed legislation.

When news surfaced that R. J. Reynolds Tobacco Holdings was one of Shandwick's major clients, ACS claimed prior ignorance and fired Shandwick. Astoundingly, ACS next hired Edelman Public Relations Worldwide, another well-known tobacco PR firm, to conduct a voter cancer education campaign for the 2000 presidential election.

Ever since von Eschenbach was appointed NCI Director, the National Cancer Program has been effectively privatized. Von Eschenbach obtained President George W. Bush's agreement to continue as vice-chairman of NDC, of which he was a main founder. NDC since has been spun off as a non-profit organization, and renamed C-Change. The group then again hired Edelman as its PR firm, following Edelman's signed pledge that it would sever its relations with the tobacco industry. Edelman represents the Brown & Williamson Tobacco Co., and the Altria Group, the parent company of Philip Morris, the largest cigarette maker in the U.S. Edelman's clients also include Kraft and other fast food and beverage companies, now targeted by anti-obesity litigation.

In July 2003, it was discovered that Edelman, in violation of its pledge, was continuing to fight tobacco control programs from its Malaysian offices. Edelman executives apologized for this "oversight," and agreed once more to terminate its support of the tobacco industry, and promised to donate this income to charity.

Commenting on the ACS and NDC relationship with Edelman, Dr. Stanton Glantz, the prominent anti-smoking activist, commented, "It's like . . . Bush hiring Al Qaeda to do PR, because they have good connections to Al-Jazeera."

Equally disturbing is the growing and secretive collaboration between the NCI and the C-Change organization. The latest example is the joint planning of a massive national tumor tissue bank for cancer drug and genetic research. According to the Washington insider *Cancer Letter,* this would cost up to $1.2 billion to operate, apart from construction costs in the billions. This initiative would be privatized, ripe with conflicts of interest, and exempt from the public scrutiny required by the Federal Advisory Committee and Freedom on Information Acts.

Behind the scenes, strong support for privatization of the cancer war comes from Michael Milken. As noted in the *Cancer Letter,* "Milken is the single most influential player in cancer politics within the last decade."

HOW TO WIN THE LOSING WAR

After all this time, we do not need another 30 years of research on cellular mechanisms of cancer and treatment, or more billions of dollars spent on illusory wonder drugs to start winning the war. The war must be fought with the right generals and right strategies. This goal should be supported by an array of interlocking initiatives.

The NCI: For over three decades, NCI generals have violated the mandates of The 1971 National Cancer Act, and its amendments, to "disseminate cancer information to the public," and to call for "an expanded and intensified research program for the prevention of cancer caused by occupational and environmental exposures to carcinogens."

The highest priority should be directed to the need for drastic changes in the NCI high command. Generals responsible for prevention should be given at least the same authority as generals responsible for damage control. Responsibility for prevention also should be extended to the 20-member National Cancer Advisory Board, as the Cancer Act requires, and to presidents of NCI's Comprehensive Cancer Centers.

NCI's generals, senior staff, and Cancer Centers presidents involved in illegal activities, or incriminated in flagrant conflicts of interest with the cancer drug industries, should resign or face dismissal.

The ACS: The public and media should be fully informed of the hostile ACS record on cancer prevention, other than the dangers of an unhealthy lifestyle. They should also be explicitly informed of flagrant conflicts of interest with the cancer drug, petrochemical, and other industries, as well as close linkage with the tobacco industry. Armed with this information, the public would then be in a position to decide whether to continue giving funds to this "charity," or to donate instead to individuals, groups, and organizations with strong scientific and public health policy concerns on cancer prevention.

Developing Grass-Roots National Support: Cancer impacts on virtually every family in the nation. Still, the epidemic is likely to be met with passivity or even denial unless citizens are provided with practical information on how to reduce their own risks. The most realistic strategy for developing broad public support for cancer prevention will stress self-interest rather than abstractions or ideology. Preventing smoking, particularly prior to addiction in adolescence, is obviously important. Much less well-recognized, though, is the critical need for user-friendly information on avoidable causes of a wide spectrum of non-smoking cancers whose incidence has escalated dramatically over recent decades.

The public's right-to-know of avoidable causes of cancer is the fundamental basis for building a national grass-roots coalition. The continuing failure of the NCI and ACS to provide the public, Congress, and regulatory agencies with such information is a flagrant denial of this right. The right can be restored by empowering consumers, citizens, workers, and patients.

Consumers have the right to information and explicit label warnings on carcinogenic ingredients and contaminants in their food, cosmetics and toiletries, and household products. Consumers then would be empowered to boycott mainstream companies selling unsafe products, and reward smaller, "green" companies marketing safe alternatives. With increasing demand for the latter, economies of scale will reduce their higher prices.

Citizens have increasing opportunities for empowerment on an individual and community basis. By plugging in their zip code into the Environmental Defense Scorecard (www.scorecard.org), citizens can obtain basic information on toxic and carcinogenic pollutants to which they are exposed by local chemical industries, and power plants. They can then organize, alert the media, and join with environmental groups to express their concerns to local and state health authorities, including state governors. Regardless of their politics, governors are generally sensitive to citizen lobbies in their states.

Workers are at particularly high risk for cancers because of longstanding exposures to a wide range of occupational carcinogens. Workers can act to reduce such exposures, individually, and through their unions and health and safety committees, once empowered by knowledge of the risks.

Patients should be advised to exercise their right-to-know by requesting full information on cancer and other risks of prescription drugs, as detailed in the "Precautions" section of the *Physicians Desk Reference* (PDR). For the wide range of common prescription drugs carrying cancer risks, safe alternatives may be requested in accordance with legal, besides ethical, requirements for informed consent. Patients should also be made aware of the carcinogenic risks of high-dose X-ray procedures, particularly pediatric CT scans, and fluoroscopy. Patients should then seek those (still few) informed radiologists and clinics practicing dose-reduction techniques, and also request dosage records for each examination.

Publicizing the Failure of the Cancer War: An aggressive critique of the cancer generals and their unwinnable strategies is well overdue. For decades, the mainstream media have mostly ignored the failed cancer policies and conflicts of interest of the cancer establishment. Activist citizen groups could generate a mounting series of reports, initially in smaller independent newspapers and radio stations nationwide, focusing on hot button topics—local or regional exposures to environmental carcinogens; "cancer clusters" in the vicinity of petrochemical and nuclear power plants; and escalating rates of cancers in children and retirees, and the known or suspect causes of such cancers.

Key to such media activities should be emphasis on the escalating rates of non-smoking cancers, along with the cancer establishment's refusal to prioritize the overdue need to reduce exposures to environmental carcinogens, and to recognize the public's right-to-know about these avoidable exposures. It might be argued that regulatory agencies, or industry itself, should be primary targets for media attention. However, considering the multibillion-dollar cancer establishment's responsibility for and control of basic information about cancer prevention, primary emphasis should be directed at exposing the establishment's non-information or, worse, willful misinformation.

Legislative Initiatives: In view of NCI's exaggerated and inconsistent claims for its prevention budget, Illinois Democrat Congresswoman Jan Schakowsky recently asked the General Accounting Office to investigate NCI's "fight against cancer." Specifically, she requested information on the dollar amounts spent on "funding for research on prevention" and "funding for outreach" to disseminate this information.

Meanwhile, Congress is investigating conflicts of interest by NCI generals and scientists with particular reference to consulting with drug industries. This should be extended, by an order of magnitude, to NCI's institutional conflicts with the multi-billion dollar Big Pharma.

Responding to Congressional concerns about NCI policies, the National Academy of Sciences (NAS) recently examined NCI's relationship with the NIH. In July 2003, the NAS reported that NCI's "special status" of independence from 26 other NIH bodies was problematic. It created "an unnecessary rift" between "the goals, mission and leadership of the NIH and those of NCI." In a startling statement, that drew minimal media attention, the NAS emphasized "Perhaps more important is the fact that the National Cancer Act has had little discernible effect on scientific and clinical progress for the diagnosis, treatment or prevention of cancer."

The NAS report makes it clear that NCI should be folded back into the NIH and integrated with the scientific community once again. But that is only the start of drastic needed reforms. Funding for cancer prevention should equal that of all other programs combined [see Chapter 2A]. Congress should direct the NCI to provide the public with all available information on avoidable and unknowing exposures to carcinogens in consumer products, prescription drugs, the workplace, and environment.

Legislative initiatives should also be developed at the state and local levels. Since the 2002 midterm elections, Congress remains divided and grid locked, and will remain even more so now. Accordingly, leadership and innovative policies on domestic agendas is likely to shift further from the national to state, county, and city levels.

The Bottom Line: Citizens, the media, and Congress must belatedly recognize that, well after three decades and spending over $50 billion, we are now further away from winning this war than when it was first declared.

Citizens, the media, and Congress must also belatedly recognize that the cancer epidemic can still be arrested and reversed. This goal will never be achieved until we recruit new generals and develop new strategies making prevention at least as urgent as damage control.

APPENDIX
Endorsers of Proposals for Cancer Policy Reform

The proposals for reforms in cancer policy made in this book have been endorsed by independent cancer prevention and public health scientists, activist groups, and nongovernmental organizations. Endorsers (in addition to the chapter authors) listed at the time of publication in the *International Journal of Health Services* for Chapters 2, 7, and 14 are given below. Endorsers of the strategies for cancer prevention outlined in Chapter 8 are available at www.preventcancer.com.

Chapter 2A

Endorsers as of mid-1992:

Jerrold L. Abraham, M.D., Department of Pathology, College of Medicine, SUNY, Syracuse

Dean Abrahamson, M.D., Ph.D., Professor of Public Affairs, University of Minnesota

Nicholas A. Ashford, Ph.D., J.D., Professor of Technology and Policy, MIT, Cambridge, Mass.

Dr. Louis S. Beliczky, United Rubber, Cork, Linoleum and Plastic Workers of America, Ohio

Rosalie Bertell, Ph.D., International Institute of Concern for Public Health, Toronto

Eula Bingham, Ph.D., Emeritus Professor Environmental Health, University of Cincinnati Medical Center, Ohio, and former Assistant Secretary of Labor, Occupational Safety and Health Administration

Elizabeth A. Bourque, Ph.D., Boston

Irwin Bross, President Biomedical Metatechnology Buffalo, and Director Biostatistics, Roswell Park Memorial Institute

Bryan O. Budholz, Ph.D., Department of Work Environment, University of Lowell, Mass.

Walter Burnstein, D.O., President, Food & Water, Inc., New York

Leopoldo E. Caltagirone, Ph.D., Chairman, Division of Biological Control, University of California, Berkeley

Barry Castleman, Ph.D., Environmental Consultant, Baltimore

Richard Clapp, Ph.D., Director, JSI Center for Environmental Studies, Boston

Shirley Conibear, M.D., Carnow, Conibear & Assoc., Chicago

Paul Connett, Ph.D., Professor of Chemistry, St. Lawrence University, Canton, N.Y.

Donald L. Dahlsten, Division of Biological Control, University of California, Berkeley

Susan Daum, M.D., Consultant in Occupational Medicine, Mt. Sinai Medical Center, New York

Brian Dolan, M.D., M.P.H., Consultant in Preventive and Occupational Medicine, Santa Monica, Calif.

Ellen A. Eisen, M.D., Professor of Work Environment, University of Lowell, Mass.

Michael Ellenbecker, Ph.D., Professor of Work Environment, University of Lowell, Mass.

Emanuel Farber, M.D., Chairman, Department of Pathology, University of Toronto

Arthur L. Frank, M.D., Ph.D., Department of Preventive Medicine, University of Kentucky College of Medicine

Richard Garcia, Ph.D., Professor of Entomology, University of California, Berkeley

Michael R. Gray, M.D., M.P.H., Chief of Staff, Benson Hospital, Benson, Ariz.

Ruth Hubbard, Ph.D., Harvard University, Cambridge, Mass.

David Kriebel, Sc.D., Professor of Work Environment, University of Lowell, Mass.

Marc Lappe, Ph.D., Professor of Health Policy and Ethics, University of Illinois College of Medicine

Marvin S., Legator, Ph.D., Professor of Preventive Medicine, University of Texas, Galveston

Stephen U. Lester, M.S., M.P.H., Falls Church, Va.

Charles Levenstein, Professor of Work Environment, University of Lowell, Mass.

Edward Lichter, M.D., Professor of Preventive Medicine, University of Illinois College of Medicine

Thomas Mancuso, M.D., Emeritus Professor of Occupational Medicine, University of Pittsburgh

Sheldon Margen, M.D., Professor of Public Health, University of California, Berkeley

Anthony Mazzocchi, Oil, Chemical & Atomic Workers Union, Denver

Myron A. Mehlman, M.D., R. W. Johnson Medical School, Piscataway, N.J.

Franklin E. Mirer, Ph.D., Health and Safety Department, International United Auto Workers, Detroit

Rafael Moure, Ph.D., Professor of Work Environment, University of Lowell, Mass.

Vicente Navarro, M.D., Professor of Health Policy and Management, Johns Hopkins University, Baltimore

Herbert Needleman, M.D., Professor of Psychiatry and Pediatrics, University of Pittsburgh

B. Paigen, Ph.D., Consultant Toxicologist, The Jackson Laboratories, Bar Harbor, Me.

Richard Piccioni, Ph.D., Senior Staff Scientist, Food & Water, Inc., Seattle, Wash.

Michael J. Plewa, Ph.D., Institute for Environmental Studies, University of Illinois, Urbana

Laura Punnett, Sc.D., Professor of Work Environment, University of Lowell, Mass.

David Rall, Former Assistant Surgeon General, and Director of The National Institute of Environmental Health Sciences

Melvin Reuber, M.D., Consultant in Carcinogenesis and Toxicology, Baltimore

Knut Ringen, M.D., Laborer's Health and Safety Fund of North America, Washington, D.C.

Anthony Robbins, M.D., Professor of Public Health, Boston University School of Medicine (Past Director, National Institute for Occupational Safety and Health)

Kenneth Rosenman, M.D., Professor of Medicine, Michigan State University, East Lansing

D. J. R. Sarma, M.D., Department of Pathology, University of Toronto

Arnold Schecter, M.D., Professor of Preventive Medicine, SUNY Health Science Center–Syracuse, Binghampton, N.Y.

Ruth Shearer, Ph.D., Consultant Toxicologist, Issaquah, Wash.

Janette D. Sherman, M.D., Consultant in Internal Medicine and Toxicology, Alexandria, Va.

Victor W. Sidel, M.D., Professor of Epidemiology and Social Medicine, Montefiore Medical Center, New York

Joseph H. Skom, M.D., Professor of Clinical Medicine, Northwestern University Medical School, Chicago

Noel Sommer, Ph.D., Professor of Environmental Science, University of California, Davis

Theodore D. Sterling, Ph.D., Professor, School of Computing Science, Simon Fraser University, Burnaby, Canada

Alice Stewart, M.D., President, Childhood Cancer Research, Boston

Joel Swartz, Ph.D., Consultant in Epidemiology, Emeryville, Calif.

David Teitelbaum, M.D., Professor of Preventive Medicine, University of Colorado, Denver

Vijayalaxmi, Ph.D., Research Geneticist, Research Triangle Park, N.C.

George Wald, Ph.D., Nobel Laureate, Harvard University. Cambridge, Mass.

Bailus Walker, Ph.D., Dean, College of Public Health, University of Oklahoma, Oklahoma City (Past Commissioner of Health, Commonwealth of Massachusetts)

David H. Wegman, M.D., Professor of Work Environment, University of Lowell, Mass.

Susan Woskie, Ph.D., Professor of Work Environment, University of Lowell, Mass.

Charles F. Wurster, M.D., Professor of Environmental Toxicology, Marine Sciences Research Center, SUNY at Stony Brook, N.Y.

Arthur C. Zahalsky, Professor of Immunology, Southern Illinois University, Edwardsville

Grace Ziem, M.D., Dr. P.H., Consultant in Occupational Medicine, Baltimore

Chapter 7

Endorsers as of mid-2002:

Margie Aliprandi, National Director, Cancer Prevention Coalition Offices, Salt Lake City, Utah

Winfield J. Abbe, Ph.D., Cancer Prevention Activist, Athens, Ga.

Nicholas Ashford, Professor Technology and Policy, Massachusetts Institute of Technology

Kenny Ausubel, President, Bioneers, and Collective Heritage Institute, Santa Fe, N.M.

Barry Castleman, Environmental Consultant

Rosalie Bertell, Ph.D., President, International Institute of Concern for Public Health, Toronto

Brent Blackwelder, President Friends of the Earth, Washington, D.C.

Judy Brady, Greenaction, and Toxic Links Coalition, San Francisco

James Brophy, Adjunct Lecturer, University of Windsor, Ontario

Irwin Bross, Ph.D., President, Biomedical Metatechnology, Inc., Buffalo, N.Y. (former Director, Biostatistics, Roswell Park Memorial Institute, Buffalo)

Chris Busby, Ph.D., M.R.S.C., Scientific Secretary, European Committee on Radiation Risks; Member, U.K. Government Committee on Radiation Risk for Internal Emitters, and U.K. Ministry of Defense Oversight Committee on Depleted Uranium

302 / Cancer-Gate

Leopoldo Caltagirone, Ph.D., Chair, Division of Biological Control, Berkeley, Calif.

Liane Casten, Publisher, Chicago Media Watch, Chicago

Richard Clapp, Ph.D., Professor of Public Health, Boston University School of Public Health, Boston; Member, Governing Board (Massachusetts) Alliance for a Healthy Tomorrow

Gary Cohen, Executive Director Environmental Health Fund, and Health Care Without Harm, Jamaica Plain, Mass.

Paul Connett, Ph.D., Professor of Chemistry, St. Lawrence University, New York; President, Fluoride Action Network

Joe Crozier, Environmental Activist, Mississauga, Ontario

Donald Dahlsten, Ph.D., Professor of Entomology, University of California, Berkeley

Alexandra Delinick, M.D., Past General Secretary, International Medical Homeopathic League

Tewolde Egziabher, General Manager, Environmental Protection Authority, Federal Democratic Republic of Ethiopia, Addis Ababa

Lynn Ehrle, M.Ed., Senior Research Fellow, Cancer Prevention Coalition, Chicago; Vice President, Cancer Alliance of Michigan

Anwar Fazal, Chair, World Alliance for Breastfeeding Action; Senior Regional Advisor, Urban Governance Initiative and United Nations Development Programme, Kuala Lumpur, Malaysia; Right Livelihood Award Laureate; Former President, International Organization of Consumers Unions

Dr. Juan Garcés, Activist Lawyer and Political Scientist; Right Livelihood Award Laureate; Former Political Advisor to President Salvador Allende of Chile

Ken Geiser, Ph.D., Professor of Work Environment, and Director, Lowell Center for Sustainable Production, University of Massachusetts, Lowell

Fernanda Giannasi, Coordinator, Virtual Citizen Ban Asbestos Network for Latin America, Brazil

Edward Golosmith, Publisher, *The Ecologist,* London.

Jay Gould, Ph.D., Founder, Radiation and Public Health Project, New York

Claus Hancke, M.D., Director, Institute for Orthomolecular Medicine, Lyngby, Denmark

Lennart Hardell, M.D., Ph.D., Professor of Epidemiology, University Hospital, Umea, Sweden

David A. Hircock, B. Pharm., Environmental Activists, Chester Springs, Pa.

Mae-Wan Ho, Ph.D., Director, Institute for Science in Society, London; Consultant, Third World Network

James Huff, Ph.D., National Institute of Environmental Health Sciences, Research Triangle Park, N.C.

Mohamed Idris, Chair, Consumers' Association, Penang, Malaysia; Co-director, Third World Network, Penang; Right Livelihood Award Laureate

Olle Johansson, M.D., Professor, Department of Neuroscience, Karolinska Institute, Stockholm

T. K. Joshi, M.B.B.S., M.S., M.Sc., Project Director, Health and Family Welfare, Delhi Government; National Consultant to the World Health Organization

Margaret Keith, Adjunct Lecturer, University of Windsor, Ontario

Marc Lappé, Ph.D., Director, Center for Ethics and Toxic Substances, Gualala, Calif.

Lynn Lawson, Chair, MCS (Multiple Chemical Sensitivity): Health and Environment, Chicago

Marvin Legator, Ph.D., Professor of Preventive Medicine, University of Texas, Galveston

Rodney Leonard, Director, Community Nutrition Institute, Washington, D.C.

Charles Levenstein, Ph.D., Professor of Work Environment, University of Massachusetts, Lowell; Editor, *New Solutions: Journal of Occupational and Environmental Health Policy*

William Lijinsky, Ph.D., Former Director, Chemical Carcinogenesis, Frederick Cancer Research Center, Frederick, Md.

Alison Linnecar, Coordinator, International Baby Food Action Network (IBFAN-GIFA); Right Livelihood Award Laureate

Helen Lynn, Health Coordinator, Women's Environmental Network, London

Elizabeth May, Director, Sierra Club of Canada, Ottawa

Anthony Mazzocchi, founder of the Labor Party, and Director of the Debs-Jones-Douglass Labor Institute

Yalem Mekonnen, M.D., Professor of Human Physiology, Addis Ababa University, Ethiopia

Gail Merrill, Environmental Activist, New Canaan, Conn.

Vicki Meyer, Ph.D., Faculty, Women's Health, DePaul University, Chicago; Founder, International Organization to Reclaim Menopause

Franklin Mirer, Ph.D., Director, Health and Safety, International United Auto Workers, Detroit

Vicente Navarro, M.D., Professor of Health and Public Policy, The Johns Hopkins University, Baltimore; Professor of Political and Social Sciences, Universitat Pompeu Fabra, Spain; Editor-in-Chief, *International Journal of Health Services*

Elizabeth O'Nan, Director, Protect All Children's Environment, Marion, N.C.

Peter Orris, M.D., M.P.H., Professor of Occupational Medicine, University of Illinois Medical School, Chicago; Professor of Internal and Preventive Medicine, Rush Medical College, Chicago; Professor of Preventive Medicine, Northwestern University Feinberg School of Medicine, Chicago

Horst Martin Rechelbacher, Environmental Activist; President, Horst Martin Rechelbacher Foundation; Founder, Aveda Corporation, Osceola, Wis.

Peter Rosset, Ph.D., Co-director, Food First/Institute for Food and Development Policy, Oakland, Calif.; Right Livelihood Award Laureate

Marjorie Roswell, Environmental Activist, Baltimore, Md.

Robert Sass, Ph.D., Professor of Occupational Health and Safety, University of Saskatchewan, Saskatoon, Canada; Former Director, Occupational Health and Safety, Saskatoon

Ruth Shearer, Ph.D., Consultant Toxicologist, Issaquah, Wash.

Janette Sherman, M.D., Consultant Toxicologist, Alexandria, Va.; Research Associate, Radiation and Public Health Project, New York

John Spratt, M.D., Professor of Surgery, James Graham Brown Breast Cancer Center, University of Louisville, Louisville, Ky.

Diane Takvorian, Executive Director, Environmental Health Coalition, San Diego, Calif.

Milton Terris, M.D., M.P.H., Editor, *Journal of Public Health Policy*; Past President, American Public Health Association

Lorenzo Tomatis, M.D., Collegium Ramazzini, Trieste, Italy; Past Director, International Agency for Research on Cancer, World Health Organization; National Institute of Environmental Health Sciences, Research Triangle Park, N.C.

Stephen Tvedten, T.I.P.M., C.E.I., Director, Institute of Pest Management, Inc., Marne, Mich.

Jakob von Uexkull, President, Right Livelihood Award Foundation, Stockholm

Quentin D. Young, Chairman, Health and Medicine Policy Research Group, Chicago, and Past President the American Public Health Association

Barbara Wilkie, Environmental Health Network of California, Larkspur

George M. Woodwell, Ph.D., Director, Woods Hole Research Center, Woods Hole, Mass.

Chapter 14

Endorsers as of late 2000:

Robert Alvarez, former Senior Policy Advisor to the U.S. Secretary of Energy; Executive Director, the STAR Foundation

Kenny Ausubel, Collective Heritage Institute/Bioneers, San Mateo, Santa Fe, N.M.

Dr. Neal Barnard, President, Physicians Committee for Responsible Medicine, Washington, D.C.

Tewolde Berhan and Sue Edwards, Institute of Sustainable Development, Addis Ababa, Ethiopia

Dr. Rosalie Bertell, International Institute of Concern for Public Health, Toronto, Canada

Barbara Brenner, J.D., Executive Director, Breast Cancer Action, San Francisco, Calif.

Dr. Barry Castleman, Environmental Consultant, Baltimore, Md.

Vera Chaney, Green Network, Leyden, Colchester, U.K.

Citizens Concerns, U.S.A.

Ronnie Cummins, National Director, Organic Consumers Association, Little Marais, Minn.

Dr. Donald Dahlsten, Professor and Associate Dean, University of California, Berkeley, Calif.

Dr. Robert Elder, Senior Microbiologist, Neogen Co., Lansing, Mich.; former Senior Scientist, Agricultural Research Service, U.S. Department of Agriculture

Dr. John Gofman, Emeritus Professor, Molecular and Radiation Biology, University of California, Berkeley, Calif.

Edward Goldsmith, M.A., Publisher and Editor, *The Ecologist,* London, U.K.

Dr. Jay M. Gould, Director, Radiation and Public Health Project, U.S.A.

Randall Hayes, President, Rainforest Action Network, U.S.A.

Luc Hens, M.D., Professor, Department of Human Ecology, Brussels Free University, Belgium

Dr. Mae-Wan Ho, Director, Institute of Science in Society, The Open University, Milton Keynes, U.K.

Jeffrey A. Hollender, President, Seventh Generation, Burlington, Vt.

Dr. Vyvyan Howard, Professor of Pathology, University of Liverpool, U.K.

S. M. Mohamed Idris, President, Consumers' Association of Penang, Sahabat Alam Malaysia (Friends of the Earth Malaysia) and Institute Masyarakat Berhad, Penang, Malaysia

Martin Khor, Director, Third World Network, Penang, Malaysia

Dr. David Kriebel, Professor of Epidemiology, University of Massachusetts, Lowell, Mass.

Lynn Landes, Founder and Director, Zero Waste America, Yardley, Pa.

Dr. Marvin Legator, Professor of Preventive Medicine, University of Texas, Galveston, Tex.

Rabbi Michael Lerner, Ph.D., Editor, Tikkun Magazine, San Francisco, Calif.

Dr. E. Lichter, Professor of Community Medicine, University of Illinois Medical School, Chicago, Ill.

Dr. William Lijinsky, former Director, Chemical Carcinogenesis, Frederick Cancer Research Center, Md.

Dr. Donald Louria, Chairman, Department of Preventive Medicine, New Jersey Medical School, Newark, N.J.

Dr. Sheldon Margen, Emeritus Professor of Public Health Nutrition. University of California, Berkeley, Calif.; Chairman, Berkeley Wellness Letter

George Monbiot, Health and Science Columnist, *The Guardian,* London, U.K.

Raymond Monbiot, Fellow of the Marketing Society, London, U.K.

Dr. Vicente Navarro, Professor of Health and Public Policy, The Johns Hopkins University, Baltimore, Md.; Professor of Political and Social Sciences, Universitat Pompeu Fabra, Spain

Dr. Herbert L. Needleman, Professor of Pediatrics and Psychiatry, University of Pittsburgh, Pittsburgh, Pa.

Debbie Ortman, National Field Organizer, Organic Consumers Association, Duluth, Minn.

Dr. Peter Phillips, Professor of Sociology, Sonoma State University, Rohnert Park, Calif.

Dr. Robert Rinehart, Emeritus Professor of Biology, San Diego State University, Calif.

Dr. Janette Sherman, Research Associate, Radiation and Public Health Project, U.S.A.; Adjunct Professor, Department of Sociology, Western Michigan University, Mich.

Dr. Vandana Shiva, Director, Research Foundation for Science, Technology and Natural Resource Policy, Dehradun, India

Dr. George Tritsch, Cancer Research Scientist, Roswell Park Memorial Institute, New York State Department of Health, N.Y.

Stephen L. Tvedten, CEO, Get Set, Inc.; President, Institute of Pest Management

Dr. Vijayalaxmi, Associate Professor, Department of Radiation Oncology, University of Texas Health Science Center, San Antonio, Tex.

Frank D. Wiewel, President, People Against Cancer, Otho, Iowa

Dr. Gesa Staats de Yanes, Professor of Fetal and Infant Pathology, University of Liverpool, U.K.

Dr. Quentin Young, Chairman, Health and Medicine Policy Research Group, Chicago; past President, American Public Health Association.

REFERENCES AND FURTHER READINGS

CHAPTER 1

1. Bridbord, K., et al. *Estimates of the Fraction of Cancer in the United States Related to Occupational Factors* (Califano Report). National Cancer Institute, National Institute of Environmental Health Sciences, and National Institute for Occupational Safety and Health, Bethesda, Md., September 25, 1978.
2. *Registrar General's Decennial Supplement for England and Wales: Occupational Mortality, 1970–1972.* Series DS, #1, OPCS, 1978.
3. National Academy of Sciences. *Diet, Nutrition and Cancer.* National Academy Press, Washington, D.C., 1982.
4. Willett, W. C., et al. Dietary fat and the risk of breast cancer. *N. Engl. J. Med.* 316: 22–28, 1987.
5. Karstadt, M., and Bobal, R. Availability of epidemiological data on humans exposed to animal carcinogens. II. Chemical uses and production volume. *Teratogenesis Carcinog. Mutagen.* 2: 151–167, 1982.
6. U.S. House of Representatives, Democratic Study Group. *Reagan's Toxic Pollution Record: A Public Health Hazard* (Special Report). Washington, D.C., July 31, 1984.
7. Greenwald, P., and Sondik, E. (eds.). *Cancer Control Objectives for the Nation, 1985–2000,* p. 101. NCI Monographs #2. National Cancer Institute, Division of Cancer Prevention and Control, Bethesda, Md., 1986.
8. Industry corrupts WHO agency (IARC). *OSHA/Environmental Watch* 1(5), September 1982.
9. Herrmann, I. Oxford medicine gains a college. *New Scientist* Match 9, 1978, p. 653.
10. Doll, R., and Peto, R. The causes of cancer: Quantitative estimates of available risks of cancer in the United States today. *JNCI* 66: 1191–1308, 1981.
11. Axelson, O. *Rebuttals of the Final Report on Cancer by the Royal Commission on the Use and Effects of Chemical Agents on Australian Personnel in Vietnam.* Linkoping University, Sweden, January 21, 1986.
12. Epstein, S. S., and Swartz, J. B. Carcinogenic risk assessment. *Science* 24: 1043–1047, 1988. [This article was co-signed by 15 nationally recognized experts in carcinogenesis, epidemiology, and public health.]

Further Reading

Ames, B., et al. Ranking possible carcinogenic hazards. *Science* 236: 271–280, 1987.
Ashford, N. A., et al. Center for Policy Alternatives of the Massachusetts Institute of Technology. *Benefits of Environmental, Health and Safety Regulation.* Report to the U.S. Senate Committee on Governmental Affairs, 96th Congress, March 25, 1980.

307

Ashford, N. A., and Caidart, C. C. The right to know: Toxic information transfer in the workplace. *Annu. Rev. Public Health* 6: 383–401, 1985.

Axelson, O. The health effects of phenoxy acid herbicides. In *Recent Advances in Occupational Health,* edited by J. M. Harrington, No. 2, Sec. 5, pp. 253–266. Churchill Livingston, New York, 1984.

Bailar, J. C., and Smith, E. M. Progress against cancer? *N. Engl. J. Med.* 314: 1226–1232, 1986. [See also comments on this article by Epstein, S. S., and Swartz, J. *N. Engl. J. Med.* 316: 753, 1987.]

Baram, M. S. Cost-benefit analysis: An inadequate basis for health, safety, and environmental regulatory decision making. *Ecol. Law Q.* 8(3): 473–531, 1980.

Boffey, P. M. Cancer progress: Are the statistics telling the truth? *New York Times,* September 18, 1984, pp. 17–20.

Boffey, P. M. Cancer survival rate progress reported, but skeptics object. *New York Times,* November 27, 1984, pp. 21–22.

Center for Science in the Public Interest. *Voodoo Science, Twisted Consumerism: The Golden Assurances of the American Council on Science and Health.* Washington, D.C., 1982.

Center for Science in the Public Interest, and others. *Petition to the Environmental Protection Agency to Develop Testing Methods to Assess Neurotoxic and Neurobehavioral Effects of Pesticide Active and Inert Ingredients.* Washington, D.C., February 1987.

Clinard, M. B., and Yeager, P. C. *Corporate Crime.* Free Press, New York, 1980.

Cohen, F. Workplace hazards: Do we have a right to know? *Hofstra Environ. Law Digest* 2: 10–11, Spring 1985.

Crawford, R. Cancer and corporations. *Society* 18: 20–27, 1981.

Davis, D. L., et al. Cancer prevention: Assessing cancer, exposure and recent trends in mortality for U.S. males, 1968–1978. *Teratogenesis Carcinog. Mutagen.* 2: 105–135, 1982.

Davis, L. N. *The Corporate Alchemists: Profit Takers and Problem Makers in the Chemical Industry.* Morrow, New York, 1984.

Diamond, S. Problem of toxic (air) emissions. *New York Times,* May 20, 1985, p. 19.

Elder, J., et al. Great Lakes Basin Working Group. *Toxic Air Pollution in the Great Lakes Basin: A Call for Action.* March 1987.

Environmental Protection Agency. *Health Assessment Document for Polychlorinated Dibenzo-p-Dioxins.* Washington, D.C., September 1985.

Epstein, S. S. Cost-benefit analysis: Inspired by rational economics or a protectionist philosophy? *Amicus J.* Spring 1982, pp. 41–47.

Epstein, S. S. *The Politics of Cancer.* Sierra Club Books, San Francisco, 1978. [Revised and expanded edition published by Anchor Press/Doubleday, New York, 1979.]

Epstein, S. S. Polluted data. *The Sciences* 18: 16–21, 1978.

Epstein, S. S., Brown, L. L., and Pope, C. *Hazardous Waste in America.* Sierra Club Books, San Francisco, 1982.

Epstein, S. S., and Swartz, J. Fallacies of lifestyle cancer theories. *Nature* 289: 127–130, 1981.

Epstein, S. S., and Swartz, J. Rebuttal to Ames on cancer and dict. *Science* 224: 660–668, 1984. [This letter was co-signed by some 20 nationally recognized authorities in the fields of public health and environmental and occupational carcinogenesis.]

Epstein, S. S., and Swartz, J. *Testimony in Support of a Zero Tolerance for EDB.* Public Hearings on Final Regulation of EDB, Massachusetts, March 19, 1984.

Freudenberg, N. Citizen action for environmental health: Report on a survey of community organizations. *Am. J. Public Health* 74: 444–448, 1984.

Friends of the Earth, Natural Resources Defense Council, Wilderness Society, Sierra Club, National Audubon Society, Environmental Defense Fund, Environmental Policy Center, Environmental Action, Defenders of Wildlife, and Solar Lobby. *Indictment: The Case Against the Reagan Environmental Record.* Washington, D.C., March 1982.

General Accounting Office. *Report on Progress in Cancer Treatment: Patterns of Survival, 1950-1982.* April 15, 1987.

Gould, J. *Quality of Life in American Neighborhoods: Levels of Affluence, Toxic Waste, and Cancer Mortality in Residential Zip Code Areas.* Council of Economic Priorities, Westview Press, Boulder, 1986.

Green, M. (ed.). *The Big Business Reader.* Pilgrim Press, New York, 1983.

Hunt, W. F., et al. Office of Air and Radiation, Environmental Protection Agency. *Estimated Cancer Incidence Rates for Selected Toxic Air Pollutants Using Ambient Air Pollution Data.* Washington, D.C., April 23, 1985.

Ives, J. H. (ed.). *The Export of Hazard: Transnational Corporations and Environmental Control Issues.* Routledge & Kegan Paul, Boston, 1985.

King, J. *Troubled Water.* Rodale Press, Emmaus, Pa., 1985.

Kjuus, H., et al. A case report study of lung cancer, occupational exposure and smoking: III. Etiologic fraction of occupational exposures. *Scan. J. Work Environ. Health* 12: 210–215, 1986.

Legator, M. S., Harper, B. L., and Scott, M. J. *The Health Detective Handbook.* Johns Hopkins Press, Baltimore, 1985.

Moertel, C. G. On Lymphokines, cytokines, and breakthroughs. *JAMA* 256: 3141, 1986.

Molinari, G. V. *A Look at Relationships between Respiratory Cancer Deaths and Petrochemical Industry Locations Affecting Staten Island, N.Y., and 155 Counties across the Nation.* U.S. Congress HR, Washington, D.C., June 15, 1985.

Morgester, J. J. Results of measurement and characterization of atmospheric emissions from petroleum refineries. In *Proceedings of Symposium on Atmospheric Emission from Petroleum Refineries, November 1979.* Environmental Protection Agency, Washington, D.C., March 1980.

Nader, R., Green, M., and Seligman, J. *Constitutionalizing the Corporation: The Case for the Federal Chartering of Giant Corporations.* Corporate Accountability Research Group, Washington, D.C., 1976.

National Research Council. *Toxicity Testing: Strategies to Determine Needs and Priorities.* National Academy Press, Washington, D.C., 1984.

New York State Department of Environmental Conservation. *Final Environmental Impact Statement on Amendments to 6 NYCRR Part 326 Relating to the Restriction of the Pesticides Aldrin, Chlordane, Chlorpyrifos, Dieldrin and Heptachlor.* Albany, N.Y., December 1986.

Occupational Safety and Health Administration. Identification, classification and regulation of potential occupational carcinogens. *Federal Register* 45(15): 5001–5296, 1980.

Office of Science and Technology Policy. Chemical carcinogens: A review of the science and its associated principles. *Federal Register 50:* 10372–10442, 1985.

Pye, V. I., Patrick, R., and Quarles, J. *Groundwater Contamination in the United States.* University of Pennsylvania Press, Philadelphia, 1983.

Saffiotti, U., and Wagoner, J. K. (eds.). Occupational carcinogenesis. *Ann. N.Y. Acad. Sci.* 271: 1–516, 1976.

Seidman, H., et al. Probabilities of eventually developing or dying of cancer: United States, 1985. *CA* 35: 35–56, 1985.

United Auto Workers. *The Case of the Workplace Killers: A Manual for Cancer Detectives on the Job.* International Union UAW, November 1980.

U.S. National Center for Health Statistics. *Age-adjusted Death Rates for 72 Selected Cancers by Color and Sex, 1979–1983.* Washington, D.C., 1985.

*The Track Record of a Cancer Educator. Letter. *Chicago Tribune,* October 13, 1979. www.preventcancer.com.
Cancer Mortality Rates. Letter. *Wall Street Journal,* December 10, 1979. www.preventcancer.com.
Make Prevention a National Priority. Editorial. *USA Today,* July 24, 1985. www.preventcancer.com.
Losing the War Against Cancer: Who's to Blame and What To Do About It. *Congressional Record,* E3449-E3654, September 8, 1987. www.preventcancer.com.

CHAPTER 2A

Have We Lost the War on Cancer? Editorial. *Chicago Tribune,* December 12, 1991. www.preventcancer.com.
Losing the Cancer War. Comment. *USA Today,* December 23, 1991. www.preventcancer.com.
Losing the War on Cancer After 20 Years. Cancer Establishment Makes False Claims: Massive Reforms Urged by Scientists, Doctors. Press release, February 4, 1992. www.preventcancer.com.
After 12 Years, Cancer is Winning. Commentary. *Los Angeles Times,* November 30, 1992. www.preventcancer.com.

CHAPTER 2E

A Needless New Risk of Breast Cancer (op-ed). *Los Angeles Times,* March 20, 1994. www.preventcancer.com/.

CHAPTER 3

1. Gofman, J. W. *Preventing Breast Cancer: The Story of a Major Proven Preventable Cause of this Disease.* Committee for Nuclear Responsibility, San Francisco, 1995.
2. Epstein, S. S., Steinman, D., and LeVert, S. *The Breast Cancer Prevention Program,* Ed. 2. Macmillan, New York, 1998.
3. Bertell, R. Breast cancer and mammography. *Mothering,* Summer 1992, pp. 49–52.
4. National Academy of Sciences–National Research Council, Advisory Committee. *Biological Effects of Ionizing Radiation (BEIR).* Washington, D.C., 1972.
5. Swift, M. Ionizing radiation, breast cancer, and ataxia-telangiectasia. *J. Natl. Cancer Inst.* 86(21): 1571–1572, 1994.
6. Bridges, B. A., and Arlett, C. F. Risk of breast cancer in ataxia-telangiectasia. *N. Engl. J. Med.* 326(20): 1357, 1992.
7. Quigley, D. T. Some neglected points in the pathology of breast cancer, and treatment of breast cancer. *Radiology,* May 1928, pp. 338–346.
8. Watmough, D. J., and Quan, K. M. X-ray mammography and breast compression. *Lancet* 340: 122, 1992.

*Letters to editors, editorials, op-eds, and press releases by Epstein and the Cancer Prevention Coalition are listed chronologically.

9. Martinez, B. Mammography centers shut down as reimbursement feud rages on. *Wall Street Journal,* October 30, 2000, p. A-1.

10. Vogel, V. G. Screening younger women at risk for breast cancer. *J. Natl. Cancer Inst. Monogr.* 16: 55–60, 1994.

11. Baines, C. J., and Dayan, R. A tangled web: Factors likely to affect the efficacy of screening mammography. *J. Natl. Cancer Inst.* 91(10): 833–838, 1999.

12. Laya, M. B. Effect of estrogen replacement therapy on the specificity and sensitivity of screening mammography. *J. Natl. Cancer Inst.* 88(10): 643–649, 1996.

13. Spratt, J. S., and Spratt, S. W. Legal perspectives on mammography and self-referral. *Cancer* 69(2): 599–600, 1992.

14. Skrabanek, P. Shadows over screening mammography. *Clin. Radiol.* 40: 4–5, 1989.

15. Davis, D. L., and Love, S. J. Mammography screening. *JAMA* 271(2): 152–153, 1994.

16. Christiansen, C. L., et al. Predicting the cumulative risk of false-positive mammograms. *J. Natl. Cancer Inst.* 92(20): 1657–1666, 2000.

17. Napoli, M. Overdiagnosis and overtreatment: The hidden pitfalls of cancer screening. *Am. J. Nurs.,* 2001, in press.

18. Baum, M. Epidemiology versus scaremongering: The case for humane interpretation of statistics and breast cancer. *Breast J.* 6(5): 331–334, 2000.

19. Miller, A. B., et al. Canadian National Breast Screening Study-2: 13-year results of a randomized trial in women aged 50–59 years. *J. Natl. Cancer Inst.* 92(18): 1490–1499, 2000.

20. Black, W. C. Overdiagnosis: An underrecognized cause of confusion and harm in cancer screening. *J. Natl. Cancer Inst.* 92(16): 1280–1282, 2000.

21. Napoli, M. What do women want to know? *J. Natl. Cancer Inst. Monogr.* 22: 11–13, 1997.

22. Lerner, B. H. Public health then and now: Great expectations: Historical perspectives on genetic breast cancer testing. *Am. J. Public Health* 89(6): 938–944, 1999.

23. Gotzsche, P. C., and Olsen, O. Is screening for breast cancer with mammography justifiable? *Lancet* 355: 129–134, 2000.

24. National Institutes of Health Consensus Development Conference Statement. Breast cancer screening for women ages 40–49, January 21–23, 1997. *J. Natl. Cancer Inst. Monogr.* 22: 7–18, 1997.

25. Ross, W. S. *Crusade: The Official History of the American Cancer Society,* p. 96. Arbor House, New York, 1987.

26. Hall, D. C., et al. Improved detection of human breast lesions following experimental training. *Cancer* 46(2): 408–414, 1980.

27. Smigel, K. Perception of risk heightens stress of breast cancer. *J. Natl. Cancer Inst.* 85(7): 525–526, 1993.

28. Baines, C. J. Efficacy and opinions about breast self-examination. In *Advanced Therapy of Breast Disease,* edited by S. E. Singletary and G. L. Robb, pp. 9–14. B. C. Decker, Hamilton, Ont., 2000.

29. Leight, S. B., et al. The effect of structured training on breast self-examination search behaviors as measured using biomedical instrumentation. *Nurs. Res.* 49(5): 283–289, 2000.

30. Worden, J. K., et al. A community-wide program in breast self-examination. *Prev. Med.* 19: 254–269, 1990.

31. Fletcher, S. W., et al. How best to teach women breast self-examination: A randomized control trial. *Ann. Intern. Med.* 112(10): 772–779, 1990.

32. Associated Press. FDA approves use of pad in breast exam. *New York Times,* December 25, 1995, p. 9Y.

33. Gehrke, A. Breast self-examination: A mixed message. *J. Natl. Cancer Inst.* 92(14): 1120–1121, 2000.
34. Thomas, D. B., et al. Randomized trial of breast self-examination in Shanghai: Methodology and preliminary results. *J. Natl. Cancer Inst.* 89: 355–365, 1997.
35. Baines, C. J., Miller, A. B., and Bassett, A. A. Physical examination: Its role as a single screening modality in the Canadian National Breast Screening Study. *Cancer* 63: 1816–1822, 1989.
36. Lewis, T. Women's health is no longer a man's world. *New York Times,* February 7, 2001, p. 1.
37. Miller, A. B., Baines, C. J., and Wall, C. Correspondence. *J. Natl. Cancer Inst.* 93(5): 396, 2001.
38. Kuroishi, T., et al. Effectiveness of mass screening for breast cancer in Japan. *Breast Cancer* 7(1): 1–8, 2000.
39. Epstein, S. S. American Cancer Society: The world's wealthiest "non-profit" institution. *Int. J. Health Serv.* 29(3): 565–578, 1999.
40. Epstein, S. S., and Gross, L. The high stakes of cancer prevention. *Tikkun* 15(6): 33–39, 2000.
41. Epstein, S. S. *The Politics of Cancer Revisited.* East Ridge Press, Hankins, N.Y., 1998.
42. Ramirez, A. Mammogram reimbursements. *New York Times,* February 19, 2001.
43. John, L. Digital imaging: A marketing triumph. *Breast Cancer Action Newsletter,* No. 62, November-December 2000.
44. Tarkan, L. An update that matters? Mammography's next step is assessed. *New York Times,* January 2, 2001, p. D5.
45. Miller, A. B. The role of screening in the fight against breast cancer. *World Health Forum* 13: 277–285, 1992.
46. Mittra, I. Breast screening: The case for physical examination without mammography. *Lancet* 343(8893): 342–344, 1994.
47. Greenlee, R. T. Cancer Statistics, 2001. *CA Cancer J. Clin.* 51(1): 15–36, 2001.

Further Reading

Mammography Radiates Doubt. Commentary. *Los Angeles Times,* January 28, 1992. www.preventcancer.com.
The Push for Mammography May Be Off Target. Commentary. *USA Today,* February 4, 1992. www.preventcancer.com.
Radiation's Risks. Letter. *New York Times,* December 28, 1993. www.preventcancer.com.
National Mammography Day. Press release, October 18, 1995. www.preventcancer.com.
Mammography's Mixed Blessings. Opinion. *Chicago Tribune,* March 14, 2001. www.preventcancer.com.
The National Breast Cancer Coalition (NBCC) Is Urged to Consider Breast Examination as a Practical Alternative to Mammography. Press release, May 3, 2001. www.preventcancer.com.
Mammography Is Dangerous Besides Ineffective. Press release, February 6, 2002. www.preventcancer.com.
Mammography Doesn't Come Without Risk. Commentary. *Los Angeles Times,* February 25, 2002. see www.preventcancer.com.
Letter. *Vitality Magazine,* September 2002. see www.preventcancer.com.
Breast Exams are Just as Effective as Screening Mammography. Press release, October 9, 2002. www.preventcancer.com.

CHAPTER 4

1. Conyers, J. Congressman. Are we really winning the war against cancer? *Congressional Rec.*, April 2, 1992, pp. E947–E949.
2. Epstein, S. S., et al. Losing the "war against cancer": A need for public policy reforms. *Int. J. Health Serv.* 22: 455–469, 1992.
3. Obey, D., Congressman. Hearings before a House Subcommittee of the Committee on Appropriations: Part 3. National Institutes of Health, National Cancer Institute, March 16, 1992.
4. The cancer war and its critics [editorial]. *Washington Post*, February 16, 1992.
5. Lawrence, J. Cancer cause and prevention [letter from the President of the American Cancer Society]. *Washington Post*, February 12, 1992.
6. Epstein, S. S. The cancer establishment [Taking Exception/Op-Ed]. *Washington Post*, March 10, 1992.
7. Greenberg, D. In tumultuous meeting at NIH severest critic gets a hearing on the war on cancer. *Sci. Government Rep.* 22(9): 1–4, 1992.
8. Greenberg, D. Washington Perspective: The two-by-four factor in cancer politics. *Lancet* 339: 1343–1344, 1992.
9. National Cancer Institute. *Cancer Control Objectives for the Nation: 1985–2000*, Monograph No. 2, pp. 1–105. Bethesda, Md., 1986.
10. U.S. Department of Health and Human Services/NCI. *Health Status Objectives. 16.1. Cancer*, pp. 416–440. Bethesda, Md., 1991.
11. National Cancer Institute. *Cancer Statistics Review 1973-1988*. NIH Publication No. 91-2789. Bethesda, Md., 1991.
12. Bailar, J. Cancer control. *Science* 236: 1049–1050, 1987.
13. Bailar, J. C. Progress against cancer? *N. Engl. J. Med.* 314: 1226–1232, 1986.
14. General Accounting Office. *Cancer Patient Survival: What Progress Has Been Made?* GAO/PEMD-87-13. Report to the Committee on Government Operations. Washington, D.C., March 1987.
15. DeVita, V. NCI response to article by Dr. Samuel S. Epstein published in the September 9, 1987 issue of the Congressional Record. Letter to Cong. H. A. Waxman, 1987.
16. Doll, R. Health and the environment in the 1990s. *Am. J. Public Health* 82: 933–941, 1992.
17. Landrigan, P. L. Commentary: Environmental disease: A preventable catastrophe. *Am. J. Public Health* 82: 941–943, 1992.
18. Davis, D. L., et al. International trends in cancer mortality in France, West Germany, Italy, Japan, England and Wales, and the United States. *Lancet* 336: 474–481, 1990.
19. Lopez, A. D. Competing causes of death: A review of recent trends in mortality in industrialized countries with special reference to cancer. *Ann. N. Y. Acad. Sci.* 609: 58–76, 1990.
20. Hoel, D. G., et al. Trends in cancer mortality in 15 industrialized countries, 1969–1986. *J. Natl. Cancer Inst.* 84: 313–320, 1992.
21. Epstein, S. S. Losing the war against cancer: Who's to blame and what to do about it? A position paper on the politics of cancer. *Congressional Rec.* September 9, 1987, pp. E3449–E3454.
22. Rifkind, R. In *Natural Obsessions: The Search for the Oncogene*, by N. Angier, p. 15. Houghton Mifflin, Boston, 1988.

23. Abel, U. *Chemotherapy of Advanced Epithelial Cancer: A Critical Survey*. Hippokrates Verlag, Stuttgart, 1990.
24. Chabner, B. A., and Friedman, M. A. Progress against rare and not-so-rare cancers. *N. Engl. J. Med.* 326: 563–565, 1992.
25. Landrigan, P. J. Testimony before NCAB, Publication Participation Hearings. Philadelphia, April 19, 1988.
26. Epstein, S. S. *The Politics of Cancer*. Anchor Press/Doubleday, New York, 1979.
27. Moss, R. W. *The Cancer Industry: Unravelling the Politics*. Paragon House, New York, 1989.
28. Epstein, S. S. Losing the war against cancer: Who's to blame and what to do about it. *Int. J. Health Serv.* 20: 53–71, 1990.
29. Epstein, S. S. Letter to J. Hallum, NIH Office of Scientific Integrity, May 7, 1992.
30. Waxman, H. Congressman. To amend the Public Health Service Act to revise and extend the programs of the National Institutes of Health and for other purposes, and report to accompany H.R. 2507. H.R. 2507, pp. 95–96. June 28, 1991.
31. Broder, S. Testimony before the House Appropriations Subcommittee on Labor, Health, and Human Services and Related Agencies. March 16, 1992.
32. Baltimore, D. In *Natural Obsessions: The Search for the Oncogene*, by N. Angier, pp. 12 and 15. Houghton Mifflin, Boston, 1988.
33. Barbacid, M. In *Natural Obsessions: The Search for the Oncogene*, by N. Angier, p. 12. Houghton Mifflin, Boston, 1988.
34. Varmus. In *Natural Obsessions: The Search for the Oncogene*, by N. Angier, p. 13. Houghton Mifflin, Boston, 1988.
35. Obey, D., Congressman. *House Congressional Rec.*, November 6, 1991, pp. H9457–H9458.
36. President's budget vs NCI's bypass: A tale of missed opportunities. *Cancer Lett.* 18(8): 4–7, 1992.
37. Doll, R., and Peto, R. The causes of cancer: Quantitative estimates of avoidable risks of cancer in the United States today. *J. Natl. Cancer Inst.* 66: 1191–1308, 1981.
38. Herrmann, I. Oxford medicine gains a college. *New Scientist*, March 9, 1978, p. 653.
39. Enstrom, J. E. Rising lung cancer mortality among non-smokers. *J. Natl. Cancer Inst.* 62: 755–760, 1970.
40. Davis, D. L., Bridbord, K., and Schneiderman, M. Cancer prevention: Assessing causes, exposures, and recent trends in mortality for U.S. males 1968–1978. *Teratogenesis Carcinog. Mutagen.* 2: 105–135, 1982.
41. U.S. Department of Health and Human Services. USDHS Report No. PHS 83-1232. Washington, D.C., December 1982.
42. Schneiderman, M. A., Davis, D. L., and Wagener, D. K. Smokers: Black and white. *Science* 249: 228–229, 1990.
43. International Agency for Research on Cancer. *Tobacco Smoking* 38: 1–421, 1986.
44. Wagoner, J., Infante, P., and Bayliss, D. Beryllium: An etiologic agent in the induction of lung cancer, non-neoplastic respiratory diseases, and heart disease among industrially exposed workers. *Environ. Res.* 21: 15–34, 1980.
45. Epstein, S. S., and Swartz, J. Cancer and diet: A rebuttal to Ames, B. *Science* 224: 660–667, 1984.
46. Perera, F. F. Presentation to the President's Cancer Panel, April 5, 1990, pp. 82–96.
47. Stocks, P. On the relations between atmospheric pollution in urban and rural localities and mortality from cancer, bronchitis and pneumonia, with particular reference to 3,4-benzopyrene, beryllium, molybdenum, vanadium and arsenic. *Br. J. Cancer* 14: 397–418, 1960.

48. National Panel of Consultants on the Conquest of Cancer. *National Program for the Conquest of Cancer*. Report to the Senate Committee on Labor and Public Welfare, November 27, 1970.

49. National Academy of Sciences. *Biologic Effects of Atmospheric Pollutants: Particulate Polycyclic Organic Matter*. National Academy Press, Washington, D.C., 1972.

50. International Agency for Research on Cancer. *Air Pollution and Cancer in Man*. Scientific Publication No. 16, 1977.

51. National Academy of Sciences. *Potential Risk of Lung Cancer from Diesel Engine Emissions*. National Academy Press, Washington, D.C., 1981.

52. National Institute for Occupational Safety and Health. *Carcinogenic Effects of Exposure to Diesel Exhaust*. NIOSH Current Intelligence Bulletin 50. Bethesda, Md., August 1988.

53. Gottlieb, M. S., et al. Lung cancer in Louisiana: Death certificate analysis. *J. Natl. Cancer Inst.* 63: 1131–1137, 1979.

54. Environmental Protection Agency. *Toxic Release Inventory*. Washington, D.C., 1990.

55. Schneiderman, M. A., Davis, D. L., and Wagener, D. K. Lung cancer that is not attributable to smoking. *JAMA* 261: 2635–2636, 1989.

56. Selikoff, I. J., and Hammond, E. C. Asbestos-associated disease in U.S. shipyards. *CA Cancer J. Clin.* 28: 87–99, 1978.

57. Infante, P. F., and Pohl, G. K. Living in a chemical world: Actions and reactions to industrial carcinogens. *Teratogenesis Carcinog. Mutagen.* 8: 225–249, 1988.

58. Maltoni, C., and Selikoff, I. J. Living in a chemical world: Occupational and environmental significance of industrial carcinogens. *Ann. N. Y. Acad. Sci.* 534: 1–1045, 1988.

59. National Institute for Occupational Safety and Health. *NIOSH National Occupational Hazard Survey* (NOHS). Bethesda, Md., 1982.

60. Peto, R., and Schneiderman, M. A. Afterword. In *Quantification of Occupational Cancer*, Banbury Report 9, edited by R. Peto and M. A. Schneiderman, pp. 695–697. Cold Spring Harbor, N.Y., 1981.

61. Landrigan, P. J., and Markowitz, S. Current magnitude of occupational disease in the U.S.: Estimates from New York State. *Ann. N. Y. Acad. Sci.* 572: 27–45, 1989.

62. Nicholson, W. J., Perkel, G., and Selikoff, I. J. Occupational exposure to asbestos: Populations at risk and projected mortality, 1980–2030. *Am. J. Ind. Med.* 3: 259–311, 1982.

63. O'Leary, L. M., et al. Parental occupational exposures and risk of childhood cancer: A review. *Am. J. Ind. Med.* 20: 17–35, 1991.

64. Peto, R. Saturated fat avoidance. *Science* 235: 1562, 1987.

65. Kolata, G. Dietary fat: Breast cancer link questioned. *Science* 235: 436, 1987.

66. Willett, W. C., et al. Dietary fat and the risk of breast cancer. *N. Engl. J. Med.* 316: 22–28, 1987.

67. Henderson, B. E., Ross, R. K., and Pike, M. C. Toward the primary prevention of cancer. *Science* 254: 1131–1138, 1991.

68. Marshall, E. Breast cancer: Stalemate in the war on cancer. *Science* 254: 1719–1720, 1991.

69. General Accounting Office. *Breast Cancer, 1971–1991, Prevention, Treatment and Research*. GAO/PEMD-92-12. Report to the Committee on Government Operations. Washington, D.C., December 1991.

70. Epstein, S. S. Mammography radiates doubt [Op/Ed]. *Los Angeles Times*, January 28, 1992.

71. Walker, A. I. T., et al. The toxicology and pharmacodynamics of dieldrin: Two year oral exposures of rats and dogs. *Toxicol. Appl. Pharmacol.* 15: 345–373, 1969.
72. National Cancer Institute. *Bioassay of Chlordane for Possible Carcinogenicity.* Carcinogenesis Technical Report Series No. 8. Bethesda, Md., 1977.
73. Rall, D. Laboratory animal toxicity and carcinogenesis testing: Underlying concepts, advantages and constraints. *Ann. N. Y. Acad. Sci.* 534: 78–83, 1988.
74. Scribner, J. D., and Mottet, N. K. DDT acceleration of mammary gland tumors induced in the male Sprague-Dawley rat by 2-acetamidophenanthrene. *Carcinogenesis 2*: 1235–1239, 1981.
75. Wasserman, M., et al. Organochlorine compounds in neoplastic and adjacent apparently normal breast tissue. *Bull. Environ. Contam. Toxicol.* 15: 478–484, 1976.
76. Falk, F., et al. Pesticides and PCB residues in human breast lipids and their relation to breast cancer. *Arch. Environ. Health* 47: 143–146, 1992.
77. Westin, J. B., and Richter, E. The Israeli breast-cancer anomaly. *Ann. N. Y. Acad. Sci.* 609: 269–279, 1990.
78. Hertz, R. The estrogen-cancer hypothesis with special emphasis on DES. In *Origins of Human Cancer, Book C, Human Risk Assessment,* edited by H. H. Hiatt, et al., pp. 1665–1682. Cold Spring Harbor Laboratory, Cold Spring Harbor, N.Y., 1977.
79. Segaloff, A., and Maxfield, W. S. The synergism between radiation and estrogen in the production of mammary cancer in the rat. *Cancer Res.* 31: 166–168, 1971.
80. Shellabarger, C. J., Stone, J. P., and Holtzman, S. Rat strain differences in mammary tumor induction with estrogen and neutron radiation. *J. Natl. Cancer Inst.* 61: 1505–1508, 1978.
81. Dao, T. The role of ovarian hormones in initiating the induction of mammary cancer in rats by polynuclear hydrocarbons. *Cancer Res.* 22: 973–984, 1962.
82. National Academy of Sciences. *The Effects on Populations of Exposure to Low Levels of Ionizing Radiation.* Report to the Advisory Committee on the Biological Effects of Ionizing Radiation (BEIR). National Research Council, Washington, D.C., November 1972.
83. Berlin, N. Quoted in Greenberg, D. S. X-ray mammography: A background to decision. *Med. Public Aff.* 295: 739–740, 1976 [1973].
84. Bailar, J. C. Mammography: A contrary view. *Ann. Intern. Med.* 84: 77–84, 1976.
85. Greene, F. L., et al. Mammography, sonomammography and diaphanography (light scanning). *Am. Surg.* 51: 58–60, 1985.
86. LaFreniere, R., Ashkar, F. S., and Ketcham, A. S. Infrared light scanning of the breast. *Am. Surg.* 52: 123–128, 1986.
87. Bailar, J. C. Mammography before age 50 years. *JAMA* 259: 1548–1549, 1988.
88. Breast cancer screening in women under 50 [editorial]. *Lancet* 337: 1575–1576, 1991.
89. Smigel, K. Breast cancer prevention trial takes off. *J. Natl. Cancer Inst.* 84: 669–670, 1992.
90. Epstein, S. S., and Rennie, S. A travesty at women's expense [Op-Ed]. *Los Angeles Times,* June 22, 1992.
91. Fugh-Berman, A., and Epstein, S. S. Tamoxifen: Disease prevention or disease substitution [Viewpoint]. *Lancet* 340: 1143–1145, 1992.
92. Han, X., and Liehr, J. G. Induction of covalent DNA adducts in rodents by tamoxifen. *Cancer Res.* 52: 1360–1363, 1992.
93. ICI Pharmaceutical Group. Data presented at the FDA Oncology Drugs Advisory Committee Meeting, Bethesda, Md., June 29, 1990.
94. Nayfield, S. G., et al. Potential role of tamoxifen in prevention of breast cancer. *J. Natl. Cancer Inst.* 83: 1450–1459, 1991.

95. Tamoxifen trial controversy. *Lancet* 339: 735, 1992.

96. Rutqvist, L. E., et al. Contralateral primary tumors in breast cancer patients in a randomized trial of adjuvant tamoxifen therapy. *J. Natl. Cancer Inst.* 83: 1299–1306, 1991.

97. Gusberg, S. B. Tamoxifen for breast cancer: Associated endometrial cancer. *Cancer* 65: 1463–1464, 1990.

98. National Research Council. *Toxicity Testing: Strategies to Determine Needs and Priorities.* National Academy Press, Washington, D.C., 1984.

99. Tomatis, L. The contribution of the IARC Monographs program to the identification of cancer risk factors. *Ann. N. Y. Acad. Sci.* 534: 31–38, 1988.

100. National Academy of Sciences. *Regulating Pesticides in Food: The Delaney Paradox.* National Academy Press, Washington, D.C., 1987.

101. Natural Resources Defense Council. *Intolerable Risks: Pesticides in Our Children's Food.* February 27, 1989.

102. Epstein, S. S., and Feldman, J. Opening the door for carcinogens: Assaults on nation's food safety laws multiply [Op-Ed]. *Los Angeles Times*, February 27, 1989.

103. Epstein, S. S., and Feldman, J. "Negligible Risk" is still much too great [Op-Ed]. *Los Angeles Times*, November 16, 1989.

104. National Coalition Against the Misuse of Pesticides. Testimony of NCAMP before the Senate Subcommittee on Toxic Substances, Environmental Oversight, Research and Development, Committee on Environment and Public Works, May 9, 1991.

105. Blair, A., et al. Cancer among farmers: A review. *Scand. J. Environ. Health* 11: 397–407, 1985.

106. Brown, L. M., et al. Pesticide exposures and other agricultural risk factors for leukemia among men in Iowa and Minnesota. *Cancer Res.* 50: 6585–6591, 1990.

107. Hayes, H. M., et al. Case control study of canine malignant lymphoma: Positive association with dog owners use of 2,4-dichlorophenoxyacetic acid herbicides. *J. Natl. Cancer Inst.* 83: 1226–1231, 1991.

108. Fisher, L., Environmental Protection Agency. Communication to Senate Committee on Labor and Human Resources, March 30, 1992.

109. Epstein, S. S. Carcinogenicity of heptachlor and chlordane. *Sci. Total Environ.* 6: 103–154, 1976.

110. Epstein, S. S. Testimony on H.R. 262, House Subcommittee on Health and the Environment, Committee on Energy and Commerce, June 24, 1987.

111. National Research Council. *Chlordane in Military Housing.* Committee on Toxicology, National Academy of Sciences, Washington, D.C., 1979.

112. National Academy of Sciences. *An Assessment of the Health Risks of Seven Pesticides Used for Termite Control.* National Academy Press, Washington, D.C., August 1982.

113. U.S. Air Force. Review of NCI proposed protocol for epidemiological feasibility study. Memo, Chappell, B. R., to AFMSC/SGPA, February 6, 1984.

114. Hoar, S. K. Letter to USAF Colonel Smead, September 19, 1983.

Further Reading

Distinguished Experts Call on President Clinton to Redirect War on Cancer. Press advisory and conference. June 24, 1993. www.preventcancer.com.

The Cancer Prevention Coalition (CPC) Calls for the Replacement of the National Cancer Institute Chief. CPC Charges Dr. Broder With Cover Up and Scientific Fraud. Press release, June 9, 1994. www.preventcancer.com.

"Research Cures Cancer" Campaign Misleads Public and Congress. Press release, January 25, 1995. www.preventcancer.com.

Why We Are Losing the War Against Cancer. Aging Population, Smoking, Don't Explain Away Rise: Leading Physician to Discuss Preventable Causes of Cancer. Press breakfast. Environmental Media Services, February 6, 1996. www.preventcancer.com.

Cancer War Is Threatened by Recommendations of Presidential Commission. Press release, August 30, 1996. www.preventcancer.com.

We Are Losing the Winnable War Against Cancer. Press release, December 18, 1996. www.preventcancer.com.

Cancer "Report Card" Gets Failing Grade. Press release, April 1, 1998. www.preventcancer.com.

The Cancer Drug Industry's "March" Seriously Misleads the Nation. Press release, September 24, 1998. www.preventcancer.com.

Prestigious International Award for U.S. Expert Who Advocates Emphasis on Cancer Prevention Rather than Just on Damage Control, Diagnosis and Treatment. Press release, December 7, 1998. www.preventcancer.com.

Environmental Cancer: Science, Not Politics. Letter. *The Wall Street Journal,* March 15, 1999. www.preventcancer.com.

Legislative Proposals for Reversing the Cancer Epidemic. Keynote address, All Parliamentary Cancer Group, U.K., July 1, 1999. see www.preventcancer.com.

UIC Cancer Prevention Champion Received "Alternative Pulitzer." Press release, April 10, 2000. www.preventcancer.com.

The CPC Charges National Academy of Sciences with Proposing Secret World Science Court. Press release, May 11, 2000. www.preventcancer.com.

The Politics of Cancer. Letter. *JAMA* 284: 4. July 26, 2000. www.preventcancer.com.

CHAPTER 5

1. Bennett, J. T. Health research charities: Doing little in research but emphasizing politics. *Union Leader,* Manchester, N.H., September 20, 1990.

2. Bennett, J. T., and DiLorenzo, T. J. *Unhealthy Charities: Hazardous to Your Health and Wealth.* Basic Books, New York, 1994.

3. Hall, H., and Williams, G. Professor vs. Cancer Society. *The Chronicle of Philanthropy,* January 28, 1992, p. 26.

4. DiLorenzo, T. J. One charity's uneconomic war on cancer. *Wall Street Journal,* March 15, 1992, p. A10.

5. Salant, J. D. Cancer Society gives to governors. Associated Press Release, March 30, 1998.

6. Epstein, S. S., Steinman, D., and LeVert, S. *The Breast Cancer Prevention Program.* Macmillan, New York, 1997.

7. Epstein, S. S. Losing the war against cancer: Who's to blame and what to do about it. *Int. J. Health Serv.* 20: 53–71, 1990.

8. Epstein, S. S. Evaluation of the National Cancer Program and proposed reforms. *Int. J. Health Serv.* 23(1): 15–44, 1993.

9. American Cancer Society. Upcoming television special on pesticides in food. Memorandum from S. Dickinson, Vice-President, Public Relations and Health, to C. W. Heath, Jr., M.D., Vice-President. *Epidemiology and Statistics,* March 22, 1993.

10. American Cancer Society. *Cancer Facts & Figures—1998,* pp. 1–32, Atlanta, 1998.

11. Kaplan, S. PR Giant makes hay from client cross-pollination: Porter/Novelli plays all sides. *PR Watch,* First quarter, 1994, p. 4.
12. Kaplan, S. Porter-Novelli plays all sides. *Legal Times* 16(27) :1, November 23, 1993.
13. Moss, R. W. *Questioning Chemotherapy.* Equinox Press, Brooklyn, N.Y., 1995.
14. U.S. Congress Office of Technology Assessment. *Unconventional Cancer Treatments.* U.S. Government Printing Office, Washington, D.C., 1990.
15. Moss. R. W. *Cancer Therapy: The Independent Consumer's Guide to Non-toxic Treatment and Prevention.* Equinox Press, Brooklyn, N.Y., 1992.
16. Castellucci, L. Practitioners seek common ground in unconventional forum. *J. Natl. Cancer Inst.* 90: 1036–1037, 1998.

Further Reading

Breast Cancer Unawareness Month. Press release, October 14, 1994. www.preventcancer.com.
National Mammography Day. Press release, October 18, 1994. www.preventcancer.com.
Letter to President Clinton Regarding Proposed Recommendation of Dr. Gilbert Omenn as FDA Commissioner, Stressing His Flawed Science and Major Conflicts of Interest. May 30, 1997. www.preventcancer.com.
Awareness Month Keeps Women Perilously Unaware. Editorial. *Chicago Tribune,* October 26, 1997. www.preventcancer.com.
U.K. Charities Indicted for Losing the Winnable War Against Cancer. Press release, September 13, 1999. www.preventcancer.com.
The Cancer In Our Charities. Article. *The Times*, U.K., September 17, 1999. www.preventcancer.com.
American Cancer Society Indicted by the Cancer Prevention Coalition for Losing the Winnable War Against Cancer. Press release, October 25, 1999. www.preventcancer.com.
University of Illinois Chicago Cancer Prevention Champion Receives "Alternative Pulitzer" Prize for Article, "American Cancer Society: The World's Wealthiest Non-profit Institution." Press release, April 10, 2000. www.preventcancer.com.
The American Cancer Society Is Threatening the U.S. National Cancer Program. Press release, June 12, 2001. www.preventcancer.com.
American Cancer Society Misleads the Public in the May 26 Discovery Health Channel Program. Press release, May 24, 2003. www.preventcancer.com.

CHAPTER 6

1. Epstein, S. S. *The Politics of Cancer Revisited.* East Ridge Press, Fremont Center, New York, 1998. Web site: www.preventcancer.com
2. Epstein, S. S., Steinman, D., and Le Vert, S. *The Breast Cancer Prevention Program,* Ed. 2. Macmillan, New York, 1998.
3. Epstein, S. S. American Cancer Society: The world's wealthiest "non-profit" institution. *Int. J. Health Serv.* 29: 565–578, 1999.
4. Cancer Prevention Coalition. American Cancer Society Indicted for Losing the Winnable War Against Cancer. PR Newswire press release, October 25, 1999.
5. Walker, M. Sir Richard Doll: A questionable pillar of the cancer establishment. *The Ecologist* 28: 82–92, 1998.

6. Epstein, S. S. U.K. Cancer Charities Indicted for Losing the Winnable War Against Cancer. PR Newswire press release and press conference, Imperial College, London, September 13, 1999.
7. Thorpe, B. European Initiative as a New Chemical Policy: Phasing Out Carcinogens. Working Paper. Clean Action Production, Montreal, 1999.
8. Epstein, S. S. *The Politics of Cancer.* Sierra Club Books, San Francisco, 1978.
9. Fagin, D., Lavelle, M., and the Center for Public Integrity. *Toxic Deception: How the Chemical Industry Manipulates Science, Bends the Law and Endangers Your Health.* Carol Publishing Group, Secaucus, N.J., 1996.
10. Commonwealth of Massachusetts. *Toxic Use Reduction Act (TURA),* 1989.
11. Massachusetts Department of Environmental Protection. 1997 Toxics Use Reduction Information Release, March 23, 1999.
12. Something else that can be reduced: Costs. *International Herald Tribune,* June 7, 1999, p. 11.
13. Interface, Inc. Sustainability Report. Atlanta, 1999.
14. Selling not products, but services. *International Herald Tribune,* June 7, 1999, p. 11.
15. Friendlier technology, or the E2 P2 factor. *International Herald Tribune,* June 7, 1999, p. 2.
16. Steinman, D., and Epstein, S. S. *The Safe Shoppers Bible: A Consumer's Guide to Non-Toxic Household Products, Cosmetics and Food.* Macmillan, New York, 1995.
17. Hawken, P., Lovins, A., and Lovins, L. H. *Natural Capitalism: Creating the Next Industrial Revolution.* Little, Brown, Boston, 1999.
18. Moore, T. J. *Prescription for Disaster.* Simon and Schuster, New York, 1998.
19. Gage, K., and Epstein, S. S. The Federal Advisory Committee System: An assessment. *Environmental Law Reporter* 7(2): 50001–50012, 1977.
20. Verall, J. V. *The Manipulation of Codex Alimentarius.* Report to Mr. R. J. Santer, President of the European Commission, March 31, 1999.
21. Castleman, B. J., and Lemen, R. A. The manipulation of international scientific organizations. *Int. J. Occup. Environ. Health* 4: 53–55, 1998.
22. Epstein, S. S. Testimony on White Collar Crime (H.R. 4973) before the Subcommittee on Crime of the Committee on the Judiciary. Washington, D. C., December 13, 1979.
23. Epstein, S. S. Corporate crime: Why we cannot trust industry-derived safety studies. *Int. J. Health Serv.* 20: 443–458, 1990.
24. Epstein, S. S. Implants pose poorly recognized risks of breast cancer. *Int. J. Occup. Med. J.* 4: 315–342, 1995.
25. *Mangini vs. R. J. Reynolds Tobacco Company.* Case No. 939359, Superior Courts of the State of California, November 2, 1998.
26. Fugh-Berman, A., and Epstein, S. Tamoxifen for breast cancer prevention: A precautionary review. *Rev. Endocrine-Related Cancer* 43: 43–53, 1993.

Further Reading

An Ounce of Prevention. Op.-ed, Sunday Opinion. *Los Angeles Times,* August 31, 2003. see www.preventcancer.com.
U.K. Cancer Charities Indicted for Losing the Winnable War Against Cancer. P.R. Newswire Press Release, September 13, 1999. www.preventcancer.com.

CHAPTER 7

1. Ries, L. A. G., et al. *SEER Cancer Statistics Review, 1973–1999.* National Cancer Institute, Bethesda, Md., 2002.

2. Dinse, G. E., et al. Unexplained increases in cancer incidence in the United States from 1975 to 1994: Possible sentinel health indicators? *Annu. Rev. Public Health* 20: 173–209, 1999.
3. Edwards, B. K., et al. Annual report to the nation on the status of cancer, 1973–1999, featuring implications of age and aging on the U.S. cancer burden. *Cancer* 94(10): 2766–2792, 2002.
4. Davis, D., and Hoel, D. (eds.). *Trends in Cancer Mortality in Industrial Countries.* New York Academy of Sciences, New York, 1990.
5. National Cancer Institute and American Cancer Society. *Report Card.* Bethesda, Md., March 12, 1998.
6. Stolberg, S. G. New cancer cases decreasing in U.S. as deaths do, too. *New York Times,* March 13, 1998.
7. Bailar, J., and Gornik, H. L. Cancer undefeated. *N. Engl. J. Med.* 336(22): 1569–1574, 1997.
8. Clapp, R. W. The decline in U.S. cancer mortality from 1991 to 1995: What's behind the numbers? *Int. J. Health Serv.* 28(4): 747–755, 1998.
9. National Cancer Institute. *Cancer Progress Report.* Bethesda, Md., 2001.
10. Greenberg, D. *Science, Money, and Politics.* University of Chicago Press, Chicago, 2001.
11. Kolata, G. Test proves fruitless, fueling new debate on cancer screening. *New York Times,* April 9, 2002.
12. Fellers, L. Taxol is one of the best cancer drugs ever discovered by the federal government: Why is it beyond some patients' reach? *Washington Post Magazine,* May 31, 1998.
13. Epstein, S. S. *The Politics of Cancer, Revisited.* East Ridge Press, Fremont Center, N.Y., 1998.
14. Doll, R., and Peto, R. The causes of cancer: Quantitative estimates of avoidable risks of cancer in the U.S. today. *J. Natl. Cancer Inst.* 66: 1191–1308, 1981.
15. Stallones, R. A., and Downs, T. A. *A Critical Review of Estimates of the Fraction of Cancer in the U.S. Related to Environmental Factors.* Report to the American Industrial Health Council. University of Texas School of Public Health, Houston, 1979.
16. Landrigan, P. Commentary: Environmental disease: A preventable epidemic. *Am. J. Public Health* 82(7): 941–943, 1992.
17. Anderson, S. J., et al. *Expanding the Public's Right-to-Know: Materials Accounting Data as a Tool for Promoting Environmental Justice and Pollution Prevention.* Inform, New York, 2000 (www.informinc.org).
18. Doody, M. M., et al. Breast cancer mortality after diagnostic mammography: Findings from the U.S. scoliosis cohort study. *Spine* 25(16): 2052–2063, 2000.
19. Ford, L. Letter to J. W. Stratton, Interim Director, California Environmental Protection Agency, Sacramento, June 23, 1995.
20. Greaves, P., et al. Two-year carcinogenicity study of tamoxifen in Alderley Park Wistar-derived rats. *Cancer Res.* 53(17): 3919–3924, 1993.
21. Kliewer, E. V., and Smith, K. R. Breast cancer mortality among immigrants in Australia and Canada. *J. Natl. Cancer Inst.* 87(15): 1154–1161, 1995.
22. Lichtenstein, P., et al. Environmental and heritable factors in the causation of cancer: Analyses of cohorts of twins from Sweden, Denmark, and Finland. *N. Engl. J. Med.* 343(2): 78–85, 2000.
23. Willett, W. C. Balancing life-style and genomics research for disease prevention. *Science* 296: 695–698, 2002.
24. Epstein, S. S. Evaluation of the National Cancer Program and proposed reforms. *Am. J. Ind. Med.* 24: 109–133, 1993.
25. National Cancer Institute. *Cancer Facts.* Bethesda, Md., May 25, 2001.

26. Baker, B. P., et al. Pesticide residues in conventional, integrated pest management (IPM)-grown and organic foods: Insights from three U.S. data sets. *Food Additives Contaminants* 19(5): 427–446, 2002.
27. American Cancer Society. *Cancer Facts and Figures 2002*. Atlanta, 2002.
28. White, J., CEO, Canadian Cancer Society. Letter to *Guelph Mercury* (Ontario), April 9, 2002.
29. Government of Canada. Discussion Document. Ottawa, September 2001.
30. Sierra Club of Canada and Canadian Cancer Society. Environmentalists Join Canadian Cancer Society in Call for Ban on Cancer-Causing Lawn Pesticides. Press release, March 1, 2002.
31. Ministry of Health, Government of Canada, 2002.
32. Epstein, S. S., and Hauter, W. Preventing food poisoning: Sanitation not irradiation. *Int. J. Health Serv.* 31(1): 187–192, 2001.
33. Eli Lilly and Co. Evista. Unpublished report, December 15, 1997, p. 13.
34. National Toxicology Program. *Toxicology and Carcinogenesis Studies of Methylphenidate Hydrochloride in F 344/N Rats and B6C3F₁ Mice.* Technical Report Series No. 439. Bethesda, Md., July 1995.
35. International Agency for Research on Cancer. *Atrazine.* IARC Monograph, Vol. 73, pp. 59–113, 1999.
36. Associated Press. Weed killer found to sexually deform frogs. *New York Times,* April 17, 2002.
37. Hayes, T. B., et al. Hermaphroditic, demasculinized frogs after exposure to the herbicide atrazine at low ecologically relevant doses. *Proc. Natl. Acad. Sci.* 99(8): 5476–5480, 2002.
38. Wilson, D. *Fateful Harvest: The True Story of a Small Town Global Industry, and a Toxic Secret.* HarperCollins, New York, 2001.
39. Epstein, S. S. *Got (genetically engineered) Milk! The Monsanto rBGH/BST Milk Wars Handbook.* Seven Stories Press, 2001 (www.sevenstories.com).
40. Gould, J. M., et al. Strontium-90 in deciduous teeth as a factor in early childhood cancer. *Int. J. Health Serv.* 30(3): 515–539, 2000.
41. Epstein, S. S. Legislative proposals for reversing the cancer epidemic and controlling run-away industrial technologies. *Int. J. Health Serv.* 30(2): 353–371, 2000.
42. Public Broadcasting Service. Kids and chemicals. *Now with Bill Moyers,* May 10, 2002.
43. ACS-led national cancer dialogue beset by patient mistrust, lack of openness. *Cancer Letter* 26(3): 1–12, January 21, 2000.
44. Epstein, S. S. American Cancer Society: The world's wealthiest "non-profit" institution. *Int. J. Health Serv.* 29(3): 565–578, 1999.
45. PR firm hired by American Cancer Society also represents "Team Kool Green." *Cancer Letter* 26(4): 1–3, January 28, 2000.
46. Love, J. P. Testimony before the House Subcommittee on Business Opportunities and Technology of the Committee on Small Business. Washington, D.C., July 11, 1994.
47. Lomborg, B. *The Skeptical Environmentalist.* Cambridge University Press, Cambridge, 2001.
48. Castleman, B. WTO confidential: The case of asbestos. *Int. J. Health Serv.* 32(3): 489–501, 2002.
49. Doll, R. Mortality from lung cancer in asbestos workers. *Br. J. Ind. Med.* 12: 81–86, 1955.
50. *Times* (London), June 8, 1967.
51. *Daily Telegraph,* January 7, 1976.

52. Castleman, B. Re: Doll's 1955 study on cancer from asbestos. *Am. J. Ind. Med.* 39: 237–240, 2001.
53. *Daily Telegraph,* February 7, 1983.
54. Society for the Prevention of Asbestos and Industrial Disease. Letter to *Sunday Times* (London), April 26, 1985.
55. Doll, R. Letter to Hon. Mr. Justice Phillip Evatt, December 4, 1985.
56. Forman, D., et al. Cancer near nuclear installations. *Nature* 329: 499–505, 1987.
57. Darby, S. C., Kendall, G. M., and Doll, R. A summary of mortality and incidence of cancer in men from the United Kingdom who participated in the United Kingdom's atmospheric nuclear tests and experimental programs. *BMJ* 296: 332–338, 1988.
58. *Sunday Telegraph,* November 26, 1989.
59. Doll, R. Effects of exposure to vinyl chloride and assessment of the evidence. *Scan. J. Work Env. Health* 14: 61–78, 1988.
60. *Daily Mail,* June 3, 1992.
61. Doll, R. Deposition, *Carlin Staples et al vs. Dow Chemical Co.,* District Court Brazoria County, Texas, January 27, 2000.
62. U.K. Ministry of Health. Letter to Samuel Epstein, M.D., May 21, 1999.
63. Tomatis, L. The IARC Monographs Program: Changing attitudes towards public health. *Int. J. Occup. Environ. Health* 8(2): 144–152, 2002.

Further Reading

PUBLIC POLICY

Reversing the Cancer Epidemic. *TIKKUN,* May/June 2002. www.preventcancer.com.
Escalating Incidence of Childhood Cancer Is Ignored by the National Cancer Institute and American Cancer Society. Press release, May 9, 2002. www.preventcancer.com.
New Report "The Stop Cancer Before It Starts Campaign" Released Today: Report Demonstrates Cancer Epidemic Continues Despite Allocation of Billions of Taxpayer Dollars. Press release, February 20, 2003. www.preventcancer.com.
U.S. Losing War on Cancer, Ignoring Prevention. Press release, February 20, 2003. www.preventcancer.com.
National Cancer Institute Leadership is Out of Touch with Reality. Press release, February 25, 2003. www.preventcancer.com.
Environmental Causes of Cancer Neglected Say U.S. Campaigners. Press release, March 27, 2003. www.preventcancer.com.
Escalating Incidence of Childhood Cancer Is Ignored by the National Cancer Institute and American Cancer Society. Press release, May 8, 2003. www.preventcancer.com.
The Sad Truth About the Stark Rise in Childhood Cancer. Opinion. *Chicago Tribune,* June 17, 2003. www.preventcancer.com.
An Ounce of Prevention: Billions Spent on Finding Cures, Little on Keeping Cancer from Occurring. Commentary. *Los Angeles Times Sunday Opinion,* August 31, 2003. www.preventcancer.com.
National Academy of Sciences Challenges the "Special Status" of the National Cancer Institute. Press release, September 30, 2003. www.preventcancer.com.

Spinning the Losing War on Cancer. Press release, November 4, 2003.
www.preventcancer.com.
Spinning the Losing Cancer War. Press release, February 23, 2004.
www.preventcancer.com.
Conflicts of Interest in the Losing Cancer War. Press release, March 4, 2004.
www.preventcancer.com.

FOOD CONTAMINANTS

EDB and Other Hazards. Letter. *Washington Post,* February 25, 1984.
www.preventcancer.com.
Opening the Door for Carcinogens. Editorial. *Los Angeles Times,* February 27, 1989. see
www.preventcancer.com.
Negligible Risk Is Still Much Too Great. Editorial. *Los Angeles Times,* November 16,
1989. www.preventcancer.com.
Get the Cancerous Pesticides Out of Our Food. Letter. *New York Times,* February 8, 1993.
www.preventcancer.com.
What About "Putting People First"? Editorial. *Los Angeles Times,* September 8, 1993.
www.preventcancer.com.
All We're Doing is Rearranging the Deck Chairs on a Seafood Titanic. Editorial. *Los
Angeles Times,* February 18, 1994. www.preventcancer.com.
New Study Feeds Pesticide Debate. Letter. *Chicago Sun Times,* March 12, 1994.
www.preventcancer.com.
Study Offers Strong Evidence in a Cancer Debate. Letter. *New York Times,* April 20, 1994.
www.preventcancer.com.
Pesticides Not Cleared of Breast Cancer Link. Letter. *New York Times,* April 25, 1994.
www.preventcancer.com.
Pesticides Pose a Lifelong Threat. Letter. *The York Times,* August 24, 1994.
www.preventcancer.com.

COSMETICS AND TOILETRIES

So You Consider Hair Dye Safe? Letter. *New York Times,* February 8, 1994.
www.preventcancer.com.
Dusting with Cancer: Coalition Urges Chicago Drug Stores to Label Talc. Press release
and citizen petition, November 17, 1994. www.preventcancer.com.
Cancer Group and Ralph Nader Release First Annual "Dirty Dozen" Consumer Products
List. Press release, September 21, 1995. www.preventcancer.com.
They Make You Smell, Feel and Look Good, but Can Cosmetics Increase Your Risk
of Cancer? Cancer Prevention Coalition Calls for Tough Cosmetic Standards. Press
release, October 22, 1996. www.preventcancer.com.
Formaldehyde-Releasing Preservatives. Appendix XIV "Shopper Beware" of *The Politics
of Cancer*, Revisited. 1998. www.preventcancer.com.
Major Cosmetic and Toiletry Ingredients Pose Avoidable Cancer Risks. Press release,
February 22, 1998. www.preventcancer.com.
Perfume:Cupid's Arrow or Poison Dart? Press release, February 7, 2000.
www.preventcancer.com.
Undisclosed Carcinogens in Cosmetics and Personal Care Products. Press release, January
15, 2001. www.preventcancer.com.
Carcinogenic Hazards of Mainstream Industry Personal Care and Cosmetic Products. Press
release, September 16, 2001. www.preventcancer.com.

Phthalates in Cosmetics Are Suspect, But Carcinogens Even More So. Press release, July 11, 2002. www.preventcancer.com.

Coalition Calls for Labeling of Cosmetics and Toiletries, Citing Cancer and Other Health Risks. Press release, August 15, 2002.

Environmental Working Group Report on Personal Care Products: Ambitious, But Flawed. Press release, July 2, 2004. www.preventcancer.com.

High Time to Label Fragrance Allergens. Press release, August 6, 2004. www.preventcancer.com.

Europe Leads the Way in Consumer Product Safety. Press release, October 13, 2004. www.preventcancer.com.

MEDICAL

A Travesty at Women's Expense. Editorial. *Los Angeles Times,* June 22, 1992. www.preventcancer.com.

Radiation Risks. Letter. *New York Times,* January 6, 1994. www.preventcancer.com.

Women at Risk Are Still in the Dark. Editorial. *Los Angeles Times,* September 9, 1994. www.preventcancer.com.

$4.25 Billion Implant Settlement Ignores Risk of Breast Cancer. Press release, September 13, 1994. www.preventcancer.com.

Lice Won't Kill You, but Its Treatment Can: Experts Call for Ban on Lindane Shampoos. Press release, and citizen petition, January 17, 1995. www.preventcancer.com.

Cancer Expert Calls Dow Breast Implant Ads Deceptive. Press release, May 11, 1995. www.preventcancer.com.

Seeking Medical Alert for all Women with Silicone Gel & Polyurethane Breast Implants. Citizen petition, May 12, 1995. www.preventcancer.com.

No Safety in These Implant Numbers. Editorial. *Chicago Tribune,* June 3, 1995. www.preventcancer.com.

Breast Implant Dangers. Letter. *New York Times,* October 26, 1995. www.preventcancer.com.

New Study Warns Implants Pose Risk of Breast Cancer. Press release, November 8, 1995. www.preventcancer.com.

New Drug Poses Risks of Ovarian Cancer. Press release, February 4, 1998. www.preventcancer.com.

Failure to Fully Document Risks of Osteoporosis Drug Is Reckless. Editorial. *Chicago Tribune,* April 19, 1998. www.preventcancer.com.

FDA Advisory Committee Urged to Reject Zeneca's Application of Tamoxifen for Preventing Breast Cancer in Healthy Women as the Drug is Ineffective and Dangerous. Press release, September 1, 1998. www.preventcancer.com.

The Cancer Drug Industry Seriously Misleads the Nation. Press release, September 24, 1998. www.preventcancer.com.

Misleading Claims by an Industry-Sponsored Study on the Safety of the Pill. Press release, January 27, 1999. www.preventcancer.com.

Genetically Engineered Anti-Aging Medication Poses Undisclosed Cancer Risks. Press release, March 14, 2000. www.preventcancer.com.

Jury Still Out on Trials of Breast Cancer Drug. Letter. *The Wall Street Journal.* June 9, 2000. www.preventcancer.com.

"Reading, Writing and Ritalin" TV Program Overlooks Evidence on Cancer Risks in Children. Press release, April 10, 2001. www.preventcancer.com.

American Academy of Pediatrics Guidelines for Treating Behavioral Disorders in Children with Ritalin Ignores Evidence of Cancer Risks. Press release, October 4, 2001. www.preventcancer.com.

Risks of Ovarian Cancer from Commonly Prescribed Drug Evista Supported by Recent Evidence. Press release, October 24, 2002. www.preventcancer.com.

Anti-Aging Medicine and Monsanto Milk Are Major Risks of Breast Cancer. Press release, May 19, 2003. www.preventcancer.com.

CHAPTER 9

1. Epstein, S. S. Legislative proposals for reversing the cancer epidemic and controlling run-away industrial technologies. *Int. J. Health Serv.* 30(2): 353–371, 2000.
2. Rio Declaration on Environment and Development, Principle 15, June 14, 1992.
3. UNCED. Convention on Biological Diversity, preamble, June 5, 1992.
4. UNCED. Agenda 21, June 13, 1992.
5. Consolidated version of the Treaty Establishing the European Community, Art. 174(2), 1993.
6. Commission of the European Communities on the Precautionary Principle. COM (2001). Brussels, February 2, 2000.
7. European Commission. *White Paper: Strategy for a Future Chemicals Policy.* COM (2001) 88, final. Brussels, February 27, 2001.
8. Christoforou, T. The precautionary principle and democratic expertise: A European legal perspective. *Sci. Public Policy* 30(3): 205–211, 2003.
9. Allanou, R., et al. *Public Availability of Data on EU High Production Volume Chemicals.* European Commission, European Chemicals Bureau, EUR 18996 EN, Brussels, 1999.
10. Environmental Protection Agency. *Chemical Hazard Data Availability Study.* Office of Pollution Protection and Toxics, Washington, D.C., 1988.
11. Wilde, M. *Locus Standi* in Environmental Torts and the Potential Influence of Human Rights Jurisprudence. *Reciel* 12(3): 284–294, 2003.
12. European Chemical Industry Council. *Discussion Paper: The Scope of the Future Chemicals Legislation and Its Elements.* May 15, 2002. www.cefic.org
13. American Chemistry Council. *Comments on the EC Proposal Concerning the Registration, Evaluation, Authorization and Registration of Chemicals.* Arlingtron, Va., July 10, 2003.
14. Luxton, J. C., et al., Washington Legal Foundation Advocate for Freedom and Justice, and the *Ad Hoc* Metals Coalition. New European chemical policy imperils U.S. Economic Growth. *Legal Backgrounder* 18(33): 1–4, 2003.
15. Loewenberg, S. Precaution is for Europeans. *New York Times,* May 18, 2003.
16. Brown, V. REACHing for Chemical Safety. *Environ. Health Perspect.* 111(14): A767–769, 2003.
17. DiGangi, J. *US Intervention in EU Chemicals Policy.* Environmental Health Fund, Jamaica Plain, Mass., September 2003.
18. U.S. opposes effort to test chemicals for health hazards. *Wall Street Journal,* September 9, 2003.
19. Greenwatch Today. *Bush Administration Presses European Union to Weaken Proposed Regulations, Lest They Affect U.S.* Washington, D.C., January 26, 2004.
20. Chemical Policy Alert. *Senators Seek Investigation of TSCA Shortfalls for Possible Legislative Overhaul.* January 8, 2004.
21. Democrats eye revisions to toxic law based on draft European policy. *Inside EPA,* November 10, 2003.

22. Trans-Atlantic Business Dialogue. *Recommendations Regarding Exemptions and Exclusions*. March 29, 2002.
23. Environmental Working Group. Media advisory. November 20, 2003.
24. Epstein, S. S., et al. The Stop Cancer Before It Starts Campaign. Cancer Prevention Coalition report, February 2003, Appendix 7. www.preventcancer.com.
25. European Commission. *Staff Working Paper: Extended Impact Statement*. COM (2003) 644, final. Brussels, October 29, 2003.
26. Epstein, S. S. *The Politics of Cancer, Revisited*. East Ridge Press, Hankins, N.Y., 1998.
27. Musu, T. *REACH, The Future EU Policy for Chemicals*. European Trade Union Technical Bureau report, November 7, 2003.
28. World Bank. *The Global Burden of Disease*. Based on analysis of Murray & Lopez, 1996.
29. Zeliger, H. I. Toxic effects of chemical mixtures. *Arch. Environ. Health* 58(1): 23–29, 2003.
30. Commonwealth of Massachusetts, Toxics Use Reduction Act, 1989.
31. Toxics Use Reduction Institute, 2003. www.turi.org.
32. Greenpeace. Safer Chemicals within REACH: Using the Substitution Principle to Drive Green Chemistry, October 2003. www.cleanproduction.org.
33. Swedish Government. *Swedish Views on the Authorization System and Comments on Accelerated Risks Management*. Stockholm, November 2002.
34. Royal Commission on Environmental Pollution. *Chemicals in Products: Safeguarding the Environment and Human Health*. London, 2003.
35. DeSimone, J. M. Practical approaches to green solvents. *Science* 297: 799–803, 2002.
36. Poliakoff, M., et al. Green chemistry: Science and politics of change. *Science* 297: 807–810, 2002.
37. Pacala, S. W., et al. False alarms over environmental false/alarms. *Science* 301: 1187–1188, 2003.
38. EPA. The Benefits and Costs of the Clean Air Act, 1970–1990. http://yosemite.epa.gov/ee/epa.
39. Kinzig, A., et al. Coping with uncertainty: A call for a new science-policy forum. *Ambio* 32(5): 330–335, August 2003.
40. Viel, J. F., et al. Soft tissue sarcoma and non-Hodgkin's lymphoma clusters around a municipal solid waste incinerator with high dioxin emission levels. *Am. J. Epidemiol.* 152(1): 13–19, 2000.
41. Floret, N., et al. Dioxin emissions from a solid waste incinerator and risks of non-Hodgkin's lymphoma. *Epidemiology* 14: 392–398, 2003.
42. Hardell, L., and Eriksson, M. Is the decline of the increasing incidence of non-Hodgkin's lymphoma in Sweden and other countries a result of cancer preventive measures? *Environ. Health Perspect.* 111(14): 1704–1706, 2003.
43. Remontet, L., et al. Cancer incidence and mortality in France over the period 1978–2000. *Rev. Epidemiol. Sante Publ.* 51: 3–30, 2003.
44. Watson, R. EU advisory committees declare their interests. *BMJ* 320: 826, 2000.
45. Burton, A. Is industry influencing IARC to downgrade carcinogens? *Lancet Oncol.* 4: 4, 2003.
46. Tomatis, L. The IARC Monograph Programme: Changing attitudes towards public health. *Int. J. Occup. Environ. Health* 8(2): 144–152, 2002.
47. Commission Working Group on the Classification and Labelling of Dangerous Substances. Guidelines for Setting Specific Concentration Limits for Carcinogens

in Annex I of Directive 67/548/EEC: Inclusion of Potency Considerations. http://europa.eu.int.
48. Michaels, D., and Wagner, W. Disclosure in regulatory science. *Science* 302: 2073, 2003.
49. Epstein, S. S. Testimony on Corporate Criminal Liability (H.R. 4973) Before the Subcommittee on Crime of the U.S. House Committee on the Judiciary, December 13, 1979.
50. Italian chemical plant managers accused of mass manslaughter. *Edie Weekly Summaries,* November 17, 2000.
51. European Convention for the Protection of Human Rights and Fundamental Freedom (Rome 4 November, 1950) (ECHR), Art. 8(1).
52. National Cancer Institute. Surveillance, Epidemiology and End Results Cancer Statistics Review (SEER). Bethesda, Md., 1975–2000.
53. National Institutes of Health/National Cancer Institute. *Atlas of Cancer Mortality in the United States.* Bethesda, Md., 1950–1994.
54. Earth Crash Earth Spirit. *Documenting the Collapse of a Dying Planet.* November 17, 2000. www.eces.org.
55. European Commission, Radiation Protection 129. Directorate-General Environment Unit C.4—Radiation Protection.
56. Pobel, D., and Viel, J. F. Case-control study of leukemia among young people near LaHague nuclear waste reprocessing plant (France). *J. Epidemiol. Community Health* 55: 101–106, 2001.
57. Guizard, D. V., et al. The incidence of childhood leukemia around the LaHague nuclear waste reprocessing plant (France). *J. Epidemiol. Community Health* 55: 469–474, 2001.
58. Gardner, M. J. Review of reported increases in childhood cancer rates in the vicinity of nuclear installments in the U.K. *J. R. Stat. Soc.* 152: 307–385, 1989.
59. Mangano, J., et al. Elevated childhood cancer incidence proximate to U.S. nuclear power plants. *Arch. Environ. Health* 58: 74–82, 2003.
60. Hattchouel, J. M., et al. Cancer mortality around French nuclear sites. *Ann. Epidemiol.* 6: 126–129, 1996.
61. LeGuen, B., et al. French approach for the distribution of iodine tablets in the vicinity of nuclear power plants. *Health Phys.* 83: 293–300, 2002.
62. Verger, P., et al. Thyroid cancers in France and the Chernobyl accident. *Health Phys.* 85: 323–329, 2003.
63. European Commission on Radiation Risks. *Regulators' Edition.* Brussels, 2003.
64. Shellabarger, C. J., et al. Experimental carcinogenesis in the breast. In *Radiation Carcinogenesis,* edited by A. C. Upton et al. Elsevier, New York, 1986.
65. Directive du Conseil, 90/394/EEC, June 1990.
66. Aubrun, J. C., et al. Occupational cancer in France: Epidemiology, toxicology, prevention and compensation. *Environ. Health Perspect.* 107(Suppl. 2): 245–252, 1999.
67. Brugère, J., and Naud, C. *Recognition of Occupational Cancers in Europe.* Trade Union Technical Bureau Newsletter, No. 21, June 2003.
68. Goldberg, M. *Risques Professionals.* Rapport Pour le Groupe Technique National, January 2003.
69. Imbernon, E. *Estimation du Nombre de Cas de Certain Cancers Attributable a des Facteurs Professionals en France.* Institut de Veille Sanitaire, Paris, 2002.
70. Viel, J. F., et al. Brain cancer mortality among French farmers: The vineyard pesticide hypothesis. *Arch. Environ. Health* 53(1): 65–70, 1998.

71. Fabro-Peray, P., et al. Environmental risk factors for non-Hodgkin's lymphoma: A population-based case control study in Languedoc-Roussillon, France. *Cancer Causes Control* 12: 201–212, 2001.
72. Boffetta, P., and Kogevinas, M. Occupational cancer in Europe. *Méd. Lavo.* 86: 236–262, 1995.
73. Germany confronts the work taboo. *Financial Times,* January 15, 2004.
74. Thévonon, E. Railing against cancer. *Label France* Magazine, No. 51, July 2003.
75. Daston, G., et al. A framework for assessing risks to children from exposure to environmental agents. *Environ. Health Perspect.* 112(2): 238–256, 2004.
76. Landrigan, P. J., et al. Children's health and the environment: Public health issues for risk assessment. *Environ. Health Perspect.* 112(2): 257–265, 2004.
77. LaRonda, L., et al. Hazard identification and predictability of children's health risk from animal data. *Environ. Health Perspect.* 112(2): 266–271, 2004.
78. Ginsberg, G., et al. Incorporating children's toxicokinetics into a risk framework. *Environ. Health Perspect.* 112(2): 272–283, 2004.
79. Hardell, L., et al. Increased concentrations of polychlorinated biphenyls, hexachlorobenzene, and chlordane in mothers of men with testicular cancer. *Environ. Health Perspect.* 111(7): 930–934, 2003.
80. Eurostat. The United Nations, Population Reference Bureau, 2001. gapminder.org.
81. Christoforou, T. The precautionary principle, risk assessment and the comprehensive role of science in the European Community and the U.S. legal system. In *Green Giants,* edited by N. J. Vig and M. G. Faure. MIT Press, Cambridge, Mass., 2004.

Further Reading

REACHing for Control of Carcinogenic Chemicals. Press release, May 5, 2004. www.preventcancer.com.

CHAPTER 10A

1. Food and Drug Administration. Talk Paper. August 4, 1989.
2. U.S. House of Representatives, Committee on Government Operations. Twenty-seventh Report: Human Food Safety and Regulation of Animal Drugs. 99th Congress, Washington, D.C., December 31, 1985.
3. Animal Health Institute. Bovine somatotropin (BST). Report No. 1-5/88-15M, 1988.
4. Kronfeld, D. S. The challenge of BST. *Large Animal Veterinarian,* November/December 1987, pp. 14–17.
5. Pursel, V., et al. Genetic engineering of livestock. *Science* 244: 1281–1288, 1989.
6. Brown, D. L., et al. Influence of sometribove USAN on the body composition of lactating cattle. *J. Nutr.* 119: 633–638, 1989.
7. Kronfeld, D. S. BST milk safety. *J. Am. Vet. Med. Assoc.* 195: 288–289, 1989.
8. Mepham, T. B. Criteria for the public acceptability of biotechnological innovations in animal production. In *Biotechnology in Growth Regulation,* edited by R. B. Heap, C. G. Prosser, and G. E. Lamming, pp. 203–212. Butterworths, London, 1989.
9. Collins, J. S. (Impro Inc., Minnetonka, Minn.). Data on somatotropin hormone research in dairy cows. Personal communication, August 31, 1989.
10. Chalupa, W., et al. Responses of dairy cows to somatotropin. *J. Dairy Sci.* 70(Suppl. 1, Pt. 216): 176, 1987.

11. Palmquist, D. L. Response of high producing cows given daily injections of recombinant bovine somatotropin from D 30-296 of lactation. *J. Dairy Sci.* 71(Suppl. 1, Pt. 261): 206, 1988.
12. Samuels, W. A. Long term evaluation of sometribove, USAN treatment and prolonged release system for lactating cows. *J. Dairy Sci.* 71(Suppl. 1, Pt. 271): 209, 1988.
13. Singer, P. L. BST: How does it affect calving interval? *Hoards Dairy Man,* July 1989, p. 55.
14. Bitman, J., et al. Blood and milk lipid responses induced by growth hormone administration in lactating cows. *J. Dairy Sci.* 67: 2873–2880, 1984.
15. Baer, R. J., et al. Composition and flavor of milk produced by cows injected with recombinant bovine somatotropin. *J. Dairy Sci.,* 1989, in press.
16. Kronfeld, D. S. Biologic and economic risks associated with use of bovine somatotropin. *J. Am. Vet. Med. Assoc.* 192: 1693–1696, 1988.
17. Prosser, C. G., et al. Changes in concentrations of IGF-1 in milk during BGH treatment in the goat. *J. Endocrinol.* 112(March Suppl.): Abstract 65, 1987.
18. Prosser, C. G. Bovine somatotropin and milk composition. *Lancet,* November 19, 1988, p. 1201.
19. Davis, S. R., et al. Effects of injecting growth hormone or thyroxine on milk production and blood plasma concentrations of insulin-like growth factors I and 11 in dairy cows. *J. Endocrinol.* 114: 17–24, 1987.
20. Editorial: Bovine somatotropin and human health. *Lancer,* August 13, 1988, p. 376.
21. Brunner, E. Safety of bovine somatotropin. *Lancet,* September 10, 1988, p. 629.
22. Food and Drug Administration. Letter from G. B. Guest, Director for Veterinary Medicine, FDA, to Senator W. P. Winkle, State Capitol, Madison, Wisc., May 9, 1989.
23. Agscene. Will junkie cows get the go ahead? *Compassion in World Farming,* March 1988, p. 5.
24. Monsanto. BST Food Wholesomeness Summary. March and May 1987.
25. Rogol, A. D. Growth hormone: Physiology, therapeutic use, and potential for abuse. *Exercise and Sport Sciences,* edited by K. Randall, pp. 353–377. Williams & Wilkins, Baltimore, 1989.
26. Forsham, P. H., et al. Nitrogen retention in man produced by chymotrypsin digests of bovine somatotropin. *Metabolism* 7: 726–764, 1958.
27. Kennelly, J. J., and deBoer, G. Bovine somatotropin. In *Proceedings of the Alberta Dairy Seminar,* Banff, Alberta, March 9–11, 1988.
28. Eppard, P. J., et al. Effect of dose of bovine growth hormone on lactation of dairy cows. *J. Dairy Sci.* 68: 1109–1115, 1985.
29. Peel, C. J., et al. Lactational response to exogenous growth hormone and abomasal infusion of a glucose-sodium caseinate mixture in high yielding cows. *J. Nutr.* 112: 1770, 1982.
30. Fronk, C. J., et al. Comparison of different patterns of exogenous growth hormone administration on milk production in Holstein cows. *J. Anim. Sci.* 57: 699, 1983.
31. McBride, B. W., et al. The influence of bovine growth hormone in animals and their products. *Res. Dev. Agric.* 5: 1–21, 1988.
32. Honegger, R., and Humbel, R. L. Insulin-like growth factors I and II in fetal and adult bovine serum. *J. Biol. Chem.* 261: 569, 1986.
33. Glimm, D. R., et al. Effect of bovine somatotropin on the distribution of immunoreactive insulin-like growth factor 1 in lactating bovine mammary tissue. *J. Dairy Sci.* 71: 2923–2935, 1988.
34. Eli Lilly and Company. Human Growth Hormones: A Controlled Clinical Comparison of Immunogenicity. Indianapolis, Ind., 1987.

35. Otterby, D. E., et al. *J. Dairy Sci.* 72(Suppl. 1): 329, 1989.
36. Morbeck, D. E., et al. *J. Dairy Sci.* 72(Suppl. 1): 345.
37. Prosser, C. G., et al. *J. Dairy Res.* 56: 17–26, 1989.

Further Reading

Growth Hormones Would Endanger Milk. Editorial. *Los Angeles Times,* July 27, 1989. www.preventcancer.com.
FDA Is Ignoring Dangers of Bovine Growth Hormone. Editorial. *Austin American-Statesman,* June 2, 1990. www.preventcancer.com.
Approval of Cow Hormone Imperils Our Milk. Letter. *New York Times,* December 11, 1990. www.preventcancer.com.
Forum on RBGH Milk and Breast Cancer. Press release, March 14, 1994. www.preventcancer.com.
A Needless New Risk of Breast Cancer. Editorial. *Los Angeles Times,* March 20, 1994. www.preventcancer.com.
New Study Warns of Breast and Colon Cancer Risks from RBGH Milk. Press release and conference, January 23, 1996. www.preventcancer.com.
Public Health and Veterinary Risks of RBST Dairy Products. Presentation to the U.K. House of Commons Committees on Agriculture and Health, December 11, 1996. www.preventcancer.com.

CHAPTER 11

1. Epstein, S. S. Potential public health hazards of biosynthetic milk hormones. *Int. J. Health Serv.* 20(1): 73–84, 1990.
2. Epstein, S. S. Polluted data. *The Sciences* 18(6): 16–21, 1978.
3. Epstein, S. S. *The Politics of Cancer.* Anchor Press/Doubleday, New York, 1979.
4. Doyle, J. Corporation on campus: Bio-science for sale. *Not Man Apart,* July/August 1987, pp. 10–11.
5. Castleman, B. Toxic pollutants, science and corporate influence. *Arch. Environ. Health* 44(2): 68, 127,1989.
6. Epstein, S. S. Losing the war against cancer. *Int. J. Health Serv.* 20(1): 53–71, 1990.
7. Kronfeld, D. S. The challenge of BST. *Large Animal Veterinarian* 42: 14–17, November/December 1987.
8. Kronfeld, D. S. Biologic and economic risks associated with the use of bovine somatotropins. *J. Am. Vet. Med. Assoc.* 192: 1693–1696, 1988.
9. Kronfeld, D. S. The continuing challenge of BST. *Large Animal Veterinarian* 44: 6–7, September/October 1989.
10. IGF-1: Troublesome BGH hormone residue. *The Milkweed* 126: 4–5, November 1989.
11. Burroughs, R., ex-Veterinary Medical Office, Center for Veterinary Medicine, FDA, Washmgton, D.C. Personal communication.
12. New Animal Drug Application Data and internal FDA documentation, Washington, D.C.
13. Ingersoll, B. Milk is found tainted with a wide range of drugs farmers give cattle. *Wall Street J.,* December 29, 1989.
14. Schneider, J. FDA accused of improper ties in review of drugs for milk cows. *New York Times,* January 12, 1990.
15. U.S. House of Representatives, Committee on Government Operations. Twenty-seventh Report: Human Food Safety and Regulation of Animal Drugs. 99th Congress, Washington, D.C., December 31, 1985.

CHAPTER 12

1. Epstein, S. S. Potential Public Health Hazards of Biosynthetic Milk Hormones. Letter and report to FDA Commissioner Frank Young, July 19, 1989.
2. Epstein, S. S. Potential public health hazards of biosynthetic milk hormones. *Int. J. Health Serv.* 20: 73–84, 1990.
3. Epstein, S. S. Questions and answers on synthetic bovine growth hormones. *Int. J. Health Serv.* 20: 573–581, 1990.
4. Food and Drug Administration. Interim guidance on the voluntary labelling of milk and milk products from cows that have not been treated with recombinant bovine somatotropin. *Federal Register* 59(28): 6279–6280, 1994.
5. Epstein, S. S. A needless new risk of breast cancer (commentary). *Los Angeles Times*, March 20, 1994, p. M5.
6. Matthews, I. S., Norstedt, G., and Palmiter, R. D. Regulation of insulin-like growth factor I gene expression by growth hormone. *Proc. Natl. Acad. Sci. USA* 83: 9343–9347, 1986.
7. Sekyi-Otu, A., et al. Metastatic behavior of the RIF-1 murine fibrosarcoma: Inhibited by hypophysectomy and partially restored by growth hormone replacement. *J. Natl. Cancer Inst.* 86: 628–632, 1994.
8. Isgaard, J., et al. Pulsatile intravenous growth hormone (GH) infusion to hypophysectomized rats increases insulin-like growth factor I messenger ribonucleic acid in skeletal tissues more effectively than continuous GH infusion. *Endocrinology* 123: 2605–2610, 1988.
9. Honegger, A., and Humbel, R. R. Insulin-like growth factors I and II in fetal and adult bovine serum. *J. Biol. Chem.* 261: 569–575, 1986.
10. McBride, B. W., Burton, J. L., and Burton, J. H. The influence of bovine growth hormone (somatotropin) on animals and their products. *Res. Dev. Agricult.* 5: 1–21, 1988.
11. Prosser, C. G., et al. Changes in concentration of insulin-like growth factor I (IGF-1) in milk during bovine growth hormone treatment in the goat. *J. Endocrinol.* 112(March Suppl.), Abstr. 65, 1987.
12. Prosser, C. G. Bovine somatotropin and milk composition. *Lancet* 1: 1201, November 19, 1988.
13. Prosser, C. G., Fleet, I. R., and Corps, A. N. Increased secretion of insulin-like growth factor I into milk of cows treated with recombinantly derived bovine growth hormone. *J. Dairy Res.* 56: 17–26, 1989.
14. Mepham, T. B. Public health implications of bovine somatotropin use in dairying: Discussion paper. *J. R. Soc. Med.* 85: 736–739, 1992.
15. Juskevich, J. C., and Geyer, C. G. Bovine growth hormone: Human food safety evaluation. *Science* 249: 875–884, 1990.
16. Frystyk, J., et al. Free insulin-like growth factors (IGF-1 and IGF-II) in human serum. *FEBS Lett.* 348: 185–191, 1994.
17. Hansen, M. K. *Biotechnology and Milk: Benefit or Threat?*, p. 6. Consumer Policy Institute, New York, 1990.
18. Schams, D. Secretion of somatotropin and IGF-1 into milk during BST administration. In *Sometribove: Mechanism of Action, Safety and Instructions for Use*. Monsanto, Basingstoke, 1991.
19. Mepham, T. B., et al. Safety of milk from cows treated with bovine somatotropin. *Lancet* 2: 197, 1994.
20. National Institutes of Health. Technology Assessment Conference Statement on Bovine Somatotropin. *JAMA* 265: 1423–1425, 1991.

21. Daughaday, W. H., Kapadia, M., and Mariz, I. Serum somatomedin binding proteins: Physiologic significance and interference in radioligand assay. *J. Lab. Clin. Med.* 109: 355–363, 1987.

22. Mesiano, S., et al. Failure of acid-ethanol treatment to prevent interference by binding proteins in radioligand assays for the insulin-like growth factors. *J. Endocrinol.* 119: 453–460, 1988.

23. Francis, G. L., et al. Insulin-like growth factors 1 and 2 in bovine colostrum— Sequences and biological activities compared with those of a potent truncated form. *Biochem. J.* 251: 95–103, 1988.

24. Gardner, M. L. Gastrointestinal absorption of intact proteins. *Annu. Rev. Nutr.* 8: 329–350, 1988.

25. Levinsky, R. J. Factors influencing uptake of food antigens. *Proc. Nutr. Soc.* 44: 81–86, 1985.

26. Roberton, D. M., et al. Milk antigen absorption in the preterm and term neonate. *Arch. Dis. Child.* 57: 369–372, 1982.

27. Reinhardt, M. C. Molecular absorption of food antigens in health and disease. *Ann. Allergy* 53: 597–601, 1984.

28. Udall, J. N. Human digestion and absorption of milk and its components at different stages of development: Protein hormones and growth factors. In *NIH Technology Assessment Conference, Bovine Somatotropin*, pp. 91–97. Bethesda, Md., 1990.

29. Lee, E. J., and Heiner, C. Allergy to cow's milk—1984. *Pediatr. Rev.* 7: 195–203, 1986.

30. Teske, R. H., Center for Veterinary Medicine FDA. Letter to S. Epstein, March 7, 1994, in response to Epstein's February 14, 1994, letter to FDA Commissioner Dr. Kessler.

31. FAO/WHO, Expert Committee on Food Additives. Evaluation of certain veterinary drug remedies in food. *WHO Tech. Rep. Ser.* 832, 4/5, pp. 113–142, 1992.

32. Collier, R. J. Qualitative and quantitative changes in hormones and growth factors in milk as affected by the administration of rBST to cattle. In *NIH Technology Assessment Conference*, pp. 45–49. Bethesda, Md., 1994.

33. Hammond, B., Manager, Toxicology, Monsanto Agriculture Co. Letter to Jerry Elliott, Program Analyst, Office of Medical Applications of Research, NIH, December 19, 1990.

34. Hansen, M. K. Letter to FDA, May 24, 1993.

35. Epstein, S. S. Polluted data. *The Sciences* 18: 16–21, 1978.

36. Carver, P., Staff Director to Rep. D. Obey, D-Wis., House Subcommittee on Labor, Health and Human Services. Personal communication, May 30, 1994.

37. Armstrong, J. D., et al. (Hoffman-LaRoche/Monsanto). Effects of sometribove or immunization against growth hormone releasing factor (GRFi) on milk yield and composition, calf gain, insulin and metabolites in multiparous beef cows. *J. Dairy Sci.* 77(Suppl. 1): 182, 1994.

38. Glimm, D. R., Baracos, V. E., and Kennelly, J. J. Effect of bovine somatotropin on the distribution of immunoreactive insulin-like growth factor-1 in lactating bovine mammary tissue. *J. Dairy Sci.* 71: 2923–2935, 1988.

39. Furlanetto, R. W., and DiCarlo, J. N. Somatomedin-C receptors and growth effects in human breast cells maintained in long-term tissue culture. *Cancer Res.* 44: 2122–2128, 1984.

40. Gregor, P., and Burleigh, B. D. Presence of high affinity somatomedin/insulin-like growth factor receptors in porcine mammary gland. *Endocrinology* 116(Suppl. 1), Abstr. 223, 1985.

41. Campbell, P. G., and Baumrucker, C. R. Characterization of insulin-like growth factor-1/somatomedin-C receptors in bovine mammary gland. *J. Dairy Sci.* 69(Suppl. 1), Abstr. 163, 1986.

42. Ullrich, A., and Schessinger, J. Signal transduction by receptors with tyrosine-kinase activity. *Cell* 61: 203–212, 1990.

43. Lippman, M. E. The development of biological therapies for breast cancer. *Science* 259: 631–632, 1993.

44. Pappa, V., et al. Insulin-like growth factor-1 receptors are overexpressed and predict a low risk in human breast cancer. *Cancer Res.* 53: 3736–3740, 1993.

45. Reynolds, R. K., et al. Regulation of epidermal growth factor and insulin-like growth factor I receptors by estradiol and progesterone in normal and neoplastic endometrial cell cultures. *Gynecol. Oncol.* 38(3): 396–406, 1990.

46. Rechler, M. M., and Nissley, S. P. The nature and regulation of the receptors for insulin-like growth factor. *Annu. Rev. Physiol.* 47: 425–442, 1985.

47. Osborne, C. K., Clemmons, D. R., and Arteaga, C. L. Regulation of breast cancer growth by insulin-like growth factors. *J. Steroid Biochem. Mol. Biol.* 37: 805–809, 1990.

48. Rosen, N., et al. Insulin-like growth factors in human breast cancer. *Breast Cancer Res. Treat.* 18(Suppl.): 555–562, 1991.

49. Pollak, M. N., Huynh, H. T., and Lefebvre, P. Tamoxifen reduces insulin-like growth factor I (IGF-1). *Breast Cancer Res. Treat.* 22: 91–100, 1992.

50. Baxter, R. C., et al. High molecular weight somatomedin-C/IGF-1 from T47D human mammary carcinoma cells: Immunoreactivity and bioactivity. In *Insulin-like Growth Factors/Somatomedins: Basic Chemistry, Biology, Clinical Importance*, edited by E. M. Spencer, pp. 615–618. DeGruyter, New York, 1983.

51. Huff, K. K., et al. Secretion of an insulin-like growth factor-1-related protein by human breast cancer cells. *Cancer Res.* 46: 4618–4619, 1986.

52. Harris, J. R., et al. Breast cancer. *N. Engl. J. Med.* 7: 473–480, 1992.

53. Lippman, M. Growth factors, receptors and breast cancer. *J. Natl. Inst. Health Res.* 3: 59–62, 1991.

54. Ekbom, A., et al. Evidence of prenatal influence on breast cancer risk. *Lancet*, October 24, 1992, pp. 1015–1018.

55. Epstein, S. S. Environmental and occupational pollutants are avoidable causes of breast cancer. *Int. J. Health Serv.* 24: 145–159, 1994.

56. Elwood, J. M., Cox, B., and Richardson, A. K. The effectiveness of breast cancer screening by mammography in younger women. *Online J. Current Clin. Trials* 193, No. 32, 1993.

57. Corps, A. N., and Brown, K. D. Stimulation of intestinal epithelial cell proliferation in culture by growth factors in human and ruminant mammary secretions. *J. Endocrinol.* 113: 285–290, 1987.

58. Playford, R. J., et al. Effect of luminal growth factor preservation on intestinal growth. *Lancet* 2: 843–848, 1993.

59. Chaurasia, O. P., et al. Insulin-like growth factor I in human gastrointestinal exocrine secretions. *Regul. Pept.* 50: 113–119, 1994.

60. Olanrewaju, H., Patel, L., and Siedel, E. R. Trophic action of local intraileal infusion of insulin-like growth factor 1: Polyamine dependence. *Am. J. Physiol.* 263: E282–E286, 1992.

61. Challacombe, D. N., and Wheeler, E. E. Safety of milk from cows treated with bovine somatotropin. *Lancet* 344: 815–816, 1994.

62. Coghlan, D. Arguing till the cows come home. *New Scientist*, October 26, 1994, pp. 11–12.

63. Lahm, H., et al. Growth regulation and co-stimulation of human colorectal cancer cell lines by insulin-like growth factor I, II and transforming growth factor alpha. *Br. J. Cancer* 65(3): 341–346, 1992.

64. Guo, Y. S. Insulinlike growth factor-binding protein modulates the growth response to insulinlike growth factor 1 by human gastric cancer cells. *Gastroenterology* 104(6): 1595–1604, 1993.

65. Burton, J. L., et al. A review of bovine growth hormone. *Can. J. Animal Sci.* 74: 167–201, 1994.

66. American Medical Association Council on Scientific Affairs. Biotechnology and the American agricultural industry. *JAMA* 265: 1429–1436, 1991.

67. Juul, A., et al. The ratio between serum levels of IGF-1 and the IGF binding proteins decreases with age in healthy patients and is increased in acromegalic patients. *Clin. Endocrinol.* 41: 85–93, 1994.

68. Tremble, J. M., and McGregor, A. M. Epidemiology, complications and mortality. In *Treating Acromegaly*, edited by J. A. H. Wass, pp. 5–12. Journal of Endocrinology, Bristol, England, 1994.

Further Reading

Epstein, S. S. *The Politics of Cancer*, Revisited, East Ridge Press, Fremont Center, N.Y., 1998, Appendix XII, p. 600.

Hormonal Milk Poses Prostate Cancer and Other Cancer Risks. Press release, March 30, 1998. www.preventcancer.com.

Monsanto's Hormonal Milk Poses Serious Risks of Breast Cancer Besides Other Cancers. Press release, June 21, 1998. www.preventcancer.com.

International Scientific Committee Warns of Serious Risks of Breast and Prostate Cancer from Monsanto's Hormonal Milk. Press release, March 21, 1999. www.preventcancer.com.

Monsanto's Genetically Engineered Modified Milk Ruled Unsafe by the United Nations. Press release, August 18, 1999. www.preventcancer.com.

Editorial Postscript to August 18, 1999 Press release: Truth or Fact. Editorial. August 25, 1999. www.preventcancer.com.

Statement on the Public Health Hazards of GE (genetically engineered) Milk and Food. Press release, November 18, 1999. www.preventcancer.com.

Austria Urged to Take Initiatives to Protect the Public Against Cancer and Other Risks of Monsanto's Genetically Engineered Modified rBST Dairy Products. Press release, Vienna. January 18, 2000. www.preventcancer.com.

Got (genetically engineered) MILK! The Monsanto rBGH/BST Milk Wars Handbook. E-book, available from Seven Stories Press, 2001. www.preventcancer.com.

Role of Insulin-Like Growth Factors in Cancer Development and Progression. Letter. *Journal of the National Cancer Institute* 95(3): 238, February 7, 2001. www.preventcancer.com.

Anti-Aging Medication and Monsanto Milk are Major Risks of Breast Cancer. Press release, May 19, 2003. www.preventcancer.com.

CHAPTER 13

1. Epstein, S. S. Potential public health hazards of biosynthetic milk hormones. *Int. J. Health Serv.* 20(1): 73–84, 1990.

2. Hertz, R. The estrogen-cancer hypothesis with special emphasis on DES. In *Origins of Human Cancer,* edited by H. H. Hiatt, J. D. Watson, and J. A. Winston, pp. 1665–1682. Vol. 4 of *Cold Spring Harbor Conference on Cell Proliferation.* Cold Spring Harbor Laboratory, 1977.
3. U.S. House of Representatives, Committee on Government Operations. Twenty-seventh Report: Human Food Safety and the Regulation of Animal Drugs. 99th Congress, Washington, D.C., December 31, 1985.

Further Reading

Europe's Worries About U.S. Meat Should Be Our Worry Too. Editorial. *Los Angeles Times,* January 30, 1989. www.preventcancer.com.
Europe's Ban on Hormone-Raised Beef is Based on Sound Science. Press release, October 8, 1996. www.preventcancer.com.
Testimony in Support of the EU Ban on Trade in Hormone Beef. Submitted to the WTO. February 5, 1997. www.preventcancer.com.
None of Us Should Eat Extra Estrogen. Commentary. *Los Angeles Times,* March 24, 1997. www.preventcancer.com.
Statement to the European Parliament in Support of the EU Ban on Trade in Hormonal Beef. May 21, 1997. www.preventcancer.com.
New Challenges on the Safety of U.S. Meat: Oprah Right for Other Reasons. Press release, February 2, 1998. www.preventcancer.com.
Epstein, S. S. *The Politics of Cancer, Revisited,* East Ridge Press, Fremont Center, N.Y., 1998, Appendix XI, p. 585.
FAO/WHO's Joint Expert Committee on Food Additives Report on Hormonal Meat Is Scientifically Invalid and Fails to Warn Consumers of Cancer Risks. Press release, May 4, 1999. www.preventcancer.com.
The European Ban on Hormonal Meat Is Based on Valid Scientific Evidence. Press conference, Salzburg, Austria, May 31, 1999. www.preventcancer.com.
Genetically Engineered Anti-aging Medication Poses Undisclosed Cancer Risks. Press release, March 14, 2000. www.preventcancer.com.
McDonald's Is Leading the Way, But Hasn't Gone Far Enough Yet. Press release, July 1, 2000. www.preventcancer.com.

CHAPTER 14

1. Congress pressures FDA for softer labeling of irradiated foods. *FDA Week,* May 12, 2000, pp. 9–10.
2. Federation of American Societies for Experimental Biology. *Evaluation of the Health Aspects of Certain Compounds Found in Irradiated Beef.* Report to the U.S. Army Medical Research and Development Command, Bethesda, Md., August 1977.
3. U.S. Food and Drug Administration. *Recommendations for Evaluating the Safety of Irradiated Food.* Final Report of FDA's Irradiated Food Committee. Washington, D.C., July 1980.
4. Epstein, S. S., and Gofman, J. W. Irradiation of food. *Science* 223: 1354, 1984.
5. Sun, M. *Science* 223: 1354, 1984.
6. van Gemert, M. *Memorandum Re: Final Report of the Task Group for the Review of Toxicology Data on Irradiated Food.* U.S. Food and Drug Administration, Washington, D.C., April 9, 1982.
7. van Gemert, M. Letter to New Jersey Assemblyman John Keller, October 19, 1993.

8. Public Citizen's Critical Mass Energy and Environment Program and the Cancer Prevention Coalition. *A Broken Record: How the FDA Legalized and Continues to Legalize Food Irradiation without Testing It for Safety.* Special report. October 2000.

9. Piccioni, R. Food irradiation: Contaminating our food. *Ecologist* 18(2): 48–55, 1988.

10. Vijayalaxmi and Srikantia, S. G. A review of the studies on the wholesomeness of irradiation wheat conducted at the National Institute of Nutrition, India. *Radiat. Phys. Chem.* 34(6): 941–952, 1989.

11. Murray, D. R. *Biology of Food Irradiation.* RSP Research Studies Press, Taunton, Somerset, England, 1990.

12. Food Chemical News: Irradiation compounds vitamin loss from cooking. *Agricultural Research Service Reports,* November 10, 1986, p. 42.

13. USDA Food Safety Inspection Service. *Irradiation of Red Meat: A Complication of Technical Data for Its Authorization and Control.* International Consultative Group on Food Irradiation, August 1996.

14. Trager, E. A. *Review of Events at Large Pool-Type Irradiators.* Office of Analysis and Evaluation of Operational Data, U.S. Nuclear Regulatory Commission, Washington, D.C., March 1989.

15. Alvarez, R. Food irradiation: 50 years of hollow promises. *Bull. Atom. Sci.* 2000, in press.

16. Elder, R. O., et al. Correlation of enterohemorrhagic *E. coli* 0157 prevalence in feces, hides and carcasses of beef cattle during processing. *Proc. Natl. Acad. Sci. U.S.A.* 97(7): 2999–3003, 2000.

17. Diaz-Gonzalez, F., et al. Grain feeding and the dissemination of acid-resistant *Escherichia coli* from cattle. *Science* 281: 1666–1668, 1998.

18. *Analysis of Ontario* E. coli *Walkerton Pollution Disaster.* The Gallon Environmental Letter. Montreal, Quebec.

Further Reading

Irradiation of Foods. Letter. *Science* 223: 1354, 1984. www.preventcancer.com.

Risks of Radiation: Too Many Questions About Food Safety. Comment. *USA Today.* January 22, 1992. www.preventcancer.com.

The CPC and Public Citizen Charge Congress with Proposing Deceptive Labeling of Irradiated Food, Besides Ignoring Its Risks to Health and the Environment. Press release, June 6, 2000. www.preventcancer.com.

FDA Legalized Food Irradiation Without Adequately Evaluating Its Risks, Dismissed Evidence of Serious Public Health Hazards. Press release, October 3, 2000. www.preventcancer.com.

Administration Proposal to Serve Irradiated Beef to School Children Poses Cancer, Genetic and Other Risks. Press release, April 8, 200 1. www.preventcancer.com.

FDA, USDA Officials Dismiss Citizens'Concerns About Irradiated Food at Symposium. Press release, June 18, 2001. www.preventcancer.com.

The CPC and Illinois Food Safety Coalition Announce a Public Information Campaign to Warn of Serious Dangers of Food Irradiation. Press release, January 17, 2002. www.preventcancer.com.

Food Irradiation Threatens Public Health, National Security. Press release, March 8, 2002. www.preventcancer.com.

USDA's Allowing Schools to Serve Irradiated Meat is Reckless. Press release, November 1, 2002. www.preventcancer.com.

Jewel-Osco's Sale of SureBeam's Irradiated Meat Threatens Consumer Health. Press release, December 4, 2002. www.preventcancer.com.
Beware of Irradiated Dietary Supplements. Press release, May 23, 2003. www.preventcancer.com.

CHAPTER 15

1. Abelson, P. H. Cancer phobia. *Science* 237: 473, 1987.
2. Ames, B., et al. Ranking possible carcinogenic hazards. *Science* 236: 271–280, 1987.
3. Epstein, S. S., and Swartz, J. B. Carcinogenic risk assessment. *Science* 240: 1043–1045, 1988. [This article was co-signed by some 15 nationally recognized experts in carcinogenesis, epidemiology, and public health.]
4. Abelson, P. H. Product liability in a litigious society. *Science* 240: 1589, 1988.
5. National Center for State Courts. 1. A Preliminary Examination of Available Civil and Criminal Trend Data in State Trial Courts for 1978, 1981, and 1984. April 1986.
6. Kakalik, J. S., and Pace, N. M. Cost and Compensation Paid in Tort Litigation. Rand Institute, 1986.
7. Hensler, D. R., et al. Trends in Tort Litigation: The Story Behind the Statistics. Rand Institute, 1987.
8. Broad, W. J. Question of scientific fakery is raised in inquiry. *New York Times,* July 12, 1989, p. 18.

CHAPTER 16

1. Epstein, S. S. Polluted data. *The Sciences* 18: 16–21, 1978.
2. Epstein, S. S. *The Politics of Cancer.* Anchor Press/Doubleday, New York, 1979.
3. Castleman, B. I., and Ziem, G. E. Corporate influence on threshold limit values. *Am. J. Ind. Med.* 13: 531–559,1988.
4. National Academy of Sciences, National Research Council, Committee on Toxicology. An *Assessment of the Health Risks of Seven Pesticides Used For Termite Control.* National Academy Press, Washington, D.C., August 1982.
5. Orkin Pest Control, National Service Department. Effective Slab Treatment. Confidential Technical Bulletin T-11(65) September 2, 1965.
6. Orkin Pest Control, National Service Department. Confidential Technical Bulletin, November 9, 1979.
7. Calo, C. J. (Velsicol). Chlordane Residue in Air of Homes in Wright Patterson Air Force Base. Confidential memorandum, November 8, 1974.
8. U.S. Air Force, Office of Surgeon General. *Evaluation of Cleaning Effectiveness to Reduce Wall/Floor Surface Chlordane Levels Within Military Family Housing.* Wright Patterson Air Force Base, 1974.
9. Livingston, J. M., et al. *Airborne Chlordane Contamination in Houses Treated at a Midwestern Air Force Base.* USAF Report No. OEHL 82-11, February 1981.
10. National Academy of Sciences, National Research Council, Committee on Toxicology. *Chlordane in Military Housing.* National Academy Press, Washington, D.C., June 4, 1979.
11. General Accounting Office. Need for Formal Risk Benefit Review of the Pesticide Chlordane. Letter to EPA, August 5, 1980.
12. Khasawinah, A. M. (Velsicol). Chlordane: Air Concentration in Treated Homes: Assessment and Significance. Unpublished report, August 1982.

13. Velsicol Chemical Corporation. Standard for Technical Chlordane. Confidential report, 1971.
14. Stumphy, M. K., and Atallah, G. H. Air and Surface Residues in Houses after Application of Heptachlor. Confidential Velsicol report 190, November 10, 1975.
15. Atallah, G. H., et al. Heptachlor and Chlordane Residues in Houses Treated with One of Three Termite Preparations. Unpublished Velsicol report, March 3, 1982.
16. Raltech Scientific Services. Applicator and Inhalation Exposure to Chlordane During and After Termiticide Application in California. Unpublished report to Velsicol, October 8, 1979.
17. Huntington Research Center. Chlordane: A 90-Day Inhalation Toxicity Study in the Rat and Monkey. Unpublished report to Velsicol, June 26, 1984.
18. Kettering Laboratories (University of Cincinnati). The Physiological Effects of the Introduction of Heptachlor into the Diet of Experimental Animals in Varying Levels of Concentration. Unpublished report to Velsicol, August 17, 1955.
19. Kettering Laboratories. The Physiological Effects of the Introduction of Heptachlor and Heptachlor Epoxide in Varying Levels of Concentration into the Diet of CFN Rats. Unpublished report to Velsicol, November 10, 1959.
20. Kettering Laboratories. The Effects of Feeding Diets Containing a Mixture of Heptachlor and Heptachlor Epoxide to Female Rats for Two Years. Unpublished report to Velsicol, January 28,1966.
21. International Research Development Corporation. Eighteen Month Oral Carcinogenic Study in Mice. Unpublished report to Velsicol, September 26, 1973.
22. International Research Development Corporation. Eighteen Month Oral Carcinogenic Study in Mice. Unpublished report to Velsicol, December 14, 1973.
23. Japanese Research Institute for Animal Science in Biochemistry and Toxicology. Chronic Toxicity and Tumorigenicity Test in Mice and Rats with Chlordane Technical. Unpublished report to Velsicol, December 1, 1983.
24. Kettering Laboratories. The Physiological Effects of the Introduction of Heptachlor Epoxide in Varying Levels of Concentration into the Diet of CFN Rats. Unpublished report to Velsicol, 1959.
25. Ingle, L. Effects of Chlordane Upon Reproduction among Albino Rats. Unpublished report to Velsicol, 1966.
26. Kettering Laboratories. The Effects Exerted on the Fertility of Rats and upon the Viability of Their Offspring by the Introduction of Heptachlor and Its Epoxide into Their Daily Diets. Unpublished report to Velsicol, February 27, 1967.
27. Kettering Laboratories. The Effects Exerted upon the Fertility of Rats and upon the Viability of Their Offspring by the Introduction of Heptachlor into Their Daily Diets. February 27, 1967.
28. International Research Development Corporation. Teratology Study in the Dutch Rabbit. Unpublished report to Velsicol, March 21, 1969.
29. Velsicol Chemical Company. Notes on the Chlordane-Heptachlor Review, Ontario, Canada: Pesticides Advisory Committee Meeting, Toronto, Ontario, Canada, Wednesday, November 15, 1972. Confidential memorandum, undated.
30. Epstein, S. S. The carcinogenicity of heptachlor and chlordane. *The Science of the Total Environment* 6: 103–154, 1976.
31. Quarles, J. (Assistant Administrator, EPA). Testimony Before the Sub-Committee on Health, Senate Committee on Labor and Public Welfare, January 10, 1976.
32. *Mullaney vs. Velsicol/Orkin,* 1987.
33. Nisbet, I., and Epstein, S. S., in preparation.
34. Polen, P. (Velsicol). Heptachlor Petitions: Drew and Baker, Jr., Letter, December 23, 1970. Memorandum to K. L. Schutz, January 12, 1971.

35. Calo, C. J. Monthly Velsicol Report: Toxicology, August 21 to September 20, 1972. Internal memorandum to K. L. Schulz, September 20,1972.
36. Plaintiff Exhibit No. 41. *Moore vs. Velsicol Chemical Company.* U.S. District Court for the District of Connecticut, C. A. #H-80-415, 1985.
37. Rust, J. H. (University of Chicago). Letter to C. J. Calo, Manager of Toxicology, Velsicol Chemical Company, December 29, 1972.
38. Newberne, P. M. (Massachusetts Institute of Technology). Letter to C. J. Calo, January 9, 1973.
39. Calo, C. J. Monthly Velsicol Report: Toxicology, December 20, 1972, to January 16, 1973. Internal memorandum to K. L. Schulz, January 18, 1973.
40. *USA vs. H. S. Gold, et al.* U.S. District Court, Northern District of Illinois, Eastern District 77CR 1073.
41. *Pesticide and Toxic Chemical News,* December 14, 1977, pp. 17–18.
42. *Federal Reporter* 561, second series, 1977, p. 671.
43. *Velsicol Chemical Company vs. Hon. J. B. Parsons, Chief Judge, U.S. District Court for the Northern District of Illinois.* U.S. Court of Appeals, Seventh Circuit, Nos. 77-1433, 77-1434, 1977.
44. Shindell and Associates. Report of Epidemiological Study of the Employees of Velsicol Chemical Company Plant, Marshall, Illinois, January 1946–December 1979. Unpublished report to Velsicol, 1980.
45. Shindell, S., and Ulrich, S. Mortality of workers employed in the manufacture of chlordane: An update. *J. Occup. Med.* 28: 497–501, 1986.
46. Infante, P., and Freeman, C. Cancer mortality among workers exposed to chlordane. *J. Occup. Med.* 29: 908–909, 1987.
47. Kasik, J. H. Letter to Louis F. Wilks, Velsicol, July 10, 1969.
48. O'Connor, C. A. III. (Sellers, Conner, and Cuneo, Washington, D.C.). Letter to C. J. Calo, Velsicol, with attached memorandum on interviews with Drs. Goldberg, Becker, and Shubik, August 19,1975.
49. Butler, W. H. (St. George's Hospital Medical School, London, England). Letter to Neil Mitchell, Esq., Counsel, Velsicol, May 10, 1976.
50. Ackerley, R. L. (Sellers, Conner, and Cuneo). Letter to Neil Mitchell, Esq., Counsel, Velsicol, June 23, 1975.
51. Polen, P. (Velsicol expert witness, Ex. 13). *EPA Final Brief, Chlordane/Heptachlor Cancellation Proceedings.* FIFRA Docket No. 384, 1975.
52. Whitacre, D. M. (Velsicol expert witness). Testimony in *Moore vs. Velsicol,* July 12, 1982.
53. Nisbet, I., Simon, R., and Epstein, S., in preparation.
54. Richmond, W. R. (Sidley and Austin, Chicago). Re *Moore vs. Velsicol:* Supplemental Answers to Interrogatories. October 24, 1985.
55. Hollingsworth, J. G. (Spriggs, Bode, and Hollingsworth, Washington, D.C.). Re *Dine vs. Western Exterminating and Velsicol:* Response to Interrogatory, 1987.
56. Morris, R. M., et al. Chlordane: Strictly Personal and Confidential. Velsicol internal memorandum, September 6, 1972.
57. Lorant, B. H. Velsicol internal memorandum, February 18, 1970.
58. Anderson, R. A. (Vice President for Research, Velsicol). Letter to W. A. Crawford, Health Commission of New South Wales, Australia, September 29, 1976.
59. Conley, B. E. The present status of chlordane. *JAMA* 158: 1364–1367, 1955.
60. Olson, R. *McFarlin vs. Velsicol, et al.,* 1983.
61. Hyde, K. M., and Falkenberg, R. L. Neuroelectrical disturbances as indicators of chronic chlordane toxicity. *Toxicol. Appl. Pharmacol.* 37: 499–515, 1976.
62. Environmental Protection Agency. *Pesticide Incident Monitoring System.* Report No. 360, 1981.

63. Velsicol Chemical Company. Bulletin 502-35R. February 1981.
64. Al-Hachim, G. M., and Al-Baker, A. Effects of chlordane on conditioned avoidance response, brain seizure threshold, and open-field performance of prenatally-treated mice. *Br. J. Pharmacol.* 49: 311–315, 1973.
65. Cerey, K., et al. Effect of heptachlor on dominant lethality and bone marrow in rats. *Mutat. Res.* 21: 26, 1973.
66. Cranmer, J. M., et al. Prenatal chlordane exposure: Effects on plasma corticosterone concentrations over the lifespan of mice. *Environ. Res.* 35: 204–210, 1984.
67. Wallingford, K. M., and Handke, J. L. *Indoor Exposure to Chlordane at a Family Planning Clinic.* National Institute for Occupational Safety and Health, Health Hazard Evaluation, May 1985.
68. Wang, H. H., and MacMahon, B. Mortality of pesticide applicators. *J. Occup. Med.* 21: 741–744,1979.
69. Wang, H. H., and MacMahon, B. Mortality of workers exposed in the manufacture of chlordane and heptachlor. *J. Occup. Med.* 21: 745–748, 1979.
70. Hiatt, H. H. (Dean, Harvard School of Public Health). Letter to B. MacMahon, October 2, 1978.
71. Blair, A., et al. Lung cancer and other causes of death among licensed pest control operators. *J. Natl. Cancer Inst.* 71: 31–37, 1983.
72. Beyer, S. (Sidley and Austin, Chicago). *Slowey vs. Velsicol Chemical Co.,* C.A. No. 85-680 N., Tr. pp. 835–842, July 17, 1986.
73. MacMahon, B. Review of Lung Cancer and Other Causes of Death among Licensed Pesticide Applicators by A. Blair, et al., *J. Natl. Cancer Inst.,* 1983; 71: 31–37. Report to Velsicol Chemical Company, October 13,1983.
74. Epstein, S. S., and Ozonoff, D. Leukemias and blood dyscrasias following exposure to chlordane and heptachlor. *Teratogenesis Carcinog. Mutagen.* 7: 527–540, 1987.
75. Schneider, D. (Manager, Technical Services, Velsicol). *Mullaney vs. Velsicol/Orkin,* October 28,1986.
76. Velsicol Chemical Company. Inspection Training Manual for Termite Control Operators, Inspectors, Salesmen, and Servicemen, 1974.
77. Velsicol Chemical Company. Safe Application Is No Accident: A Residue Management Guide for Professional Pest Control Operators. Velsicol bulletin, 1984.
78. Velsicol Chemical Company. Advertisement in *Pest Control Technology,* March 1981.
79. Velsicol Chemical Company. Chlordane Fact Sheet. Undated, but later than 1982.
80. Velsicol Chemical Company. Gold Crest Product Information Guide. Undated, but later than 1982.
81. Velsicol Chemical Company. Termiticide Clean-up Manual. Undated, but later than 1982.
82. Velsicol Chemical Company. Letter to Pest Control Professionals, March 12, 1985.
83. Velsicol Chemical Company. Attachment to Minutes of Chemical Risks Assessment Committee Meeting, March 3, 1980.
84. Hearings on H. R. 2664, "Corporate Criminal Liability Act of 1987." U.S. House of Representatives, Committee on the Judiciary, November 1987.

Further Reading

Epstein, S. S. Criticizes Insurers. Letter. *Business Insurance,* April 30, 1979. www.preventcancer.com.
Testimony on White Collar Crime (H.R. 4973) Before the Subcommittee on Crime of the Committee on the Judiciary. December 13, 1979. www.preventcancer.com.

Cancer War Is Threatened by Environmental Protection Agency Proposals. Press release, August 16, 1996. www.preventcancer.com.

Cancer War Is Threatened by Recommendations of Presidential Commission. Press release, August 30, 1996. www.preventcancer.com.

Monsanto Charged with White Collar Crime. Appendix V of e-book, GOT (genetically engineered) MILK! The Monsanto rBGH/BST Milk Wars Handbook. Seven Stories Press, 2001. www.preventcancer.com.

"Trade Secrets:" The Latest in a Long Line of Conspiracies. Press release, March 23, 2001. www.preventcancer.com.

IBM's Corporate Recklessness: From the Holocaust to Occupational Cancer. Press release, August 16, 2004. www.preventcancer.com.

CHAPTER 17

1. Sleisenger, M. H., and Fordtran, J. S. (eds.). *Gastrointestinal Disease,* Ed. 3. W. B. Saunders, Philadelphia, 1983.

2. Steinhorn, S. C., et al. Characteristics of colon cancer patients reported in population-based tumor registries and comprehensive cancer centers. *J. Natl. Cancer Inst.* 70: 629–634, 1983.

3. Hill, M. J. The etiology of colon cancer. *CRC Crit. Rev. Toxicol.* 4: 31–82, 1975.

4. Boyle, P., Zaridye, D. G., and Smans, M. Descriptive epidemiology of colorectal cancer. *Int. J. Cancer* 36: 9–18, 1985.

5. Devesa, S. S., et al. Cancer incidence and mortality trends among whites in the United States, 1947–84. *J. Natl. Cancer Inst.* 79: 701–770, 1987.

6. Schottenfeld, D., and Fraumeni, J. F. (eds.). *Cancer Epidemiology and Prevention.* W. B. Saunders, Philadelphia, 1982.

7. Stavraky, K. M. The role of ecological analysis in studies of the etiology of disease: A discussion with reference to large bowel cancer. *J. Chron. Dis.* 29: 435–444, 1976.

8. Haenszel, W., and Correa, P. Cancer of the colon and rectum and adenomatous polyps: A review of epidemiologic findings. *Cancer* 28: 14–24, 1971.

9. Najem, G. R., et al. Gastrointestinal cancer mortality in New Jersey counties and the relationship with environmental variables. *Int. J. Epidemiol.* 12: 276–289, 1983.

10. Bailar, J. A., and Smith, E. M. Progress against cancer? *N. Engl. J. Med.* 314: 1226–1232, 1986.

11. Epstein, S. S. *Congressional Record,* September 9, 1987, E3449–E3454.

12. Epstein, S. S. *The Politics of Cancer.* Anchor Press/Doubleday, New York, 1979.

13. Committee on Diet, Nutrition, and Cancer. *Diet, Nutrition, and Cancer.* National Academy Press, Washington, D.C., 1982.

14. Haenszel, W., et al. Large bowel cancer in Hawaiian Japanese. *J. Natl. Cancer Inst.* 51: 1765–1779, 1973.

15. Mason, T. J., et al. *Atlas of Cancer Mortality for U.S. Counties, 1950–1969.* U.S. Department of Health, Education, and Welfare, Publication No. 75-780, Washington, D.C., 1975.

16. Pickle, L. W., et al. *Atlas of U.S. Cancer Mortality Among Whites, 1950–1980.* U.S. Department of Health, Education, and Welfare, Publication No. 87-2900, Washington, D.C., 1987.

17. Correa, P. Comments on the epidemiology of large bowel cancer. *Cancer Res.* 35: 3395–3397,1975.

18. Cannon-Albright, L. A., et al. Common inheritance of susceptibility to colonic adenomatous polyps and associated colorectal cancers. *N. Engl. J. Med. 319:* 533–537, 1988.

19. Mecklin, J. P., Jarvinen, H. J., and Peltokalio, P. Cancer family syndrome: Genetic analysis of 22 Finnish kindreds. *Gastroenterology* 90: 328–333, 1986.

20. Lionas, D. A., et al. Cholecystectomy and carcinoma of the colon. *Lancet* 2: 379–381, 1981.

21. Vernick, L. J., and Kuller, L. H. Cholecystectomy and right sided colon cancer. *Lancet 2:* 381–383, 1981.

22. Adami, H. O., et al. Colorectal cancer after cholecystectomy: Absence of risk increase within 11–14 years. *Gastroenterology* 85: 859–865, 1983.

23. Willett, W. C., and MacMahon, B. Diet and cancer: An overview. *N. Engl. J. Med.* 310: 633–638, 697–703, 1984.

24. Saracci, R. The interaction of tobacco smoking and other agents in cancer etiology. *Epidemiol. Rev.* 9: 175–193, 1987.

25. Enstrom, J. E. Colorectal cancer and beer drinking. *Br. J. Cancer* 35: 674–683, 1977.

26. Breslow, N. E., and Enstrom, J. E. Geographic correlations between cancer mortality rates and alcohol-tobacco consumption in the U.S. *J. Natl. Cancer Inst.* 53: 531–539, 1974.

27. Dean, G., et al. Causes of death of blue-collar workers at a Dublin brewery, 1954–1973. *Br. J. Cancer* 40: 581–589, 1979.

28. Jensen, O. M. Cancer morbidity and causes of death among Danish brewery workers. *Int. J. Cancer* 23: 454–463, 1979.

29. Jenson, O. M. *Cancer Mortality and Causes of Death Among Danish Brewery Workers.* International Agency for Research in Cancer, Lyon, France, 1980.

30. Seitz, H. K., et al. Enhancement of 1,2-dimethylhydrazine-induced rectal carcinogenesis following chronic ethanol consumption in the rat. *Gastroenterology* 86: 886–891, 1984.

31. Garabrant, D. H., et al. Job activity and colon cancer risks. *Am. J. Epidemiol.* 119: 1005–1014, 1984.

32. Vena, J. E., et al. Lifetime occupational exercise and colon cancer. *Am. J. Epidemiol.* 122: 357–365, 1985.

33. Wynder, E. L., and Shigematsu, T. Environmental factors of cancer of the rectum and colon. *Cancer* 20: 1520–1561, 1967.

34. Neugut, A. I., and Wylie, P. Occupational cancers of the gastrointestinal tract, Part 1: Colon, stomach, and esophagus. *Occup. Med.: State-of-the-Art Rev.* 2: 109–135, 1987.

35. Berg, J. W., and Howell, M. A. Occupation and bowel cancer. *J. Toxicol. Environ. Health* 1: 75–89, 1975.

36. Davis, D. L., Bridbord, K., and Schneiderman, M. Cancer prevention: Assessing causes, exposures, and recent trends in mortality in U.S. males, 1968–1978. *Teratogenesis Carcinog. Mutagen.* 2: 105–135, 1982.

37. Mausner, J. S., and Kramer, S. *Epidemiology.* W. B. Saunders, Philadelphia, 1985.

38. Levine, D. S. Does asbestos exposure cause gastrointestinal cancer? *Dig. Dis. Sci.* 30: 1189–1198, 1985.

39. Morgan, R. W., Foliart, D. E., and Wong, O. Asbestos and gastrointestinal cancer. *West. J. Med.* 143: 60–65, 1985.

40. Miller, A. B. Asbestos fiber dust and gastrointestinal malignancies: Review of the literature with regard to cause/effect relationship. *J. Chron. Dis.* 31: 23–33, 1978.

41. McNeil, B. J., and Eddy, D. M. The costs and effects of screening for cancer among asbestos-exposed workers. *J. Chron. Dis.* 35: 351–358, 1982.

42. Selikoff, I. J., Seidman, H., and Haond, E. C. Mortality of cigarette smoking among amosite asbestos factory workers. *J. Natl. Cancer Inst.* 65: 507–513, 1980.

43. Donham, K. J., et al. T'he effects of long-term ingestion of asbestos on the colon of F344 rats. *Cancer* 45: 1073–1084, 1980.

44. Amacher, D. E., Alarif, A., and Epstein, S. S. Effects of ingested chrysotile on DNA synthesis in the gastrointestinal tract and liver of the rat. *Environ. Health Perspect* 9: 319–324, 1974.

45. Volkheimer, G. Persorption. *Acta Hepato-Gastroenterol.* 20: 361–352, 1973.

46. Ehrlich, A., Rohl, A. N., and Holstein, E. C. Asbestos bodies and carcinoma of colon in an insulation worker with asbestos. *JAMA* 254: 2932–2933, 1985.

47. O'Berg, M. T. Epidemiological study of workers exposed to acrylonitrile. *J. Occup. Med.* 22: 245–252, 1980.

48. International Agency for Research in Cancer. *Some Monomers, Plastics, and Synthetic Elastomers, and Acrolein.* I.A.R.C. Monographs on the Evaluation of Carcinogenic Risk of Chemicals in Humans, Vol. 19. Lyon, France, 1979.

49. Quast, J. F., et al. *A Two Year Toxicity and Oncogenicity Study with Acrylonitrile Incorporated in the Drinking Water of Rats: Final Report.* Toxicology Research Laboratory, Dow Chemical, Midland, Mich., 1980.

50. National Toxicology Program. *Fourth Annual Report on Carcinogens,* Summary 1985. U.S. Department of Health and Human Services, NTP Publication No. 85-002, Research Triangle Park, N.C., 1985.

51. National Institute for Occupational Safety and Health. *Recommended Standard for Occupational Exposure to Acrylonitrile.* Department of Health, Education, and Welfare, NIOSH Publication No. 78-116, Washington, D.C., 1978.

52. Werner, J. B., and Carter, J. T. Mortality of United Kingdom acrylonitrile polymerization workers. *Br. J. Ind. Med.* 38: 247–253, 1981.

53. Hochheiser, S. Cast Sheets, Cockpits, and Juke Boxes: The Development of Plexiglas (R) in the United States. Presentation to the History of Science Society, Norwalk, Conn., October 28,1983.

54. National Toxicology Program. Draft Technical Report on the Carcinogenesis Bioassay of Ethylacrylate in F344 Rats and B6C3F2 Mice. U.S. Department of Health and Human Services, NTP Technical Report Series, No. 259, Research Triangle Park, N.C., 1983.

55. DeFonso, L. R., Maher, K., and Kelton, S. C. Interim Communication on the Results of a Mortality Study of Bristol Plant Employees Hired Prior to 1946. Bristol Plant Mortality Study (1966–1975). Health Protection Research Report Nos. 8 and 8A, Rohm and Haas Co., Philadelphia, 1976.

56. DeFonso, L., and Maher, K. A Matched Case-control Study Nested Within a Historical Cohort Study of Acrylate/Methacrylate Workers. Rohm and Haas Co., Philadelphia, January 1986.

57. Vobecky, J., et al. An occupational group with high risk of large bowel cancer. *Gastroenterology* 75: 221–223, 1978.

58. Vobecky, J., Caro, J., and Devroede, G. A case controlled study of risk factors for large bowel carcinoma. *Cancer* 51: 1958–1963, 1983.

59. Vobecky, J., Devroede, G., and Caro, J. Risk of large bowel cancer in synthetic fiber manufacturer. *Cancer* 54: 2537–2542, 1984.

60. Hoar, S. K., and Blair, A. Death certificate case-control study of cancers of the prostate and colon and employment in the textile industry. *Arch. Environ. Health* 39: 280–283, 1984.

61. Torkelson, T. R., et al. Toxicologic investigation of dibromochloropropane (DBCP). *Toxicol. Appl. Pharmacol.* 3: 545–559, 1961.

62. Hearn, S., et al. Mortality experience of employees with occupational exposure to DBCP. *Arch. Environ. Health* 39: 49–55, 1984.
63. Occupational Safety and Health Administration. Emergency temporary standard for occupational exposure to dibromochloropropane: OSHA hearings. *Federal Register* 42: 15536–15548, 1977.
64. Salg, J. *DBCP Register: Report Summarizing Activities Through January, 1981.* Department of Health and Human Services, NIOSH, Washington, D.C., February 5, 1982.
65. Wharton, D., et al. Infertility in male pesticide workers. *Lancet* 2: 1259–1261, 1977.
66. Southern Research Institute. *Contract Report to the E.P.A. Carcinogen Assessment Group: Preliminary Report on D.B.C.P.* Washington, D.C., September 1977.
67. Wong, O., et al. Mortality of workers potentially exposed to organic and inorganic brominated chemicals, DBCP, TRIS, PBB, and DDT. *Br. J. Ind. Med.* 41: 15–24, 1984.
68. Ditraglia, D., et al. Mortality study of workers employed at organochlorane pesticide manufacturing plants. *Scand. J. Work Environ. Health* 7(S4): 140–146, 1981.
69. Greene, M. H., et al. Cancer mortality among printing plant workers. *Environ. Res.* 20: 66–73, 1979.
70. Lloyd, J. W., Decouffle, P., and Saivin, L. G. Unusual mortality experience of printing pressmen. *J. Occup. Med.* 19: 543–550, 1977.
71. Swanson, G. M., and Belle, S. H. Cancer morbidity among woodworkers in the U.S. automotive industry. *J. Occup. Med.* 24: 315–319, 1982.
72. Swanson, G. M., Belle, S. H., and Burrows, R. W. Colon cancer incidence among model makers and patternmakers in the automotive manufacturing industry. *J. Occup. Med.* 27: 567–569, 1985.
73. Robinson, C., Waxweller, R. J., and McCammon, C. S. Pattern and model makers: Proportionate mortality, 1972–1978. *Am. J. Ind. Med.* 1: 159–165, 1980.
74. Demers, R. Y., et al. Prevalence of colorectal polyps among Michigan pattern and model makers. *J. Occup. Med.* 27: 809–812, 1985.
75. Delzell, E., and Monson, R. R. Mortality among rubber workers: Processing workers. *J. Occup. Med.* 24: 539–545, 1982.
76. McMichael, A. J., Spirtas, M. S., and Kupper, L. L. An epidemiologic study of mortality within a cohort of rubber workers: 1964–1972. *J. Occup. Med.* 16: 458–464, 1974.
77. Norell, S., et al. Oesophageal cancer and vulcanization work. *Lancet* 1: 462–463, 1983.
78. Parkes, H. G., et al. Cancer mortality in the British rubber industry. *Br. J. Ind. Med.* 39: 209–220, 1982.
79. Morgan, R. W., Kaplan, S. D., and Gaffey, W. A general mortality study of production workers in the paint and coating manufacturing industry. *J. Occup. Med.* 23: 13–21, 1981.
80. Miller, B. A., Blair, A., and McCann, M. Mortality patterns among professional artists: A preliminary report. *J. Environ. Pathol. Toxicol. Oncol.* 6: 303–313, 1985.
81. Polednak, A. P., Stehney, A. F., and Rolland, R. E. Mortality among women first employed before 1930 in the U.S. radium dial-painting industry. *Am. J. Epidemiol.* 107: 179–195, 1978.
82. Spiegelman, D., and Wegman, D. H. Occupation related risks for colon cancer. *J. Natl. Cancer Inst.* 75: 813–821, 1985.
83. Decoufle, P. Cancer risks associated with employment in the leather and leather products industry. *Arch. Environ. Health* 34: 33–37, 1979.

84. Bendix, S. Firefighter exposure to environmental carcinogens. *J. Combustion. Toxicol.* 6: 127–135, 1979.
85. Decoufle, P. Further analysis of cancer mortality patterns among workers exposed to cutting oil mists. *J. Natl. Cancer Inst.* 61: 1035–1039, 1978.
86. Wang, J. D., Wegman, D. H., and Smith, T. I. Cancer risks in the optical manufacturing industry. *Br. J. Ind. Med.* 40: 177–181, 1983.
87. International Agency for Research in Cancer. *Some Aromatic Amines, Hydrazine and Related Substances, N-Nitroso Compounds, and Miscellaneous Alkylating Agents.* I.A.R.C. Monographs on the Evaluation of Carcinogenic Risk of Chemicals to Man, Vol. 4. Lyon, France, 1974.
88. International Agency for Research in Cancer. *Some N-Nitroso Compounds.* I.A.R.C. Monographs on the Evaluation of Carcinogenics Risk of Chemicals to Man, Vol. 17. Lyon, France, 1978.
89. Decoufle, P., and Stanislawczy, K. *A Retrospective Survey of Cancer in Relation to Occupation.* U.S. Department of Health, Education, and Welfare, NIOSH Publication No. 77-178, Washington, D.C., 1977.
90. Blair, A., Decoufle, P., and Grauman, D. Causes of death among laundry and dry cleaning workers. *Am. J. Public Health* 69: 508–511, 1979.
91. National Toxicology Program. Toxicology and Carcinogenesis Studies of Bromodichloromethane in F344/N Rats and B6C3F Mice. U.S. Department of Health and Human Services, NTP Publication No. 88-2537, Research Triangle Park, N.C., 1988.
92. International Agency for Research in Cancer. *Some Halogenated Hydrocarbons.* I.A.R.C. Monographs on the Evaluation of Carcinogenic Risk of Chemicals to Man, Vol. 20. Lyon, France, 1982.
93. Tokudome, S., and Kuratsune, M. A cohort study on mortality from cancer and other causes among workers at a metal refinery. *Int. J. Cancer* 17: 310–317, 1976.
94. Kaminski, R., Geissert, K. S., and Dacey, E. Mortality analysis of plumbers and pipefitters. *J. Occup. Med.* 22: 183–189, 1980.
95. Dolan, B. P., and Dolan, D. C. California Pipes Trade Council Health Survey. Final unpublished report, 1980.
96. Schwartz, E., and Grady, K. *Patterns of Occupational Mortality in New Hampshire, 1975–1985.* New Hampshire Division of Public Health Services, Concord, 1986.
97. Savitz, D. A., and Moure, R. Cancer risk among oil refinery workers. *J. Occup. Med.* 26: 662–670, 1984.
98. Hanis, N. M., Stavraky, K. M., and Fowler, J. L. Cancer mortality in oil refinery workers. *J. Occup. Med.* 21: 167–174, 1979.
99. Rushton, L., and Alderson, M. R. An epidemiologic survey of eight oil refineries in Britain. *Br. J. Ind. Med.* 38: 225–234, 1981.
100. Walrath, J., and Fraumeni, R. Mortality patterns among embalmers. *Int. J. Cancer* 31: 407–411, 1983.
101. Levine, R. J., Andjelkovich, D. A., and Shaw, L. K. The mortality of Ontario undertakers and a review of the formaldehyde related mortality studies. *J. Occup. Med.* 26: 740–746, 1984.
102. Heldaas, S. S., Landard, S. L., and Andersen, A. Incidence of cancer among vinyl chloride and polyvinyl chloride workers. *Br. J. Ind. Med.* 41: 25–30, 1984.
103. King, J. *Troubled Water.* Rodale Press, Emmaus, Pa., 1985.
104. Council on Environmental Quality. *Contamination of Ground Water by Toxic Organic Chemicals.* U.S. Government Printing Office, Washington, D.C., January 1981.

105. Isacson, P., Bean, J. A., and Splinter, R. Drinking water and cancer incidence in Iowa: Association of cancer with incidence of contamination. *Am. J. Epidemiol.* 121: 856–859, 1985.

106. Environmental Studies Board Commission on Natural Resources. *Chloroform, Carbon Tetrachloride, and Other Halomethanes: An Environmental Assessment.* National Academy of Sciences, National Research Council, Washington, D.C., 1978.

107. Page, T., Harris, R. H., and Epstein, S. S. Drinking water and cancer mortality in Louisiana. *Science* 193: 55–57, 1976.

108. Cantor, K. P. Epidemiological evidence of carcinogenicity of chlorinated organics in drinking water. *Environ. Health Perspect.* 46: 187–195, 1982.

109. Cantor, K. P., et al. Associations of cancer mortality with halomethanes in drinking water. *J. Natl. Cancer Inst.* 61: 979–985, 1978.

110. Velema, J. P. Contaminated drinking water as a potential cause of cancer in humans. *J. Environ. Sci. Health* C5: 1–28, 1987.

111. Carly, G. L., and Mettlin, C. J. Cancer incidence and trihalomethane concentrations in a public drinking water system. *Am. J. Public Health* 70: 523–525, 1980.

112. Cantor, K. P., et al. Bladder cancer, drinking water source, and tap water consumption: A case-control study. *J. Natl. Cancer Inst.* 79: 1269–1279, 1987.

113. Crump, K. S., and Guess, H. A. Drinking water and cancer: Review of recent epidemiological findings and assessment of risks. *Ann. Rev. Public Health* 3: 339–357, 1982.

114. Young, T. B., Kanarek, M. S., and Tsiatis, A. A. Epidemiologic study of drinking water chlorination and Wisconsin female cancer mortality. *J. Natl. Cancer Inst.* 67: 1191–1195, 1981.

115. Gottlieb, M. S., Carr, J. K., and Clarkson, J. R. Drinking water and cancer in Louisiana. *Am. J. Epidemiol.* 116: 652–667, 1982.

116. Gottlieb, M. S., Carr, J. K., and Morris, D. T. Cancer and drinking water in Louisiana: Colon and rectum. *Int. J. Epidemiol.* 10: 117–125, 1981.

117. Wilkens, J. R. III, Reiches, N. A., and Kruse, C. W. Organic chemical contaminants in drinking water and cancer. *Am. J. Epidemiol.* 110: 420–448, 1979.

118. Lawrence, C. E., et al. Trihalomethanes in drinking water and human colorectal cancer. *J. Natl. Cancer Inst.* 72: 563–568, 1984.

119. Sandler, R. S., and Sandler, D. P. Radiation induced cancers of the colon and rectum: Assessing the risks. *Gastroenterology* 84: 51–57, 1983.

120. Schull, W. J. Atomic bomb survivors: Patterns of cancer risk. In *Radiation Carcinogenesis: Epidemiologic and Radiologic Significance,* edited by J. D. Boice and J. F. Fraumeni. Raven Press, New York, 1984.

121. Kato, H., and Schull, W. J. Studies of the mortality of A-bomb survivors: Mortality 1950–1978, cancer mortality. *Radiat. Res.* 90: 395–432, 1982.

122. Dickson, R. J. Late results of radium treatment of carcinoma of the cervix. *Clin. Radiol.* 23: 528–535, 1972.

123. Smith, P. G., Doll, R., and Radford, E. P. Cancer mortality among patients with ankylosing spondylitis not given x-ray therapy. *Br. J. Radiol.* 50: 728–734, 1977.

124. Smith, P. G., and Doll, R. Late effects of x-irradiation in patients treated for metropathia hemorrhagica. *Br. J. Radiol.* 49: 224–232, 1976.

125. Committee on the Biologic Effects of Ionizing Radiation. *The Effects on Populations of Exposures to Low Levels of Ionizing Radiation: 1980.* National Academy Press, Washington, D.C., 1980.

126. Denmar, D. L., Birchner, F. R., and Osborne, J. W. Induction of colon adenocarcinoma in the rat by x-irradiation. *Cancer Res.* 38: 1899–1905, 1978.

127. Confonti, P. M., Kanarek, M. S., and Lackson, L. A. Asbestos in drinking water and cancer in the San Francisco Bay area: 1969–1974. *J. Chron. Dis.* 34: 211–224, 1981.
128. Levy, B. S., Sigurdson, E., and Mandel, J. Investigating possible effects of asbestos in city water: Surveillance of GI cancer incidents in Duluth, Minnesota. *Am. J. Epidemiol.* 103: 362–368, 1976.
129. Polissar, L., Seversons, R. K., and Boatman, E. S. A case-control study of asbestos in drinking water and cancer risks. *Am. J. Epidemiol.* 119: 456–471, 1984.
130. Marsh, G. M. Critical review of the epidemiologic studies related to ingested asbestos. *Environ. Health Perspect.* 53: 49–56, 1983.
131. Occupational Safety and Health Administration. Identification, classification, and regulation of potential occupational carcinogens, Part VII. *Federal Register* 45: 5001–5296, 1980.
132. International Agency for Research in Cancer. *Overall Evaluations of Carcinogenicity: An Updating of I.A.R.C. Monographs, Volumes 1 to 42.* I.A.R.C. Monographs on the Evaluation of Carcinogenic Risks to Humans, Suppl. 7. Lyon, France, 1987.
133. International Agency for Research in Cancer. *Some Naturally Occurring Substances.* I.A.R.C. Monographs on the Evaluation of Carcinogenic Risk of Chemicals to Man, Vol. 10. Lyon, France, 1976.
134. Goodman, D. G., et al. *Chemically Induced and Unusual Proliferative and Neoplastic Lesions in Rats: Digestive System.* Registry of Veterinary Pathology, Armed Forces Institute of Pathology, Washington, D.C., 1984.
135. Newberne, P. M., and Rogers, A. E. Rat colon carcinogenesis associated with aflatoxin and marginal vitamin A. *J. Natl. Cancer Inst.* 50: 439–448, 1973.
136. Sloan, D. A., et al. Increased incidence of experimental colon cancer associated with long-term metronidazole therapy. *Am. J. Surg.* 145: 66–69, 1983.
136. Rustia, M., and Shubik, P. Induction of lung tumors and malignant lymphomas in mice by metronidazole. *J. Natl. Cancer Inst.* 48: 721–729, 1972.
137. Beard, C. M., et al. Cancer after exposure to metronidazole. *J. Natl. Cancer Inst.* 48: 721–729, 1972.
138. Beard, C. M., et al. Cancer after exposure to metronidazole. *Mayo Clin. Proc.* 63: 147–153, 1988.
139. Beard, C. M., et al. Lack of evidence for cancer due to use of metronidazole. *N. Engl. J. Med.* 301: 519–522, 1979.
140. Gilbertsen, V. A., et al. Colon cancer control study: An interim report. In *Colorectal Cancer: Prevention, Epidemiology, and Screening,* edited by S. Winawer, D. Schottenfeld, and P. Sherlock. Raven Press, New York, 1980.
141. Winawer, S. J., et al. Progress report on controlled trial of fecal occult blood testing for the detection of colorectal neoplasia. *Cancer* 45: 2959–2964, 1980.
142. Bertario, L., et al. Sensitivity of hemoccult test for large bowel cancer in high-risk subjects. *Dig. Dis. Sci.* 33: 609–613, 1988.
143. Tedesco, F. J., et al. Diagnostic implications of the spatial distribution of colonic mass lesions (polyps and cancers). *Gastrointest. Endosc.* 26: 95–97, 1980.

CHAPTER 18

1. Steinberg, K. K., et al. A meta analysis of the effect of estrogen replacement therapy on the risk of breast cancer. *JAMA* 264: 2648–2653, 1990.
2. Henderson, B. E., Ross, R. K., and Pike, M. C. Toward the primary prevention of cancer. *Science* 254: 1131–1138, 1991.

3. WHO collaborative study of neoplasia and steroid contraceptives. *Contraception* 45: 299–312, 1992.
4. National Womens Health Network. Use of Depo-provera for contraception. Testimony to the Advisory Committee on Fertility and Maternal Health Drugs, Food and Drug Administration, June 19, 1992.
5. General Accounting Office. *Breast Cancer, 1971–1991: Prevention, Treatment and Research.* GAO/PEMD-92-12. Report to the Committee on Government Operations. Washington, D.C., December 1991.
6. Harris, J., et al. Breast cancer. *N. Engl. J. Med.* 327: 319–328, 1992.
7. National Cancer Institute. *Cancer Statistics Review, 1973–1989.* NIH Publication No. 92-2789. Bethesda, Md., 1992.
8. Davis, D. L., et al. International trends in cancer mortality in France, West Germany, Italy, Japan, England and Wales, and the United States. *Lancet* 336: 474–481, 1990.
9. Kohlmeier, L., Rehn, J., and Hoffmeister, H. Lifestyle and trends in world-wide breast cancer rates. *Ann. N.Y. Acad. Sci.* 609: 259–268, 1990.
10. Epstein, S. S. Evaluation of the National Cancer Program and proposed reforms. *Int. J. Health Serv.* 23(1): 15–44, 1993.
11. Fitzhugh, O. G., et al. Chronic oral toxicity of aldrin and dieldrin in rats and dogs. *Food. Cosmet. Toxicol.* 2: 551–562, 1964.
12. Walker, A. I. T., et al. The toxicology and pharmacodynamics of dieldrin: Two year oral exposure of rats and dogs. *Toxicol. Appl. Pharmacol.* 15: 345–373, 1969.
13. National Cancer Institute. *Bioassay of Chlordane for Possible Carcinogenicity.* Carcinogenesis Technical Report Series No. 8, Bethesda, Md., 1977.
14. Japanese Research Institute for Animal Science and Biochemistry and Toxicology. *Thirty Month Chronic Toxicity and Tumorigenicity Test in Rats with Chlordane Technical.* Confidential Report to Velsicol Chemical Co. December 1983.
15. Rall, D. Laboratory animal toxicity and carcinogenesis: Under-lying concepts, advantages and constraints. *Ann. N.Y. Acad. Sci.* 534: 78–83, 1988.
16. Scribner, J. D., and Mottet, N. K. DDT acceleration of mammary gland tumors induced in the male Sprague-Dawley rat by 2-acetamido-phenanthrene. *Carcinogenesis* 2: 1236–1239, 1981.
17. Wasserman, M., et al. Organochlorine compounds in neoplastic and adjacent apparently normal breast tissue. *Bull. Environ. Contam. Toxicol.* 15: 478–484, 1976.
18. Falck, F., et al. Pesticides and polychlorinated biphenyl residues in human breast lipids and their relation to breast cancer. *Arch. Environ. Health* 47: 143–146, 1992.
19. Mussalo-Rauhamaa, et al. Occurrence of beta-hexachloro-cyclohexane in breast cancer patients. *Cancer* 66: 2124–2128, 1990.
20. Epstein, S. S. Carcinogens in Israeli milk [in Hebrew]. *Harefuah* 94: 42–44, 1978.
21. Westin, J. Carcinogens in Israeli milk: A study in regulatory failure. *Int. J. Health Serv.* 23(3): 497–517, 1993.
22. Davis, D. L., et al. Medical hypothesis: Xeno-estrogens as preventable causes of breast cancer. *Environ. Health Perspect.* 101(5): 372–377, 1993.
23. International Agency for Research on Cancer. *Occupational Exposures in Insecticide Application, and Some Pesticides: Atrazine* 53: 441–466, 1991.
24. Donna, A., et al. Triazine herbicides and ovarian epithelial neoplasms. *Scand. J. Work Environ. Health* 15: 47–53, 1989.
25. Epstein, S. S. The chemical jungle: Today's beef industry. *Int. J. Health Serv.* 20(2): 277–280, 1990.

26. Hertz, R. The estrogen-cancer hypothesis with special emphasis on DES. In *Origins of Human Cancer, Book C: Human Risk Assessment*, edited by H. H. Hiatt et al., pp. 1665–1682. Cold Spring Harbor Laboratory, Cold Spring Harbor, N.Y., 1977.
27. Segaloff, A., and Maxfield, W. S. The synergism between radiation and estrogen in the production of mammary cancer in the rat. *Cancer Res.* 31: 166–168, 1971.
28. Shellabarger, C. J., Stone, J. P., and Holtzman, S. Rat strain differences in mammary tumor induction with estrogen and neutron radiation. *J. Natl. Cancer Inst.* 61: 1505–1508, 1978.
29. Dao, T. The role of ovarian hormones in initiating the induction of mammary cancer in rats by polynuclear hydrocarbons. *Cancer Res.* 22: 973–984, 1962.
30. Ekbom, A., et al. Evidence of prenatal influences on breast cancer risk. *Lancet* 340: 1015–1018, 1992.
31. Griffith, J., et al. Cancer mortality in U.S. countries with hazardous waste sites and groundwater pollution. *Arch. Environ. Health* 44: 69–74, 1989.
32. Sternglass, E., and Gould, J. M. Breast cancer: Evidence for a relation to fission products in the diet. *Int. J. Health Serv.* 23(4): 783–804, 1993.
33. National Toxicology Program. *Carcinogenesis Studies of 1,2-Dichloropropane in F344/N Rats and B6C3F1 Mice (Gavage studies).* Technical Report No. 263. Department of Health and Human Services, Research Triangle Park, N.C., 1986.
34. Wong, et al. Chronic Inhalation Study of 1,2-Dibromoethane in Rats with and without Dietary Disulfiram. Midwest Research Institute, Contract No. 210-76-0131. National Institute for Occupational Safety and Health, Department of Health, Education and Welfare, 1980.
35. National Cancer Institute and National Toxicology Program. *Bioassay of 1,2-Dibromoethane for Possible Carcinogenicity (Inhalation Study).* Publication No. (NIH)80-1766. Department of Health, Education and Welfare, 1980.
36. Olson, W. A., et al. Incidence of stomach cancer in rats and mice by halogenated aliphatic fumigants. *J. Natl. Cancer Inst.* 51: 1993–1995, 1972.
37. National Toxicology Program. *Carcinogenesis Studies of Dibromochloropropane in F344 Rats and B6C3F1 Mice (Inhalation Study).* Technical Report Series No. 206. Department of Health, Education and Welfare, 1982.
38. Manz, A., et al. Cancer mortality among workers in chemical plant contaminated with dioxin. *Lancet* 338: 959–964, 1991.
39. Hall, N., and Rosenman, K. Cancer by industry: Analysis of a population-based cancer registry with an emphasis on blue collar workers. *Am. J. Ind. Med.* 19: 145–159, 1991.
40. Walrath, J., et al. Causes of death among female chemists. *Am. J. Pub. Health* 75: 883–885, 1985.
41. International Agency for Research on Cancer. *Occupational Exposures of Hairdressers and Barbers and Personal Use of Hair Colourants* 57: 43–118, 1993.

Further Reading

Awareness Month Keeps Women Perilously Unaware (op-ed). *Chicago Tribune,* October 26, 1997. www.preventcancer.com.
A Needless New Risk of Breast Cancer (op-ed). *Los Angeles Times,* March 20, 1994. www.preventcancer.com.
Breast Cancer, The Environmental Connection. Presentation at The American Association for the Advancement of Science (AAAS), San Francisco, February 22, 1994. www.preventcancer.com.
Breast Cancer Deaths Linked to Nuclear Emissions. Press release, September 8, 1994. www.preventcancer.com.

INDEX

351

Praise for Recent Books by Samuel S. Epstein

The Safe Shopper's Bible (1995)

> . . . **The most important book a shopper will ever own.** *The Safe Shopper's Bible* is a number-one recommendation on my reading list for all my patients and their families. *Use it!*
>
> Jay Gordon, M.D.
> Medical Correspondent, ABC Television

> Dr. Sam Epstein's writing is, like his medical advice, good for your health. **Read him carefully and the chances are you'll live longer.**
>
> Studs Terkel

> **A long overdue and indispensable reference book** important to all who are interested in reducing their risk of exposure to harmful chemicals found in most household products, cosmetics, and food. I cannot think of anyone who would not benefit from this book.
>
> Aexander G. Schauss, Ph.D.
> Executive Director, Citizens for Health

> *The Safe Shopper's Bible* is the consumer's action handbook for the '90's: comprehensive, well-documented, with all the appropriate warnings—a compendium of reasonable alternatives. **A must for all who care about their health.**
>
> Gary Null, Ph.D.
> WBAI National Radio

> **The ultimate shopper's guide.** A book that should help you get your money's worth every time you shop while safeguarding your family's health.
>
> Earl Mindell, R.Ph.
> Author, *The Vitamin Bible*

371

The Breast Cancer Prevention Program (1998)

This book is more than a remarkable study. **It is a prescription that may save your life.**

Studs Terkel

What a tremendous book, on every level.

Townsend Letter for Doctors and Patients

A marvelous book—intelligent, courageous, and practical.

Barbara Seaman
Co-founder, National Women's Health Network
Author, *The Doctor's Case Against the Pill*

A comprehensive picture of probably all the factors in the home, the immediate area, the workplace and in food that have been linked with breast cancer . . . Full of stimulating ideas for action.

Helen Lynn and Ann Link
Women's Environmental Network

The Politics of Cancer, Revisited (1998)

Every journalist reporting on cancer (as it should be covered) has within easy reach, a shop-worn, dog-eared, heavily underlined 1978 edition of Sam Epstein's *Politics of Cancer*. For twenty years we have waited impatiently for the day when we would no longer have to update old findings. Our wait is over. Not only has Dr. Epstein provided new data, charts, epidemiology, and science, **but he has refortified his contention that the war on cancer is unfinished, and far from triumphant.**

Mark Dowie
Former publisher and editor, *Mother Jones*
Author, *Losing Ground: American Environmentalism
at the Close of the Twentieth Century*

Cancer continues to be the scourge of many workplaces; **this book is an extraordinary weapon to mount an attack on this deadly disease. It minces no words in indicting the cancer establishment whose misdirected efforts have contributed to the ongoing cancer epidemic.**

Dr. Epstein's work is a strong rebuttal to the self-interested Pollyannas in the cancer establishment and provides worker advocates with essential knowledge that will serve to protect the lives of those we represent.

Robert Wages
President, Oil, Chemical, and Atomic Workers
International Union, AFL-CIO

Some twenty years later, we have a most worthy sequel to the 1978 ground-breaking *The Politics of Cancer*. This work is muscular, relentless, and compelling. Its thesis: billions of public dollars are being misspent in an ill-conceived "war on cancer"—a war we are losing because we are not addressing the increasingly carcinogenic environment that man has created. In failing to allocate these resources for prevention, we are fighting the wrong war. The author documents that opposition from powerful corporate interests, and their allies in government and the academy, has sustained this strategy.

We have here a must-read for the scientist and the citizen concerned with the public's health.

Quentin D. Young, M.D.
President, American Public Health Association

A remarkable scientifically documented analysis of the failing war against cancer and the reasons for the failure. This book also provides a practical road map for personal and political opportunities for turning the tide of the modern cancer epidemic.

Devra Lee Davis, Ph.D., M.P.H.
World Resources Institute, Washington, D.C.

A unique and superbly documented indictment of the National Cancer Institute and the American Cancer Society for their reckless indifference to cancer prevention, for their incestuous relationship with the cancer drug industry, and for their false claims for miracle cancer drugs and for winning the war against cancer. **This is essential reading for every concerned woman and man on how to reverse the cancer epidemic by personal and political initiatives.**

Barbara Seaman
Co-founder, National Women's Health Network
Author, *The Doctor's Case Against the Pill*

In *The Politics of Cancer, Revisited*, Professor Samuel Epstein delivers a devastating attack on the cancer establishment. He provides damning evidence, in extraordinary detail, of the rising tide of cancer incidence and death. With scholarly precision, he delivers a ringing indictment of the National Cancer Institute and the American Cancer Society. Epstein details their fixation on diagnosis and treatment, and their complete failure to focus on prevention by research and education on eliminating the poisons from our food, air, water, and environment.

While the original *Politics of Cancer* was a tremendously important work, as influential as Rachel Carson's *Silent Spring*, *The Politics of Cancer, Revisited* is even more chilling—in the face of rising cancer incidence and death, Epstein documents that the cancer establishment resists all efforts toward reform and continues its failed policies of the past.

As a nation, we cannot afford to overlook Epstein's recommendations. To the health of our nation this is a book of tremendous importance.

Frank D. Wiewel
Founder, People Against Cancer

Samuel Epstein's book *The Politics of Cancer* blew the lid off the "cancer establishment" when it was published in 1978. Twenty years later, the new *Politics of Cancer, Revisited* is a blockbuster. It exposes the rampant industrial pollution that causes many preventable cases of cancer. It also shows the frightening power of industry in keeping us from winning the war against cancer. **We all owe Professor Epstein a debt of gratitude for almost single-handedly keeping this issue alive and before the public for all these years.**

Ralph W. Moss, Ph.D.
Director, *The Moss Reports*

Praise for *Cancer-Gate*

Cancer has surpassed heart disease as America's #1 killer, but the National Cancer Institute continues to hope that miraculous "magic bullets" will save us. For more than three decades, Prof. Samuel S. Epstein has shown that many kinds of cancer can be prevented by simply eliminating carcinogens in the air, food, water, and workplace. Vested interests have blocked this strategy. Sam Epstein is a national treasure and his *Cancer-Gate* is simply magnificent—a battle cry for activists to reclaim the failing war against cancer.

Ralph W. Moss, Ph.D.
President, Cancer Communications, Inc., Lemont, Pennsylvania
Director, *The Moss Reports,* Author, *The Cancer Industry*

Professor Epstein's scientifically accurate yet highly readable book is an extraordinarily important depiction of the failure of President Nixon's 1971 "War on Cancer." This has been due to concentration on highly questionable treatment and a monumental neglect of preventing environmental and other avoidable causes of cancer. Like the "War on Terrorism," which has been sidetracked into a war on Iraq and on human rights, the "War on Cancer" has enriched powerful special interests and stifled the free flow of public information. This book provides recommendations and inspiration for, at long last, transforming the largely futile, and inflationary, cancer war into realistic strategies to prevent the nation's leading cause of suffering and premature death.

Victor W. Sidel, M.D.
Distinguished University Professor of Social Medicine,
Montefiore Medical Center/Albert Einstein College of Medicine
Past President, American Public Health Association

There is less and less effort to inform workers and their families, and the general public, about avoidable environmental and occupational causes of cancer. This book will make you pause and think—especially if you have, or a loved one has, cancer.

Eula Bingham, Ph.D.
Professor Emerita of Environmental Health,
University of Cincinnati Medical Center
Former Assistant Secretary of Labor, Occupational
Safety and Health Administration

As *Cancer-Gate* details, the National Cancer Institute and American Cancer Society have narrowly focused their policies and resources on promoting highly profitable Big Pharma "miracle" drugs in largely unsuccessful efforts to cure cancer. What's more, in defiance of the Human Rights Covenants, they have denied the public its right to know of available information on the causes and prevention of cancer.

Dr. Rosalie Bertell
Former President, International Institute of Concern for Public Health
Member, National Association for Public Health Policy,
International Science Oversight Committee

Dr. Epstein is a scientist/scholar/activist who devotes his life 24/7 to informing the public about what really causes cancer, and how we can protect ourselves. In this brilliant and compelling book, in spite of the silence of the National Cancer Institute and attacks by industry, he has established guidelines on the public's undeniable right to know about avoidable causes of cancer in the environment, workplace, hormone replacement therapy and other prescription drugs, and consumer products.

Barbara Seaman
Co-Founder, National Women's Health Network
Author, The Doctor's Case Against the Pill

Dr. Epstein's factual exposé of the National Cancer Institute and American Cancer Society—their conflicts of interest, co-option by the pharmaceutical and petrochemical industries, and indifference to cancer prevention—is riveting. Dr. Epstein reaches for the law to turn the issue of public health into one of human rights. This book belongs on the bookshelf of every lawyer and teacher of environmental law or public health, in every law library, and on the reading lists of all law school classes.

George S. Grossman
Professor of Law and Director, Law Library,
University of California, Davis

Cancer-Gate is Dr. Epstein's heroic effort to show us how to reduce our risks of cancer. Motivated by compassion and concern, he does not fail to deeply impress. In both print and film, he is as remarkable in his command of scientific data as in his ability to present them in a way that is both convincing to the public health community and accessible to the general public. He has shared these powerful insights in my recent documentary, *The Corporation*.

Mark Achbar
Executive Producer and Co-Director, The Corporation
Recipient of 22 international awards

Dr. Epstein's new masterpiece, *Cancer-Gate,* takes the onus from an industry that tries to keep us in the dark about the war on cancer and puts the information right into our hands. This well-researched book acts as a roadmap, showing what is being done and what can be done regarding the war on cancer. The importance of becoming proactive gets even more personal as Dr. Epstein reveals the role that the cosmetics industry plays in the cancer epidemic, in my forthcoming documentary *America the Beautiful.*

Darryl Roberts
Producer, Sensory Overload Productions